WAITING FOR THE PEOPLE

WAITING FOR THE PEOPLE

The Idea of Democracy in Indian Anticolonial Thought

∞ NAZMUL SULTAN

THE BELKNAP PRESS OF HARVARD UNIVERSITY PRESS

Cambridge, Massachusetts, & London, England

2024

Library of Congress Cataloging-in-Publication Data

Names: Sultan, Nazmul, author.

Title: Waiting for the people : the idea of democracy in Indian anticolonial thought / Nazmul Sultan.

Description: Cambridge, Massachusetts ; London, England : The Belknap Press of Harvard University Press, 2024. | Includes bibliographical references and index.

Identifiers: LCCN 2023008350 | ISBN 9780674290372 (cloth)

Subjects: LCSH: Democracy—India. | Sovereignty. | Liberalism—India—History. | Self-determination, National—India. | Anti-imperialist movements—India. | Decolonization—India. | Postcolonialism—India. | India—Politics and government—19th century. | India—Politics and government—20th century.

Classification: LCC JQ281 .S85 2024 | DDC 320.454—dc23/eng/20230705

LC record available at https://lccn.loc.gov/2023008350

CONTENTS

WAITING FOR THE PEOPLE

VLADIMIR: ... What do we do now?

ESTRAGON: Wait.

VLADIMIR: Yes, but while waiting.

—Samuel Beckett, *Waiting for Godot*

INTRODUCTION

Waiting for the People

IN 1887—STILL the early years of organized anticolonial politics in India—Bipin Chandra Pal (1858-1932) observed that "the glorious annals of the Hindoo and Mahomedan periods of Indian history have recorded the achievements of priests and princes, of skillful generals and wise statesmen, and profound thinkers, but the name of the *people* is nowhere to be found in them." Pal surmised that "the *Indian people*" simply did not exist as a political entity prior to British rule. For all his discontent with the colonial state, the future "prophet of [Indian] nationalism" concluded that the Indian people were being "called into existence" by the British.[1] By this point, Pal's argument was widely shared by political thinkers across the imperial divide. Two decades before Pal, Edwin Arnold, a noted Indologist and historian of British India, had proudly claimed: "We are making a people in India where hitherto there have been a hundred tribes but no people. . . . We are introducing an idea unknown to the East, as it was unknown to Europe before commerce—the idea of popular rights and equality."[2] Hidden in his mammoth history of Governor Dalhousie's regime in India, Arnold's celebration of the democratic "contribution" of colonialism was very much a distillation of the argument that foundational British political thinkers such as John

Stuart Mill and Thomas Babington Macaulay had already helped establish. Yet the question of the Indian people—despite its putative historical nonbeing—proved to be both tenacious and decisive. This book is the story of the abstract figure that shaped the terms of anticolonial struggle and the pursuit of democracy in India: the people.

The Indian anticolonial democratic project would be fundamentally driven by the perceived need to transform the historically "backward" and politically amorphous colonial "masses" into *the* people: this I call the problem of peoplehood. There was more to the problem than the challenge of constituting preexisting groups into a cohesive people, which is an indispensable element of democratic politics anywhere. Rather, because the political qualities of peoplehood themselves appeared to be a product of historical development, the project of turning the masses into the people became embroiled in a set of paradigmatic problems ultimately to do with the conditions of possibility of democracy in the colonial world. As a conceptual dilemma proper, this problem of peoplehood transcended its British uses as a legitimating trope. Nearly all the canonical anticolonial thinkers—ranging from Surendranath Banerjea (1848-1925) to Jawaharlal Nehru (1889-1964)—struggled with the seemingly irrefutable premise of an absent Indian peoplehood. Having offered compelling arguments for Indian self-rule, thinkers as different as Dadabhai Naoroji (1825-1917) and Bal Gangadhar Tilak (1856-1920) found themselves left with a "not-yet" people whose right to self-government could not be articulated in sovereign terms. B. R. Ambedkar (1891-1956), after submitting the draft constitution of the new republic of India, considered it necessary to remind his audience that Indians were still not a people at home with the demands of democracy.[3] The figure of the people—the sine qua non of modern democracy—had turned out to be the marker of an enduring problem in India.

Contrary to the well-worn trope, the history of popular sovereignty in the colonial world was not simply one of sovereignty denied (by empire) and reclaimed (by anticolonial actors). The structure of the "denial" unalterably transformed the meaning of popular sovereignty and democratic government for Indian political thinkers. Modern colonialism was not simply a new spin on the timeless trope of conquest, nor was anticolonial political thought a mere exercise in overcoming foreign rule. From the nineteenth century onward, colonialism was understood and justified in what might be called democratic terms. Central to the democratic signification of colonialism had been the framework of developmentalism, whose historical and analytical purchase surpassed its use as an imperial promise of progress. That British rule was an undemocratic form of foreign rule was not in doubt. Yet the developmental horizon initially claimed by the empire ultimately became inseparable from the emergence of democracy as a globally legible category. The developmental vision located the source of global political differences in different stages of peoplehood, thereby rendering the globe politically thinkable as a hierarchy of peoples.

The question of the people consumed Indian political life well before its juridical triumph at postcolonial founding: the force of its purported absence had already begun to shape political imagination in the nineteenth century. That the power exercised by "the authority of the 'absent people'" is a constitutive element of modern parliamentary democracy has been underscored by scholars of democracy.[4] Its reach, however, was deeper in colonial India and of a fundamentally different sort, for it originated a political tradition where democracy itself was experienced in a distinct manner. Thanks to the diagnosis that the people as a political entity was lacking in India, the premise of sovereign peoplehood could not be taken for granted; it had instead turned into the goal to be aspired for. Self-government, then, appeared to be something not so much authorized by the people as generative of sovereign peoplehood. Against this backdrop, Indian political thinkers took it upon themselves not just to reclaim the sovereignty denied to their people but also to address the theoretical assumptions that rendered the democratic ideal compatible with the imperial geography of the globe. At once the ground and promise of colonialism, the figure of the people came to be central to Indian anticolonial thinkers' quest for democracy in a world fractured along the purportedly measurable capacity for self-rule.

THE GLOBAL CAREER OF POPULAR SOVEREIGNTY

Though the study of popular sovereignty has long been beset with fundamental disagreements, the conflicting series of propositions associated with the discourse of popular sovereignty have propelled, rather than stymied, its emergence as the ground of modern democracy. Popular sovereignty thrived, as it were, on its many claimants and detractors. Reflecting on the revolutionary origins of the idea of popular sovereignty, Hannah Arendt speculated that "if this notion [*le peuple*] has reached four corners of the earth, it is not because of any influence of abstract ideas but because of its obvious plausibility under conditions of abject poverty."[5] I do not share the assumption that "abstract ideas" of the people were unimportant in the global career of popular sovereignty, or that "abject poverty" has a universal political import.[6] However, Arendt's underscoring of the singular global reach of the popular sovereignty discourse captures a point of utmost importance: if democracy has now acquired the status of the sole "secular claimant" of political legitimacy,[7] it is primarily because of the incontestability of the foundation of popular sovereignty.

While representative and centralized forms of democratic government faced much skepticism in the global nineteenth and twentieth centuries, the sovereignty of the people, as an ideal, met with no meaningful normative challenge. After storming the heaven of sovereignty,[8] the "people" seemed to have conquered the globe—sometime between the great eighteenth-century revolutions and mid-twentieth-century decolonization, and somewhere behind the main stage of social and economic history. The story of this singular conquest is generally told with reference to the tremendous social and economic transformations of the nineteenth and twentieth centuries. But alongside these changes, the global rise of the people was also a story of intellectual transformations. The stubborn persistence of diffusionist approaches in the global history of democracy means that the framework of dissemination and reception tends to obfuscate the transformation and reconstitution of democratic ideas themselves. As we shall see, anticolonial aspirants for popular sovereignty were locked in a conflict with an imperial project that had—however contradictorily—sought to derive its legitimacy from a contesting, global narrative of peoplehood. It is partly due to the history of this conflict that the age of decolonization doubled as the global vindication of popular sovereignty.

The strength and ubiquity of popular sovereignty lies in its roots as a discourse of authorization. The modern recognition that the figure of the people no longer amounts to a "visibly identifiable gathering of autonomous citizens"[9] shifted the primary stake of the popular sovereignty discourse to the processes of claiming authorization from the abstraction called "the people." Invocations of the people in political modernity are necessarily an exercise in speaking in the name of an entity that does not empirically exist as a homogeneous, empirically locatable subject. This foundational abstraction of "the people" notwithstanding, much of the contemporary theoretical dispute around popular sovereignty concerns not whether the people is the ultimate political authority but instead how to enact and institutionalize the authority vested in it. Regardless of how critical of popular rule a contemporary liberal political thinker might be, the procedure of popular consent—which traces the sovereignty of the state to the people—is essential.[10] Radical democrats—while overwhelmingly critical of representative democracy—articulate their extra-institutional vision of democracy through the figure of the people.[11] Deliberative democratic theorists too find it necessary to account for a procedural authorization of rights and laws in the will of the people, notwithstanding their attempts to render the people as "'subjectless' forms of communication circulating through forums and legislative bodies."[12] Though disagreements over what exactly constitutes popular authorization—and how it must be politically instituted—are abundant,[13] what has come to be beyond dispute, barring some residual protestations, is the idea that democratic legitimacy requires an authorization from the people.

The distinction between sovereignty and government was crucial to the formation of modern popular sovereignty as an authorizing ideal. The concept of sovereignty, since its medieval origin, had implied that "*authorising* the actions of a government" is not the same as "governing." Sovereignty thus meant not so much the holding of political offices as the power to decide who would constitute the government and to pass fundamental legislation. As Richard Tuck has shown, the sovereignty-government distinction was constitutive of the idea of popular sovereignty since Jean Bodin and ran through canonical modern political philosophers ranging from Thomas Hobbes to Jean-Jacques Rousseau.[14] The very emergence of a constitutional theory of public authority in the early modern era was likewise indebted to the incipient doctrine of popular sovereignty. The limited government of the constitutional order had become theoretically possible owing to the "unlimited" power ascribed to the people.[15] It was, however, only with the two classical revolutions of the late eighteenth century—the French and the American—that popular sovereignty began to acquire the public legitimacy that it now enjoys. The French and American revolutionaries vigorously debated the meaning of popular sovereignty, taking paths that were neither identical nor short of novel challenges. The limited government of American constitutionalism and the transformative vision of French republicanism both nevertheless emboldened the idea that the people are the source of authority and the foundation of legitimacy.

For all its centrality to the modern constitutional order, popular sovereignty has been no less salient to extraconstitutional claims of political authorization. The invocation of popular sovereignty both by institutional and extra-institutional actors, as Jason Frank has argued, is enabled by the fact that "the people" is more of a claim than a determinate object. The "constitutive surplus" of popular sovereignty—the surplus that remains despite institutional authorization derived from the people—tends to outlive the founding event and continues to serve as a reservoir for popular claim-making.[16] Modern democracy rode the waves of many popular insurrections, and the founding power associated with the self-authorizing people shaped institutional ideals of democracy as much as the dictions of popular politics. To complicate the matter further, the essential claimability of the people means that both governmental and extragovernmental actors could invoke the name of the people, thus transcending strict constitutional protocols for popular authorization. Indeed, as Bryan Garsten argues, the multiplication and contestability of "governmental claims to represent the people" is a germane feature of modern representative democracy.[17]

The figure of the insurrectionary people no doubt coexists with the specter of the riotous mob. The "strong cleanser of rationality and the stiff brush of virtue" notwithstanding, the idea of the people has proved to be hard to sanitize,[18] resisting its circumscription to either constitutional or extraconstitutional guises. Though the power of the people may seem to be anchored in a naturalized "folk foundationalism," the plural purchase of popular sovereignty is more than a symptom of its intellectual deficiency.[19] The concept of the people works as more of a "bedrock" (in a Wittgensteinian sense) than as a transparent epistemic foundation: it is the ground where "the spade turns," not so much because it is an intrinsically self-justifying foundation but rather because it is "held fast by what lies around."[20] The concept of the people operates as the legitimating ground for almost all modern democratic reasoning and practices, from the constitution to routine electoral politics. The self-evident character of popular sovereignty owes essentially to the way in which the complex order of modern democratic norms and institutions trace their ultimate foundation in it.

That the question of popular sovereignty also animated the modern history of colonialism and anticolonial resistance in all its messiness has been less studied and less understood. This is in part because in the colonial world the emergence of the people was neither historically parallel nor conceptually analogous to the European experience. The beginning of the British conquest of India in the mid-eighteenth century triggered thorny questions of conquest and legitimacy (without any meaningful reference to popular sovereignty), leading to Edmund Burke's famous trial of Warren Hastings and the larger "scandal of empire."[21] The framework of ancient constitutionalism shaped the terms of the dispute concerning what gave the British the right to rule over India in the final decades of the eighteenth century.[22] As the self-understanding and legitimating discourses of imperial rule went through a transformation in the early nineteenth century, the question of the people—or rather its absence in India—slowly emerged as the main framework for the political legitimation of British rule. The British claim that the justification of imperial rule consisted in developing the people so as to make India fit for self-government paradoxically conceded the supremacy of the principle of popular sovereignty. A principle but not a fact, the question of peoplehood turned into the end goal of foreign government. In this way, as we shall see throughout the book, the modern distinction between sovereignty and government found a new expression in the colonial world. This colonial birth of popular sovereignty was not centered on debates around democracy ancient and modern; rather, it was born out of a paradigmatic conviction about the untimeliness of democracy in the backward non-European world vis-à-vis the European world.

"The people," argues Bernard Yack, "exists in a kind of eternal present. It never ages or dies."[23] Though Yack notes that the concept of the people is of relatively modern origin, its conceptual significance, he contends, is primarily spatial, not temporal. In its global unfolding, the concept of the people, on the contrary, has been entangled in temporal—or to be more specific, developmentalist—concerns. To be sure, in normative and constitutional reasoning, the people necessarily features as a given entity. While one might dispute who the "real" people are and what their authority may entail, the question as to the *existence* of the people is not a problem that one is ordinarily faced with. This was precisely the assumption that came to be undone in the colonial world. In colonial India, as we shall see, the name of the people was replete with temporal markers—its existence as a recognizable political entity was rendered conditional on prior historical criteria. The conceptual birth of the people in India, strangely, amounted to its historical absence.

From the nineteenth century onward, the figure of the Indian people came to descriptively embody the underdevelopment ascribed to its moral and material history. If, in the modern European history of popular sovereignty, the sociological deprivation and historical subjection of the masses bolstered the argument concerning their unrealized sovereignty,[24] these same phenomena would stand for the disqualification of the sovereign claim of the people in India. The social lack attributed to the Indian people directly undermined its claim to "political abstraction."[25] Throughout the colonial era, representations of mass underdevelopment pervaded Indian political thought: expressions such as "the starving millions" and "ignorant masses" bled into the characterization of the Indian people as politically unfit. Likewise, the diversity of India across regional and religious lines appeared as evidence of the absence of a unified entity called the people. Normatively, the perceived inadequacy of Indian peoplehood helped legitimate the suspension of their sovereignty, for only a fit people could institute and practice self-government. The institution of self-government among a backward people was claimed to be not just impractical but, more damningly, a hindrance toward the growth of developed peoplehood. The ultimate promise that the empire made was not simply the prosaic objective of training a people in the institution of self-government; it was to bring into being the Indian people itself.

In established accounts of anticolonial political thought, the nationalist claim to popular sovereignty is understood to be central to overturning imperial sovereignty in the twentieth century, with little or no differentiation between the "nation" and the "people."[26] In *Waiting for the People* I present a different story. The democratic dilemma that was constitutive of modern colonialism can scarcely be captured through the category of the nation. From Bipin Chandra Pal to Jawaharlal Nehru, Indian political thinkers, despite their qualified acceptance of "anticolonial nationalism," struggled to posit sovereign authority in the Indian people. For most of the colonial era, the questions pertaining to the boundary and common belonging of the people—the standard elements of nationhood—were recognized and yet understood in relation to the broader normative horizon centered on the problem of the democratic fitness of the Indian masses. The entanglement of the concept of the people with a powerful narrative concerning the global progression of democracy meant that Indian political thinkers could not simply claim the atemporal universality of popular sovereignty, turning a blind eye to their all-too-developmental existence. What they did—and what I recover in this book—is wrestle with the terms and times of modern popular sovereignty, and thereby investigate the meaning of democracy itself.

DEVELOPMENTALISM AND THE DEMOCRATIC LEGITIMATION OF EMPIRE

Adam Smith famously characterized the twin events of "the discovery of America, and that of a passage to the East Indies by the Cape of Good Hope" as two of the "greatest and most important events recorded in the history of mankind."[27] The European discovery of the rest of the world eventually metamorphized into global imperial projects, leaving in its trail a set of entwined questions about the expanded vista of the globe and the bounded political community. The archive of modern European political thought faithfully reflects the force of Smith's observation. European political thinkers before and after Smith, from Francisco de Vitoria to Karl Marx, directly or indirectly reckoned with the inescapable problem of Europe's imperial expansion. Despite the obvious continuity of the themes of conquest and colonization, the stake of the empire question was never static or self-evident.[28] The many material and intellectual problems traveling to and from the non-European world normatively challenged the established natural law framework, gave impetus to the Age of Enlightenment, and shaped the cores of the developmentalist paradigm. It is curious, then, that for most of the twentieth century, an age of global democracy marked by innumerable anticolonial rebellions and foundings, the problems of empire and anticolonialism posed questions pertaining to the applicability of ideas and norms rather than foundational matters in the discipline of political theory. This neglect had much to do with the political success of anticolonialism. The rise of new postcolonial states, along with the normative codification of the right to self-determination in the international domain, had seemingly settled the colonial question. It had become simply a "morally objectionable form of political relation": the unjust domination of one people over another.[29] The moralization of the question of colonialism, however, runs a distinct risk: it obscures how colonial rule in Asia and Africa was fundamentally predicated on claims about the condition of possibility of the otherwise unquestioned (moral) norm of democratic self-rule.

The reinvention of empire in the age of the democratic revolution transformed the ideal of democracy as much as it remade the meaning of imperial rule. The temporal texture of the democratic revolution—that the rise of equality was the sign of a universal future to come—not only facilitated a new approach to pre-democratic pasts but also rendered philosophically superfluous the question concerning the immediate universality of political norms. The lesson of the nineteenth century, John Stuart Mill once noted revealingly, was to historicize the "ought": "different stages of human progress not only *will* have (which must always have been evident), but *ought* to have, different institutions."[30] The norms were not to be simply relativized; if anything, the universality of a political norm such as self-government rested directly on the necessarily provisional history of its antecedent. The entwined history of empire and democracy lay in this very conjuncture.

In the wake of the postcolonial turn later in the twentieth century, historians debated the exact manner in which colonialism constituted a break with the precolonial past and the new forms of practice globalized through colonial governmentality.[31] The ensuing reconsideration of colonial statehood and ideology further established that colonialism could be neither reduced to universal sociology nor analytically circumscribed to the realm of exceptions. Political theorists have also amply demonstrated that the extraordinary confidence with which European empires ruled over the world was not unrelated—to put it mildly—to the heartland of European intellectual preoccupations, be it liberalism or the rise of social theory.[32] The result has been a coming together of otherwise sequestered worlds of political thought. In particular, the framework of liberalism, thanks to its overt commitment to the idea of progress, has inspired some of the most powerful observations on the mutual constitution of the metropolitan and colonial intellectual worlds. The pioneering work on liberal imperialism has recovered the pivotal role that the discourses of progress and development played in nineteenth-century legitimations of empire. These explorations of the intimacy between progress and empire laid bare the formative reconciliation of the despotic fact of imperial rule with the norms of liberalism.[33]

Though European imperial expansion flourished in the age of democratic revolutions, the question of democracy has mostly been a footnote to the scholarship on liberal imperialism.[34] Beneath the liberal motifs of civilization and progress, as we shall see from the colonial vantage point, lay the foundational problem of democracy. In this book's telling, the category of the people was central to the theoretical assimilation of progress and empire in democratic thought. In the global nineteenth century, democracy was neither simply a humanistic category nor merely a problem of reason and cognition. Whether we look at Tocqueville's *Democracy in America* or Mill's *Considerations on Representative Government*, democracy was ineluctably mired in a paradoxical struggle with its own historical conditions. This struggle simultaneously necessitated the containment of the people possessed by sovereign drives in the metropolitan world, and the prioritization of the development of modern peoplehood elsewhere. The progressive ordering of the people, forged in the global landscape of empire, resulted in an ingenious democratic gloss on foreign despotism. The argument that despotism was necessary for certain stages of historical development *for* the sake of democracy itself was no doubt a sleight of reason, but it was a move that capitalized the immanent contradictions of democratic thought. The liberal-imperial discourse of progress, in the process, essentially performed a "democratic" justification of imperial rule.

Perceptive liberal imperialists like Mill, not to mention Indian political thinkers, found it difficult to ignore the patent despotism of

British rule in India. Mill also understood that the fact of imperial rule needed to be reconciled with the norm of representative government. The answer to this challenge was to be found in the theory of representative government itself—a form of rule that required an appropriate "will and capacity" among the people for its actualization.[35] India appeared unfit for representative democracy primarily because of the historical deficit of a set of democratic qualities in the people—for example, public spirit, popular unity, institutional competence, and so on. Conversely, what entitled the British to rule over India was not simply civilizational superiority; more specifically, it pertained to their claim to be a people historically advanced and trained in representative government. In other words, the developmental account of colonialism could operate as a discourse of political legitimation because of its translation into the terms of peoplehood. In this way, modern colonialism not only acknowledged its own violation of norms but derived its legitimacy from that very acknowledgment.

The intellectual reconsideration of the empire question in the recent past has brought the far-flung regions of the world once more into contiguity with the mainstream of modern political thought. Conceptual proximity, however, can be deceptive, for the archive of anticolonial political thought is often susceptible to interpretation as answers to the problems or blind spots of modern European political thought. There is no doubt that anticolonial thinkers often recognized the weak foundations of essentialist discourses (such as "civilization") in contemporary European political thought. But what rendered their attempts to critique imperial thought more challenging is the imperially inflected nature of democratic norms—the same norms that were at the center of anticolonial political claims since the nineteenth century also helped legitimate imperial rule abroad. The anticolonial answer to this problem, as a result, required an examination of the normative foundations of modern democracy.

Such an approach to the global history of democratic thought calls for attentiveness to the varying purchase of notions of "progress," "improvement," "development," and other cognate ideas. Before the rise of notions of progress and development, the discourse of improvement functioned as an idiom of moral good, independent of the paradigm of historical development. When the idea of historical progress—that is, the assumption that differences observed across the globe could be understood as advancement or backwardness on a shared scale—flourished in the nineteenth century, its reach encompassed the moral and the material equally. Together with moral confidence in the universality of liberal norms, the "rapid transformations of the external conditions of life" constituted a self-evident proof of the general progress of the age in the nineteenth century.[36] The idiom of improvement, too, came to be defined by this newfound sense of progress. Questions of economy, institutions, education, customs, and culture all lent themselves to the mediation of progress.

The term "development," which is more a twentieth-century term, shares a great deal of the theory of history with nineteenth-century ideas of progress. Though "progress" and "development" are often interchangeable terms, the latter is arguably less beholden to a strong teleological orientation to the future. The rise of the idea of development accompanied the growing dominance of the economy-centric accounts of relative advancement and backwardness, while its relationship to the moral components of nineteenth-century theories of progress also proved to be uneasy. With postcolonial foundings and the institution of universal suffrage, the political implications of the moral and educational components of developmentalism became even more debatable. Though "progress" was far from a purely descriptive term, the politics facilitated by it did not exactly have a voluntarist approach, as evident in the progressive justification for imperial tutelage. The idea of development, in contrast, is more overtly committed to the agency of conscious willing.[37] As I reconstruct the arc of Indian anticolonial political thought in this book, the continuities and ruptures in the connected thread of the ideas of progress and development—and the implications of these shifts for the question of democracy—will also be an important element of my narrative.

THE COLONIAL PROBLEM OF PEOPLEHOOD

As the promise of transforming the Indian masses into a people fit for self-government emerged as the main British claim to rule, the open-ended discourses of improvement and progress became subordinate to the higher goal of developing the people. When India transferred from Company rule to the British Crown in 1858, the British administration began to publish a yearly report under the suggestive title "Statement

Exhibiting the Moral and Material Progress and Condition of India." Crucially, the developmental project was no longer a British concoction grafted onto Indian society. The intellectual climate of the urban centers was awash in various projects of "social reform." Myriad reflections on progress saturated the sociological, historical, and moral imaginations of the age.[38] What offered such an enduring life to developmental ideals of imperial provenance was their widespread purchase among Indians themselves. The significant Indian excitement over the diffusion of modern knowledge was initially independent of the problem of historical development. By the middle of the nineteenth century, however, these manifold ruminations on the pressing necessity of progress began to coalesce around one overarching political "object": "[the improvement of] the natives of India as a people."[39]

As Indian political thinkers began to make claims for self-rule, their agenda would become absorbed in a recurring question: What are the political qualities that could transform an amorphous mass into a people? This was an unavoidable question concerning the formation of the democratic subject, and yet it also reinforced the premise of imperial rule. From moral to material underdevelopment, the state of colonial peoplehood seemed to contradict the political ground on which contemporary Euro-American democracies were standing. To be clear, the "people" that Indian liberal thinkers found wanting was not so much an insurrectionary crowd, for the period was rife with the news of peasant insurgencies and revolts.[40] For many, such "pre-political" actors only affirmed the overwhelming discourse of the Indian unfitness for self-government.[41] In fact, Indian reformists, much to the embarrassment of later nationalist historiography, widely disavowed the most serious insurrectionary challenge to British rule—the Rebellion of 1857, which, among other things, sought to restore Mughal power. It was instead the people underlying representative government—a historically "fit" authority capable of grounding self-government through its political will and institutional competence—that informed nineteenth-century accounts of an absent Indian peoplehood. Understood primarily as the bearer of "indirect sovereignty" in nineteenth-century British thought,[42] this "fit" people figured as the prior condition of self-government. For all its similarities to British political thought, the fitness of the people was a problem posed in strikingly different ways in India: while British intellectuals back in the metropolis might have doubted the democratic capacity of Britain's working classes, the presence of a people broadly commensurate with the requirements of self-government was never seriously questioned. Thus, even as Victorian British politics itself was consumed by debates between different approaches to representing the people in Parliament,[43] Indians found themselves stuck on the prior problem of peoplehood, a problem that posited the wholesale transformation of the masses as a precondition of self-government.

Even so, this problem did not exactly block the political aspiration of the first generation of political thinkers associated with the Indian National Congress. This group of thinkers—Dadabhai Naoroji, Surendranath Banerjea, and R. C. Dutt (1848–1909), among others—would creatively exploit the gap between sovereignty and government that emerged in the wake of the democratic legitimation of empire. Throughout the latter half of the nineteenth century, they relentlessly pushed for new forms of political participation in colonial government and forged multiple strategies for persuading the British to concede Indian demands. This particular mode of politics—variously characterized as "constitutional agitation," "gradual reformism," and (as execrated by later critics) "political mendicancy"—was directly tethered to visions of a democratic future. Surendranath Banerjea suggestively recapitulated his generation's fascination with the ideal of popular "enthronement" in the latter half of the nineteenth century. Banerjea was an ever-present figure in Indian political life for about half a century, roughly between the 1870s and the 1920s. Revisiting these early years in a later memoir, Banerjea keenly underscored the mutual imbrication between the early politics of gradual reformism and the ideal of "popular domination":

> We not only wanted to be members of the bureaucracy and to leaven it with the Indian element, but we looked forward to controlling it, and shaping and guiding its measures and eventually bringing the entire administration under complete popular domination. It was a departure hardly noticed at the time, but [was] fraught with immense possibilities. Along with the development of the struggle for place and power to be secured to our countrymen, there came gradually but steadily to the forefront the idea this was not enough. . . . The demand for representative government was now definitely formed.[44]

In concrete terms, the pursuit of the "place and power" of the Indian people meant the demand for limited representation and administrative roles, albeit with the long-term aim to prepare them for full self-government. The demand for Indian representation soon became the rallying cry of Indian liberals.[45] But this claim of representation had little to do with representing the will of the people; it was instead framed as a step toward developing an Indian people out of a backward, inchoate mass. It was only by participating in the government—Naoroji, Banerjea, and other Indian liberals maintained—that the advanced section of Indians could learn to practice self-government. This was not elitism for its own sake: Indian liberals presented themselves as the best mediator between the age of progress and the "teeming" and "dumb millions" resigned to destitution.[46] In this way, the demand for political representation and minimal self-government doubled as an investment in the formation of a developed Indian people. Such claims for Indian representation received little vindication from the empire, and the attempts to institutionally influence colonial administration rarely succeeded. Some Indian actors, such as Naoroji, sought representation in the British Parliament, while others pursued additional means for appealing to the English people directly. The idea of directing political propaganda at the British people was expressive of a deeper predicament of late nineteenth-century Indian political thought: the people who could authorize Indian representation and self-government resided in England, not in India.

Despite all the disputes regarding the nature of the distinction between sovereignty and government, the priority of sovereignty over government has been more or less assumed in modern political thought. Indian liberals did not consciously aim to reverse the order, but their politics of appealing to the English people enacted precisely such a situation. Though they unfailingly extolled the empire for its promise of self-government, their political imagination was not of naive faith. In foregrounding the empire's promise of its own dissolution, Indian liberals constructed a discursive space where the development of the people figured as the ultimate end of all political measures. In the meantime, however, they had to negotiate with an administration hardly bound to the promises ascribed to the imperial ideal. Through the practical business of making their case and pleas to the empire, Naoroji and his colleagues fashioned self-government as an exercise in the generation of that which, in principle, is prior to it: popular sovereignty. This history is one important reason the meaning of the idea of democracy (either as a form of government or as a form of society) in India would elude our understanding if isolated from the distinct, but fundamentally related, concerns over peoplehood and popular sovereignty.

The turn-of-the century Indian political scene was an intellectually bustling and rich domain, whose center of gravity revolved around the invocation and dissection of said imperial promises. Before they made an alternative anticolonial promise, a group of gifted thinkers and "impatient" political actors—Bal Gangadhar Tilak, Bipin Chandra Pal, and Aurobindo Ghose, among others—discovered the humiliation of appealing to the foreign conqueror for India's own democratic salvation. The rejection of the appeal to the empire amounted to a refusal to wait for self-government, a point on which an aging Naoroji eventually converged with the "extremists." Naoroji's unexpected call for "swaraj" (which he understood to be equivalent to a limited form of institutional self-government) *without* delay, in 1906, sparked a wider demand for the Indian control of the government and has been rightly recognized as a watershed moment in Indian political history. However, to refuse to wait for self-government, as the swaraj thinkers found out, did not mean a resolution of the questions of peoplehood and sovereignty. Instead, the urgent search for self-government anticlimactically laid bare the absent ground of popular sovereignty. Early twentieth-century Indian political thinkers drifted restlessly between the two poles of the political world—the present yet unacceptable imperial sovereignty and the normatively desirable yet absent popular sovereignty. The developmentalist paradigm blurred the space between "the people" as a descriptive marker and as a normative marker, thus signifying the poverty and illiteracy of the masses as proof of their unfitness for sovereignty. For all their radical denunciations of imperial sovereignty, neither Pal nor Tilak fully broke from the terms of the problem of peoplehood. After claiming swaraj, they found themselves circling around the absent figure of the sovereign people, who alone could authorize self-government. In their search for an authorizing ground for self-rule, these swaraj thinkers ultimately ended up either unhappily restoring the authority of imperial sovereignty or reluctantly deferring the time of popular sovereignty.

This colonial paradox of peoplehood ran through the long career of the anticolonial democratic project. The eminently claimable entity called the people—the modern foundation of legitimacy and marker of resistance—had turned out to be unclaimable in its colonial iteration. The outcome was a language of politics that shaped the broader understanding of self-government as a process generative of peoplehood. Democratic theorists know well that there is a necessary incompleteness to many of the germane concepts of modern democracy. The people, one might reasonably say, is never fully present anywhere.[47] But the generic dilemmas of democratic thought in colonial India were compounded by a specifically historical expectation concerning the backwardness of the people. The trope of waiting for the people did not amount to a suspension of the search for sovereignty, much less a tame submission to empire. Rather, it was the prompt that forced Indian political thinkers to work through the foundational grammar of sovereignty and government anew. Still, the dilemmas underwritten in the trope of waiting for the people required more than just a declaration of the people's arrival, for what they signaled was neither a mere ideological obfuscation nor a straightforward by-product of political repression. This was precisely the inheritance that shaped the terms of twentieth-century Indian political thinkers' momentous effort to dissociate modern democracy from its imperial moorings.

TWO TRADITIONS OF INDIAN ANTICOLONIAL POLITICAL THOUGHT

Though it threw up more questions than answers, the swaraj moment left Indian political thinkers with the realization that the overwhelming challenge for the anticolonial agenda lay in the difficult project of recovering "sovereignty" from the troubled enterprise of "self-government." This endeavor brought Indian political thinkers to critically reflect on the relationship between sovereignty and government, especially the nineteenth-century inheritance that self-government was the means to the end of popular sovereignty. Because the question of sovereignty was inseparable from the problem of peoplehood, the reexamination of the very concept of the people became pivotal to these different endeavors. It was also in this context that the respective orientations of what might be characterized as "two traditions" of Indian anticolonial political thought—"development-critical" and "development-affirming"—would crystallize. Politically consequential as it was, the split of the Congress in 1907 between moderatism and extremism is not necessarily central to this distinction, for both parties shared a paradigmatic faith in the project of developing the people. Nor was the question of political opposition to empire the decisive test. Many who chose to work within the developmental paradigm had no patience whatsoever for the imperial attachment. The developmental framing of the problem of peoplehood instead drove the most significant theoretical wedge between twentieth-century Indian political thinkers.

If the Indian nineteenth century was fervently beholden to developmentalism, the arrival of the next century was announced by a thinker singularly unpersuaded by it: Mohandas Karamchand Gandhi (1869–1948). Though the critical tradition found its prophet in Gandhi, its appeal had a wide reach, including a great many of Gandhi's contemporaries, such as Rabindranath Tagore and Brajendranath Seal. Gandhi's rejection of developmentalism entailed a fundamental skepticism toward the prevalent framing of the problem of peoplehood, and he deliberately put forward a theory of action rooted in the primacy of the present. Responding to the same problem, federalists such as Seal would seek to pluralize the path of development with a recuperative, rather than transformative, focus. Broader global shifts in theoretical imaginations of the future, on the other hand, would transform the development-affirming tradition in the interwar era. How progress occurs and to what extent political agency can shape it were questions long understood with reference to Europe's transition from the premodern to the modern age. It generated the expectation that a slow and drawn-out process might also be necessary for the arrival of democracy in India. In the interwar decades, however, this assumption rapidly fell apart, allowing for new ways of imagining the agency of the government as well as that of the people. Nehru, in particular, carved out new ways of thinking about the movement of the figure of the people in time: his agenda for "carrying" the people at an accelerated pace gave a new meaning to (anticolonial) sovereignty. The difference between the two traditions of Indian political thought was not about determining immediate political alliances (Nehru and Gandhi, for all their disagreements, mostly worked together). Rather, what was at stake was the problem of articulating a temporal orientation to democracy. The "development-affirming" tradition saw democratic government as a vehicle to a developed people; the "development-critical" tradition was united by a suspicion of that framing.

No other thinker exemplified the perplexities of the anticolonial democratic project as much as Gandhi. Evidently a thinker of individual moral action, Gandhi's extraordinary role in democratizing the Indian anticolonial movement has long perplexed historians of modern South Asia, whose analyses have ranged from an interest-based explanation to accounts of Gandhi's free-floating signification among the peasants to various accounts of the "spiritualization" of politics.[48] Gandhi entered the Indian intellectual scene in the first decade of the twentieth century, with his powerful 1909 pamphlet *Hind Swaraj*. Before his emergence, the world of Congress politics had bifurcated between the "moderates," who still clung onto gradual reformism, and the "extremists," who were unable to summon popular authorization on developmentalist grounds. Gandhi was able to clearly explicate how the extremist claim for Indian control over government shared the premise of development with the moderate subscription to the imperial script of gradual reformism. In his telling, the politics of waiting for the people suffered from the same externalization of authority that pervaded the practice of appealing to a remote imperial authority. Read in this context, Gandhi's reconfiguration of self-rule as a rule over the individual self appears to be more than just a moral turn escaping the political world. The key to understanding Gandhi's political thought, in my reading, is the problem of political authorization. His turn to the self-authorizing individual actor unexpectedly suspended the development–democracy nexus that his predecessors had found difficult to break through. The result was the anticolonial movement breaking free from its own discursive constraints and opening up to the masses, who did not need to show any proof of their fitness (even as Gandhi himself remained wary of the mob and eschewed the invocation of the people as a collective actor).

Gandhi's singular diagnostic brilliance resided in his audacious probing of the developmental framework through which the problem of popular authorization was articulated. The Mahatma's far-reaching critique of developmentalism—often incorrectly reduced to a critique of the more essentialist problem of civilization—questioned the reliance of the anticolonial democratic project on the higher claims of a developed future. Instead of working within the problem-space of developmentalism, Gandhi embraced an almost impossible project of displacing the collective condition of politics onto the individual moral actor. Toward the end of *Hind Swaraj*, following a summary of the duties incumbent on anticolonial actors, the Reader, Gandhi's imagined interlocutor, asks: "This is a large order. When will *all* carry it out?"[49] Gandhi's answer was curious: individual actors have nothing to do with others.[50] Self-rule could be enacted only by taking the self as the source of authorization—by way of ruling the self. There was thus no need to wait for a people to arrive. Having demonstrated the developmental entanglement of colonial peoplehood, Gandhi proposed an ethical vision of individual self-rule as a pointed answer to the political crisis of collective authorization. In so doing, his intervention creatively interrupted the hegemony of the developmental framework in Indian political life. Although Gandhi's intervention was not merely an ethical flight away from politics, the very nature of his account of self-rule, as we shall see, resisted its consolidation as an institutionalized ideal.

Around the same time, the time of peoplehood would be scrutinized with more systematic intent by another discerning school of Indian political thought—pluralist federalism (I will be simply calling them the Indian "federalists"). Whereas Gandhi sought to displace the question of collective peoplehood, the federalists aimed to transform the very concept of the people. Announcing a sharp break from the nineteenth century, they perspicaciously questioned the picture of a single and undivided peoplehood. The intellectual fount of the federalist school was the Bengali philosopher Brajendranath Seal (1864–1938), a close and critical reader of Hegel, and its philosophical and political champions were, respectively, Radhakamal Mukerjee (1889–1968) and Chittaranjan Das (1870–1925). The federalists were in dialogue with British pluralist and American progressive thought. But the distinctive dimension of their project was nested in the contention that the ideal of representative government is rooted in the paradigmatic discourse of "unilinear" development. Their (anti-) Hegelian origins made the pluralists keenly aware of the discourse of development that underwrote the expansionist view of representative government: the idea that centralized representative government was the end toward which the rest of the world was traveling could be a meaningful proposition only if world history was thought of as a linear progression. They suggested instead that the trajectory of development intrinsic to the Indian people had been blocked by colonial rule. Armed with this argument, the federalists drew inspiration from the burgeoning literature on the Indian village republic to articulate a project of diffused self-rule. Mukerjee and Das, in particular, argued that the people should be conceptualized as many-willed and dispersed. They also resisted the conception of the people as an entity unified by a determinate boundary—or as a territorial object that could be divided into the majority and the minority.

The pluralist reconceptualization of the question of peoplehood allowed the federalists to challenge the nineteenth-century order of sovereignty and government. Insofar as the people was many-willed and the time of development multilinear, the criteria of popular fitness and unity, they argued, should cease to matter. For these federalists, pluralist sovereignty and self-government on a small scale were one and the same. Yet for all their scrupulously formulated objections against monist sovereignty, the one-and-undivided figure of the people—perhaps the most captivating modern incarnation of monist sovereignty—was hard to give up. The problem manifested in the attempts to rearticulate federalism as a discourse of resistance against British rule. If the people were many-willed and scattered, where could *collective* authorization against imperial rule be found? This tension led the federalist leaders, especially C. R. Das, to supplement pluralist sovereignty with the provisional figure of a "one" people coming together to end imperial subjection. The federalist attempt to combine a pluralist theory of peoplehood with the "resistance" discourse of popular sovereignty ended in a theoretical stalemate.[51] Their rejection of the one people as a constituted entity stood in uneasy tension with their reliance on the unified voice of the "one people." This dilemma undercut the federalist aim to compete with the parliamentarian mainstream. It also revealed the Janus-faced nature of popular sovereignty in the age of open conflict between imperial and anticolonial politics.

Whereas Gandhi and the federalists endeavored to step outside of the developmental narrative of peoplehood, the development-affirming approach found a new lease of life when Jawaharlal Nehru arrived on the scene in the 1920s. Nehru was critical of the moral texture of Gandhian swaraj as well as the federalist affirmation of divided sovereignty. He made an emphatic, but qualified, return to the developmental premise of the pre-Gandhian era. The reason for this renewed turn to developmentalism was the emerging possibility of imagining social and political transformation as a process amenable to rapid acceleration. The timeline of development now appeared to be malleable if guided by a state free of imperial constraints. In political terms, Nehru's founding promise amounted to a project for asserting sovereign control over the time of development. This also constituted Nehru's break from the pre-Gandhian account of development. Nehru questioned the idea that independence meant the control of the colonial government; rather, the point was to rethink the meaning of sovereignty itself. He resignified the question of sovereign statehood as that which could rise above the slow pace of history. Postcolonial founding could be articulated as an immediately attainable ideal precisely because of the new claim that the sovereign state would make possible an accelerated route to democracy proper.

So far as the question of peoplehood was concerned, Nehru split the people into its present immiserated body and the future abundant body. The rapid pace of development, on his view, would eventually generate a people one with itself. However, he also maintained that if the postcolonial state was to assert sovereignty over the time of development, the unity of the Indian people was a necessary requirement. Nehru's return to monist peoplehood invited spirited rejoinders from the critics of the Indian National Congress—above all, B. R. Ambedkar and Muhammad Ali Jinnah (1876–1948). Drawing from the modern anxiety over majoritarian rule, Jinnah argued that the institution of unitary parliamentary rule among an underdeveloped people would only lead to "communal majoritarianism," as opposed to a political majority. Ambedkar incisively articulated the tension between the two times of the people: the people as a "fit" political actor and as a single cohesive entity. Single-minded striving toward the abundant future, he argued, would only reproduce the caste hierarchy that had reduced the Indian masses into a graded order. The eventual partition of Indians as a people, rather than simply India as a territory, stemmed from the clash between the two times of the people—one pertaining to the development of the people, the other pertaining to the boundary of the people.

The larger interpretive problem that plagues the study of anticolonial thought—what we might think of as a problem of the belated universal—is particularly strong in the case of Nehru and his generation. A closer reading of their political thought reveals that postcolonial founding was neither a sudden realization of a preexisting ideal nor the natural outcome of being "schooled" in democracy under colonialism. For Nehru as for many other postcolonial founders, sovereign statehood figured as the vehicle that would propel the people to the future. With this move, independence and democracy ceased to be ideals that would be available only after the consummation of the development of the masses; they were transformed instead into a transitional answer to the very problem of underdevelopment. The postcolonial developmental state would not merely translate or represent popular will; it would work as a mediator to make the people one with itself. Though the people were not to be the passive object of development, the primary developmental agency was located in the planning state. The critical tradition of Indian political thought found no match for Nehru's rejuvenation of developmentalism and rapidly faded in the 1940s. Its intellectual inheritance, too, lost some of its intelligibility, though it never quite disappeared from the theater of postcolonial democracy. On the other hand, the enduring inheritance of Indian anticolonial thought—the priority of government over sovereignty—found a different life in the moment of founding. The people had finally arrived as a trace of the future, to authorize the postcolonial state's accelerated travel through the time of development.

ANTICOLONIAL VISIONS AND THE POSTCOLONIAL LIFE OF DEMOCRACY

Writing in response to the post–World War I international situation, W. E. B. Du Bois observed that "despite the attempt to prove that its practice [democracy] is the secret and divine gift of the few, no habit is more natural or more widely spread among primitive people, or more easily capable of development among masses."[52] A few years earlier, firing the opening salvos of a new revolutionary era, V. I. Lenin had famously proclaimed that every cook can govern: 'We demand an immediate break with the prejudiced view that only the rich, or officials chosen from rich families, are capable of administering the state, of performing the ordinary, everyday work of administration. We demand that . . . a beginning be made at once in training all the working people, all the poor, for this work. . . . Is there any way other than practice by which the people can learn to govern themselves and to avoid mistakes?"[53] In India itself, Gandhi made it a commonplace to question the assumption that self-government was the result of civilizational progress. As another influential Indian political actor of the era, C. R. Das, put it: "Nobody really believes that the time has not come [for self-government]. It is a matter of immediate necessity and we must have it."[54] Self-government meant different things to these disparate thinkers, but it captured an emerging consensus on a global scale. After a century of enthrallment with developmentalism, the tide, it may seem, was turning in the interwar era. The success of decolonization in a few decades—including the global rise of universal suffrage—seems only to confirm that the developmental disqualification of self-government had lost its once-ubiquitous purchase.

And so, by the end of the Great War the argument that people can only learn self-government by practicing it—tirelessly put forward by nineteenth-century Indian liberals, even in the face of widespread metropolitan disbelief—had finally become widely acceptable. Lest it be taken as affirming the self-fulfilling, progressive narrative of democratization, it is worth recalling that the question of self-government was not the same as that of sovereignty and that the theory of developmentalism continued to play a powerful role in the understanding of self-government. As the specific history leading to postcolonial founding shows, the affirmation of mass capacity for self-government coexisted with the belief that the work of government is to develop the conditions that are necessary for the full exercise of popular sovereignty. This distinction between self-government and its historical conditions is one reason the postcolonial states that were born on the ruins of empire across Asia and Africa have predominantly understood themselves in developmentalist terms. Indeed, it was entirely uncontroversial in the late twentieth century to observe that postcolonial "reality" itself had been "colonized" by the "development discourse," in everything from economic planning to techniques of governance.[55] The emphatic continuity of the developmental paradigm *after* the end of its normative attachment to the criterion of self-government also had to do with the changing meaning of self-government. Beginning in the interwar era in particular, the significance of the legislative operations of parliament attenuated, while the expectation that the independent state should develop the masses grew. In other words, the developmental approach to peoplehood did not need to be abandoned to disqualify the claim that only developed peoples are fit for self-rule. As we will see with Nehru, parliamentary democracy could now be re-signified as one component of the developmental project of the postcolonial state. Instead of stopping at the elitist or paternalistic nature of postcolonial states, we must reckon with this internal dynamic of postcolonial democracy.

The developmental character of postcolonial democracy has spawned a whole body of scholarship. Historians, political economists, and anthropologists have extensively studied the developmental discourses and practices of postcolonial political life over the last few decades.[56] The rebirth of developmentalism as the reigning ideology of international organizations and as a quantifiable index of postcolonial governance, however, has resulted in a forgetting of its earlier roots in the imperial, and global, history of popular sovereignty. Seen in the light of its longer history, developmentalism turns out to be neither merely a product of the postwar reordering of the world nor simply an institutional inheritance of colonial governance. It is more fundamental: the political grounding of developmentalism on the figure of the people rendered it central to the very imagination of democracy in the colonial and postcolonial world.

The somewhat unceremonious entrance of the postcolonial masses into the fold of representative democracy had a more far-reaching, transformative effect than originally envisioned. Once the language of development was separated from the persistence of imperial rule, it could no longer be readily translated into an indictment of postcolonial peoplehood. The neat imperial solution—foreign government as a developing agent of the yet-to-be sovereign people—had finally fallen apart. Only a reductive understanding of political transformation at postcolonial founding could lead to the conclusion that the imperial and postcolonial states were essentially continuous. As the imperial uses of developmentalism subsided and its progressivist theory of history receded into the background, its effect on democratic politics in the postcolonial world took new forms. It was the priority of development that shifted the focus of postcolonial politics away from traditional parliamentarism to a dynamic executive promising to address developmental deficit. The older conception of government as that which would be generative of peoplehood seeped into political language and imagination without positing a dichotomy between substantive development and juridical sovereignty of the people.

Much of this has to do with the democratization of a developmental form of claim-making and authorization in the postcolonial period. With the institution of universal franchise and electoral democracy, the masses—hitherto the marker of a deferred sovereignty—began to participate in the messy terrain of representative democracy with great energy, dashing in the process the residual hold of the fitness discourse. In the early years of independence, postcolonial founders such as Nehru would put a great emphasis on ensuring the temporal concord between the planning state and the masses of the people. The preeminent democratic responsibility of the postcolonial state appeared to be the establishment of a reciprocity between the future-oriented, technologically driven objectives of the planners and the political consciousness of the people. To make the people "plan-conscious"—as Nehru put it—was to "produce a sensation in [the people] that they are partners in the vast undertaking of running a nation."[57] In the postcolonial world, though, the internal logic and force of electoral democracy quickly came to take precedence over the utopian project of social transformation led by a planning state standing beyond the ordinary preoccupations of "political democracy."[58] The name of the people continues to be routinely invoked to authorize the mandate for various forms of developmental projects, while the postcolonial masses themselves now also question the authority and legitimacy of instituted power on developmentalist grounds.[59]

This postcolonial politics of development—whether involving economic or sociocultural issues—is hardly reducible to the familiar framework of redistributive politics or even to the framework of justice *stricto sensu*. The specific language of postcolonial democracy, in my telling, emanates from the (anti)colonial conception of the people as a developmental entity. The sovereign place of the people is rarely questioned in postcolonial democracy; but the primary way the people appears is not so much as the idealized source of will to be translated into laws. Rather, the people figures as the actor who authorizes or denies the terms of its own development. This deeply developmental character of postcolonial democracy cannot thus be explained away as an effect of modern governmentality or as a by-product of the problem of poverty.

The broader aim of this study of the Indian anticolonial democratic project is to offer an intellectual genealogy for the form of postcolonial democracy we now see in South Asia and beyond. The postcolonial revolution severed the immediate imperial political implication of deferred peoplehood, but the deeper conceptual inheritance proved to be stubborn. In its postcolonial iteration, development has been not just a medium through which democracy speaks but also the language that shapes the meaning of democracy. The global career of modern democracy cannot be understood through the framework of the belated universal implicit in the commonplace uses of descriptive devices such as "democratization" or "developing world." Postcolonial democracy was born out of a struggle against an imperial rule that drew its legitimacy from a developmentally integrated vision of the world. In the end, the promises of development turned out to be less a guiding star that could lead the people beyond the messiness of popular politics, becoming instead the stuff of politics itself.

THE ANTICOLONIAL MOMENT IN MODERN POLITICAL THOUGHT

This book ultimately calls for framing the problem of anticolonialism in a new key. Working simultaneously in the shadows of the British Empire and of the epistemic claims of European modernity, Indian political thinkers scarcely found any historical parallel to their political struggle. The developmental comparison with the progressive Europe might have condemned India's past, but it did not decode the mystery of its political future. Though the thinkers I study in this book invariably took pride in the resources of their ancient past, no claims of political or intellectual continuity across time were meaningful enough. It was, of course, not unusual for Indian thinkers to place their struggle in historical continuity with modern European democratic revolutions. Still, as I argue in Chapter 2, such attempts ultimately led to the realization that India's subjection owed to the rise of democracy and development in Europe. While Indians did discover a unity of purpose with other Asian and African subject peoples in the interwar era, it was understood to be a parallel born out of common present struggles and enmities. The discovery of distant companions across continents only accentuated the perception that the anticolonial project was a historic venture into the unknown, to a promised land where independence (from empire) and democracy must coincide.

Following the track of the term "colonialism," "anticolonialism" turned up as a descriptor of India's long history of grappling with the British Empire only in the second half of the twentieth century. The rise of "the colonial" as a preferred descriptor for British rule, from the second quarter of the twentieth century in India, accompanied the understanding that distinct phenomena such as foreign subjection, democratization, racial hierarchy, and modernity collapsed into the world-historical enterprise of the British Empire.[60] It is against this diagnosis of colonialism that modern Indian political thought developed. The scholarly approach to this body of political thought, however, sprang from a well-worn idea with a complex nineteenth-century history: nationalism. Propelled by the highly influential work of scholars such as Elie Kedourie, Benedict Anderson, Ernest Gellner, and others, the conceptual device of nationalism sought to account for the paradigmatic location of anticolonial thought in the global history of ideas. The founding of new bounded territories centered on collective national identity became the defining logic rather than a mere outcome of the long anticolonial movement. The parochial remit of nationalism, in a way, stood as evidence for the expansion of the universality of the modern form of political community, where sovereignty, constitutional democracy, and bounded identity came together.

For their part, postcolonial founders in India and elsewhere were fairly wary of the language of nationalism and often balked at its normative poverty even when they were forced to affirm its apparent historical necessity. As Adom Getachew has demonstrated in her recent study, anticolonial thinkers, far from being parochial nationalists, actively sought to democratize the international order.[61] Indeed, even "official nationalists" like Nehru found it difficult to reflect on nationalism without foregrounding its normative limits. This critical history notwithstanding, the rise of nationalism as a catch-all category subsumed the anticolonial pursuit of democracy into the framework of territorial-national sovereignty and the attendant challenge of overcoming cultural and psychological burdens of imperial subjection. For late twentieth-century scholars of empire and anticolonialism, the conceptual token of nationalism allowed for a qualified historical vindication of the anti-colonial project, all while enlisting the pantheon of anticolonial nationalist thinkers in an intellectual tradition without "grand thinkers."[62]

In a classic study of Indian anticolonial thought, Partha Chatterjee influentially recapitulated the problem of anticolonialism as a simultaneous rejection and acceptance of the "dominance, both moral and epistemic, of an alien culture."[63] In the struggle between the nation and the empire, Chatterjee diagnosed a pervasive problem of derivativeness that cut across different moments of anticolonial thought. Chatterjee's formulation had the virtue of pushing back against the diffusionist narrative of anticolonialism; he rightly placed anticolonial thinkers' paradoxical struggle with imperial modernity at the center of their intellectual endeavor. But the foregrounding of the nationalist framework meant that the anticolonial search for popular sovereignty was made to amount to the more prosaic quest as to whether "a backward nation could 'modernize' itself while retaining its cultural identity."[64] Although anticolonial thinkers asserted their sovereign subjectivity as a nation, the "object in nationalist thought is still the Oriental, who retains the essentialist character depicted in Orientalist discourse."[65] The anticolonial project, then, turned on the affirmation of the national self against the imperial other. In the process, the theoretical ambitions of Indian anticolonial thinkers to reinvent the meaning of democracy became secondary to the narrative.

As this history of democratic thought in India shows, the intellectual anxiety over derivativeness involved not so much the ignominy of borrowing from the imperial other but rather a foundational concern over the time and place of political ideas in an uneven globe. The nineteenth-century optimism about political progress, though already charged with imitativeness, turned into a full-blown anxiety over derivativeness by the early decades of the twentieth century, especially for those who concerned themselves with the intellectual world of political thought. There is perhaps no better exemplar of this tension than the historian Bimanbehari Majumdar's 1934 volume *History of Political Thought from Rammohan to Dayananda (1821–1883)*, arguably the first significant attempt at writing the history of modern Indian political thought. Majumdar's now-forgotten intellectual history is exceptionally erudite, with a remarkable command over an archive scattered in monographs and periodical articles in multiple Indian regions and languages. This otherwise exemplary act of writing the history of political thought from the non-European world started with a telling apology. The "title of the work," Majumdar noted, required "some explanation":

> Political thought in the modern academic sense is a development possible only in a free state working out its destiny, or in a new state in process of formation out of the chaos of political strifes. In a country like ours, amongst a people who have for ages been ruled over by a succession of foreigners no other political development is normally possible except acquiescence . . . a development of political thought has taken place, through criticism and appreciation of the British administrative system in all its different and expanding spheres, for that is the only way in which political thought can grow in a subject country, as it grew in the subject medieval countries of Central Europe through discussions of questions affecting the Papal and Empire government.[66]

Some three decades later, when Majumdar published a new edition of the volume in independent India, the title of the volume had been changed to *History of Indian Social and Political Ideas*. This titular modification had to do with the consideration that the term "political ideas" is more "modest" than "political thought." He reiterated the troubled relationship of the backward peoples with the enterprise of political thought as they had to "give expression to their political ideas often in the garb of an essay on society, its functions and reforms needed."[67]

Majumdar's agenda in the book, however, was anything but modest. In the preface to the first edition, having felt it necessary to justify the title of the book, he emphatically argued that the contributions of a number of Indian political thinkers preceded their British counterparts: "I have shown how even before Austin, Raja Rammohun Roy made a reconciliation between the historical and analytical schools of jurisprudence and distinguished Law from Morality, how Akshaykumar Dutta preached the organismic theory of state before Herbert Spencer . . . and how Bankimchandra presented a new theory of Nationalism."[68] In the span of two paragraphs, Majumdar's shift from doubting the very possibility of "political thought" in the colonial world to its historical precedence captures a constitutive anxiety of writing the history of modern non-European political thought.[69] Majumdar's apprehension was shared by the majority of political thinkers he so carefully studied in the volume. This anxiety over the comparative location of Indian political thought is more than simply a testament to the necessarily comparative dimension of any political thought.[70] As Majumdar's *History* reveals, non-European political thought since the nineteenth century has largely felt the comparative weight of ideas in developmental terms. The specter of a delayed restaging of European ideas forced a spirited engagement with the abstract order of the globe as much as it facilitated an anxious tabulation of intellectual precedence. To be sure, the global landscape of modern political thought posed new challenges to both European and non-European political thinkers, though for the latter the comparative weight of backwardness generated a strong sense of doubt concerning the possibility of transcending their own historical particularity—and living up to what Leigh Jenco has characterized as the "deterritorialized claims" of political theory.[71]

This struggle to locate their own ideas attuned anticolonial political thinkers to the work of temporal visions in democratic politics. In fact, it can be argued that the greatest contribution of the anticolonial archive to the history of political thought lies in its treatment of the temporal background of political ideas. As we also shall see, the reckoning with the temporal vision of democratic thought necessarily meant a confrontation with its global landscape. In recent years, David Scott's work has done much to bring the temporal structure of anticolonial political thought into view. In revisiting C. L. R James's two narratives of the Haitian Revolution, Scott distinguishes the romantic, "vindicationist" aspiration of anticolonialism from the tragic sensibilities of the postcolonial era: the anticolonial search for sovereignty—the "answer" to the "question" of colonialism—was a "romantic" aspiration for overcoming of the "negative" power of colonialism.[72] For Scott, anticolonial emplotment was essentially romantic owing to its juxtaposition of the negative power of colonialism with the vision of a "positive and regenerative counter-power."[73] It is true that the midcentury postcolonial founders broadly shared Frantz Fanon's account of colonialism as a "totalizing structure" of subjection and fashioned the discourse of founding as a narrative of overcoming.[74] In India, too, the exhilaration of enacting sovereign self-rule among those who had long been deemed unqualified for it was palpable.

Important as the negative picture of colonialism was (especially at the moment of postcolonial founding), anticolonial thinkers, as we shall see throughout this book, sought to advance their political projects through self-conscious attempts to transform the terms of the postimperial future set by modern justifications of empire. For the Indian thinkers I study in this book, empire certainly had to be overcome, but no less important was the challenge of finding theoretical premises resistant to the ideals that had originally rendered empire compatible with democracy. To reflect on this problem was to grapple with developmentalism as a philosophical abstraction: the vision of the global where political orders were understood as either relatively advanced or backward. The greatest success of modern empires, after all, lay not in mere territorial possession but in the imposition of the view that the globe has a certain order of progression. By and large, Indian anticolonial thinkers agreed that the overcoming of developmentalism was never simply a matter of counterposing the precolonial against the colonial. Nor was it simply a matter of seizing the deferred future. What was required was a capacious way of thinking together the past and the future—which once mapped onto a world of "advanced" and "backward" peoples—that would resist the collapse of global difference into a political hierarchy. This foundationally global concern of anticolonial political thought is not reducible to an appreciation of transnational connections or to the fact that different parts of the globe were interlocked in a dynamic process. In thinking about the developmental order, anticolonial political thinkers repetitively stumbled on a picture of the globe that was, at once, hierarchical and integrated. What they demanded was a scrutinization of this global picture presupposed by modern political thought, even while the focus was limited to a local or national context. Ideologically internationalists or not, anticolonial political thinkers invariably grappled with the developmental background of political ideas—and ideals. Absent this consideration, the historiography of anticolonial political thought runs the risk of missing how central a transformative approach to the terms of the political future was to the anticolonial project.

This specifically required a subtle examination and reconstruction of the political ideals that anticolonial movements shared with modern

European democratic thought. Indian anticolonial political thinkers had an overlapping agreement that democratic self-rule was the only legitimate answer to imperial rule, but they were wary of approaching democratic ideals as ahistorical, portable artifacts. This is the concern that led Gandhi to argue that representative democracy reproduces the ills of modern civilization, and to redefine self-rule as a norm resistant to deferral of action. The federalists' critique of collective sovereignty owed no less to the unilinear narrative encoded within the ideal of representative government. Many others accepted the philosophical foundation of developmentalism as a condition of democracy, but they too had fashioned their ideals to address the hierarchical global background of the colonial present and postcolonial future. Nehru, for instance, strongly felt that democracy had to be theorized anew for a world where the juridical enshrining of popular sovereignty was insufficient. Insofar as the anticolonial project had to substantively remake its historical conditions, it required a democratic theory sensitive to its own paradigmatic contexts. The cumulative result of these endeavors was a sustained reckoning with the global terms of modern democratic political ideals. These different thinkers often disagreed on the fundamental premises of political theorization; their differences—we will see in following chapters—were often more important than their shared inheritance. But as far as the historiography of anticolonial political thought is concerned, it is worth underscoring that they all undertook, with varying degrees of success, the task of remaking the ideals of democracy in response to a powerful narrative about how democracy would unfold globally.

The broader point here lies in the fact that Indian anticolonial thinkers gave equal importance to democracy as a norm and as a historical phenomenon. The transcontinental backdrop of imperial subjection attuned Indian political thinkers to the global assumptions and entanglements of their democratic agendas. The democratic horizon of their expectations, at the same time, rendered the problem of anticolonialism beyond the culturalist matrix of nationalism and the mere replacement of imperial sovereignty. The chapters that follow reconstruct how these entwined concerns shaped modern Indian theorizations of the foundational political concepts of sovereignty, government, peoplehood, and self-rule. Alive to the fact that the imperial unification of the world dissociated modern democracy from many of its given contexts and aspirations, the Indian anticolonial thinkers studied here tackled head-on the new problems and forms of inequalities that trailed the globalization of democratic ideas. In tracing this history buried in the depths of the anticolonial archive, *Waiting for the People* aims to recover the meaning of what anticolonialism was and the intellectual inheritances it left behind for the world that was born in its wake.

CHAPTER 1

A GLOBAL HIERARCHY OF PEOPLES

The Rise of Developmentalism in the Nineteenth Century

DURING HIS FIRST encounter with a group of Europeans—an early mission of Portuguese Jesuits—in 1573, the Mughal emperor Akbar reportedly showed great interest in learning about the "wonders of Portugal and manners and customs of Europe." Writing on this encounter, his vizier Abul Fazl noted in passing that the emperor "desired to make this inquiry [about Europe] as a means for taming this barbarian group."[1] Abul Fazl seemed to have found it necessary to justify the undue interest the emperor had shown in the European missionaries. His concern was not entirely surprising. The Mughals, after all, considered themselves to be one of the greatest empires of the known world.[2] The discovery of an oceanic route to India in 1498 brought European traders into the already flourishing transnational commercial world of early modern India. Throughout the seventeenth and eighteenth centuries, the European traders based in India slowly became integrated into the commercial life of coastal Indian cities. Although the British traders began to found their own enclaves with the permission of native rulers, they "played virtually no political role outside their enclaves" until "the middle of the eighteenth century."[3] Europeans were subjects of ethnographic curiosity, theological exchanges, and trade-related tensions, but no overpowering political or epistemic framework became synonymous with Europe for Indians.[4]

It was only in the mid-eighteenth century with the British conquest of Bengal—which began as a relatively local political victory—that the Indian political and intellectual horizon became fatefully interlocked with the history of Europe.[5] For the British, no inherited imperial framework could be sufficient to understand how to rule over a complex society situated across the globe. The transplantation of the British political system in India appeared to be as untenable as the continuation of what the British deemed as "corrupt" and "despotic" forms of native rule. In the latter half of the eighteenth century, as British rule in India slowly expanded, the Montesquieu-inspired climatological account of civilizational difference wielded significant influence over British understanding of Indian difference.[6] For Indians, still steeped in the Persianate world of the Mughal Empire, the ambitions of great empires and the politics of conquest were not especially unfamiliar. Before the "great divergence" fully took off, the sense of difference between Indians and their European rulers was not yet mediated by any seemingly providential spin of progress.[7]

The reckoning with the colonial encounter in European political thought had begun much earlier. The colonization of the Americas—marked by the discovery of a new world and the brutal subjection of the native inhabitants—posed an altogether novel set of questions for early modern European political thought. The process of making the unfamiliar familiar—what the historian Anthony Pagden terms the "principle of attachment"—went through multiple phases over the long history of European expansion in the world.[8] In the wake of the early Spanish colonization of the Americas in the sixteenth century, the preexisting Thomist natural law framework, for instance, shaped efforts to render the Amerindians commensurable with Europeans.[9] As the Age of Enlightenment commenced and natural law traditions declined, the conjectural history framework would centralize the figure of the human in its approach to the non-European world. The construction of the purportedly primitive peoples as closer to the natural could allow for both their glorification as noble and their condemnation as ignoble, depending on how the distinction between the natural and the social was normatively evaluated.[10] It even made possible the signification of

Europeans as a corrupted version of the pristine nature of an original humankind. In the latter half of the eighteenth century, a number of Enlightenment thinkers would mount severe criticisms of European domination over the non-European world, often by stressing the shared ground of "cultural humanity."[11] Still, even as the Enlightenment critique of empire acquired momentum in late eighteenth-century European thought, the "second" imperial expansion of Europe was acquiring new momentum in Asia and Africa.[12]

All of this was to change in the nineteenth century—in the metropolis and colonies alike. The discourse of historical development—what I will simply call developmentalism—emerged as the overarching paradigm for cognizing and theorizing global difference in the nineteenth century.[13] The distinctive marker of developmentalism was the assumption that different points of a shared time could be located in different sites of the world. As the vast majority of the non-European world was quickly being turned into European imperial possessions, the developmental resolution of global difference brought together hitherto historically incommensurable traditions in a shared scale of backwardness and forwardness. As the historian Jürgen Osterhammel observes, the "closing of distance" that began from the late eighteenth century—thanks to the simultaneous expansion of global empires and capitalism—conferred a strong sense of urgency on the problem of global difference. What followed was nothing short of a "transformation of the world" itself.[14] Neither the framework of shared "cultural humanity" nor the guidance of universal morality proved to be sufficient to navigate the (imperial) world brought together on an unprecedented scale. In the shadow of the developmental turn, the non-European world no longer remained merely other. In becoming the prehistory of European modernity, India also integrated more directly with Europe. The one world and one time of developmentalism reinforced a theoretical commitment to global oneness as much as it legitimized a division of the globe between the dyad of "progressive" and "backward." This dual pull of developmentalism would remain a feature of its complex history over the rest of the century and beyond, complicating attempts to simply reduce it to—or neatly disentangle it entirely from—empire.

Although political thought was not unique in coming under the profound influence of the developmental description of the world, it played a foundational role in shaping the meaning of developmentalism itself. Not simply an intellectual reflection of economic and social transformations, developmentalism took part in the making of a new world. There was no purportedly objective fact that led nineteenth-century British— and Indian—thinkers to conclude that India should be fashioned in the political image of Britain. It was rather the developmentalization of the norm of self-government—a proof by "ought" rather than "is"—that paved the way for the characterization of non-European political institutions and practices as not simply despotic but also backward. Developmentalism offered no positive norm of its own, but it foregrounded a temporal logic for the rise of democracy in Europe as well as for the continued hold of despotism among subject peoples elsewhere. The paradigmatic function of developmentalism meant that it is not best approached simply as a matter of self-conscious ideological subscription, for it imbued political imagination with a new orientation to the past and the future alike. In this chapter, then, I take up the question of how the developmental view of global difference entered into political theorization and how each shaped the other.

The category of the people was at the center of how the developmental description of the globe found its way in political thought. In the hands of liberal imperialists, I suggest, the hierarchy of civilizations amounted to a hierarchy of peoplehood. The result was what I call the democratic justification of imperial rule. I follow the distinct careers of Rammohun Roy (1772–1833) and John Stuart Mill (1806–1873) to recuperate the entwined origins of developmentalism and democracy for colonial India. Though separated by a few decades, Rammohun and the younger Mill intellectually inhabited different ages and were united only by a brief moment of intellectual overlap—and a missed personal encounter—at the height of the 1832 Reform Bill agitations. The brief intersection in their political and intellectual preoccupations, however, captured the emerging centrality of the category of the people in the formation of the developmental paradigm.

Rammohun was arguably the last major thinker in the British Empire to operate with an eighteenth-century, Enlightenment approach to the question of global difference. Rammohun's reason-centric approach to difference ascribed the limitations of India to its "excess," rather than to its lack, of civilization. The normative horizon within which he operated was that of "good government," where global empires posed a particular challenge to the ideals of the separation of powers and civil liberty. The younger Mill—for all his longing for the eighteenth century—would establish himself as the most articulate defender of the globe-spanning developmental hierarchy of peoples. With John Stuart Mill, the emerging view that the non-European world was lacking in civilization—not in the eighteenth-century sense but in the newfound sense of historical progress—reached its philosophical epitome. Yet Mill's developmental justification of empire could be so strident because of his disavowal of the universal principle of empire; his confidence stemmed instead from the normative subservience of empire to the higher ideal of self-government.

The transformative nature of the developmental turn appears most sharply when we trace how it rendered secondary—even obsolete—the political questions and problems of the preceding era. The political thought of Rammohun Roy offers a key to this turning point. In Rammohun's work, the Indian masses—the "natives," in the parlance of his days—figured as agents whose exercise of reason was crucial to the institution of good government. For him, the question was whether Indians could exercise reason without abandoning inherited resources—their "ancient traditions." The overarching concerns of Rammohun's vision of good government were the separation of powers and civil rights. The improvement of the (subject-) people was a given responsibility of the government; the state of peoplehood had no bearing on the abstract norms that constituted the universal criteria of good government. Thus, the trans-imperial scope of Rammohun's politics was unencumbered by both self-government and developmentalism. As his indirect encounter with James Mill will help illustrate, there were only faint traces of the emerging paradigm of developmentalism in his thought. Indeed, his belated appreciation of the norm of self-government quite directly led to a developmental approach to the question of Indian peoplehood. Contrary to the long-held scholarly consensus, I suggest in this chapter that Rammohun marked the end, not the beginning, of an era.

Next, I explore how the developmental unevenness of the globe received a collectivist resignification from British liberal imperialists. The seemingly self-evident progressive state of the European world was here inextricably linked to the development of the collective capacity of its peoples. Although his liberal imperialism was not quite unique in Victorian Britain, John Stuart Mill occupies a special place both for his salience in the history of political thought and for his singular presence in nineteenth-century Indian political thought. The younger Mill's emphasis on the necessity of a correspondence between the level of historical development and the form of political institutions would project self-government as the highest ideal for the colonies and yet defer it to a distant future. Mill singled out certain qualities of peoplehood, from collective will to capacity for cooperation, as the ultimate political markers of historical development. The rise of democratic government in England owed to the relative progress of its people, just as the necessity for enlightened imperial rule in India stemmed from its backward peoplehood. The aim of British rule, then, was not simply to train the Indians into self-government. More fundamentally, it involved the challenge of transforming its amorphous masses into a people fit for self-government. This is how empire and democracy came to be co-constitutive for the global political horizon of the nineteenth century.

BEFORE DEVELOPMENTALISM: RAMMOHUN ROY'S EMPIRE OF LIBERTY

> From the late unhappy news [the overthrowing of the Neapolitan constitutional government], I am obliged to conclude that I shall not live to see liberty universally restored to the nations of Europe and Asiatic nations, especially those that are European colonies . . . I consider the cause of the Neapolitans as my own, and their enemies, as ours.
>
> —Rammohun Roy, 1821[15]

Rammohun Roy's visit to England in 1831—officially as an ambassador of the moribund Mughal Empire—generated great public interest in the heart of the British Empire. This long tour—his first and last (he died in Bristol in 1833)—brought him into conversation with the luminaries of British public life, including Jeremy Bentham, Benjamin Disraeli, William Godwin, Robert Owen, and James Mill. Bentham floated the idea of Rammohun standing for elections to the British Parliament, while the phrenologists obsessed over the learned Hindu to prove or disprove hypotheses about race and intelligence. For his part, Rammohun vigorously campaigned for the political demands of Indians, and enthusiastically took up the cause of the Reform Bill.[16] During the tour, he was invited by a Select Committee of the House of Commons to share his opinions on several India-related issues. He was asked pointedly about the "conditions" of the Indian people—physical, material, and moral. While his response to the queries relating to the physical condition of the people focused primarily on climate and diet, he found it rather difficult to answer the question concerning the "moral condition of the people" in a straightforward manner.[17] Rammohun first noted that European opinions about "native" peoples, both favorable and unfavorable, were based on faulty generalizations, resulting in a monolithic view of the native population. In contrast, he chose to answer the question by dividing the broad category of the native people into different classes: villagers, city-dwellers, and professional classes. The peasants and villagers, Rammohun observed, "are as innocent, temperate, and moral in their conduct as the people of any country whatsoever."[18] The city-dwellers and professionals who were in interaction with people from different "civilizations" tended to be inferior in their moral commitments. Nonetheless, Rammohun added, there were plenty of people from these two classes who had "real merit, worth and character." The Select Committee probed further the economic and cultural practices of the natives, leading to the question: "What capability of improvement do they [the Indian people] possess?" Rammohun's terse answer could not have been more unequivocal: "They have the same capability of improvement as any other civilized people."[19] Such a confident dismissal of the inferiority of the Indian people would not be repeated again with the same force in the rest of the century.

Rammohun Roy is often posited as the determinate origin point of the Indian liberal tradition that culminated later in the century. His writings are also read as the epitome of a precocious nineteenth-century liberalism, untainted by the "indigenist nationalism" of his successors.[20] Given Rammohun's enduring status as the originator of all things modern in colonial India, very few of his interpreters have paused to ask: What exactly did "improvement" or "civilization" mean for Rammohun? How did he evaluate the criteria of "inferiority" or the very notion of the "native" people? The stakes of here are more than scholastic. Rammohun's work is crucial to understanding the ascendance of developmentalism in Indian political thought, even as his own intellectual preoccupations predated and only passingly grappled with emerging developmental tropes. He witnessed the crumbling of the precolonial political order as well as the emergence of a novel form of transnational imperial rule in early colonial India. He shared the eighteenth-century Enlightenment faith in the universal purchase of reason and hoped to institute political liberty across imperial space. His work also illustrates how the framework of universal liberty came to be displaced by a developmental vision of democracy. My aim is thus not to posit Rammohun as a lost alternative to developmentalism or to judge Rammohun's successors in the mirror of his thought, for the meaning of imperial subjection would sharply change in the decades following his death.

Born in the early years of British rule in Bengal in the 1770s, Rammohun's extraordinary intellectual training spanned the major intellectual traditions of precolonial India (Sanskrit, Persian, and Arabic) as well as contemporary European Enlightenment thought. As we shall see, his intellectual foundations—especially the framework of reason and the politics of liberty—were primarily inherited from the eighteenth century. Rammohun wrote extensively on the terms of interpreting India's ancient resources while responding creatively to the imperial remaking of the world. He campaigned for the reform of Hinduism, agitated against the curtailing of press freedom, demanded the separation of powers, and enthusiastically embraced the cause of the British Reform Bill of 1832. Rammohun's global intellectual interests would come to be matched by a "transnational fame."[21]

Rammohun's humanist approach to global difference emerged out of his background in monist theology. His early intellectual training was in Islamic theology, and he wrote primarily in Persian.[22] At this early stage of his career, Rammohun was preoccupied with resolving the tension between "reason" and "tradition." When exactly he began to be acquainted with contemporary European thought is a matter of contention among scholars.[23] Very little of his writings from the first phase of his career survived. The earliest surviving text, *Tuhfat-ul-Muwahhidin* (translated both as *A Gift to Monotheists* and as *A Gift to Deists*), written in Persian with an Arabic preface, offered a rationalist defense of monotheism. The text disqualified special claims of revelation and proposed that metaphysical as well as moral principles should be premised on reason. Organized between the dyad of "nature" and "custom," the *Tuhfat* attributes to the latter the plural character of religious beliefs and practices across societies.[24] Rammohun found belief in a supreme being and the soul to be the touchstones of rational theology, but he also observed that the dominance of custom—which makes "individuals of mankind blind and deaf notwithstanding their having eyes and ears"[25]—had historically obfuscated the enterprise of reason across the globe. In this early work, the problem of custom was essentially one of "deception." Indeed, Rammohun divides humankind into four groups: the deceiver, the deceived, the self-deceived who help delude others, and the undeceived.[26] But he argued that inductive reason is sufficient to avoid deception and demystify the "wonderful inventions of the people of Europe" or "the dexterity of jugglers."[27] The text is also striking for its deployment of the tropes of conjectural history to explain how different religions evolved into customs detached from reason.[28] There are thus good reasons to assume that Rammohun was somewhat familiar with the conjectural-historical style of eighteenth-century European Enlightenment thought by the time he wrote the *Tuhfat*.

Rammohun's mature theological writings would depart from this strong opposition between reason and custom (tradition), though the former continued to be central to his thought. Throughout the 1820s and 1830s he would publish widely in Bengali and English to advance a new understanding of the Hindu scriptures, especially the Vedanta. Rammohun's overarching goal in these numerous treatises and translations was to defend a nondualist interpretation of divinity in the Hindu scriptures. Instead of directly controverting the authority of the scriptures, he now took them as an ancient repository of reason. Moving away from the deception-centric framework, he suggested that the "idolatrous" portions of the scriptures are "allegorical adoration of the true Deity": their purpose was to guide "those whose limited understandings rendered them incapable of comprehending . . . the invisible Supreme Being."[29] A careful reading of the scripture ultimately reveals nothing contrary to reason. This argument was not limited to the Hindu scriptures. Rammohun would publish his own version of the New Testament, a collection of moral precepts devoid of miraculous and Trinitarian elements.[30] Yet he also added that reason by itself is inadequate for the purpose of interpretation, as it generates "universal doubt, incompatible with principles on which our comfort and happiness mainly depend." This realization led Rammohun to attribute special importance to the "traditions of ancient nations," where "reason" and "common justice" are both latent.[31] In the words of one of his foremost nineteenth-century interpreters, B. N. Seal, Rammohun understood traditions to be "embodiments of the collective sense of [the] races of mankind."[32]

This orientation found its most powerful expression in Rammohun's writing against *sati*, or widow-burning. His relentless campaign against sati was the source of his fame and notoriety in India. Crucially, in his copious writings on the issue, Rammohun steered clear of any invocation of the civilization/barbarism dichotomy. In his heated debate with the traditionalist pandits, Rammohun refused to concede scriptural legitimation of sati: he found it be at once against "all scriptures and all reason."[33] He gathered evidence in support of the rights of widows from scriptures and offered alternative explanations of the passages that might appear to support sati. For example, he argued that most compelling evidence in support of sati characterizes it as a lesser good compared to virtuous living of widows and, at any rate, requires the consent of the widow. As these provisions had never been respected, widows thus could not possibly have consented to their own immolation.[34] In another instance, Rammohun connected the exclusion of women from their right to property as the debilitating circumstance that had led to the perpetuation of sati.[35]

Rammohun thus did not approach the Indian past as a "lack" of civilization. On the contrary, the "degradation" of the Indian society, as he once put it, had to do with its "excess in civilization."[36] He was not keen on the legal resolution of the problem of sati, especially because of the charge of an external imposition of norms that the supporters of sati were likely to bring against it (though he did support the law when it was instituted in 1829).[37] Rammohun ultimately held that practices such as sati and the exclusion of women from property rights are against "both common sense and the law of the land."[38] The consolidation of such practices did not have much to do with the absence of enlightened norms in India. It was instead rooted in the wrong interpretation of scriptures put forward by the Brahmins, "self-interested guides" who "[had hidden] the true substance of morality."[39] Some recent interpreters of

Rammohun, such as Andrew Sartori, have taken his critique of "priestly cunning" to be proof of his reproduction of a "classic trope" of "British liberalism."[40] This characterization of Rammohun as a "sincere liberal imperialist" is highly debatable.[41] For James Mill, "priesthood" is a marker of historical backwardness (rather than mere deception) and is "generally found to usurp the greatest authority, in the *lowest* state of society."[42] Likewise, the discourse of "priestcraft" served as evidence of backwardness in Macaulay's developmental narrative of Indian society. For Rammohun, on the contrary, priestcraft "hid" the source of reason *already* latent in Indian tradition. It had no bearing on the purported civilizational location of a people. Rammohun himself was clear about his own intellectual affinities with eighteenth-century European Enlightenment thinkers. In a pseudonymously published essay, he placed himself in the company of British and French Enlightenment philosophers: "We Hindoos regard him in the same light as Christians do Hume, Voltaire, Gibbon and other sceptics."[43]

But Rammohun had eventually outgrown the Voltairean denigration of religion that marked his *Tuhfat* phase. In fact, the desire to reconcile universal reason and plural human societies led him to defend Christianity against its strictly rationalist critics. Rammohun's exchange with the utopian socialist Robert Owen is suggestive here. In spite of his openness to Owen's socialist ideas, Rammohun could not reconcile himself to Owen's rejection of religion. After multiple dialogues, Rammohun decided that he would no longer engage with Owen. The reason for his abstinence was Owen's rejection of the "Precepts of Christianity."[44] In a follow-up letter to Owen's son, Robert Dale, Rammohun revisited the gist of his disagreement with the elder Owen: "It is not necessary either in England or in America to oppose religion in promoting the social domestic and political welfare of their inhabitants particularly a system of religion which inculcates the doctrine of universal love and charity . . . more than two thousand years ago wise and pious Brahmans of India entertained almost the same opinion which your father offers though by no means were destitute of religion."[45] Owen's religious views were controversial in his day. Rammohun's global fame also partly owed to the unitarian excitement over a non-European proponent (Ralph Waldo Emerson characterized him as a rare "trophy" for Unitarians).[46] That Rammohun, notwithstanding his earlier denunciation of religion, was skeptical of Owen's critique of religion might seem unsurprising. But Rammohun's charge against Owen becomes more interesting when we take into account the point that the thinker who so mercilessly satirized the missionary universalization of Christianity was also its defender in the European context.[47] This was more than a strictly theological issue. As Rammohun's invocation of the ancient Brahman suggests, the "common basis" across religious traditions operated as a shared ground from which the uneven imperial world could be brought into a commensurable dialogue. Respect for Christianity in Europe was essential to render legible the reason inherent in Indian religious traditions. This was how Rammohun worked out his vision of Enlightenment universalism, which was the bedrock of his political turn in the 1820s.

Rammohun's clash with the emerging discourse of progressive imperialism took place in the wake of Grant's Jury Bill in the British Parliament. The bill would allow Indians to serve on the grand jury (including in the trials of Christians) as well as the Office of the Justice of the Peace. The right to serve as jurors was central to Rammohun's political activism in the 1820s. Upon his arrival in England, he collaborated with Charles Grant (a member of Parliament who belonged to the famous Clapham Sect) to amend the current jury act. The East India Company led the opposition to the bill. The dispute around the bill boiled down to a fraught set of arguments concerning whether the "natives" were advanced enough to serve on the jury and in the magistracy. In the pages of the *Morning Chronicle,* a proxy encounter took place between Rammohun Roy and James Mill. The *Chronicle*'s opposition to the bill, Rammohun wrote in a letter, had been "stirred up" by James Mill—a friend of the editor, John Black.[48] The *Chronicle* made a twofold argument against opening up the Office of the Justice of the Peace to the natives. First, it suggested that the system in Britain itself was beleaguered by feudal remnants as well as by less than ideally trained magistrates. Second, Indians being in "possession of proper qualifications" for the office would be nothing short of a "fortunate accident."[49] The two prongs of the argument ultimately united on the question of public "intelligence." With the growing dissemination of legal knowledge and "increased intelligence" in Britain, even unqualified magistrates were forced to take heed of public opinion.

Among a backward people unacquainted with "English law," on the other hand, the introduction of native magistrates "would be, of all monstrosities ever conceived, the most monstrous."[50] The editorial's approving invocation of the importance of an advanced stage of civilization and the questioning of the intellectual qualification of Indians carried the imprint of James Mill's arguments in *The History of British India*. In fact, the editorial approvingly quoted the rebuttal of the bill offered by the East India Company's Court of Directors (a document that may well have been prepared by James Mill, Chief Examiner of the Company's correspondence with India at the time).

Directly following the Court of Directors' observations, the *Chronicle* presented a long quotation from Charles Grant's rejoinder. Grant affirmed that the intellectual capacity of "respectable natives" should not be doubted; in fact, he argued, the proof was already abundant in the public services for which they were currently eligible. In the original rebuttal to the Company, Grant borrowed a number of his arguments directly from Rammohun's lengthy testimony and the response he had drafted against the Court of Directors' letter.[51] Following Rammohun, Grant found "gratuitous" the assumption that Indians would not make any willing sacrifice to serve voluntarily or would be unable to learn the intricacies of English law.[52] There was another point on which Rammohun disagreed even more decisively with James Mill and the East India Company. The jury system, he argued, was nothing alien to the Indian tradition: "the principle of juries under certain modifications has from the most remote periods been well understood in this country under the name of Punchayet." The tracing of the jury system to a traditional Indian village council is representative of Rammohun's overarching aim to unify reason and tradition. His assertion that "respectable and intelligent natives" were qualified to serve as jurors did not simply appeal to their knowledge of English law and language. The expertise of Indians in precolonial legal practices was also significant to Rammohun's argument, for the principles of justice were ultimately the same.[53] Thanks, in part, to Rammohun's effort, Grant's Jury Bill was enacted in 1832.

Rammohun's defense of the "common basis" of justice was consistent with his faith in the universal scope of liberty. The two poles of his normative universe were "liberty" and "despotism." As his early interpreters noticed, Rammohun's political thought bore unmistakable marks of Montesquieu's theorization of liberty.[54] Along Montesquieuian lines, the question of liberty, for Rammohun, figured as the challenge to institute the separation of powers and civil rights. Much of his criticism of British policies in the 1820s concerned the despotic potential involved in empowering the British administration in India with legislative as well as judicial power. Rammohun's persistent pursuit of trial by jury emerged out of the belief that the "[combination] of Legislative and Judicial power . . . is destructive of all Civil Liberty."[55] The concern with the separation of powers was also at the forefront of Rammohun's other political preoccupation: the freedom of the press. His writings in opposition to the 1823 restrictions on vernacular press freedom foregrounded the universal indefensibility of despotic rule, along with the enlightening qualities of free speech. The curtailing of free speech ultimately was a manifestation of the dangers of concentrating all forms of political power in the administration. Rammohun maintained that the restriction on the freedom of the press was a direct result of the executive authority's assumption of legislative power.[56] As he often argued, the main danger of such a concentration of power was the violation of civil rights. On the same grounds, Rammohun protested the establishment of a legislative authority in India, which he feared would result in a further conflation between legislative power and executive power. Instead, he preferred the British Parliament exercising legislative powers from a distance.[57] What it also shows is that he was open to creatively using the global distance between India and Britain to find novel ways to constrain the despotic drives of Company rule over India. The same concern with the separation of powers also informed Rammohun's scant writings on the political history of ancient India. In Rammohun's conjectural narrative, the conflict introduced by caste in an "early age of civilization" was resolved only when legislative and executive authority were shared between two separate "tribes." It was only then that India "enjoyed peace and comfort for a great many centuries." As this arrangement collapsed and one group came to control both executive and legislative authorities, India entered into a millennium of tyranny.[58]

This preoccupation of Rammohun's political thought also helps to explain his controversial position on the colonization of India by European settlers. Rammohun's support of European colonization has long troubled the project of assimilating him to a progressive narrative of anticolonial political thought.[59] Rammohun's case for colonization was different from that of the free traders, who had also been campaigning for the abolition of the East India Company's monopoly.[60] The free traders held that the opening up of the Indian market would lead to widespread European colonization and help India advance. Rammohun did not agree with this argument. He observed that "persons of lower class" would be likely to give in to racial and religious discrimination. The only colonization that could be endorsed was that of "higher and better educated classes of Europeans."[61] Rammohun hoped that a "free and extensive communication" between European settlers and the natives would free the latter's "mind from superstition and prejudices" and improve their knowledge of agriculture and the mechanical arts.[62] The aim of this otherwise tacit legitimation of the civilizing mission concerned the facilitation of reason already present in Indians rather than an appeal to uplift them to a higher stage of historical development. What Rammohun valued in colonization was the benefits of exposure to new technical and rational knowledge, which he considered to be easily transmittable from one people to another.

Alienating some of his allies who were invested in prioritizing free trade, Rammohun made the question of the separation of powers central in this debate on colonization. The European settlers, who would bring their rights with them, would be a guard against the "abuse of power" by the Company-State. The increased intercourse between India and Britain through the settlers, Rammohun further hoped, would enable Parliament to legislate more proficiently on Indian issues. Once again, Rammohun underscored the remedy it would offer to help overcome the "mercy of the representations of a comparatively few individuals."[63] On the other hand, the "turbulence" likely to follow from European colonization could be preemptively remedied by enacting "equal laws, placing all the classes on the same footing as to civil rights, and the establishment of trial by jury."[64]

This further illustrates that Rammohun was willing to go so far as to alter the makeup of the Indian people for the sake of civil rights and the separation of powers. The pursuit of liberty in an imperial context counterintuitively presented the prospect of European colonization to be the antidote to despotic rule. What it also helps us to see is the relative distance between Rammohun's politics of liberty and the emerging ideal of self-government. His was a form of politics unconcerned with the source of sovereignty.[65] Much like Montesquieu, Rammohun made no meaningful distinction between sovereignty and government, beyond the legislative–executive distinction.[66] He did not think it necessary to respond to the unique challenge of instituting liberty in a global empire— where sovereignty was located in another corner of the world—by questioning imperial sovereignty itself. The "principles of good government" concerned the separation of powers and civil rights, which Rammohun hoped to institute within the imperial form.[67] This is also precisely why imperial subjection could not stand in the way of the universal import of liberty. To refer back to the epigraph to this section, Rammohun experienced no temporal lag between the liberty of the Neapolitans and his own.

As Rammohun took his politics of liberty to the imperial heartland, British politics was undergoing its own reckoning with the question of democracy, namely the Reform Bill of 1832. This democratic experience sowed the seeds of developmental reasoning in the final phase of Rammohun's thought. An enthusiast for the Reform Bill, Rammohun vowed to sever connections with England if the bill failed in Parliament.[68] The signs of a more uncertain future, however, could also be found in his interpretation of the Reform Act. As it turned out, the normative affirmation of self-government could not quite be separated from the developmentalization of the ideal itself. In the midst of the dual victories of the Reform Bill and the Jury Bill, it became evident that the success of the people of England had paradoxically deferred the project of instituting liberty in India. Cautioning against excessive excitement over the passing of the Jury Bill, Rammohun wrote: "The voice of the mighty people of England grows every day stronger in proportion to the growth of their intelligence. I must at the same time confess that the progress we have made in India as to knowledge or politics is by no means equal to that made here by the English. . . . We should not be too hasty and too sanguine in raising our condition, since gradual improvements are most durable."[69] He even directly attributed the rise of popular power in England to its historical advancement: "England is now arrived at that degree of civilization which places the reign of opinion on a permanent basis."[70]

Rammohun passed away soon after, leaving behind a set of unforeseen legacies. He would be hailed variously as the "father of modern

India," the first liberal, and even the real originator of the idea of swaraj.[71] As Partha Chatterjee rightly observes, such recruitments of Rammohun in the "nationalist modern" tend to elide his distinct historical moment.[72] Rammohun's political thought, barring the late hesitations, was not concerned with self-government or developmentalism. Much in the vein of eighteenth-century British thought, Rammohun's work is replete with the term "improvement." He did hold that the "object of the Government" was the "improvement of the native population."[73] It is worth keeping in mind, however, that the term "improvement" originated in the seventeenth century and gained widespread currency as a general metaphor for "betterment."[74] In the history of British political thought, the term can be found in abundance from John Locke to Edmund Burke. As Rammohun was writing, the meaning of "improvement" was becoming more than a marker of open-ended "betterment"; the collective stage of improvement of a people would soon come to be the precondition of self-government. Rammohun's political thought predated this turn in nineteenth-century imperial as well as anticolonial thought. In the age of self-government, scholars struggled to explain the absence of the idea in Rammohun Roy's work. The editor of his collected works, Jogendra Chunder Ghose, argued that the "germs" of representative government could already be seen in the reforms he proposed toward the end of his life.[75] Others, such as Bimanbehari Majumdar, conjectured that Rammohun did not make the demand because he realized that India was not yet fit for self-government.[76] These attempts to offer an alibi for Rammohun, however, only registered the central place that the idea of self-government would retrospectively come to occupy in the narratives of nineteenth-century Indian political thought.

LIBERAL IMPERIALISM AND THE MAKING
OF HIERARCHICAL PEOPLEHOOD

As Rammohun Roy was campaigning for religious reform and civil rights, the ideology of British rule in India was undergoing a significant transformation. Already in the late eighteenth century, the novel challenge of ruling over the far-flung world of India—teeming as it was with a dizzying variety of regions and cultures—posed a set of difficult questions to the British. Unlike the settler colonial expansion into the new world, the loosely integrated territory of India, and its complex political geography, immediately appeared to make the direct transplantation of English law unfeasible. Yet, as Robert Travers argues, the long-standing British tradition of viewing Asiatic societies as "despotic" meant that the continuation of precolonial juridical and administrative traditions was not a viable alternative either.[77] To reconcile empire with liberty, eighteenth-century British theorists of empire turned to the idea of "ancient constitutionalism," an artifact of their own metropolitan political context. Espoused most famously by Edmund Burke, the framework allowed the British to draw legitimacy from the "genius" of India embodied in the "ancient Mughal constitution" without directly transposing British norms onto India. The widespread purchase of a Montesquieuian, climatological view of Indian difference helped explain the supposedly organic roots of its "despotic" form of government, whereas ancient constitutionalism emphasized the possibility of retrieving the uncorrupted higher norms buried in the Indian past.[78] The trial of Warren Hastings—which brought the Company's violence and unchecked exploitation into British view—burst open this tension inherent in late eighteenth-century British rule in India.[79]

In the period following the trial of Hastings (and the major economic reform ushered in by Lord Cornwallis) and amid the decline of the ancient constitutionalism framework, imperial administrators in India showed a renewed resistance to "applying British constitutional principles to the Indian administration."[80] Instead, these imperial actors found it more plausible and reasonable to retain the supposedly "Indian tradition of personal government . . . and notions of Indian 'difference.'"[81] The consolidation of Indian "difference" coexisted often with a defense of British Empire as an agent of improvement, though this moral idiom of *improvement* was still far removed from developmentalism. In marked contrast from what James Mill would soon argue, some of these imperial administrators, such as Thomas Munro, found "India so distant from Britain, and so different, that it must have its own futures, one that built upon a foundation of Indian institutions, cultures and peoples under the watchful hand of architects like himself."[82] Such a vision of global difference did not necessarily undermine the imperial project, but it imbued it with a specific set of priorities. For these imperial administrators, the question at stake was how Britain should manage the otherness of

India for the sake of consolidating and expanding British rule. The developmentalist question par excellence—How could India be made historically commensurate with the advanced nations of the world?—was still an unaskable one. As we have seen, for all his faith in the universal validity of good government, Rammohun, too, neither considered it necessary for India to radically rebuild itself on supposedly advanced British foundations nor found the fact of imperial hierarchy to be indicative of any necessary developmental hierarchy.

It was in this context that James Mill's monumental *History of British India*—published in 1817 (though he started working on it from 1806)—sought to offer a new basis to British rule in India. Though Mill's text was very much an intervention in the British debates over its Indian empire, it also signaled the transformation of the question of empire into a philosophical problem of foundational import. To rule over India was no longer simply a matter of imperial governance and expansion; it involved the question of how the globe should be thought of as a coherent entity. Marked by an "uneasy alliance" between utilitarianism and conjectural history, James Mill's global view of progress was more an initiator of liberal imperialism than a continuation of the theories of his eighteenth-century Scottish predecessors.[83] The text launched a full-fledged assault on the orientalists, such as William Jones, who found precolonial Mughal and ancient Indian literary and philosophical resources worthy of intellectual respect and valuable for imperial governance. Consider, for example, this passage: "As the manners, institutions, and attainments of the Hindus, have been stationary for many ages. . . . By conversing with the Hindus of the present day, we, in some measure, converse with the Chaldeans and Babylonians of the time of Cyrus; with the Persians and Egyptians of the time of Alexander."[84] In this effortless global measuring of developmental progress, Mill showed no qualms in equating contemporary India with the times of Alexander. This way of approaching global difference quickly assumed a life beyond Britain. As the explanatory power of a common process of progressive development ascended, the once-venerated non-European objects of knowledge were soon consigned to the prehistory of Europe.[85] From G. W. F Hegel to J. S. Mill, nineteenth-century theorists of historical development relied heavily on the imperially mediated knowledge of the non-European world, and in particular that of India, to fashion the paradigm of developmentalism.[86] In any case, the liberal-imperialist turn in the more abstract ideologies of empire coincided with the desire to institute a new order in India, even if the liberal imperialists had no overwhelming control over concrete administrative policies.[87]

The globe was no longer a space marked by irreducible human or cultural difference; all such differences, on the contrary, could be classified in a shared scheme of developmental progress. The elder Mill, however, neither grappled with the philosophical stakes of a global discourse of development nor historicized the categories of developmental comparison. His relatively "underdeveloped" account of historical development collapsed the cognitive, material, and customary dimensions of non-European peoples to create a straight line of progress—an almost dyadic conception of progress that often distilled into a crude separation between civilization and barbarism. This analytical poverty of the elder Mill's conception of progress would be the subject of his Whig contemporaries' withering criticism; it was not lost on his son either. Having consigned India to the prehistory of Europe, James Mill's utilitarian suggestion was "light taxes and good laws; nothing more is wanting for national and individual prosperity all over the globe."[88] The purpose of such good government would be to maximize the "happiness" of Indians. The aim of political—or rather civilizational—reform was to elevate the state of Indians, but the elder Mill's utilitarian priorities led him to posit good government—rather than self-government—as the end of imperial rule.

For the next generation of liberal imperialists, the normative value of self-government transcended the question of utility.[89] For T. B. Macaulay as for J. S. Mill, the project of self-government—understood as parliamentary representative government—was at the heart of the process of progress. This political meaning of progress—as opposed to the strict utilitarian account of the elder Mill—would exert an extraordinary influence over the rest of the century. The emerging centrality of the figure of the people in progressive legitimation of empire was eloquently captured in Macaulay's famous speech at the British Parliament on the Government of India Act in 1833. Macaulay's starting point was similar to James Mill's: the patent backwardness of India (in fact, he lauded the elder Mill, otherwise his rival, as the greatest expert on India).[90] Taking liberties with orientalist caricatures, he observed that Indians were a people "debased by three thousand years of despotism and priestcraft."[91] Macaulay's repeated reference to the Indian "people" moves suggestively between the descriptive and normative senses of the term. Descriptively, "the people" embodied a backward temporality. Macaulay pondered whether the anarchic period between the decline of the Mughal Empire and the consolidation of British rule had been enough to "throw the people back whole centuries."[92] The figure of the people, then, was a repository of civilizational progress (or its lack thereof). The normative implication of the developmental location of a people became obvious when Macaulay asked: "[Is] representative government practicable in India?" "In Europe," he observed, "the people are everywhere perfectly competent to hold some share . . . of political power." Owing to the backwardness of the Indian people, the fitness for representative government was utterly absent there. The form of rule that would fit the (not-yet) people was "enlightened and paternal despotism."[93] In Macaulay's account, British rule over India took the form of an advanced people ruling over a backward people. The British were making a despotic exception (albeit a despotism of "good government") for the purpose of self-government itself: "by good government we may educate our subjects into a *capacity* for better government; that, having become instructed in European knowledge, they may, in some future age, demand European institutions."[94] This framework of hierarchical peoplehood helped resolve, however contentiously, the tension between empire and self-government. In the process, it transformed a debate about the status of Indian civilization into a developmental narrative of peoplehood.

While revisiting his intellectual break from strict utilitarianism, John Stuart Mill singled out the question of representative democracy thus: "In politics . . . I no longer accepted the doctrine of the *Essay on Government* as a scientific theory. . . . I ceased to consider representative democracy as an *absolute* principle, and regarded it as a question of time, place, and circumstance."[95] For all his disagreements with Macaulay's Whiggism, this is one crucial point on which the younger Mill's ideas converged with Macaulay's: the progressive conception of peoplehood and its implication for the institution of self-government. Mill's turn to the developmental conception of (representative) self-government, too, took place amid the turbulent times of the 1832 Reform Bill agitations. We have already seen how the traces of this argument (that the time of self-government depends on the historical state of a given peoplehood) made their way into the private letters of Rammohun Roy around the same time. Although Rammohun frequented the same social gatherings as the younger Mill (who was aware of the Raja's high-profile visit to England), Mill had seemingly shown no interest in the Indian pandit. As Lynn Zastoupil notes, Mill's "neglect" of Rammohun was rather "astounding."[96] But in another sense, this was not surprising either. The reason-centric, universal "good government" of Rammohun—which is what Mill may have encountered in Rammohun's public writings—would have failed to speak to Mill's incipient developmental view of self-government, regardless of his concurrent attempts at that time to incorporate the eighteenth-century emphasis on the sedimented qualities of human experience. With his discovery of the centrality of "time, place, and circumstance" in theorizing the global scope of representative government, John Stuart Mill had begun to fashion himself as the philosophical purveyor of a new global, and imperial, era.

Indeed, by the time Mill came to write the essay "Civilization" in 1836, his understanding of progress had taken a more pronounced collectivist turn. Mill was alive to the different uses of the term "civilization"; he keenly recognized the ongoing resignification of the term in reference to the framework of historical development.[97] Taking the developmental meaning of civilization as his starting point (as a contrast to "rudeness or barbarism"), Mill asked: What are the most important elements of civilization? The simple answer Mill offered—property and mental powers—was a familiar one in 1830s Britain, but the other substantive point he underscored captured a turning point in the political meaning of civilization: the rise of the masses. With the advent of civilization, Mill argued, "the power passes more and more from individuals, and small knots of individuals, to masses."[98] He established the point by examining the cases of backward peoples. The "savage" communities are "poor and feeble" because of their "incapacity of co-operation."[99] Had this not been the case, the Indian states would not have surrendered so easily to the English.[100] Conversely, the capacity for cooperation increases with the progress of civilization. The "triumph of democracy" in advanced nations, too, was an effect of their historical development, which had generated in a wider dissemination of knowledge, communication, and wealth.[101]

Mill noted that the rise of democracy originated not from the opinions of the few but from the wider reach of social and moral progress. Once again, he digressed to the non-European world to establish the point: "There is no danger of the prevalence of democracy in Syria or Timbuctoo."[102] It is worth dwelling upon this striking statement. The seemingly random coupling of two quite different communities—Syria and Timbuktu—is representative of how the flattening of distinctions between different non-European peoples coexisted with the attentiveness he showed to the complexity of progress in the European context.[103] But this excursion into the remote world of Africa and Asia also represents another crucial point. It signaled the deep entanglement between historical backwardness and collective subjection: the imperial subjection of much of Asia and Africa was a result of their developmental lack as a political collectivity. At the same time, the fact that democracy was a meaningful proposition in Europe—as opposed to in the backward regions—owed to the progressive rise (however incomplete) of the masses.

The framework of hierarchical peoplehood would find its fullest expression in what arguably was John Stuart Mill's most important work of political theory. Published in 1861, *Considerations on Representative Government* was purportedly a theoretical exploration of the enterprise of representative government. The text, however, turned out to be as much a commentary on the power that lies "outside the machinery of representative government."[104] The "power outside" referred above all to the people, especially whether they are developed enough to meet the demands of representative government. The *Considerations*, as a whole, is replete with comparison between peoples belonging to different stages of progress. The co-constitutive relationship between progress and peoplehood that Mill had already sketched out in his earlier works would receive a more theoretically sustained treatment in this text. The opening chapters (especially chapters 1 to 4), in particular, sought to specify the criteria of peoplehood necessary for representative government. This was, however, less a ground-clearing operation than an introduction of the motifs that would pervade the rest of the text.

In the *Considerations*, the concept of the people primarily figured as the bearer of historical progress and, by extension, as the key determinant of whether the project of representative government is admissible in a given political community. Mill considered the criteria of peoplehood to be fundamentally dependent on the given "social conditions." In the standard Victorian mode, Mill understood "social conditions" to comprise both moral and material elements. Progress on one side, however, does not guarantee advancement on another. For Mill, the line that demarcates popular fitness for representative government from unfitness is rarely clear-cut, but its fuzziness does not make it any less important. He abstracted three criteria of democratic peoplehood:

> [Representative government] must be unsuitable in any case in which it cannot permanently subsist—i.e. in which it does not fulfil the three fundamental conditions. . . . 1. That the people should be willing to receive it. 2. That they should be willing and able to do what is necessary for its preservation. 3. That they should be willing and able to fulfil the duties and discharge the functions which it imposes on them.[105]

Mill substantiated this argument concerning popular fitness for representative government with reference to evidence drawn primarily from the non-European world. The first condition of democratic peoplehood—the popular will to "receive" representative government—turned out to be an issue beyond the voluntary will of a given people. While earlier in the text Mill emphasized the power of (individual) will as a public opinion-shaping force, he found the vanguardism of individual reformers inadequate for willing representative government into being in an overarchingly backward society. Insofar as the people of a society are indifferent to and unaware of the operations of representative government, they are more likely to be an obstacle to, rather than authorizers of, such government. The first steps toward representative government are instead to be found in its limited and unwilled imposition by an enlightened despotism. Collective political will can only emerge after "a central power, despotic in principle though generally much restricted in practice, was mainly instrumental in carrying the people through a necessary stage of improvement."[106] Even if somehow a people lagging behind in progressive qualities were to turn to a representative form of government, their deficit in progress would quickly bring the experiment to an end.[107]

The question of "capacity," for Mill, stems even more directly from a people's "stage of civilization." Consider what he took to be one of the most important prerequisites in the people for representative government—obedience to political authority. Such a quality is unlikely to be present in the "savage" stage of civilization where the struggle with nature and neighbors is the main preoccupation.[108] But the global state of progress is more of a spectrum than a binary: respect for and compliance with laws were missing not only among "semi-barbarous" Hindus, but also among the relatively more advanced peoples of Southern Europe who had sanctioned private retribution up until a recent time.[109] The criterion of nationality, too, was not entirely separable from the processes of progress.[110] Mill observed that the sense of peoplehood ("a multitude of insignificant political units be welded into a people"), which should ideally precede representative government, comes most advantageously from the experience of being ruled by a centralizing authority in an earlier stage of progress.[111] In other words, the political qualities that constitute the people—will, capacity, belonging, obedience, and so on— variously result from their state of civilizational progress. As I argued above, Mill already located the evidence of progress in the ascendance of the collective. In the *Considerations,* he pursued the argument further to demonstrate the inseparability of the fact of progress from the norms of democratic peoplehood.

Mill's "Germano-Coleridgean" turn had deepened his commitment to appreciations of "the laws of historical development and of the filiation of the different states of man and society."[112] Echoing Hegel and Comte, he likened the movement of progress to a mobile "van," which moves from one "advanced guard of the species" to another.[113] His appreciation of the role of antagonism as the "real security for continued progress" led to a more stubborn notion of historical development, though it was also a richer account than those of his British contemporaries.[114] Nevertheless, his stress on the sedimented, emotional qualities of societal and individual lives did not contradict a progressivist vision of historical development.[115] Mill's contribution to the Great Indian Education Debate of the 1830s is suggestive here. Against Macaulay's Anglicist position, he argued that the "moral and intellectual improvement of the people of India" requires a "cultivation of the Oriental languages." Mill found it "chimerical" that the "mental cultivation" of Indians could be facilitated without taking vernacular languages and customs into account.[116] This argument relates to Mill's later attempts to analytically separate the question of civilization from that of national character. His remarks on France, in particular, show an unwillingness to reduce the question of national character to the question of developmental progress.[117] While Mill took France to be more or less on the same level of historical development as England, he found their "national character" to be at odds with the ethos of representative government. The tendency in the French "character" to seek distinction and wield political power disrupted the possibility of consolidating representative government.[118]

It is interesting to note that this argument concerning French difficulties in instituting stable representative government appeared in the chapter where Mill elaborated on the political unfitness of backward non-European peoples. There is, however, a significant difference. The main problem of a people such as Indians lies in their backwardness, even as progress by itself might not necessarily generate a character best suited for representative government. Thus, Mill held that the people who generally lack the will and capacity befitting an advanced civilization are categorically excluded from the realm of representative government; it is worth pointing out that the same commitment to the framework of historical development allowed him to staunchly argue against the naturalist defense of slavery.[119] Furthermore, even if an otherwise backward people acquire the "special requisites" needed for representative government, its institution might clash with the prior necessity of civilizational advancement.[120] Mill treated the problem of national character, on the other hand, as an essentialist inheritance (or, at any rate, national traits that change only very slowly). For a nation such as France, its national character deters it from making the "best use" of representative government.[121]

Because the sources of progress are not equally distributed across the world, the backward, "not-yet" peoples require an external intervention to evolve into *the* people: "their improvement cannot come from themselves, but must be superinduced from without."[122] Mill credits despotic regimes with advancing a people prior to the emergence of representative government, but he is rather ambivalent about the extent to which native, non-European despotisms can accomplish such a task. In the above-quoted disclaimer in *On Liberty,* he had singled out Charlemagne and

Akbar as two examples of progressive despotism. In the *Considerations,*
while discussing how native despotic rulers occasionally facilitated
great improvements, Mill omits Akbar and instead discusses Charlemagne
and Peter the Great.[123] This was not a mere oversight. Mill directly addressed the limits of progress under Asian despotism earlier in the
text. He noted that "Egyptian hierarchy" and the "paternal despotism of
China" were "fit" for carrying those peoples to a limited extent. But
because of their lack of "mental liberty and individuality," these institutions failed to make further progress. He then contrasts the "stationary"
Hindu civilization with the Jewish tradition. The "antagonism of influence" internal to the Jewish tradition, Mill observed, propelled it to
continual progression. The lack of such intrinsic progressive drive, in
contrast, was what made Indians, Chinese, and other Asian peoples
stagnant.[124] This argument also shows the limits of Mill's cultural pluralism, as he clearly found certain traditions to be a hindrance to the
march of progress.

While Mill's preferred solution for places such as India was enlightened rule by the advanced British, he posited independent self-
government—and not any imperial federation—as the end of progress
under imperial rule. He emphatically argued that "the conquerors and
the conquered cannot ... live together under the same free institutions."[125] He was also critical of the prospect of a shared and united
political sovereignty for Britain and its distant colonies, since the latter
were "separated by half the globe" and lacked a common "public."[126] Crucially, Mill considered parliamentary rule over India—which would
amount to the British people (through their representatives) ruling over
Indians—to be detrimental to the development of the colonies. Given the
shortsightedness and self-interest of a foreign people, their direct rule
was unlikely to be beneficial for India. He instead preferred rule by his
employer, the East India Company—a private enterprise more directly engaged with Indian problems and supposedly less susceptible to popular
opinions. Mill's criticism of "direct" rule by the British people themselves
has led Nadia Urbinati to argue that he considered empire and representative government to be fundamentally incompatible, as his defense of
East India Company rule was predicated on the necessity to avoid "im-
perialistic domination by the English people through the political
branches of their government."[127] However, as we saw above, Mill's

defense of direct rule by the Company was based on pragmatic grounds, not on a fundamental questioning of the sovereignty of an advanced people over an inferior one. Furthermore, what ultimately made an English private potentate such as the Company a legitimate ruler was their position as the indirect agent of an advanced people. Mill's resistance to parliamentary rule over India thus does not challenge—but instead is enabled by—the global hierarchy of peoplehood.

Over the past few decades, much has been written on the imperial thought of John Stuart Mill. In fact, the proliferation of empire scholarship in political theory in the recent decades owes a special debt to the rediscovery of the imperial investments of Mill—the patron saint of modern liberalism. I have revisited above this well-trodden territory with a new question in mind: How exactly did the historical backwardness ascribed to the colonial world translate in political terms? As we saw, the reinscription of the imperial globe as a hierarchy of peoples brought normative commitments to democracy on the same temporal plane as that of empire. In Mill's eloquent formulation, representative government was not a universal norm but instead a matter of time and place. But the time of representative government was dependent on the still more fundamental premise of peoplehood. It is in this dynamic that the political meaning of developmentalism found its full expression.

True to its global scope, the developmental conception of the people also bled into Mill's account of metropolitan democracy. The progress of the metropolitan people as a collective entity was what made democracy a meaningful proposition in Britain as opposed to the backward nations of the world. At the same time, for all their relative progress, the majority of the metropolitan people were yet to acquire sufficient economic advancement and moral cultivation. The force and appeal of the "language of capacity"—so central to Victorian political thought—cannot thus be fully understood without reference to the progressive vision of modern peoplehood.[128] Mill feared that the homogenization of the English masses—a by-product of the very progress of the people—would halt metropolitan progress and result in a stationary state.[129] His support of proportional representation and plural voting stemmed in part from the desire to resist the anti-progressive potentials of the English masses. While reluctant to allow universal suffrage at once in England, Mill was not principally opposed to it; he considered universal and equal suffrage a desirable possibility in a more advanced stage of progress.[130] The progressive history of peoplehood—though not fully realized or secure anywhere—helped make sense of imperial domination and subjection while also enabling the stitching together of democracy at home and despotic rule abroad.

CONCLUSION

As European imperialism was bringing almost all of Asia and Africa under its rule, the "shrinkage of the globe"—to use Hannah Arendt's expression—imputed a new urgency to the question of global difference.[131] The broadly Enlightenment horizon of Rammohun Roy, where the framework of universal reason conditioned the approach to civilizational difference, would give way to a developmental view of global difference. As Rammohun's late hesitations illustrate, the force of developmental reasoning sprang directly from the desire to emulate the historical conditions that rendered self-government plausible in Europe. Around the same time, the younger Mill also found the rise of the people to be an inexorable force unleashed by the advent of progress. Though the rise of the people simultaneously propelled and endangered metropolitan democracy, the question it generated for India was different. If developed peoplehood was to be India's destiny, what first needed to be determined was the form of nonpopular government that would be best suited for the development of a backward people. The hierarchy between the Indian (non-)people and the English people was no mere manifestation of the objective discrepancies in their economic and social states. Instead, the language of peoplehood rendered Britain and India— the two representatives of the two worlds translatable in shared terms.

The final chapter of Mill's *Considerations* offered a defense of the East India Company rule following the Sepoy Rebellion of 1857 in India. The sudden challenge to the seat of British power in India sent shock waves through the imperial heartland, leading to the dissolution of the Company and the transfer of the formal sovereignty of India to the British Crown. Mill himself deemed the Rebellion to be an anomaly, representative neither of the essential nature of British rule nor of any coherent political expression of Indians.[132] As an essayist for the *Westminster Review* observed soon after the Rebellion, "the question of retaining India or not is at least of as much interest to the natives of the country as to ourselves." The question of Indian independence was a mere "chimera," because there was "no people" in India to begin with: "'the people of India' has no existence . . . if, by [the] people, we mean a distinct, cohesive, syngeneous [sic] polity. We shall never understand India rightly, unless we accept the full significance of its 'no people.'"[133] This revelatory screed of the respected *Westminster Review* ultimately underscored a more widely shared point: Britain could not leave India because there was no people to replace itself with.

The preeminent Indian journalist of the era, Grish Chunder Ghose, wrote an impassioned rejoinder to the *Westminster Review*. In his withering critique he noted that "it requires not Aristotle's Categories, Bacon's universal principle of Induction, Kant's Pure Reasoning or Cousin's Emperico-Philosophical analysis to demonstrate the national existence of the people of India."[134] Interestingly, however, Ghose's evidence for the fact of Indian peoplehood was overwhelmingly drawn from the list of Indian service to the British Empire. One could easily see evidence of the existence of the Indian people, he observed, from their contributions to the "life and blood of the English Government in this country." If the Indian people did not exist, the parliamentary deliberations on Indian affairs, too, must be taken as a grand act of self-deception. Drawing evidence from the British archive, Ghose concluded that "there is a people of India. . . . Niggers or nobodies, they are in veritable corporeal existence."[135] Ghose's arguments for the "corporeal existence" of the Indian people responded to a genuine problem: in moments of crises and exigencies, the imperial project—notwithstanding its promise of self-government—was quick as ever to reduce the Indian people to a juridical nonbeing. What was no less important, however, was Ghose's hesitation in making a self-referential, political case for the Indian people's existence. After all, the *Westminster Review* dismissed the claims of Indian peoplehood on the ground of its national amorphousness and unfitness for establishing and maintaining independence.

The commonplace collapsing of developmentalism into the longer arc of the modern imperial expansion of Europe tends to stretch the former from the Age of Enlightenment to the horrors of the twentieth century, resulting in a confusion regarding the historical provenance of the developmental view of global difference. As I have argued through my reading of J. S. Mill, the liberal imperialists had overcome the democratic dilemma of development (that is, the universality of norms versus the unevenness of the facts of progress) by arguing that different developmental locations necessitate different political arrangements. The central place of the category of peoplehood emerged in this conjuncture. In fact, developmentalism came to be profoundly imbricated with empire only after the resignification of global difference as a graded hierarchy of peoples. The recasting of empire in terms of peoplehood would arguably be the most significant inheritance for anticolonial thinkers from the age of Macaulay and Mill. The dispute over the terms of peoplehood would be at the heart of the political struggle for the founding generation of the Indian National Congress in the second half of the nineteenth century. In many ways, the Indian liberals would lay the foundations for the anticolonial democratic project. Those foundations, however, were as much defined by a deep-seated tension over the meaning of peoplehood as they were shaped by a reorientation of the Indian critique of empire.

CHAPTER 2

THE BIRTH OF THE PEOPLE

Liberalism and the Origins of the Anticolonial
Democratic Project in India

> Head bowed, they stand
> Speechless—In their pale faces
> A chronicle of agony, centuries old
> The weight on their shoulder piles high; sluggish,
> They toil on till the last breath.
> . . .
> To these benighted, emaciated, dumb faces
> Speech must be given—
> Inside these exhausted, sapless, broken hearts
> Hope has to be voiced.
>
> —Rabindranath Tagore, "Turn Me Back Now"

THESE VIVID LINES are from a well-known Bengali poem by Rabindranath Tagore. Written in the final decade of the nineteenth century, it addressed the poet's struggle between worldly and otherworldly impulses. The figure of the people appeared as a synecdochic marker of the world outside—the oppressed yet voiceless masses standing for the urgency of worldly action. This jarring picture of the Indian masses echoed the more prosaic rhetoric of Tagore's contemporary political thinkers: the people, the supposed sovereign of the democratic age, appeared to be so miserable as to be incapable of assuming their political mantle. From Dadabhai Naoroji to R. C. Dutt to Surendranath Banerjea, Indian political thinkers of the time would work relentlessly to insert this figure of the Indian masses into the world of empire and liberalism. The people appeared in the guise of an amorphous collective—starving and speechless. Still, this was no longer the poverty of mere subjects, but that of the (not-yet) people whose plight had a new political meaning.

In the second half of the nineteenth century, the concept of the people made an unceremonious entrance into Indian political thought with all its normative weight and historical traces. The rise of the economic critique of British rule in the period powerfully brought into view an immiserated "social" body of the people.[1] The lesson of political modernity, Pierre Rosanvallon argues, is that "the people is a political proposition before it is a sociological fact."[2] Indian liberals such as Naoroji and Banerjea were acutely aware of the distinction between the people as a "sociological fact" and the people as a "political proposition." But they held that a progressive transformation of the social body of the people was the prior condition of its claim to political sovereignty. Indian liberals' diagnosis of the backwardness of their own people was conducted from the economic (Naoroji and Dutt) as well as the political-pedagogic (Banerjea) vantage point, though they also affirmed the mutual dependence between the two. The problem of transforming the masses into *the* people thus came to be at the center of the nineteenth-century Indian project of self-government. Forged in a fraught exchange with British liberal thought, this account of self-government was not so much about affirming the right of a people to form its own government; it was instead an argument for self-government for those who had not yet earned the right to sovereignty. Instead of contesting the contemporary British liberal account of the backward Indian masses, the Indian liberals turned the premise of backwardness against the colonial administration to justify Indian claim for self-government. This political opening, an immanent critique of empire if there ever was one, would mark the uncertain inauguration of organized anticolonial politics in India.

Between the rise of British rule in the eighteenth century and the heady decades of anticolonial resistance in the twentieth, the nineteenth century hangs in suspended animation in the historiography of colonial India. More often than not, the century stands as the proverbial midwife between a past that was fait accompli (imperial subjection) and a future that was still distant (postcolonial founding). As we shall see, the conceptual contours of the anticolonial democratic project were already well articulated by the end of the nineteenth century. The program of representative government emerged as the stated ideal of political action, as did the broader framework for critiquing imperial rule. However, these Indian actors' concrete political agenda was decidedly minimalist and posed no challenge to imperial sovereignty. To explain the political fortunes of the period, historians have traditionally relied on processes of social transformation, ranging from the narratives of stunted modernization to accounts based strictly on social interest.[3] By all accounts, nineteenth-century Indian thinkers fell short of both the standards of emerging anticolonialism and contemporary European liberalism. For most of the twentieth century, then, this archive of political thought was read in reference to what it was not.

With the global turn in the scholarship on imperial and anticolonial thought, intellectual historians have made a new effort to reconsider the political thought of nineteenth-century India. The category of liberalism has been central to this new turn. The narratives of Indian liberalism usually begin with the early nineteenth-century thinker Rammohun Roy and partially conclude in the early twentieth century with the emergence of what is generally categorized as anticolonial nationalism. The reckoning with the imperial entanglements of European liberal thought enabled historians of Indian political thought to place the arguments of nineteenth-century Indian thinkers in the context of a global discourse of liberalism as opposed to that of twentieth-century anticolonial thought. In particular, C. A. Bayly pioneered the revival of the study of Indian liberalism. He frames the problem of Indian liberalism as a "pursuit of social and political liberty" in a colonial context. For Bayly, Indian liberalism was marked by an attempt to "rewrite the liberal discourse so as to strip it of its coercive colonial features and re-empower it as an indigenous ideology, but one still pointing towards universal progress."[4] According to another recent interpretation put forward by Andrew Sartori, nineteenth-century Indian liberalism was defined by the "use" of the "logic of commercial society" to fashion political and ethical imagination.[5]

In this chapter I share in the aim to read nineteenth-century Indian thought on its own terms, but I depart from the ways in which Indian liberalism is usually periodized and its global exchanges theorized. The loosely defined yet overarchingly deployed framework of liberalism has obscured from view the distinctive formation of the democratic ideal in nineteenth-century India. From the first half of the nineteenth century to the second, the discursive horizon of Indian political thought went through a fundamental transformation. For the Indian political thinkers of the second half of the nineteenth century, the promise of the new political horizon was encapsulated in the term "self-government"—an ideal that captured their aspiration for representative democracy.[6] The project of self-government would simultaneously excite and invite a great deal of self-critical, and occasionally satirical, political reflection in late nineteenth-century India.[7] The turn to self-government would, however, instantly drive a wedge between the two prongs of modern democracy: self-government (understood as Indian participation in administration and legislation) and popular sovereignty. As Naoroji noted in 1867, the long experience of "despotic" rule had left India a "degraded nation": the "mass of the people," lacking the "political aid which is so vital to the growth and welfare of any nation," were in a static state.[8] The economic exploitation and political exclusion under the British, they further argued, resulted in a "drain" of the moral and material resources of India. Nevertheless, Naoroji and his colleagues readily accepted that the Indian masses were not developed enough to exercise sovereignty: the state of Indian people-hood failed to meet the demand of the democratic norm. Still, they refused to leave the task of transforming the masses to the British. Instead of deriving the claim for self-government from the prior ground of popular sovereignty, they proposed that the practices of self-government would pave the way for the development of the sovereign authority of the Indian people. To this end, they fashioned a set of minimalist programs for In-dian self-government, from the Indianization of the civil services to limited legislative representation. The end goal of such minimalist pro-grams, as one major late nineteenth-century Indian political thinker put it, was the distant horizon of "complete popular domination."[9] The emer-gence of this democratic ideal, however, paradoxically pushed the actual institution of democracy into a distant future.

As Duncan Bell has shown in the Euro-American context, the for-mation of liberalism as an expansive category—from laissez-faire capi-talism to individual rights—is mostly a twentieth-century affair.[10] In twentieth-century India, the retrospective gaze of the liberal framework in the twentieth century pulled Rammohun and his contemporaries closer to their late nineteenth-century successors, undermining their moorings in the age of reason. Though I will be using the phrase "Indian liberals" to refer to late nineteenth-century Indian thinkers who self-consciously, and often critically, identified with contemporary British liberalism (namely, Naoroji, Banerjea, and Dutt), my aim is not to adjudicate their liberal credentials but instead to demonstrate how their pursuit of self-government in terms of contemporary British liberalism generated a split between popular sovereignty and self-government. I also aim in this chapter to trace the subtle transformation of the normative assumptions of Indian political thought between the two halves of the nineteenth century. The immediate successors of Rammohun Roy saw no necessary connection between the imperative of improvement and the rule of the East India Company. Given their reason-centric approach, it appeared to them that "improvement" did not need to be a long, arduous process or a replication of Europe's historical trajectory. But, like for Rammohun, their political agenda turned on the question of "good government" rather than self-government. As we will see in the following section, Dakshinaranjan Mukherjee's sharp indictment of British rule in the 1830s and 1840s made no reference to the state of Indian peoplehood. He instead proposed that the norms of good government, being universal, applied as much to ancient India as they did to nineteenth-century Europe. Mukherjee's British critics, however, already presaged the beginning of an age of the people amid the flourishing of global empires. They objected to his blistering charges not by contradicting the substance of the allegations but by attributing those deficiencies to the state of the Indian people. The question of the people worked as an alibi for empire, but it also functioned as a negative theology of sort: its absence was as meaningful as its presence. Although the modern history of popular sovereignty is mostly told in terms of the emphatic self-presentation of the people, this "absent" history was no less significant in its global career.

With the developmental justifications and critiques of empire, imperial subjection no longer appeared to be a fact of the world that needed to be constitutionally regulated so as to maintain the liberty of subjects. Empire instead came to be interpreted as the consequence of the historical absence of Indian peoplehood and as a preparation for future democracy. The second part of this chapter traces how Indian liberals put forward the diagnosis that the continued underdevelopment of the Indian masses was the result of excluding the "advanced" sections of the society from the government. Against this backdrop they turned to the work of British liberal thinkers, especially John Stuart Mill, to mount a developmental defense of self-government. But the surprising appropriation of Mill for the project of Indian self-government would result in a rather unwitting vindication of the still more fundamental premise of Millian liberalism: sovereignty of advanced peoples over their backward counterparts. The Indian liberals accepted the deferred sovereignty of the underdeveloped people but departed from Mill's aim to shelter imperial rule abroad from the internal dynamics of British democracy. Unmediated access to the "English people," as opposed to an enlightened intermediary, was to be the political hallmark of Indian liberalism. The project of Indian self-government thus came to base itself on an affirmation of the sovereign authority of the English people over the Indian people. The modern career of democracy in India began with a constitutive split between sovereignty and government, one that found its original expression in nineteenth-century Indian liberalism.

LIBERALITY BEFORE LIBERALISM: THE GOVERNMENT AND THE PEOPLE

Before the adjective "liberal" meant anything politically specific, it stood for the virtues of generosity and measured judgment. Rammohun Roy, for instance, frequently appealed to liberal "manner" and "principles" in the eighteenth-century sense of an enlightened attitude and moderation. An apt illustration of this understanding is his account of Ranjit Singh, the contemporary Sikh king from western India. Rammohun noted that Singh's regime was founded on "arbitrary rule" and the "idea of constitutional government [is] entirely foreign to his mind." And yet he found Singh to be "prudent" and "moderate," and thus "inclined towards liberal principles."[11] Notwithstanding his later status as the progenitor of Indian liberalism, Rammohun, as we saw in Chapter 1, was far removed from the main preoccupations of the nineteenth-century liberalism organized around the ideal of representative government.

Much the same can be said for his younger political followers in Bengal, who went further than the Raja in their condemnation of British rule. The Young Bengal group—whose complicated historical legacy owes to their impetuous iconoclasm and public disavowal of inherited customs—were less invested than Rammohun in maintaining a delicate balance of reason and tradition.[12] Though they are now remembered as the Europe-enchanted first generation of modern Indian intellectuals, some of the Young Bengal members were, in fact, sternly critical of imperial rule. Over the 1830s and 1840s the contentious public spheres of urban India—especially in Bengal and Maharashtra—were replete with the charges of illiberal attitude against the "body of merchants" reigning over India. The rule of the East India Company, the Young Bengal editors of the *Gyananneshun* (Quest for Knowledge) argued in the 1830s, was barely distinguishable from the tyranny of self-interest. For the Company, these critics held, the dictum of profit almost always overrode the "distribution of justice."[13] Much like a host of other journals mushrooming in Kolkata in the period, the *Gyananneshun* hoped to facilitate the improvement of the natives through diffusion of knowledge and cultivation of dialogues and discussions. It understood improvement primarily in moral and intellectual terms, although material requisites for the growth of Indians also received some sparse attention. The "liberality" that this group of political commentators venerated was still a matter of sentiments and morals, and increasingly dovetailed with the virtue of promoting improvement. It is an appellation they bestowed freely to European as well as Indian individuals, and occasionally to the specific policies and actions of the administration.

Though Rammohun passed over the opportunity to make any public comment on the Indian policies of James Mill, the editors of *Gyananneshun* saw no need to mince words when the historian "known [for his] liberality" opposed the employment of Indians in the public service.[14] In a testimony at the British Parliament on the issue, the elder Mill plainly dismissed the integration of Indians in the administration; he argued that the economic and material advancement of the natives should be the priority, and that opening government employment to Indians would only distract them from focusing on "[elevating] their own resources, their industry and economy."[15] The *Gyananneshun* found this argument highly tendentious: "We shall beg of him to conceive that the

English nation was conquered by a foreign people, and all the employments in public service were held by the latter. What, we ask, would be the condition of England?" Neither James Mill's utilitarian view of government nor his prioritization of the economic over the political appeared to be particularly persuasive. For the *Gyananneshun*, the problems of India, plenty as they were, required moral and political education.[16] Such an education was not predicated on the continuation of imperial rule. The meaning of improvement, in other words, was yet to be overdetermined by the discourse of historical development. Indeed, British rule and the question of improvement appeared to be fairly distinct issues in 1830s India.

The best exemplar of the critique of British rule in terms of "good government" was Dakshinaranjan Mukherjee's 1843 paper "On the Present State of the Honorable East India Company's Court of Judicature and Police, under the Bengal Presidency."[17] Mukherjee's now-forgotten paper, which he delivered at a gathering of the "Hindoo Society for Acquisition of General Knowledge," was one of the most sophisticated pieces of political writings from the era. The paper began with a nod to eighteenth-century conjectural history: Mukherjee observed that the need for a regulated system of rules emerged out of humanity's striving to leave behind the state of barbarism. He proposed that the idea of a "code" regulating the "rights between man and man" is what should be defined as "Government."[18] The fundamental duty of a government, it then follows, is to protect the powerless from the powerful. Even a despotic government is constrained by this duty: "At the onset of social advancement, it was apprehended that all Governments were bound, conformably to the tenor of the laws under which they were called into existence, to render equal justice to their subject."[19] Mukherjee, however, was keen to assert that this core principle of government, which arose at the early stage of civilization, was not displaced in later stages; instead, the truth realized at the earliest stage became refined and grew into dominance with the progress of civilization. The principle of "equal justice" thus had a universal purchase and had no necessary tension with progress. Turning to India, Mukherjee found the evidence of this understanding of government in its ancient texts and scriptures. In fact, the principle of government survived the history of the Muslim conquest of India.[20] Insofar as this meaning of government had been forgotten in India,

Mukerjee claimed, the responsibility lay with the "thralldom of priest-craft" rather than with India's Muslim conquerors. This same priest-craft was also the progenitor of the "unnatural and unholy distinction of caste," which, for Mukerjee, undermined the divine human equality present at the dawn of Indian civilization.[21]

On this premise Mukherjee launched his fierce critique of British rule. In British India, he argued, there was a "thorough dominion of vice, in its most unblushing form" at every step of the way. His detailed analysis focused particularly on the judiciary and police. Echoing Ram-mohun's stress on the separation of powers, Mukherjee argued that the lack of meaningful separation between the court and the police corrupted the justice system as a whole. The European officers' lack of vernacular knowledge, coupled with a lack of education, led to a rule of discretionary power rather than that of justice. The contemptuous European administrators were themselves "semi-barbarous": they pos-sessed no superiority in knowledge or wealth compared to their native subjects and usually arrived in India only with the aim to "[gratify] their love of gold." The "all-devouring revenue enactments" of the Company ground the peasantry to dust, leaving no time or opportunity for them to publicly take up the fight against the corrupt court and police.[22] Fur-thermore, the exclusionary nature of the administration—in which the governed had no share— sapped Indians of their public spirit. Mukherjee concluded that without a "cordial intercourse between the delegated rulers and the ruled . . . no Government can maintain any permanent hold on, the affections and sympathies of its subjects, whatever security it may enjoy in its physical strength."[23] It is worth noting that this sharp condemnation of British rule made no distinction between the superior norms of the British and their corrupt application in India—a rhetorical trope that would become prevalent later in the century. Mukherjee was unconcerned with what exact promise that the Government of India had made. His universal origin narrative of government meant that he did not take British and Indian ideas of government to be essentially dif-ferent. In his conjectural history, the basic principle of government was shared across civilizations.

Mukherjee's paper triggered something of a controversy in the British imperial world. The presentation of the paper itself was inter-rupted halfway by one of the distinguished members of the audience—the principal of Hindu College, Captain Richardson. As a "sincere advocate of the cause of native education," Richardson found himself unable to withstand how "the spread of intelligence among young natives, had taken a direction and resulted in effects, contrary to his expectations."[24] While Mukherjee's paper was "correct in its style and tolerably chaste," the substance of his claims amounted to "treason." In facilitating the spread of knowledge, the British were already resigned to the fact that it would be "fatal to the existence of their own power . . . that hereafter the people might be qualified to govern themselves." After all, Richardson argued, the diffusion of knowledge and the general progress of the English people had made them increasingly more critical of their government. For an Indian, however, it was rather absurd to hold the British administration responsible for the defects of governance. The source of those defects, he concluded, lie in "the people themselves than . . . Government."[25] In response to Richardson's charge of Indian ungratefulness, the president of the meeting, Tarachand Chakrabarty, pointed out that his outburst exhibited the vices that he attributed to educated Indians.[26] Mukherjee, on his part, contended that Richardson was wrong in holding the people themselves responsible for the defects of their government. His distance from the emerging age of progress could further be seen in the assertion that followed: he was "no enemy to British rule nor to any other rule that was upright and impartial." Regardless of the specific form of the government, what really mattered was the performance of justice. Having made this point, Mukherjee recited a suggestive couplet from Alexander Pope: "For forms of Government let fools contest;/Whate'er is best administered is best."[27]

The London-based *Asiatic Journal* was affronted by Mukherjee's temerity. Without the government that he abused, the *Journal* opined, Mukherjee and his people would have been in a "state of slavery, with a scanty rag round their loins."[28] The locally based *Friend of India* was particularly appalled by the loud applause that greeted the most critical segments of Mukherjee's "most unqualified abuse of the Government of India." The *Friend of India*'s substantive disagreement with Mukherjee's paper, however, returned to the rift between the government and the people: "It is public opinion, and not the fear of legal consequence, which keeps the Bench in England pure. That opinion is wanting here. . . . The more they [the educated Indian youth] examine the state of courts, the more will they discover, that the remedy of existing evils lies more in the hands of the people, than of the government."[29] This commentary was prompted by a second speech by Mukherjee a week later, where he expressed the hope that the "public opinion" of Indians would soon rise to the challenge and help eradicate the evils of bad government.[30]

And so the debate over the corrupt governance of the British in India came to be bifurcated between two poles: the government and the people. The gulf between Mukherjee and his critics was not simply one of disagreement. The problem at stake was the philosophical foundation of government. In his universal but pre-democratic conception of government, Mukherjee saw no reason to ground his political norms on the state of development of the Indian people. The focus on the people, whose lack of improvement he otherwise accepted, appeared to be a deflection from the problem of unjust rule. Mukherjee was certainly right in pointing out that the name of the people had become an excuse and an alibi. But his aggressive British critics were more than just shoring up the empire. Their confident rebuttals emanated instead from an ongoing collapse of the ideal of popular sovereignty into that of empire. In this inverted history of popular sovereignty, the location of a given people in the scale of historical development directly determined the scope of what a government could do.

The futility of the pursuit of liberality in the global era of developmentalism—where the ethos of enlightened generosity could no longer override the higher premise concerning the state of peoplehood—would soon be evident to midcentury Indian political thinkers. Mukherjee would rediscover himself as a staunch defender of the British Empire after the Rebellion of 1857. He now concluded that "the British Nation is intended by God to resuscitate the moral and intellectual energies of our race, and to lead us gradually to appreciate and to deserve the social and political rights which they possess in their native land."[31] As Mukherjee's arguments in the wake of the Rebellion signaled, the providential spin on the developmental claims of British rule would come to entail a resignification of the Muslim era in India as a stunted chapter of progress.[32] The desirable social and political rights could no longer be located in the imaginary origins of Indian civilization; the historical trajectory of modern Europe had by then become a necessary condition for the practicability of self-government.

Though fundamentally skeptical of direct popular participation in governance and embroiled in empire, mid-nineteenth century European accounts of liberalism were premised on a set of claims concerning democratic peoplehood. For the colonial world, however, the people existed more as a promissory future norm than as a present fact. The effect of this colonial reconfiguration of the concept of the people was most palpable in the ways in which it shaped Indian political expectations vis-à-vis their foreign government. The principles of universal justice ceased to be an immediate—or sufficient—criterion for evaluating the success of foreign rule; the facilitation of the development of the people was where its ultimate challenge lay. Unsurprisingly, then, the age of Rammohun and Mukherjee quickly evanesced. The points of departure for the Indian political thinkers of the latter half of the century would be dramatically different. Empire itself had turned into a promise for future self-government. This complex nexus of self-government, development, and empire allowed for newer possibilities for critiquing British rule in India. However, as the successors of Rammohun and Mukherjee would soon find out, critiques of empire had a strange knack of metamorphizing into pious offerings to imperial sovereignty in the age of democracy's tortured globalization.

EMPIRE AND THE SOCIAL BODY OF THE PEOPLE

In May 1881, the Pune-based political journal *Mahratta*—edited by, among others, Bal Gangadhar Tilak—published an article on the political nature of British rule in India. It took issue with a certain Sergeant Atkinson, who in a recent series of lectures had argued that India should be considered a limited monarchy since it was a dependency of Britain. Chastising the sergeant for his superficial understanding of Bentham and Austin, the unsigned editorial argued, first, that Britain was a republic, as "the sovereignty of England is distributed into the hands of the many." The same did not extend to India: "Having shown that the British Government is a republic, we do not at once proceed to say, after the fashion of Mr. Atkinson, that the Government of the Indian Empire is also a republic, because India is a dependency of England." The form of rule in India was "despotic" not so much because of the lack of the separation of powers or the prevalence of arbitrary rule but instead because it paid no attention to "the will and the wishes of the ruled." No matter how "good" imperial rule was, it could not be compared with the legitimacy granted by self-government. The form of the government of India was thus claimed to be "republican foreign despotism."[33] Two weeks later, the same journal published another editorial on the question of representative government in India. Its conclusion ran thus: "A day will certainly come, however distant it may be, on which the 'mistress of the ocean' will confer upon us this grand privilege [representative government]. In the meantime we must pass through many preparatory stages."[34]

These seemingly contradictory editorial stances toward the same question—imperial rule was normatively unjustified, but imperial tutelage was accepted as a "preparatory" work toward the overcoming of empire—was not an isolated instance. A year later, the Bengali novelist and essayist Bankimchandra Chatterjee would publish *Anandamath* (The Abbey of Bliss)—perhaps the best-known political novel of nineteenth-century India. Situated in the tumultuous period of the 1770s, when Muslim rule in Bengal was crumbling and the British were in ascendance, this novel tells the story of a famine-stricken Brahmin who joined a rebellious group of militant ascetics called *Santandal* (the party of the children) in order to resist the allegedly decadent Muslim regime. Although controversial for its unrestrained invocation of a primordial rivalry between Hindus and Muslims, Bankim's celebration of physical resistance to foreign rule would also make the novel an acclaimed source-text for later nationalists. Written in the genre of the romance novel, *Anandamath* narrated a somewhat anticlimactic story. Just as the militant ascetics precipitated the collapse of the Muslim regime, a divine voice intervened to dissuade Satyananda, the leader of the group, from fighting the ascendant British: "The English are learned in the knowledge of the external world and skilled at educating the public. We will make them the new rulers of this country. . . . Until the day Hindus fully acquire knowledge, strength, and the qualities [needed for that purpose], the English shall rule over this country."[35]

Such was the political horizon of late nineteenth-century India, a world steeped in the ubiquity of a developmental imagination and yet quietly indignant at the fact of foreign subjection. By the 1860s the normative horizon of "good government" had receded, along with the idea that empire could ever be congruent with liberty proper. Nor was there any dearth of critical reflection on the illiberal "machinery" of British rule in India.[36] Whereas Rammohun and Mukherjee once could criticize their foreign government in legal and administrative terms, their political successors found it more reasonable to ground the critique of empire on the unfulfillment of the development it promised. The figure of the Indian people was once again central to the transformation. From a mere object of improvement, the people had transformed into the reason for improvement itself. As we saw in Chapter 1, the co-constitution of empire and democracy meant the resignification of (imperial) government as that which would form the masses into a people commensurate with the time of democracy. Their contemporaneous Indian liberal thinkers—Dadabhai Naoroji, Surendranath Banerjea, and R. C. Dutt, among others—arrived at a similar point, albeit through a reckoning with the failure of imperial governance.

For these Indian thinkers, the imperial habit of collapsing developmental claims into civilizational essentialism remained an enduring problem. Even as both Macaulay and Mill staunchly opposed biologically essentialist explanations of global difference, the theme of civilizational essentialism persisted in their own language and in the more prosaic workings of imperial domination. Naoroji and his colleagues took it upon themselves to thoroughly critique the civilizational—and cognitivist—aspects of Victorian developmentalism. Perhaps the most iconic moment of this endeavor was Naoroji's brilliant rebuttal to John Crawfurd, the president of the London Ethnological Society. In February 1866, Crawfurd delivered a paper before the Society titled "On the Physical and Mental Characteristics of the European and Asiatic Races of Man." The paper engaged in rather crude ethnological and biological generalizations, to prove that the "Asiatic races" are intellectually, morally, and physically much inferior to their European counterparts. Crawfurd concluded that the difference is ultimately "innate."[37] In his response, speaking for multiple Asian civilizations all at once, Naoroji found little credence to the claim that Asiatic races were intellectually and physically inferior. The chief mistake of Crawfurd's argument, Naoroji claimed, was the assumption that "diversity" of peoples necessarily implies an innate hierarchy.[38]

At the same time, Naoroji maintained that while Indians were not innately inferior, they indeed were underdeveloped compared to the

Europeans: if modern Europe was developmentally advanced, it was because of the contingency of history, not because of any essential quality of its civilization.[39] The nineteenth-century picture of Britain stood as the self-evident proof of its superiority, but a synchronic comparison between contemporary Britain and India could scarcely capture the different historical fortunes these countries had experienced over a longer scale of time. As he put it: "It would be almost as fair to compare India in the sixteenth with England in the nineteenth centuries, as it would be to compare the two countries in the first centuries of the Christian era when India was at the top of civilization, and England at the bottom." The nineteenth century, then, was not the same for India and England; their calendrical contemporaneity belied a historical non-contemporaneity.[40]

This critique of civilizational essentialism usually coexisted with an economic account of the relative development of Europe and backwardness of India. After its trail was blazed by Dadabhai Naoroji and R. C. Dutt, the economic critique of British rule became fairly widespread in turn-of-the-century India. Naoroji's classic *Poverty and Un-British Rule in India,* marshaling formidable statistical evidence, documented the ways in which Britain was draining India. Although the origins of the "drain theory" goes back to 1840s western Indian writings, Naoroji radically expanded upon the theory in light of new political economy literature and with the help of a vast body of statistical data.[41] Rammohun's faint optimism about the prospect of free trade had given way to an anxiety regarding the depletion of Indian industries in an economically uneven world. In this new era, the economic problem of India could neither be understood in Malthusian terms nor attributed to the size of its markets.[42] The source of Indian poverty instead lay in the economic structure of the empire. Naoroji did not share Mill's claim that India was an economic burden to England, but he drew on Mill's work to argue that the problem of the Indian economy emanated from the state of its capital. British economic policies had actively diminished Indian capital, which also weakened the labor market. The Indian economy was thus a "candle that [burned] at both ends."[43] Thanks to the capital-starved economy, foreign trade for India only meant the flourishing of the channel through which "in addition . . . [to] profits, a portion of the production itself is also swept away."[44] In the imperial context, he argued, free trade practically amounts to a "race between a starving, exhaust[ed] invalid, and a strong man with a horse to ride on." Naoroji thus argued for the necessity of protectionism for "young colonies."[45] He found a paradigmatic difference between the poor of India and the poor of western Europe: Indians simply lacked productive capacity, whereas the European poor "having plenty . . . [suffer] from some defect in its distribution."[46]

What is less often emphasized is Naoroji and his colleagues' articulation of a parallel account of the "moral drain" of Indians. The exclusion of Indians from political offices meant that their moral faculties—unused and untapped—were in decline. The Europeans in India, Naoroji noted, "acquire India's money, experience, and wisdom; and when they go, they carry both away with them, leaving India so much poorer in material and moral wealth."[47] Given the profound distance between Europeans and the Indian masses, the former could neither be the "natural leader of the people" nor guide the growth of Indians into modern citizens.[48] This was a task that only Indians with worldly wisdom of political experience could help inculcate in the masses. The greater implication of this argument resided in reconfiguring the relationship between the material and the moral. Naoroji did not simply affirm the primacy of the economic as the determinant of the moral condition of a people; he also characterized the moral faculty of the masses as a form of "wealth."[49] Just as trade without the growth of capital could not improve the economic condition, so education without administrative and political responsibilities would not be enough to raise the "moral wealth" of the people. This argument also signaled a growing rift between the intellectual and the moral. While the likes of Rammohun and Mukherjee tacitly accepted the mutually binding relationship between intellectual knowledge and moral reform, it now appeared that the growth of intellectual capacity had no essential bearing on the moral virtues of a people.[50] In subsuming the moral question under the economic metaphor of wealth, Naoroji exemplified the disappearance of the relative autonomy of the moral question that could be seen earlier in the century. The dovetailing of the moral with the economic further signified the attenuation of the older assumption that the growth of the moral capacity of the people could be achieved through reason and education. Instead, the moral question now became tied with the problem of self-government.

While Naoroji and Dutt were thinkers primarily focused on the material, others, such as Surendranath Banerjea, squarely centered political ethos and education of the masses in the developmental process. For Banerjea, the primary value of including Indians in the government consisted in the possibility that it could be "an instrument of political education"—that is, the diffusion of the capacity and knowledge required for modern citizenship.[51] Banerjea considered education to be the most crucial element in India's progress, and he liberally praised the British for their role in disseminating modern education in India.[52] His view of political education sought to bridge the gap between the intellectual and the moral by way of combining modern knowledge with a moral mission assigned to educated Indians. The importance of pedagogic institutions and practices appeared most strikingly in Banerjea's discussion of the question of unity among the Indian masses. Banerjea asked if the hope for an "intellectual, moral, and social union of the Indian peoples" had been the "phantom of an excited imagination."[53] After all, the diverse masses of India appear to be "separated . . . by everything that constitutes the distinctive difference between races and peoples."[54] Such a conclusion, he averred, would be misleading. Considering the contrasting cases of Swiss, Italian, and German nationhood, Banerjea found no essential linguistic or ethnic criteria for national unity. Compared to its ancient past, modern India appeared to be particularly well-suited for the cultivation of the sentiment of political "brotherhood" across its diverse regions. The "great revolution" ushered in by the British was transforming the Indian society. The introduction of English education had brought the educated groups from across India close to each other and had generated the condition of possibility for Indian unity.[55] The duty incumbent on educated Indians, in turn, was to educate and develop the masses of the people.[56] Banerjea did not take the formation of Indian unity to be simply an intellectual matter; it also required a foundation in emotion. Empowered by their English education, the leaders of the people, Banerjea suggested, must help disseminate the ideal of Indian unity. While Mazzini's role in bringing about Italian unity was Banerjea's favored reference, he suggestively located the medium of action for India not in secret societies but in the pedagogic possibility of elevating public opinion.[57] Himself a victim of anti-Indian discrimination (Banerjea, one of the first Indians to qualify for the Indian Civil Service, was summarily dismissed from his post for a clerical error), Banerjea did not doubt the greater role of the empire in enabling the formation of a cohesive Indian people.

The divine mission of British rule, in his telling, resided precisely in the formation of its other: a homogeneous Indian people.[58]

Broadly speaking, for Naoroji and his colleagues the economic misery of the people, coupled with their lack of education and their political exclusion, had stunted the growth of the Indian masses and widened their distance from the demands of the nineteenth century. The British administration was directly responsible for this misfortune, having economically impoverished and morally weakened the "dumb millions" of India.[59] Crucially, the diagnosis of the social deficiencies of the masses did not morph into an affirmation of their sovereign claims as a people, but instead boosted the case for taking them as the main object of development. While reflecting on the ancien régime administrators' portrayal of the misery of the people prior to the French Revolution, Alexis de Tocqueville observed: "Because [the people] seemed so impassive, they were deemed to be deaf. When their fate began to arouse interest, others began to speak in front of them as if they were not there."[60] The Indian liberals, who primarily wrote in English and operated in a transnational imperial realm, had found it easy to assume—to use Tocqueville's expression again—the "absence of the people from the political scene."[61]

While the administrators of the ancien régime were yet to encounter the people as a political abstraction, these late nineteenth-century Indian thinkers had no such unfamiliarity with the principle of popular sovereignty. The Indian liberals were all too aware of the two bodies of the people, especially French revolutionary experiments to "superimpose" the people as a "political abstraction on sociological specificity."[62] They occasionally contrasted their slow approach to that of the French, for the "disastrous consequence" of the French Revolution consisted in giving "self-government" all at once to the people.[63] This, however, was not the crux of their difference from the French revolutionaries or British liberals. The French revolutionary signification of poverty and misery as the legitimating premise of popular sovereignty, as Hannah Arendt influentially argued, led to a short circuit between the social and the political.[64] The popular sovereignty–inflected account of the social question would enjoy a wider life throughout the next two centuries. To be sure, nineteenth-century British liberals continued to assert close connection between social conditions and political capacity, but their skepticism regarding the political capacity of the English working classes coexisted with a strong confidence in the fitness of the middle classes. Regardless of all their hesitations on the question of universal suffrage, Reform-era British liberals found the progress of the middle classes sufficient enough to assert that the time of representative government proper had arrived there.[65] In taking it for granted that social backwardness is generative of political unfitness, Indian liberals followed their British counterparts. Importantly, however, the subject of poverty (and its constitutive political incapacity) for the Indian liberals was not a specific class but the masses as a whole. The apparent reason behind this framing was the absence of a comparable educated middle class in India, but the political effect of conceptualizing Indian masses in terms of social deprivation and historical backwardness proved to be far-reaching. Specifically, this meant that the Indian-liberal narratives of mass destitution and exploitation simultaneously indicted the colonial administration and cast doubt on the status of the Indian people as a political abstraction. The immediate transmutation of the social question into a proof of the political incapacity of the masses was the distinctive touchstone of nineteenth-century Indian political thought. To put it another way, the poverty and illiteracy of the Indian people were not simply practical problems for the functioning of a prospective democracy but also the developmental markers of their very incompleteness *as* a people.

The practical solution followed from this diagnosis: the masses had to be shaped in light of the political norms of the nineteenth century, by their advanced "natural leaders" who knew how to read the whispers of progressive history. When Surendranath Banerjea declared in his presidential speech at the 1895 Congress Session that "[no] responsible Congressman had ever asked for representative institutions . . . for the masses of our people," he was articulating a position largely taken for granted by late nineteenth-century Congress politicians.[66] The entrenched nature of this problem of peoplehood meant that the role of (self-)government had become resignified as a mover of history. It had to stand beyond the time of the Indian people to facilitate their development in history. For all their trenchant critiques of imperial policy and administration, the Indian liberals thus did not abandon, but instead clung to the promise of development. In fact, the liberals accepted that they owed the abstract lesson concerning the urgency of development to the British: the sharp indictment of the economic policy of the British administration often led to an enthusiastic affirmation of the political promise of development. Insofar as the lack of Indian peoplehood was a result of the long history of subjection, Naoroji argued, its resolution too should take place slowly, through a process of gradual reform. Having painstakingly shown how imperial rule was draining India, Naoroji credited "English rule" with "[pouring] new light . . . upon us, turning us from darkness into light and teaching us the new lesson that kings are made for the people, not peoples for their kings." Imperial rule was thus also a "blessing."[67] The British had simultaneously impoverished India and gifted it a new, though ever elusive, political ideal: self-government. For the Indian liberals, British rule, though the source of the blessing, could not by itself realize the higher promise of empire. Only (a limited form of) Indian self-government could fulfill the ultimate imperial promise: the development of the people itself.

A TALE OF TWO PEOPLES, OR JOHN STUART MILL IN INDIA

As liberal imperialism fell into decline in Britain,[68] the political thought of British liberal thinkers acquired a new life among contemporary Indian thinkers.[69] Rabindranath Tagore would later characterize this as India's turn to the "Great Englishman" (philosophers and writers) to fend off the "Little Englishman" (colonial administrators). Tagore humorously, but aptly, observed: for Indians the "Great Englishman" lived in the texts of English literature and history; for the "Great Englishman," India resided in the records and accounting books. On the other hand, Tagore added, "the 'Little Englishman' does not move. He has kept India in a state of immobility, and he has been attached to this immobile country himself, for century after century."[70] As Tagore implied, the vociferous Indian-liberal critique of colonial administrators coexisted with a reclaiming of the lessons of British liberal imperialist thinkers. By the 1850s, John Stuart Mill in particular emerged as a common reference among Indian political thinkers.[71] Macaulay's speeches and writings (especially the 1833 Government of India speech) had also exerted much influence. This turn to British liberal imperialist thinkers paradoxically emerged from the Indian pursuit of self-government—a right that had to be made admissible without reference to Indian sovereignty.

The work of self-government was still promissory—a distant ideal rather than an immediately realizable possibility. But it also had an urgent present necessity. The Indian liberals concluded that the disastrous policies of the administration—and the misery it caused in India—stemmed from the absence of Indian influence in the government. For Naoroji as for Banerjea, the best means to improve the body of the people was to politically empower its advanced section—the educated classes. What made the educated classes particularly equipped for leadership was their simultaneous appreciation of the norm of self-government and the patience required for "slowly" advancing their people.[72] In practical terms, it meant a "love" for the empire as well as for "the people."[73] Accordingly, the question of self-government came to be focused on the integration of educated Indians into the orbit of government. More specifically, it entailed the demands of Indian integration into the administration and a more muted claim for legislative representation.

There were, broadly speaking, two related avenues of authorization that early Congress thinkers pursued in their attempts to legitimize the demand for limited self-government. The first strategy was to claim that Indians should be counted as citizens of the British Empire, which would endow them with political rights.[74] To ground this claim, Naoroji, in particular, invoked the authority of the pledges that the Company and the Queen had made over the century, especially the Proclamation of 1858. Yet the 1858 Proclamation had no specific promise of self-government for Indians. Naoroji's attempt to interpret the recognition of Indians as British citizens was further debilitated by the general exclusion of non-white colonies such as India from the contemporary projects of "Greater Britain."[75] The second—and more consequential—justificatory strategy was to link political representation with the urgency of development.

A highly selective reading of John Stuart Mill laid the foundations for this argument. R. C. Dutt perhaps best exemplifies this late nineteenth-century Indian appropriation of Mill. Much like Naoroji, Dutt found the "drain [of] the resources" and "poverty of the voiceless millions" to be directly related to the "non-representation" of Indian views in the administration of the country.[76] To shore up this argument, Dutt would often summon the authority of Mill. Consider this quote from Mill's *Considerations on Representative Government* that Dutt referred to after connecting Indian underdevelopment to political nonrepresentation:

"It is an inherent condition of human affairs that no intention, however sincere, of protecting the interest of others, can make it safe or salutary to tie up their own hands."[77] Dutt argued that the experience of the last few decades vindicated Mill's point and made it imperative that "some form of representation such as it is safe and wise and practicable" should be given to India. Mill's exception for backward dependencies such as India was silently passed over. In the introduction to his acclaimed *Economic History of India*, Dutt cited Mill's arguments against the parliamentary rule of the English people over India (which arose in the context of Mill's support of the Company rule). Ignoring Mill's conclusion while invoking his authority, Dutt directed Mill's argument against parliamentary rule over India to bolster the case for Indian self-government. Similar justifications of limited Indian representation were ubiquitous in the work of Surendranath Banerjea, Naoroji, and others—whether citing Mill or not.

As we saw in Chapter 1, Mill disqualified Indians from sovereignty on developmental grounds while assigning the responsibility for their advancement to the British-led administration. His account thus deferred both the sovereignty and self-government of India. In contrast, Indian liberals posited self-government as the path toward the development of the people into a "fit" sovereign. This developmental justification of self-government both pitted the liberals against the colonial administration and reinforced their investment in imperial sovereignty. But where exactly was imperial sovereignty to be found? Naoroji argued that imperial sovereignty ultimately rested in the "hands of the Indian authorities *in England*," who were under parliamentary control.[78] As a result, the responsibility for India resided with "the English people": "One elector in England has more voice in the government of his country than the whole of the Indian people. . . . We appeal to you to exercise your power in making your Government carry out its solemn pledges."[79] The responsibility of the English people was also a matter of conscience, for they, too, once were at the same historical stage as Indians.[80] The political project of the liberals was thus to directly engage the English people in order to bolster the case of (limited) Indian self-government. This, of course, was directly against Mill's impassioned defense of non-parliamentary rule over India in the final chapter of *Considerations on*

Representative Government.[81] Indeed, the faith in the efficacy of "petitioning" and "constitutional agitation" in England was inseparable from the faith in the remote English people.[82] Because the location of the sovereign people was in another corner of the world, the Indian liberals decided to take their appeal directly to England, bypassing the colonial administration itself. Accordingly, Naoroji ran for the British Parliament, succeeding in his second attempt in 1892.

Surendranath Banerjea's response to the curtailing of the freedom of the vernacular press in 1878 provides another striking example. In a speech in front of a large gathering in Kolkata, Banerjea both disputed the evidence of Indian sedition and supplied the audience with a number of quotations from high British authorities on the loyalty of Indian subjects. The suggestive element of the speech consisted elsewhere, in his reconsideration of the meaning of the freedom of the press as a liberal principle, and the political strategy he advocated in response to its undermining. Interestingly, in contrast to Rammohun's case for a free press (as we saw in Chapter 1), Banerjea had no interest in stressing the universal scope of such political norms. The "question," he argued, "is not whether a certain number of Indians should have the right of free speech." It is rather an "essentially English question."[83] For Banerjea, the gravity of the question ultimately resided in whether the restrictions on a free press—which is "against the instinct of Englishmen"—should be enacted "in any part of the world acknowledging British rule." In so doing, Banerjea grounded the Indian claim to the freedom of the press on an English norm, which he ultimately traced back to the authority of the English people. The political duty of Indians, then, "is to appeal to the representatives of England" and to Englishmen's instinct of freedom.[84] "It is in the best interest of the millions of this country," Banerjea argued in a follow-up speech, "[to devise] means to educate English opinion on Indian questions." Given the absence of such a mission thus far, Banerjea concluded that Indians have "absolutely done nothing" to advance their cause.[85] The upshot of the meeting was a resolution to petition the British Parliament. What this also laid bare was the fundamental reliance of Indian liberal political claims on the possibility—and even necessity—of seeking authorization from the English people for the sake of Indian causes, especially that of self-government. In a recent study, Theodore Koditschek describes this form of political claim-making as strategic "calculations by trailblazing nationalists who recognized that the highest hope for Indian unity and independence lay in cultivating the British connection."[86] Whether "calculated" or not, this particular mode of political claim-making shaped the core of Indian liberalism and would have lasting consequences for the longer career of Indian democracy.

By the end of the nineteenth century, these Indian liberals had helped consolidate a picture of the people whose socioeconomic exploitation redoubled as political incapacity. Their hope to temporarily separate the political abstraction of popular sovereignty from the immiserated social body of the people turned out to be a fateful bargain. The normative pull of popular sovereignty turned them away from the people that was not-yet and toward the people that already was—to wit, the English people. The affirmation of the sovereignty of the English people in the present for the sake of the future Indian people resulted in a stark display of the hierarchy of peoples. In the process, self-government transformed into an institution historically prior to popular sovereignty. It came to be seen as a bridge that would ultimately generate Indian peoplehood itself. This curious split between sovereignty and government in nineteenth-century India was not entirely lost on the early commentators of Indian political thought. One of the first historians to identify a coherent "liberal school of political thought" in nineteenth-century India, Bimanbehari Majumdar, noted that the distinctive feature of the liberal school was their investment in "systematic propaganda in England."[87] Recent historiography of Indian liberalism, however, has lost sight of this distinctly political dimension of the problem, thanks to the emphatic prioritization of the questions of rights and political economy in the scholarship on the global career of liberalism. As we shall see in later chapters, this initial framing of the anticolonial democratic project remained a recurring question in its twentieth-century history.

The rise of the discourse of self-government fundamentally transformed the normative horizon of Indian political thought in the second half of the nineteenth century. In contrast to Rammohun and Mukherjee's pre-democratic "liberalism," Banerjea and Naoroji's framework of self-government had replaced the concerns about the separation of powers and the liberty of subjects with concern for the development of the people. Empire too had become a normatively irredeemable entity:

for all their invocation of the imperial promise, these late nineteenth-century liberals held that the only legitimate form of government was a popular one. But the project of acquiring sovereignty through self-government amounted to an undermining of Indian peoplehood. From the final decade of the nineteenth century, the main charge against the generation of Banerjea and Naoroji would precisely be the enactment of imperial hierarchy in the name of self-government. What the liberals characterized as "constitutional agitation" would be called "mendicancy" and "begging" by their "extremist" critics. The faith in the "Great Englishman" also did not escape the biting irony of critics. As Tagore put it: "You [Indians] should not clamorously run to the harbors of the West in the hope that the 'Great Englishman' will be sending us a ship laden with gifts. Remember that the 'Little Englishman' has laid mines in the Indian Ocean. It may still be possible that the broken structures of that ship, which is only what you will receive, could serve as burning woods for the funeral pyre of free *self-government*."[88]

The long-standing tradition of studying this episode in Indian political thought through the lens of nationalism meant that scholars have largely missed the tension underlying this dispute—which was essentially a dispute between contesting claims of sovereignty and government. The "extremist" critics had more than a straightforwardly nationalist charge against their predecessors: there was also the problem of popular authorization. As Aurobindo Ghose—who first articulated a critique of the Congress on this ground in the 1890s (*New Lamps for the Old*)—would write during the Swadeshi movement in 1907: "The very basis of constitutional agitation is a reliance on the foreigner and a habit of appealing to him, which is the reverse side of a distrust and certain contempt for their own people."[89] The "contempt" for the Indian people that the critics identified in the likes of Banerjea and Naoroji was no standard "liberal" distrust of the people. Naoroji, Banerjea, and Dutt understood their political agendas in foundationally popular terms, even though theirs was a people marked by sociological misery and (by extension) political incapacity. The difficult irony of nineteenth-century Indian liberalism resided in the precarious business of pursuing self-government in a world where the claim to self-government amounted to a direct sacrifice of the sovereign aspirations of the Indian people.

CODA: THE CONCEPTUAL FORMATION OF INDIAN LIBERALISM IN THE TWENTIETH CENTURY

While revisiting the 1919 Jallianwala Bagh Massacre and its aftermath in his magisterial autobiography *Toward Freedom,* Jawaharlal Nehru noted, with a tinge of amusement, that the "moderates" had begun to call themselves "Liberals."[90] Nehru found no meaningful liberal quality in his opponents' approach to politics.[91] In the next few pages Nehru would alternate between the terms "moderates" and "Liberals," ultimately settling on the latter. Nehru was referring to the founding of the "National Liberal Federation of India" in 1920. The need for a separate political platform for the more gradual reform-oriented faction of the Congress emerged out of their unease with the label "moderate." The president of its second session, Sir P. S. Sivaswamy Aiyer, suggested that they adopt either "Liberal" or "Progressive" as the name of the new political organization.[92] The conceptual intimacy between these two terms has been the subject of a great deal of writing in the history of British liberalism. In the historiography of colonial India, the term "moderates" would ultimately carry the day. For a brief period, however, the rebranding of "moderatism" generated a flurry of reflections on the history of liberalism in India.

One of the first book-length studies of the history of Indian liberalism was Maganlal Buch's *The Rise and Growth of Indian Liberalism* (1938), based on his University of London dissertation. The book was self-consciously presented as a history for the Liberal Federation.[93] Buch traced the slow but steady growth of the "liberal spirit" over all aspects of Indian life: religious, social, economic, and political. His definition of liberalism was straightforward: "the ideal of gradual attainment of fuller and fuller freedom."[94] Buch's text was ultimately a faithful meditation on the progressive nature of political development. Invariably, the distinction between Indian Liberals and their political opponents was drawn in terms of temporal markers: patient vs. impatient, forward-looking vs. past-looking, and so on. The search for the prehistory of the Liberals —or the moderates—would lead Buch to take Rammohun Roy as the beginning point of the march of progress in India (and, by extension, that of Indian liberalism). Buch's narrative gave us a taste of the future, though Rammohun's rebirth as the apostle of liberalism was yet to be set in motion. A few years later, V. N. Naik published a history of the Liberal Federation on the occasion of its silver jubilee. The volume was written amid the unraveling of the British Empire and the patent political irrelevance of the flailing Liberal Federation. Naik's text turned out to be a celebration of the "animated moderation" of Indian liberalism. His narrative also started with Rammohun, whom he presented as a moderate thinker—a proponent of "regulated liberty." Naik, however, acknowledged that Rammohun was at best a precursor of liberalism proper, as he wrote "before the dawn of liberalism in Europe and before its rise in the mid-Victorian period of English history."[95] Such qualifications notwithstanding, there was no meaningful barrier to the conscription of Rammohun into the liberal canon in the Cold War era. In his 1962 text *In Defense of Liberalism,* K. M. Panikkar would straightforwardly identify Rammohun as the "father of liberalism in India," citing his support for equality and individual rights.[96]

The meaning of liberalism in colonial India had been inseparable from the Indian investment of hope in the British Liberal Party. In nineteenth-century Britain, the meaning of liberalism was profoundly shaped by the experience of the Reform Acts. As James Fitzjames Stephen aptly put it: "'liberal' and 'liberalism' are rather proper names than significant words, and denote in politics . . . the party which wishes to alter existing institutions with the view of increasing popular power." For Stephen, the meaning of liberalism was not radically different from democracy. If liberalism was to fare better than democracy, Stephen also observed, it would need to restrain the popular power that it helped to politically integrate.[97] Throughout the nineteenth century, the older references of the term to moderation and liberty coexisted with the more precise political reference to parliamentary reform.[98] Though affiliated with the British Liberal Party, Stephen was no liberal-imperialist in the mold of John Stuart Mill; he had no illusions regarding the non-liberal roots of British imperial rule. When Stephen came out against the Ilbert Bill of 1883 (which would have allowed Indian judges to preside over the trials of British citizens), K. T. Telang—who would later be hailed as a founder of Indian liberalism—offered a scathing rejoinder: "[Stephen is] in obtrusive antagonism to the doctrines of modern liberalism, by which I do not mean what is called by that name in the jargon of English party politics, but I mean liberalism in the broader and higher sense, as signifying those political principles, which, for us here in India, are embodied in the great Proclamation of 1858."[99] For Telang, the liberal promise of empire—which for late nineteenth-century Indian thinkers, as we have seen with Naoroji, was encapsulated in the Queen's Proclamation—had no transparent relationship to domestic politics in Britain. Telang instead suggested that the higher meaning of liberalism was to be found in imperial conduct rather than in strictly domestic issues. Early twentieth-century Indian critics of liberalism would approach the question somewhat differently. Bal Gangadhar Tilak's speech "The Tenet of the New Party," delivered at the height of the Congress's moderate-extremist divide in 1907, is suggestive. While fiercely questioning Gokhale's faith in the imperial promise, Tilak singled out the moderates' enthusiasm about the "revival of Liberalism" in Britain. He suggested that liberalism as a political principle did not quite travel across the imperial space: "A Liberal Government means that the Government or the members of the Government are imbued with Liberal principles because they want to have the administration of their country conducted on those principles. They are Liberals in England, but I have seen Liberals in England come out to India to get into conservative ways."[100]

The Cold War construction of liberalism as an ideological counterpart to capitalist exchange relations would also make its entrance into the historiography of colonial India. Ranajit Guha's 1974 essay—"Neel-Darpan: The Image of a Peasant Revolt in a Liberal Mirror"—is perhaps one of the earliest academic works on nineteenth-century India that implied that the logic of capitalist class relations is built into the political idea of liberalism. At once a "liberal" and "petty bourgeois," Dinabandhu Mitra—the author of *Neel Darpan*—appeared to Guha as a paradigmatic liberal who "stands close to the power of the state seeking cover behind the law and the bureaucracy."[101] Guha is careful enough to analytically distinguish liberalism as a political idea from the larger class analysis that undergirded his argument. Thus, even though the conceptual and economic dimensions of liberalism became closely linked, Guha's account of Indian liberalism as a synonym for imperial loyalty was very much in continuity with the early twentieth-century critique of moderatism. Other historians of nineteenth-century India soon began to argue that Indian liberalism exemplified the distinct predicament of a "bourgeois-liberal" ideology lacking the attendant social transformation.[102]

Just as the postwar Euro-American debate over liberalism began to wane, the idea made its proverbially belated entrance into the scholarship of the colonial world. This turn to the history of Indian liberal thought was triggered by the rise of scholarship on "liberal imperialism" in the history of political thought and imperial history.[103] Though the historical imbrication between liberalism and empire has been the main preoccupation of this scholarship, the centering of liberalism in imperial history offered a different set of interpretive possibilities for the scholars of nineteenth-century Indian intellectual history. It allowed them to place nineteenth-century Indian thought in its contemporary global-imperial context, as opposed to the benchmark of twentieth century anticolonialism. Naoroji and his colleagues' attempt to carve out a non-European space for "constitutional liberalism" could now be seen as innovative, thus facilitating the contention that theirs was a "liberalism much more than a discourse masking the exercise of social and political power."[104]

We see, then, that the changing fortunes of Indian liberalism veered from an older discourse of historical lack (vis-à-vis contemporary European liberalism as well as twentieth-century anticolonial democratic norms) to a more globally sensitive approach that has sought to transcend the limits of ideology-critique. In contrast, my goal in this chapter has been to critically examine the very criteria through which the global scope of nineteenth-century Indian political thought has been understood. As we have seen earlier in the chapter, Mukherjee's politics of "good government" was primarily nondevelopmental, relying as it did on a universalist notion of fairness and liberality. The developmental integration of the globe, and the concomitant resignification of self-government as a historically dependent ideal, presented a different challenge to Naoroji and Banerjea's generation. The standard grouping of the likes of Rammohun and Mukherjee and their late nineteenth-century successors such as Naoroji and Banerjea under the rubric of liberalism thus tends to obscure the emergence of the democratic ideal in the interim period.

By and large, early Congress thinkers enthusiastically theorized the progressive vision of a democratic future and even accepted the violence of the empire as an unavoidable part of the progressive journey: "It has been remarked by Tennyson, somewhere in his poems, that the path of human progress is streaked with blood, and the car of human civilization rolls forward amid the corpses of men, women, and children. This remark seems to me to be pregnant with truth ... [England] has a glorious mission to fulfill here, a mission far nobler than it ever fell to the lot of Greek, Macedonian, or Roman to accomplish."[105] The political end of the progressive journey, Banerjea added later, would be a state rested on the principle of "popular domination."[106] The dogged pursuit of progress could easily lend itself to the impoverishment of the present. More consequentially, for Banerjea and his colleagues, it reinforced a move away from the people that they one day hoped to see "enthroned."[107]

The first decade of the twentieth century would usher in a new era with the outbreak of colonial India's first mass anticolonial movement. In the wake of the Swadeshi movement, the politics of waiting for the people would encounter intense criticism from a new group of political thinkers in and around the Congress. Ironically, the declaration of the demand for immediate self-government came from none other than Dadabhai Naoroji, the old guard of nineteenth-century liberals. Nevertheless, the nineteenth-century tradition of Indian liberalism rapidly went into obsolescence. The new group of anticolonial thinkers—organized around a shared rejection of appealing to the English people—would face their own struggle in conceptualizing a sovereign people. Their dramatic rise, though historically influential, would only last briefly. Out of the ruins of nineteenth-century anticolonial thought would emerge colonial India's most formidable critic of developmentalism: Mohandas Karamchand Gandhi. In Chapter 3 we turn to this story.

THE COLONIAL PARADOX
OF PEOPLEHOOD

Swaraj and the Gandhian Moment

IN HIS PRESIDENTIAL speech at the Calcutta Congress Session of 1906, Dadabhai Naoroji—at the twilight of a half-century political career—deployed the word "swaraj" in passing to describe the demand for immediate self-government: "We do not ask any favors. . . . Instead of going into any further divisions or details of our rights as British citizens, the whole matter can be comprised in one word —'self-government' or *Swaraj* like that of the United Kingdom or the Colonies."[1] The "Grand Old Man of India" delivered the speech at the height of the Swadeshi movement, an event that inaugurated the era of mass protests and raised new questions about the terms of anticolonial politics in India. For much of the speech, Naoroji painstakingly elaborated on the institutional nature of his rather minimalistic, and already familiar, account of Indian self-government. Still, his public disavowal of the temporal order of anticolonial politics (what he characterized as the necessity to wait "till all the people [were] ready" for self-government) sent seismic waves through the bustling political scene of colonial India.[2] An intense interpretative debate soon broke out over the meaning and political implications of the "dubious word" *swaraj,* ultimately leading to the splitting of the Congress in 1907.[3]

The Kolkata-based weekly *The Bengalee*—edited by Surendranath Banerjea, a leader of the moderate wing of the party—lauded Naoroji's deployment of the term, saying that it had "a fullness of meaning, a reality about it, which is denied to words drawn from an alien language."[4] At the opposite, so-called extremist spectrum of Congress politics, Aurobindo Ghose and Bipin Chandra Pal's *Bande Mataram,* despite its consistent criticism of Congress moderates, including Naoroji, found the coinage of "swaraj" to be the product of "an inspired moment."[5] Against the *Bengalee*'s contention that the term was "discovered" by Naoroji, the London-based expatriate outlet *Indian Sociologist* wryly pointed out that two regional periodicals bearing the name *Hind Swarajya* were in circulation much before the presidential address, and that one of them had in fact been involved in a well-publicized sedition case in the recent past. The author of this brief article, Shyamji Krishnavarma, explained the meaning of the term in an assured matter-of-fact manner: "The word 'Swaraj' . . . is the Sanskrit equivalent for Home Rule . . . the Latin word *suum regnum* being literally in Sanskrit *svarajyam,* i.e., one's own rule—home rule."[6] As the unfolding debate quickly demonstrated, such confident definitions of swaraj opened up more questions than answers. The word "swaraj" would soon become absorbed in questions of foundational political-theoretic import: What constituted the peoplehood of the colonized, and what would their *own* rule mean? Did "swaraj" simply mean Indian representation under imperial sovereignty? If it instead is an outright call for independence, how could the people—the "self" of self-rule—rule without any prior training in democracy?

The word "swaraj"—and the emerging concept of swaraj—entered a political terrain organized around the ideal of self-government. There was no clear indication at the outset as to whether "rule" meant something different from "government." The prefix "swa-," too, was rendered into English as both "home (rule)" and "self(-rule)." Naoroji himself seemed to have intended to use the term "swaraj" interchangeably with "self-government," but his characterization of swaraj as a matter of "here and now" already signaled a major difference from the gradual reformism associated with the agenda of self-government. In disavowing the necessity to wait for self-government, these early twentieth-century Indian political thinkers found themselves in uncharted territory where the preexisting questions of sovereignty, government, and peoplehood—no longer mediated by the slow temporality of gradual reformism—suddenly came to jostle together anew. As an aging Naoroji stepped back from the political fray after his 1906 speech at the Congress session, the increasingly contentious exchange between the vying groups of the Congress appeared to have collapsed into a restless exegetical exercise on the meaning of the word he bequeathed to them. Along the way, the problem of peoplehood would turn into a full-fledged paradox.

The charismatic group of political thinkers identified with the "extremist" side of the Congress, especially Bipin Chandra Pal and Bal Gangadhar Tilak, were the first to register the full philosophical weight of swaraj. Both Pal and Tilak readily underscored the temporal break with the older project of self-government that Naoroji's swaraj speech announced. Convinced of the futility—and political ignominy—of appealing to the British people, Pal and Tilak made impassioned cases for turning to India itself to ground the project of swaraj. It is an endeavor that necessarily intensified and dramatized the absent grammar of Indian peoplehood, especially for those who no longer subscribed to empire. Having rejected imperial sovereignty, Pal and Tilak stumbled into the now seemingly freestanding truth concerning the underdevelopment of the (not-yet) sovereign people: their search for popular authorization for swaraj struggled to brush aside the view that the norms of sovereign peoplehood had not yet organized themselves in India's political life. The call for self-government without delay pried open the still more fundamental concerns about the source of sovereignty.

Reckoning with the conflicted history of modern popular sovereignty, democratic theorists have stressed the point that the problem of authorization is ultimately rooted in the essential contestability of the concept of the people.[7] As Jason Frank argues, claims to speak in the name of the people—whether by underauthorized groups or instituted authorities—are always marked by "never fully realized reference to the sovereign people."[8] The project of anticolonial founding, too, grappled with a dilemma of authorization; the colonial dilemma followed not so much from the contesting claims of being authorized by the people, but rather from the paradigmatic presupposition that the people—because of their developmental lack—had not yet become claimable. As we saw in Chapter 2, the global hierarchy of peoples entailed the argument that the Indian masses lacked the political qualities necessary for assuming the role of sovereignty. Essentially rendered as an object of development, the figure of the Indian people fell short of the criteria of sovereign peoplehood and thus could not stand as the authorizer for the claim to self-rule. As Tilak and Pal found out, the demand of immediate self-government for the underdeveloped—and unclaimable—figure of the people unwittingly reinforced a further deferral of popular sovereignty. Conversely, the act of appealing to empire for self-rule reinstated British sovereignty and undermined the very abstraction of sovereign peoplehood that was posited as the ultimate goal. This was precisely the paradox that would shape the struggle to define swaraj.

In this chapter I delve deep into the intellectual history of swaraj and, in the process, outline the context against which Mohandas Karamchand Gandhi appeared on the Indian political scene. The word "swaraj" is now most famously associated with Gandhi, who led the Indian anticolonial movement in its name and whose influential text *Hind Swaraj* bears the term in its title. This Gandhian account of swaraj is generally contrasted with the instrumentalist approach of his predecessors in the anticolonial movement.[9] As we shall see, such a framing of Gandhi's concept of swaraj both obscures the central theoretical tension that constituted its pre-Gandhian career and elides the theoretical innovation underlying Gandhi's reinvention of the concept. By recovering his disputes with the developmental— as well as instrumental—visions of self-rule in *Hind Swaraj,* I offer a reinterpretation of the political import of Gandhi's ethical turn to the self. Gandhi's theory of action has been interpreted as an "escape" from or an "indifference" to politics.[10] Though it is evident that Gandhi largely avoided the institutional terms of modern politics, I suggest that his rejection of the developmental ideals of collective peoplehood—political fitness and unity, in particular—offered an innovative answer to the crisis of popular authorization that plagued early twentieth-century Indian politics. The question of nonviolence was no doubt an essential foundation of Gandhi's political thought, but it was his emphatic displacement of the terms of swaraj theorization that paved the way for his swift rise in a period of political crisis in early twentieth-century India.

The Gandhian recasting of the concept of swaraj displaced the mantle of authorization from the collective to the self, emphasizing the immediate possibility of self-rule if anticolonial actors took their own moral authority as the source of political action. Even Gandhi's most sustained attempt at articulating an alternative vision of a self-ruling community—that is, the village republic—was driven by self-conscious efforts to eschew the ground of collective authority. Gandhi instead turned to the cooperative power generated from individual self-sacrifice to ground an alternative collectivity. His repudiation of the co-constituted ideals of development and peoplehood helped anticolonial politics break free of the crisis encountered by early swaraj theorists. Yet the same principle would also resist institutional consolidation of the Gandhian vision of swaraj. Read in the context of his predecessors' struggle to authorize swaraj in the name of the people, Gandhi's moral theory of self-rule emerges as an attempt to displace, if not to resolve, the terms of the colonial problem of peoplehood.

SWARAJ: FROM A WORD TO AN EVENT

The politics of deferral encountered a powerful political challenge with the outbreak of the Swadeshi movement in 1905. Triggered by the partition of Bengal into two separate administrative units, the Swadeshi movement mobilized urban masses in major colonial provinces such as Bengal and Bombay, foregrounding the principles of the economic boycott of British goods and the promotion of indigenous industries and institutions.[11] The newfound political agency of the masses[12] emboldened the critics of imperial sovereignty, who began to characterize the Congress's invocations of imperial norms as a form of self-deprecating "mendicancy."[13] Amid the unfolding political unrest, the "Grand Old Man of India" was summoned from virtual retirement to preside over the yearly session of the Congress after the moderate and extremist wings of the platform failed to agree on other options.[14] To the surprise of his younger colleagues, Naoroji would explicitly distance himself from the program of gradual reformism once associated with his name.

Much of Naoroji's presidential speech reiterated the arguments he helped fashion over the final quarter of the previous century. Throughout the speech, he emphasized the mutual reinforcement between self-government and the development of the people. The author of *Poverty and the Un-British Rule in India* responded positively to Swadeshi demands by linking the lack of economic development in India to the absence of self-government: "Once self-government is attained, then will there be prosperity enough for all, but not till then."[15] He even concluded the speech with a passionate plea asserting the developmental urgency of self-government: Indians must achieve the right of self-government to save the "millions now perishing by poverty, famine, and plague, and the scores of millions that are starving on scanty subsistence."[16] Although this particular theme of the speech reproduced the more familiar aspects of his work, Naoroji's refusal to wait for self-government marked a new beginning: "It is futile to tell me that we must wait till all the people are ready. The British people did not so wait for their parliament. We are not allowed to be fit for 150 years. We can never be fit till we actually undertake the work and the responsibility."[17] This declaration indexed a rupture from the program of gradual reformism: Naoroji was no longer willing to delay Indian self-government on the ground of mass backwardness.

The speech ultimately staged an unsustainable dual commitment. The concrete elements of self-government Naoroji outlined in the speech—Indianization of civil services, political representation, and restructuring of financial policies for India—were consistent with his long-standing preoccupations.[18] In untethering those demands from an indefinite preparatory phase, Naoroji no doubt gave them a new impetus. But the political strategy he defended reaffirmed the importance of appealing to the ultimate imperial authority—the British people. The first half of the speech, summarizing his political and scholarly work over the previous few decades, elaborated an interpretation of imperial sovereignty that stressed the justness of British imperial norms. Though the developmental necessity of self-government was its main justification, Naoroji also summoned the ideal of imperial citizenship to further justify his claim. Indians, he argued, should be considered British citizens by birth, and therefore they also should enjoy the right to self-government like other colonies of the empire.[19] As always, he also meticulously reproduced the pledges of future self-government made by the Queen and colonial administrators.

Insofar as the pursuit of political authorization for the demand of self-government was concerned, Naoroji had no qualm with appealing to the British people. The much-derided "mendicant" method of politics was duly defended as an important strategy to convince the British of the justness of Indian demands: "I am not ashamed of being a mendicant. . . . I appeal to the Indian people for this [political union], because it is in their own hands . . . just as I appeal to the British people for things that are entirely in their hands."[20] It was up to Indians to overcome their differences, to peacefully agitate, and to raise funds for the political agenda. Sovereign authority nonetheless remained in the hands of the British people, and there was no alternative to convincing them of the rightness of Indian demands. Naoroji's demand of immediate self-government consciously steered clear of invoking the authority of the Indian people. Just as parliamentary government existed in England before the masses attained voting rights, "a good beginning" could be made without waiting for the full development of the Indian people.[21] Naoroji's figuration of the people as a developmentally incomplete entity enabled the demand for Indian self-government, while simultaneously affirming the positing of sovereignty in the British. Naoroji's call for swaraj, then, essentially returned to the older framework of splitting the question of (British) sovereignty from that of (Indian) self-government.

The immediate reception of Naoroji's speech reflected this tension over self-government without sovereignty. Moderates within the Congress, such as Gopal Krishna Gokhale, found common ground with specific strategies, such as the Indianization of the civil services, but Naoroji's suspension of gradualist reformism caught them by surprise. A. C. Mazumdar—a moderate Congress member himself, and a perceptive, if partisan, narrator of the Congress politics of the period—summed up the situation this way:

> The first resolution was announced by the Extremist press as the *Swaraj* resolution, though the dubious word *Swaraj* was to be found nowhere in the resolution itself, and was used only once by the President [Naoroji] in his inaugural address, of course, in a perfectly legitimate sense. The separatists evidently smarted under a sense of wrong and throughout the year that followed kept up an agitation through the columns of their papers as well as upon the platforms decrying the Congress and preaching the "utter futility" of the Congress propaganda.[22]

One of the resolutions passed by the Calcutta session— containing the demand that "the system of government obtaining in the Self-Governing

Colonies should be extended to India, and that, as steps leading to it, it urges that the following reforms should be immediately carried out"—generated much interpretative disagreement between the Congress's opposing groups.[23] The extremists dubbed it the swaraj resolution, whereas the moderates led by Gokhale stressed the absence of the word "swaraj" from the official resolution. Furthermore, endorsing gradual reformism, Gokhale interpreted Naoroji's declaration of "self-government as in the colonies" as a mere preamble to his concrete institutional demands, such as the Indianization of the civil services.[24] Congress moderates such as Gokhale found no merit in the arguments for immediate self-government, owing to the practical political problems that an underdeveloped people would encounter were it given the right to form its own government.

For the "extremists," the "politics of petition" endorsed by Naoroji was no match for the urgency he freshly attributed to the demand for swaraj. Although "extremist" political thinkers such as Bipin Chandra Pal and Bal Gangadhar Tilak would eventually—and without qualification—identify Naoroji as the originator of the political idea of swaraj, their initial reaction was rather mixed. Speaking a few days after the conclusion of the Calcutta Congress Session, Tilak offered an immediate appraisal of Naoroji's presidential speech: After spending more than a quarter century "trying to convince the English people of the injustice that is being done to us," Naoroji's retraction exemplified the end of the mode of politics that appealed to the "benevolence" and moral norms of the British.[25] Naoroji's account of swaraj, therefore, was incomplete, and his reliance on pledged rights and on the Queen's proclamation was politically naive and unhelpful to the cause of swaraj.[26] The critical ire of the extremist group was directed primarily at the faith in imperial sovereignty, especially the assumption that the British would eventually concede meaningful rights and opportunities of self-government to Indians.[27]

PAL, TILAK, AND THE PROBLEM OF POPULAR AUTHORIZATION

Bipin Chandra Pal offered one of the earliest—and influential—elaborations of the swaraj concept in his arresting series of lectures in Madras in May 1907. By the early 1900s, Pal had abandoned his imperial loyalism and emerged—along with Tilak and Lala Lajpat Rai—as a figurehead of the new Congress. The *Madras Lectures* presented a commentary on Naoroji's swaraj speech as much as a reflection on Pal's own political trajectory. Subjecting Naoroji's speech to close scrutiny, Pal found irresolvable ambiguity in the former's statement that Indians demand "self-government, as in the United Kingdom or the Colonies, i.e., Swaraj." Swaraj in the fashion of the United Kingdom would mean complete independence, including the rights of self-legislation and autonomy over foreign relations. If conceived in the form of the white British colonies, such as Australia and Canada, the extent of swaraj would be limited but still quite meaningful. Pal saw no viability of an arrangement where Britain would be in charge of foreign and military affairs while leaving the business of internal government to Indians. In such a hypothetical situation, the question regarding the source of ultimate sovereignty would be irresistible: Indian agendas of taxation and self-legislation could not but come into conflict with British interests. If this arrangement worked for white settler colonies such as Canada and Australia, Pal observed, it was because of the racial order underlying British imperialism.[28] These settler colonies accepted surplus population from Britain, and in return Britain would "help the Colonies to exterminate the native race . . . [and] strengthen the white power in distant parts of the globe."[29] He further observed that Naoroji's phrase "self-government as in the Colonies" deliberately avoided the confused phrase "Colonial self-government," which involves "the perpetuation of the relationship of the existing British Colonies with the mother country."[30] In any case, Pal had no doubt that Britain would find such an ideal of swaraj unacceptable for "black and brown" colonies.[31]

For Pal, the major "revelation" of swaraj was that "there is a natural, a fundamental conflict between the self and the not-self in the political affairs of the country."[32] He associated the language of "revelation" with swaraj self-consciously, for it dramatically broke the spell of the nineteenth-century program of "constitutional agitation." The agendas of Indian participation in imperial legislative bodies and civil services concealed the fact that the British administration—no matter how virtuous—was not authorized by the Indian people. This was where the source of the problem lay: "Good Government is not only no substitute for self-government[;] it is an exceedingly evil thing when the authority of the State rests in the hands of an irresponsible power."[33] The ideal of "good government" could only erode the urgency of swaraj in colonial India. In fact, "the ideal of swaraj has been revealed to us only recently . . . because for nearly a hundred years and more we looked upon the Government as our own."[34] The point was instead to see the British administration as a *pararashtra*—a state of others. At the highest level of abstraction, however, swaraj meant more than an opposition to foreign subjection. Its assertion of the equality of all Indians made it nothing less than a symbol of "divine democracy."[35]

In the context of foreign rule, though, its most immediate meaning pertained to the necessity to create a "big *swa* [we] whose *raj* [rule] we desire to set up and attain in this country."[36] No less importantly, this lesson of swaraj fundamentally disavowed the imperial query "Are you fit for swaraj?" Pal observed that such a question is meaningful only if one asks for authorization from an authority who is external to the Indian people. Even if Britain were to offer India "the gift of swaraj," it would be a self-defeating exercise to accept it. The swaraj that is not willed by Indians themselves would belie its very meaning. The trouble with imperial sovereignty resided precisely in its obfuscation of the self–other distinction. As long as the imperial sovereign was taken as the source of "wealth," "honor," and "strength," Indians would fail to cultivate an autonomous sense of the self.[37] The calling of swaraj was thus to "turn our faces away from the Government House . . . to the *huts of the people*."[38]

Nevertheless, Pal's rejection of the prevailing understanding of swaraj as self-government within empire did not amount to an outright call for independence. Though it was now imperative to turn to the people, the state of Indian peoplehood was yet to be commensurate with the norms of democratic self-rule proper. Pal conceded that "the freedom of the free citizen comprising a free state" had not organized itself yet in social, political, or economic life of Indians.[39] The intellectual, physical, and economic degradations of Indians under colonial rule had made swaraj in the form of independent statehood an unfeasible immediate goal. To be fit for swaraj, Indians must first register organic growth and internal development.[40] His account of swaraj was thus suggestive of what the historian Sumit Sarkar termed "constructive Swadeshi"— an approach marked by its emphasis on self-development as opposed to the reliance on British help.[41]

Pal specified two forms of "training" essential for the development process. "Subjective" training would consist in directing the sources of honor and strength to the self while cultivating an aversion to all that emanates from the empire. In contrast, "objective" training would be based on "civic organisation" outside of the machinery of the colonial state. These self-governing institutions would work as a "school of civic duties for the people."[42] In the period of training, the "longing for emancipation"—as manifested in calls for complete severance of the British connection—would play a heuristic role: it would remind Indians of "the existence of bondage and a keen sense of it."[43] Interestingly, this commitment to the primacy of organic growth of the Indian people had helped Pal support his defense of colonial government in the 1880s. After his turnaround, the possibility of organic growth, now dissociated from the empire, was linked inextricably to the practices of self-rule outside of the colonial state. In any case, Pal's account of self-rule—out of its simultaneous aversion to imperial sovereignty and acceptance of the underdevelopment of the people—ended up reinstating another deferral, albeit it was the deferral of the people as a sovereign authority but not as a self-governing entity. Before the full formation of the sovereign people, swaraj would mean extra-colonial political training, aiming to generate peoplehood without relying on the British.

Pal's "extremist" comrade from western India, Bal Gangadhar Tilak, took a slightly different approach to the problem. Tilak refused to fully externalize the pursuit of swaraj from the colonial state. If the "Old Party" sought to achieve self-government through petition and appeal to the English people, the "New Party" would do it through boycott.[44] Through the democratic pressure of boycott, Indians who worked as "useful lubricants" in the bureaucratic machinery could take control of the government itself: "I want to have the key of my house and not merely one stranger turned out of it. Self-government is our goal; we want . . . control over our administrative machinery."[45] This otherwise instrumental account of self-rule was undergirded by a rejection of the notion that development is a politically neutral issue. For Tilak, the objects of development—education, for example—could not be separated from the question of who controlled the Indian government. Because of the fundamental conflict of interest between India and its foreign rulers, the kind of education required to develop Indians as "good citizens"—and to facilitate "scientific" and "industrial" development—could never be imparted by the latter.[46] That the Indian people needed to be developed was central to Tilak's argument, but the nature of that development could no longer be an objective question. He observed that the promise of British rulers to extend the right of self-government once "the people" overcame their "social inferiority" previously legitimated colonial rule.[47] The failure of the British to advance Indian development had invalidated, on its own terms, the deferral of self-government on the same ground.

Tilak's case for self-government was thus unqualified and unapologetic. There was no basis to the (Indian) liberal optimism that "the whole British electorate" could be converted to a pro-Indian position.[48] Such an approach not only was politically unrealistic but also compromised the emerging sense of Indian nationality. Tilak suggested that the experience of imperial subjection—including the spread of "Western education"—had led to a fresh development of the "old national character" of Indians, triggering a conflict between the "national character of India and the institutions of Government."[49] While the Indian sense of nationhood progressed, the colonial administration clung onto its refusal to "give proper respect to public opinion." Drawing from a widespread nineteenth-century British argument for democracy (that the form of government must reflect the state of peoplehood), Tilak concluded that the "nature of the [Indian] people" no longer "harmonized" with their government.[50] This was the deeper truth that Tilak located in the acts of political assassination and bombing undertaken by the revolutionary terrorists in Swadeshi Bengal: "The bomb party has come into existence in consequence of the . . . obstinacy in treating public opinion with recklessness."[51] Although his own stated preference was for boycott rather than violent resistance, Tilak's bold attempt to underscore the deeper meaning of political assassinations landed him in prison on a much-publicized sedition case.[52]

Tilak's claim concerning the growth of public opinion coexisted with his (better-known) exhortation for the rejuvenation of Indian nationality. He very much shared Pal's conclusion that the separation between the national self and the imperial other could not be elided through any reimagination of imperial sovereignty, however capaciously defined. Tilak's various activities of the Swadeshi era—ranging from the Shivaji Festival to the call for a shared script for all Sanskritic languages—are usually taken to be a foundational chapter in the career of Hindu revivalism in India.[53] Indeed, he seemed to have little hesitation in affirming (Hindu) religion and inherited traditions as the necessary building blocks of the Indian national character. For all his vindication of Hindu tradition, however, Tilak—a thinker immersed in European political thought of his era—was emphatic in his separation of the question of nationality from that of (democratic) peoplehood. While he found the celebration of the Indian past to be germane to the growth of the "spirit of nationality," the point of returning to a figure such as Shivaji (the seventeenth-century Maratha ruler who was both hailed as a precursor of Indian nation-building and criticized as an emblem of sectarian Hindu revivalism in the modern era) was not to wax nostalgic for the past of the nation.[54] "We Indians," Tilak stated, "have learned at our own cost the lesson of the importance of *popular and representative Government.*"[55] As Tilak also knew, this question of "representative government"—steeped as it was in the concerns regarding socioeconomic development and political education—sustained the doubt over the fitness of the Indian people as a democratic entity. The assertion of nationality was thus no adequate answer to the problem of peoplehood.

Having simultaneously defined swaraj as the Indian control of the government and rejected the norms of imperial sovereignty, Tilak, too, encountered the problem of sovereign authorization. As we have seen, Tilak considered self-government to be an uncompromisable right, one that required no appeal to imperial sovereignty. He held that it was in the best interest of the British Empire to meet this Indian demand, for the discrepancy between the political state of a people and their government usually leads to revolution. The result of this theoretical maneuver was thus that "[swaraj] should be brought about with the consent of Government in conformity with the condition of the people."[56] This rather qualified expression—"the consent of Government in conformity with the condition of the people"—captured the uncertainty over the nature of sovereign authorization required for swaraj. The people no longer required justification for self-government, but the question of sovereignty remained an outstanding problem. Tilak's attempt to resolve the dilemma explicitly at the level of political sovereignty brought the colonial paradox of peoplehood into view once again. Singling out contemporary efforts to characterize British rule as a form of contract, he argued that the sovereignty of the emperor was not discernible through the framework of the social contract because "the word 'contract' cannot be made applicable to relations existing [between] unequals." The "English idea" of sovereignty implied that popular agitation was an attempt to "enforce the terms of . . . an agreement." The "Eastern idea," in contrast, took both the king and the subjects as part of "the Godhead." If the king strays from the principles of justice, the subjects have a duty to "control the power of the king." The abuse of the divine power given to the king transforms him into an evil force, legitimating his replacement with a new "deity."[57] Tilak, however, did not elaborate on the new "deity" required for the age of swaraj; nor did he specify whether the people themselves could take the place of the fallen deity. Rendering both the people and the king as equal parts of the godhead, Tilak, at that point, worked around the thorny question of sovereignty.

After his release from a lengthy prison sentence on sedition charges, Tilak attempted a less ambitious response to this problem. He suggested an analytical distinction between "invisible" and "visible" government to better define the elusive concept of swaraj. The emperor pertained to the invisible government, a political entity separated from the problems of administration and management. The advisory role of the invisible sovereign is needed because "what [Indians] have to do [they] must do with the help of some one or another, since [they] are in such a helpless condition."[58] It is the absence of the people's full self-dependence that necessitated the guidance of the British sovereign. The question of swaraj, in contrast, pertained to the visible government. Although the invisible government could work as a trustee of the "house," the people who lived there must control its administrative aspects. Pushing the question of sovereignty into the invisible realm, Tilak elaborated on the house metaphor:

Whatever you have to do, whatever you want—if you want to dig a well in your house—you have to petition to the Collector. . . . When a boy is young he knows nothing. When he grows up he begins to know and then begins to think it would be very good if the management of the household was carried on at least to some extent according to his opinion. Just so it is with a nation.... Let us give up the thought about invisible government, let us come within the limits of the visible government.... This is the principle of *swarajya*.[59]

In his second attempt to define swaraj, Tilak asserted the analytical distinction of the concept from sovereignty, circumscribing it to the realm of government. He contended that the Indian people were ready to run their own government with the "aid" and "help" of the "invisible" English sovereign. Swaraj would not, however, immediately mean a replacement of the "sovereign authority" of the British, which is at the "root" of the power of visible government.[60] In disavowing the claim for sovereignty, Tilak hoped to move past the questions regarding sovereign authorization that the idea of swaraj brought to the fore. For now, the people had to be content with their power over "visible government," leaving the invisible power of sovereignty with the British. This was a concession that Tilak made in order to direct political energy to the agenda of controlling government, but this framing also meant that the problem of sovereign authorization was pushed outside of the scope of swaraj. In the end, then, Tilak's account of swaraj fell back into the vicious cycle of restoring imperial authority while seeking the immediate right of self-government.

These Indian attempts to theorize swaraj throw revealing light on the specificity of the paradox of founding in the colonial world.[61] The question of founding, at least since Rousseau, has been entangled in a paradox of the people. As both the cause and the effect of founding, the figure of the people, as Rousseau underscored, has to originate a new order and yet be transformed by the order it institutes.[62] Indeed, the temporal lag between what the people is and what it ought to be underlies a number of paradoxes that continue to resonate in contemporary democratic theory.[63] This paradox could also be found in abundance in the record of modern democratic revolutions. As the Abbé Sieyès famously argued on the eve of the French Revolution, the French nation (understood as the collective body of the people) was simultaneously given ("the Third Estate is everything") and unbuilt ("the Third Estate has been nothing").[64] Indeed, modern democratic foundings invariably affirmed the sovereign claim of a people for a new founding on the premise that the existing order denied their very peoplehood.[65] The generic paradoxes of democratic founding acquired a distinct form in colonial India. As these early theories of swaraj illustrate, the developmental conception of the people resulted in an uncertainty over the presence of sovereign peoplehood itself in the colonial world. The principle of popular sovereignty appeared as an abstractly valid norm that was not concretely claimable in the name of a patently underdeveloped people. The result was a form of politics that had to appeal to nonpopular political authorities, all while professing its faith in the norm of popular sovereignty. It was precisely this not-yet-claimable authority of the people that rendered the swaraj project caught in a cycle of deferral and suspension.

For most of the nineteenth century, as we saw in Chapter 2, the Indian people figured as the object of development and the promised goal of foreign government. It was not simply that the sovereignty of the Indian people was denied: the language of peoplehood was parasitic on the developmental power invested in government. In refusing to wait for self-government, these swaraj theorists found themselves stranded with an absent figure of the people. Pal and Tilak's struggle to locate popular authorization for swaraj—the struggle that only accentuated their rejection of imperial rule—especially exemplified the deep-seated fracture between (self-)government and (popular) sovereignty. Nevertheless, the word "swaraj" came to carry the birthmark of the refusal to wait for self-government. But the persistence of the government-centric approach to development meant that there was no obvious alternative solution to the problem of peoplehood.

Marked by this debate over the meaning of swaraj, the Congress-led anticolonial movement eventually descended into a crisis with the fading of Swadeshi mass mobilization. By the end of the decade, Tilak was exiled, Pal withdrew from the scene, Aurobindo prematurely retired from active politics, and the moderates found themselves consigned to political irrelevance. The story of how an expatriate coming from South Africa, M. K. Gandhi, took Indian politics by storm a few years later and transformed the Indian anticolonial movement into one of the largest mass movements of the last century is well known.[66] Gandhi's political rise, however, was preceded by an act of genuine theoretical innovation.

THE GANDHIAN TURN: THE SELF, THE COLLECTIVE, AND THE TIME OF SELF-RULE

Although Gandhi was based at the time on the distant shores of South Africa, his attention was captured almost instantly by Naoroji's call for swaraj at the Calcutta Congress Session. Writing in the *Indian Opinion,* less than two weeks after the Calcutta Session, Gandhi noted the immense publicity that Naoroji's "forceful and effective" speech had received. In his brief review of the address, Gandhi put the word "swaraj" at the forefront: "The substance of the address is that India will not prosper until we wake up and become united. To put it differently, it means that it lies in our hands to achieve swaraj, to prosper, and to preserve the rights we value."[67] In this earliest iteration of Gandhi's account of swaraj, the term was used without registering any meaningful opposition to the instrumentalist approach to self-government. Crucially, though, Gandhi stressed that it was up to Indians to achieve swaraj, diverging from Naoroji's affirmation of the necessity of appealing to the English people. The most striking aspect of Gandhi's first—and brief—reflection on the question of self-rule was the dramatic assertion that swaraj could be achieved "this day" if Indians showed the strength of unity regardless of the fears of retribution, thereby breaking away from the long-drawn-out process of development presupposed by his predecessors. The familiar Gandhian account of swaraj was yet to be articulated, but this earliest commentary on the topic instantiated one continuous thread of his argument: that the power to establish swaraj lies in the immediate moral authority of Indians.

Gandhi first offered an embryonic version of the reworked concept of swaraj in the final installment of his Gujarati paraphrase of John Ruskin's *Unto This Last.* Addressing what by then had become a "cry for swarajya" in India, Gandhi argued that the meaning of swaraj was hardly understood.[68] If understood as a means to secure self-interest à la the Natal whites, swaraj would be "no better than hell."[69] The two existing approaches to swaraj—the instrumentalist project of physically expelling the British and the developmentalist project predicated on a faith in the politically transformative power of moral and material progress—were both misleading: "Just as we cannot achieve real swarajya . . . by killing the British—so also will it not be possible for us to achieve it by

establishing big factories in India." "Real" swaraj could be achieved neither through mere Indian control of the government nor through the
means of development. Its meaning instead consisted in moral mastery.
The agent of moral action was the individual actor, and "a nation that
has many such men always enjoys swarajya."[70]

Gandhi's intervention is often posited against the backdrop of a ste-
reotyped, instrumentalist "extremist" account. The instrumentalism
of the extremist account is usually located in the priority given to ousting
the British, regardless of the means of reaching that goal. Anthony Parel
has summarized the pre-Gandhian extremist accounts of swaraj as
"complete sovereignty achieved through constitutional means if possible, but through other means if necessary."[71] Similarly, the comparative political theorist Fred Dallmayr casts the pre-Gandhian career of
swaraj as that of a "narrowly" strategic concept, denoting "nothing more
than the expulsion of the British from India."[72] Yet neither Naoroji nor
Tilak—two of Dallmayr's examples—fits well with this characterization.
Rather, as we saw in the first section of this chapter, the relationship
between sovereignty and government had by no means been an easily
resolved issue for Gandhi's predecessors. Gandhi himself, as I have underscored above, separately underscored these two—instrumental and
developmentalist—approaches to the question of swaraj.

The archival source of such interpretations of the pre-Gandhian accounts of swaraj lies in the writings of the expatriate group associated
with the *Indian Sociologist*. Edited by Shyamji Krishnavarma, the *Indian
Sociologist* was an influential London-based periodical that also seized on
the word "swaraj" following Naoroji's speech. Gandhi came in contentious contact with the members of the India House (an Indian student
residence in London that fostered radical resistance against the British)—
Shyamji Krishnavarma, V. D. Savarkar, Har Dayal, and others—during
his two visits to London in 1906 and 1909.[73] Krishnavarma's journal was
also in circulation in the Indian community in South Africa.[74] Gandhi's
disagreement with the *Indian Sociologist* was profound. In January 1908,
the *Indian Sociologist* too publicly announced its disapproval of Gandhi's
activism in South Africa, branding him as an ideologue of empire.[75]

Shyamji Krishnavarma was an ardent follower of Herbert Spencer,
and his political trajectory was not quite representative of the swaraj
movement that was flourishing within the Congress during the same

period.[76] The main difference consisted in Krishnavarma's foregrounding of an instrumental conception of political power. Unlike the Congress theorists of swaraj, who were concerned with developing the people before claiming sovereignty, Krishnavarma defended the demand for complete independence with the claim that "given [independence], the future form of government will take care of itself."[77] One central register of developmentalist politics —education—was regularly taken up by the *Indian Sociologist*. Dismissing any relationship between education and politics, they argued, on several occasions, that what mattered was the "possession of a stake in the country," not literacy.[78] When a young India House associate assassinated the British official Curzon Wyllie in London, Krishnavarma's journal found itself engulfed in political controversy.[79] Gandhi landed in London to negotiate with British officials as a civil rights activist in South Africa amid the chaos caused by the assassination. *Hind Swaraj* would be written on the return voyage to South Africa in 1909.[80] This historical context of *Hind Swaraj* partly explains why the pre-Gandhian history of swaraj in Gandhi scholarship has often been reductive, focusing primarily on his disagreement with Krishnavarma's instrumentalist account of swaraj. The critical agenda of *Hind Swaraj*, however, was no less concerned with the developmentalist project and its constitutive crisis of political authorization.

Written in the form of a dialogue between an Editor and a Reader, the text was focused on India but was profoundly informed by the lessons of Gandhi's transnational life. Gandhi's own arguments were voiced through the Editor while the Reader borrowed arguments drawn from those with whom Gandhi disagreed, including the talking points popularized by the *Indian Sociologist*. Though he had been based in South Africa since 1893, Gandhi stayed in touch with the leadership of the Indian National Congress—especially Naoroji and Gokhale—over the years. The Reader, in contrast, was shorn of respect for the old guard of the Congress. The opening chapters of *Hind Swaraj* briefly revisited the moderate-extremist divide of the Congress. Gandhi began the text by distancing himself from the prevalent critique of the moderates without identifying with the latter. His observation that the Swadeshi era brought an end to the days of mere petitioning to the British sovereign amply signaled that Gandhi was not overly pious about the old Congress, even as he saw no compelling reason for fixating on their weaknesses. After evaluating the state of the Congress, Gandhi turned to the question that would pervade the rest of the text: What is swaraj?

Swaraj understood as mere expulsion of the British from India, Gandhi famously argued, would amount to nothing more than a form of "English rule without the Englishman."[81] This was the crux of Gandhi's dispute with the *Indian Sociologist*. For Gandhi, imitative understanding of self-government—exhibited in the desire to "copy" English institutions—was a natural accompaniment to the instrumental method through which many sought to acquire swaraj. This demand for swaraj thus boiled down to this: "Just as they do not allow others to obtain a footing in their country, so should we not allow them or others to obtain it in ours. What they have done in their own country has not been done in any other country. It is, therefore, proper for us to import their institutions."[82] In this way, Gandhi's reading of this particular "extremist" account of swaraj brought forth the underlying imitative and instrumentalist notion of rule. The argument centered on the expulsion of the British was turned upside down as Gandhi located the source of such opposition to the "Englishman" in the uncritical faith that English political institutions were India's developmental destiny. He followed up this ingenious diagnosis of the instrumentalist argument for swaraj with a dramatic, and wholesale, denunciation of the idealized British parliamentary system. Gandhi characterized the English Parliament as an infantile institution devoid of any substance, and the English people—the benchmark by which the developmentalist discourse measured colonial subjects—as fickle and zealous, and thus deserving of their political institutions.

The problem of developmentalism took center stage in the text as Gandhi turned his attention from the condition of England to that of India. In *Hind Swaraj*, Gandhi's reflections on developmentalism were tied up with his critique of civilization. The Congress-affiliated swaraj thinkers who were mired in the problem of developmentalism—specifically Tilak and Pal—did not appear directly in the text. Gandhi was personally familiar with Tilak and was certainly also aware of other extremist writings in this period.[83] It was, in all likelihood, a deliberate choice not to name them. In any case, the hallmark of the Congress extremist account of swaraj—development through India-controlled political institutions—did not fall out of the scope of Gandhi's critique.

In fact, it was key to the arguments he made later in the text. The Reader, too, began to entertain a wider range of arguments than those of the *Indian Sociologist*.

Having explained India's colonial subjection as being a result of the weakness of Indians rather than the strength of the British, Gandhi announced his rejection of all the products and agents of colonial modernity: railways and rail travelers, medicine and doctors, the legal system and lawyers, and so on.[84] These indubitable markers of the developmentalist paradigm, Gandhi proposed, were implicated in the logic of subjection. This is also why Gandhi considered modern civilization to be inimical to the cultivation of moral self-rule. The dependence on institutions such as the railways or modern medicine enabled further attrition of the individual's capacity to rule over oneself. The developmental vision, it turned out, not only was beholden to the ideals of "English rule" but was also guilty of strengthening the hold of extraneous forces on the sources of self-rule. The ideals of progress, in other words, directly erode the capacity for, and defer the arrival of, self-rule.[85] The deeper import of this claim consists in reversing the necessary connection established between material and moral development, as evident in the pre-Gandhian theories of swaraj. In addition, whereas early swaraj thinkers traced the source of India's disunity in its underdevelopment, Gandhi found social conflict to be no hindrance to the project of swaraj. It was the ability to accommodate difference—as opposed to an overarching political unity—that defined the political fitness of a nation. To be sure, Gandhi also plainly rejected the nineteenth-century consensus that no nation existed in India prior to the arrival of the British: "We were one nation before they came to India. One thought inspired us. Our mode of life was the same."[86] One part of Gandhi's argument was expressive of the desire to polemically suspend the imperial paternity claim for Indian nationhood: "It was because we were one nation that they were able to establish one kingdom. Subsequently they divided us."[87] Though these passages in *Hind Swaraj* are often taken to be evidence of his underlying nationalism, what is important to underscore here is the work that the invocations of the nation did for Gandhi. For the Hindu-Muslim question, for instance, he appealed to the prior ground of common belonging to justify separate religious and cultural practices. It was an appeal to unity that sought to legitimate substantive autonomy for different communities. He also drew inspiration for an actor-centric account of "passive resistance" from the records of the Indian nation.[88] Beyond these uses, the nation played no central role in his theory of action. Rather, the source of action, as I argue below, was vested in the individual, not in collectivities such as the people or the nation.

By rejecting the developmental paradigm *in toto*, Gandhi's account of swaraj shifted the emphasis to the self-authorizing individual. The first definition of swaraj he offered appeared to be straightforward enough: "It is swaraj when we learn to rule ourselves." This definition was followed by a more ambiguous claim: "It is, therefore, in the palm of our hands."[89] Gandhi then sharpened its critical implication for the developmentalist paradigm by arguing that swaraj was not a distant utopia, and there was no need to be "sitting still" and waiting for it.[90] What Indians needed in order to acquire swaraj was not a temporally drawn-out process of institutional training. Famously in 1920, Gandhi would promise, with a strange cadence of foreknowledge, the attainment of swaraj in one year if his programs of noncooperation were properly adopted. This sudden declaration struck contemporary political observers as unrealistic and irresponsible. Responding to "much laughter [that] has been indulged in at [his] expense," Gandhi added further fuel to the fire: he claimed that the "proposition" had a "mathematical" certainty. If individual Indians took themselves to be their own authority and acted accordingly, the "time" of swaraj would be solely dependent on them.[91]

To return to *Hind Swaraj*, Gandhi expanded on the claim that swaraj is immediately available with a pivotal move: "[it] has to be experienced by each one for himself."[92] To be able to rule over oneself, however, one must be able to exercise self-control. Gandhi's advocacy of certain practices—chastity, spinning, and fearlessness, among others—is related to the cultivation of self-control.[93] To this extent, self-rule and self-control are inseparable.[94] Critical of the defense of impatience as a political virtue,[95] Gandhi affirmed the patient work on the self needed to cultivate self-control and to avoid the temptations of instrumental action, without undermining his contention that the possibility of immediately authorizing oneself to enact swaraj is ever present. The immediate availability of swaraj meant neither an internal reservoir to be tapped nor a set of moral rules to be followed. Its most pertinent meaning resided in the claim that the source of swaraj is hiding in plain sight, in the power of moral action available to everyone. The logic of Gandhi's swaraj was fundamentally different from that of self-government, not least because the latter sought to reach a higher stage of development—moral or material—through the acquisition of Indian control over government.

This context also offers the key to understanding the formative moment of Gandhi's account of nonviolence. Gandhi's English version of *Hind Swaraj* rendered "satyagraha" (literally translatable as "truth-force") as "passive resistance." In fact, as Eijiro Hazama has shown, he would not translate it as "nonviolence" until after 1919.[96] Though the scope and content of nonviolence would eventually acquire a broader character, its early formulation was very much tied up with the problem of swaraj. In *Hind Swaraj*, he defined "passive resistance" as "a method of securing rights by personal suffering; it is the reverse of resistance by arms."[97] Unlike the means of "brute force," "passive resistance" refuses to share the terms of securing rights with the political authority in question. If an authority concedes a demand upon being overpowered by violent resistance, they only agree with the terms of violent resistance, not with the demand itself. Thanks to this diagnosis, Gandhi considered violent resistance generative of reliance on external authorities, among other things.[98]

For the present argument, an even more crucial aspect of Gandhi's turn to the self in *Hind Swaraj* is his disavowal of the problem of collective authorization—a disavowal connected with his critique of developmentalism. Gandhi reminded the Reader in *Hind Swaraj* that anticolonial actors are guilty of projecting their own weaknesses onto the masses: "Those in whose name we speak we do not know, nor do they know us."[99] He was not convinced of the narrative of mass deprivation that collapsed the material into the moral. But Gandhi went beyond simply pointing out the misunderstanding of the state of the Indian people. After repudiating the view that laws must be followed because they are issued by the government, he extended his argument against the majoritarian—and popular—conception of political authority: "It is a superstition and an ungodly thing to believe that an act of a majority binds a minority."[100] For him, swaraj constituted not only a rejection of appeal to imperial sovereignty but also a critique of the alternative, if deferred, ideal of popular sovereignty. As he put it later: "Swaraj will not be a gift from anyone. It will not fall from above, nor will it be thrown up from below."[101] The problem with the framework of rights lies in its dependence on a higher authority.[102] If individuals approach their actions as a form of self-enacted "duty" requiring no vindication from above or below, the necessity of being authorized by a higher agent is perforce bypassed.[103] It is from the "want of faith in duty" that actors "wait" for the "majority" before engaging in action.[104]

Gandhi's critique of developmentalist and instrumentalist accounts of swaraj, thus, also entailed a rejection of appealing to the people. Gandhi, of course, had no qualms about exhorting the masses or about mobilizing the masses against what he considered to be unjust policies. Where he departed from the vast majority of his colleagues was in the conviction that political action did not need to be authorized by the people. As he reminded the Reader in the conclusion to *Hind Swaraj:* "You and I have nothing to do with the others. Let each do his duty. If I do my duty, that is, serve myself, I shall be able to serve others."[105] Just as "one drowning man will never save another," swaraj, too, must be acquired by individuals before they can hope to impart it to others.[106] As Gandhi would note some three decades later: "Swaraj of a people means the sum total of the swaraj (self-rule) of individuals."[107]

By the end of the 1910s, the author of *Hind Swaraj* emerged as the undisputed leader of the Indian National Congress, which continued to frame its political objectives in terms of institutional reforms. This tension surfaced in Gandhi's 1921 preface to *Hind Swaraj,* where he made a distinction between "parliamentary" and "individual" swaraj. His use of the phrase "parliamentary swaraj" prompted Anthony Parel to argue that Gandhi sought to resolve the tension between the self and the collective by specifying two distinctive kinds of swaraj: individual and political.[108] This interpretive attempt, however, is undercut by the absence of any corresponding account of institutional politics in Gandhi's work. While it is true that Gandhi uses the term "parliamentary swaraj" in the new preface, he also distinguished between the demand of the movement he was leading "in accordance to the wishes of the people of India" and what he himself had envisioned in *Hind Swaraj* and still continued to "individually" work toward.[109] In fact, Gandhi's view of the parliament had no meaningful transformation in the intervening years. Speaking in 1918, for instance, Gandhi noted that having a parliament meant having the right to err. The place of the parliament, if India were to have one, would be no greater than its "cottages."[110] Such deflationary views of the parliament—and modern representative institutions—persisted in Gandhi's work throughout the long period he led the Congress.[111]

That Gandhi likened the parliament to Indian cottages helps reveal a fundamental refusal to take the institutional domain as a distinct or privileged site of political action. Gandhi's moral philosophy shares little with traditional moral idealism,[112] and it also challenges moral evasions of political conflicts.[113] Since his rise in the anticolonial movement, Gandhi was frequently critiqued for conflating politics with morality and spirituality. Tilak expressed a widely held opinion when he argued contra Gandhi in 1920 that "politics is a game of worldly people, not of sadhus [saints]," and that it thus requires norms and practices specific to the political domain.[114] Gandhi, in his reply, resisted the separation between the moral and the political: "it betrays mental laziness to think that the [political] world is not for sadhus."[115] Gandhi's theory of action, then, was not so much a withdrawal from politics as a refusal to accept that moral self-rule is inapplicable to the political domain.

This struggle to reconcile "individual" and "parliamentary" visions of swaraj is illustrative of a recurring question in Gandhi scholarship: What is political about Gandhi's turn to the self? For all his dramatic influence over anticolonial politics, Gandhi has long been interpreted as a moral thinker whose politics were a "consequence of his view of morality."[116] Gandhi's well-documented aversion to institutional politics, of course, easily lends itself to such interpretations. Attempts to salvage an institutional vision of politics, such as Parel's, struggle to find an appreciation of the autonomy of the political in Gandhi. In an influential study of Gandhi's political thought, Partha Chatterjee, attending closely to the "disjuncture between morality and politics" in Gandhi, attributed Gandhi's political success primarily to his capacity to mobilize "collective moral will."[117] Others focus on how Gandhi's moral theory played a transformative role in democratizing the public sphere.[118] However, as we have seen, Gandhi's reconfiguration of the problem of authorization in Hind Swaraj brings to the fore a different political dimension of his theory of self-rule. Gandhi's turn to the moral authority of the self was a simultaneous refusal of the developmentalist and instrumentalist constraints on anticolonial action. Once extricated from these constraints, anticolonial action would not need to wait for the arrival of a people developed enough to be sovereign. It is this intrinsic transformation of the temporality of anticolonial action that generated the political character of Gandhi's ethical turn. To this extent, Gandhi's reinvention of the concept of swaraj, notwithstanding its ethical form, immanently addressed the pervasive problem of peoplehood.

Given the primacy of self-authorized moral action, what then explains Gandhi's idealization of the village as a collective political form? His reflections on the village republic have led to different interpretations. Taking Gandhi's suspicion of collective political authority to its conclusion, Uday Mehta interprets his turn to the village as an exemplar of the "ethics of everyday life," indifferent to the collective terms of modern politics.[119] Karuna Mantena, in contrast, identifies in Gandhi's writings on the village republic elements of an institutional imagination: "voluntary," "antistatist," and grounded in a "non-hierarchical form of authority."[120] Indeed, as we saw above, Gandhi developed his institutional alternative to the state-form through a voluntary and individual actor-centered rethinking of political association. Yet this quest for a nondevelopmental and nonhierarchical source of action coexisted with a foundational doubt of all extra-individual sources of authority. Moving away from collective authority, Gandhi turned to the power of individual self-sacrifice to theorize the possibility of a collective bond in his ideal political community. Bridging the individual *satyagrahi* (nonviolent actor) to the wider collectivity, the cooperative power of self-sacrifice is what allowed Gandhi to make space for collectivity without undermining his individual-oriented theory of swaraj. The village—the proper site of Gandhi's constructive program[121]—is ultimately a political collectivity that is authorized and sustained by the self-sacrificing power of individual actors. Gandhi was acutely aware, though, that practices of sacrifice can facilitate sovereignty over others.[122] The challenge for him was to articulate an account of self-sacrifice that is not generative of the sovereign–subject relationship.

What binds the individual with greater entities is their willingness to "perish for the village." Indeed, the "law" that would govern "every villager is that he will suffer death in the defense of his and his village's honor."[123] As Gandhi would later elaborate, the relationship of the individual to the collective is more like an "oceanic circle" than a pyramidal structure.[124] Gandhi's elaboration of the nature of the village community in the 1940s—a theme already present in *Hind Swaraj*—further emphasized the horizontal and seamless relationship between the individual and the collective. The village community "will be an oceanic circle whose centre will be the individual always ready to perish for the village, the latter ready to perish for the circle of villages, till at last the whole becomes one life composed of individuals, never aggressive in their arrogance but ever humble, sharing the majesty of the oceanic circle of which they are integral units."[125] The authority of the self is neither undermined nor delegated to a higher level for the purpose of holding together the collective. It is instead the self-authorized sacrifice of the self that binds the collective. Although the individual actor retains sovereignty insofar as their sacrifice is willed and sustained by relentless self-discipline, the containment of sacrifice within the self is meant to resist its transformation into sovereignty over others. For Gandhi, between the singular (individual) and the universal (collective), as the philosopher Akeel Bilgrami argues, the only link is the power of setting up examples.[126] To return to Gandhi's metaphor: because one drowning person cannot save another, the best one can do is to learn how to swim and set an example for others. When anticolonial actors enact self-rule on themselves, they neither act for an already existing collective nor rationalize their action as a form of gradual development. This is also the presupposition that led Gandhi to repeatedly claim that his project of swaraj required no waiting.

THE AFTERLIFE OF GANDHI'S SWARAJ

In Gandhi the anticolonial movement acquired a popular character, opening up what had hitherto been a relatively limited terrain of high politics. The theoretical source of Gandhi's politically transformative effect, I have argued, lay in liberating anticolonial politics from its incapacitating entanglement in the colonial paradox of peoplehood. Instead of negotiating the problem from within, Gandhi rejected the ideal of collective peoplehood as the source of political authority. In a way, then, Gandhi's theory of self-rule was an attempt to break free of both the (collective) self and (developmentalist) rule. This feature of Gandhi's account of swaraj would become concretely materialized with his emergence as the main leader of the Congress in the late 1910s. As Jawaharlal Nehru recounted later, Gandhi, even at the height of the Noncooperation movement, remained "delightfully vague" regarding the institutional form of swaraj.[127] Maintaining ambiguity on the nature of post-imperial polity, Gandhi began to deploy the language of swaraj to address issues ranging from timeliness to religious tolerance. What remained consistent in his indiscriminate uses of the word, however, is the point that the power to enact self-rule lies in the moral authority of individual actors.

Even as he rejected almost every premise of imperial sovereignty in *Hind Swaraj*, Gandhi did not take the problem of empire to be the decisive test for swaraj. He continued to believe, until at least 1920, that a truly self-authorized form of swaraj could be addressed to the higher moral ideals of the British Empire. When Gandhi returned to India at the height of the Great War, the political scene was dominated by the demand for self-government within empire—a subdued inheritance from the age of swaraj. Gandhi, at that point, neither affirmed nor contested the goal of self-government within empire. Curiously, however, he took initiatives to recruit soldiers for the British army during World War I. In the course of his controversial recruitment campaign, Gandhi offered a variety of arguments, ranging from a speculative, and highly contested, defense of military service as a potential answer to the cowardice that diluted the meaning of nonviolence in India, to an emphasis on the necessary connection between the ideal of imperial citizenship and self-sacrifice for empire.[128] While the goal of self-government within empire might not have been his chosen agenda, he argued, those who aspire to it "must be equally prepared to sacrifice themselves for the Empire in which they hope and desire to reach their final status."[129] That act itself would secure the end (i.e., self-government), he suggested.[130] Instead of affirming or rejecting the "goal" of imperial citizenship, Gandhi held that it was self-authorized, "voluntary sacrifice" that would render the relationship between imperial masters and subjects obsolete.[131] His approach to the imperial question throughout the 1910s was to refuse the standing of imperial promise as an authorizing source of action while asserting the possibility that the higher moral ideals of the empire would not ultimately be opposed to the political ends sought by nonviolent actors. A decade after *Hind Swaraj,* amid the Non-Cooperation and Khilafat movements, Gandhi would eventually disavow the very legitimacy of addressing the moral ideals of the empire.[132] The result, as I have argued elsewhere, was a form of anti-imperialism that turned the moral empire into a universal addressee—an addressee of action that, regardless of the enormity of its violence, could not discount the irreducible possibility of its own conversion into nonviolence.[133]

Insofar as the question of swaraj was concerned, Gandhi's argument, however, remained fairly consistent with *Hind Swaraj.* When the goal of the anticolonial movement transformed into independent statehood in the 1930s, he saw no need to revise the theory of swaraj. For Gandhi, to conceive of the people as an authority who could bestow sovereignty is to misunderstand self-rule. He was equally apprehensive about standing for the people—or to call upon the masses before they were prepared to be the source of their own action. This no doubt presents a very idiosyncratic picture of the twentieth century's most iconic anticolonial actor. Gandhi's project does not directly fit either the problem (alien rule) or the solution (collective sovereignty) associated with the familiar picture of anticolonialism. Yet Gandhi's success as an anticolonial actor was not accidental. Modern colonialism, as we saw, not so much denied as deferred the possibility of self-rule for the colonized. Gandhi overturned the (collective) source and criteria of political action to paradoxically recover self-rule from its developmental disavowal in the colonies.

What made his account of swaraj so generative for anticolonial political action was also what resisted its consolidation in programmatic or institutional terms.[134] Consider, for example, this well-known exchange between Gandhi and Nehru (who would soon be the first prime minister of independent India). Writing to Nehru in 1945, Gandhi affirmed the vision of *Hind Swaraj,* particularly the ideal of the village republic, and suggested a Congress working committee meeting to discuss the topic. Nehru expressed disbelief in response to his mentor's continued faith in the vision of *Hind Swaraj,* which he described as "unreal" and discordant with the times: "As you know, the Congress has never considered that picture [of village republic]. . . . You yourself have never asked it to adopt it except for certain relatively minor aspects of it."[135] Nehru, accordingly, defended the importance of developmental programs to sustain and uplift the masses of the people, vetoing the proposal to initiate a conversation in the Congress around the topic of the village community.

Historically speaking, Nehru was not incorrect in recalling that neither the Congress nor Gandhi himself had pushed their political movement in the direction of the village republic. Gandhi's theory of self-rule was predicated on a disavowal of the logic of collective authorization presupposed by modem political institutions. As the leader of the anticolonial movement for nearly three decades, Gandhi encouraged individual actors to adopt the life of a satyagrahi. But he consistently refrained from invoking the collective authority of the anticolonial movement to advance the project of the village republic. Gandhi's profound rejection of collective authority took shape during the political crisis that marked the era of Pal and Tilak. And he remained faithful to this principle up to the end of his long political career (of note here is his absence from the Constituent Assembly of India).

Even if Gandhi's own account of swaraj retained its continuous thread, the broader understanding of the concept never quite moved too far from its founding ambiguity. In the early 1920s, as the Non-Cooperation and Khilafat movements were coming to a close, a Bengali political actor interviewed a number of leading anticolonial leaders about their definition of swaraj. The interviewees were a diverse pool of actors, representative of the plural constituencies of the Gandhi-led movement. They were all asked the same question: What does swaraj mean to you? The definition of swaraj varied widely—from a complete severance of the British connection, to imperial federation, to other forms of nonrepresentative political arrangement. The following question asked if Gandhi's methods were the best means for attaining swaraj. While many interviewees differed with Gandhi's view of nonviolence as a "creed" rather than a "policy," none could dismiss the extraordinary power that the Gandhian nonviolence unleashed while disarming the moral claim of the empire.[136] Gandhi's emphasis on the self-referentiality of nonviolent action—that its power comes from the moral authority of actors and not from a mere failure of the empire—bestowed a power to anticolonial action that stood in stark contrast to the era that just preceded him.

Gandhi, as I have noted above, rarely contested the "goal" of the anticolonial movement, whether it be the ideal "self-government within empire" (dominant until the 1920s) or the ideal of independent state-hood (dominant in the 1930s and 1940s). Brushing aside the importance of expressing fidelity to the goal, he continued to maintain that the "progress towards the goal will be in exact proportion to the purity of our means."[137] Still, given the ubiquitous uncertainty around the political form that swaraj would take, the concept would become suspect to the next generation of political actors.[138] Writing in 1928, Nehru stated that the older generation who had fought for swaraj had wanted the masses to participate in their fight, but had failed to consider the real economic "needs of the masses."[139] In 1929, the Congress ultimately adopted *Purna Swaraj* (officially translated as "complete independence"), where the adjective "purna" stood for the severance of "the British connection." The resolution of the problem of political sovereignty in the form of independent statehood neutralized the uncertainty over the definition of self-rule—an uncertainty that originally helped the swaraj literature thrive.

CONCLUSION

Born out of a literary digression by Naoroji, the word "swaraj" quickly transformed into a contentious concept. The transformation of a word into a concept, observes Reinhart Koselleck, takes place when "a single word is needed that contains—and is indispensable for *articulating*—the full range of meanings derived from a given sociopolitical context."[140] Indeed, the concept of swaraj enabled attempts to articulate anew the relationship among a set of ideas stuck in the rut of developmentalism: self-government, sovereignty, gradual reform, independence, and peoplehood. As we saw in Chapter 2, its conceptual predecessor—self-government—was marked by a tenuous arrangement between foreign sovereignty and limited participation in the colonial administration. As the Swadeshi critics disclosed the order of hierarchical peoplehood underlying the older agenda of limited self-government, the swaraj concept arrived with the aspiration to refuse the deferral of Indian self-rule. In their striving to turn to popular authority, the early swaraj thinkers, however, revealed the deep-seated hold of the colonial problem of peoplehood. Neither the rejection of imperial sovereignty nor the refusal to wait for self-government was sufficient for overcoming the developmentalized grammar of politics.

In fact, the unqualified disavowal of deferred self-government turned the problem of peoplehood into a full-fledged paradox, as the early swaraj thinkers found themselves forced to make an impossible choice between an unclaimable people and an illegitimate empire. In any case, the attempts by swaraj theorists—from Naoroji to Gandhi—to overcome the problem of peoplehood yielded rich insights on the distinctive trajectory of popular sovereignty in the colonial world.

The people, of course, is never a prepolitical entity; its meaning is articulated by contesting acts of claiming and speaking in the name of the people during the course of political struggle.[141] As Enrique Dussel notes, "the people is that strictly political category (because it is not properly sociological or economic) that appears as absolutely essential, despite its ambiguity."[142] The search for swaraj in early twentieth-century India unfolded in the midst of the anticolonial struggle and was faced with the necessity to conceptualize the people beyond its colonial signification. Yet the developmentalist conception of colonial peoplehood constituted a political background where claims had to be made while awaiting the arrival of a "fit" people. The dilemma of working between the "not-yet" popular sovereignty and the existing (and unacceptable) imperial sovereignty meant that the early swaraj thinkers were caught in a crisis. That this crisis of anticolonial politics was only sidestepped (though not quite resolved) after Gandhi's sweeping disavowal of the co-constituted ideals of development and peoplehood is not a historical anomaly.

Gandhi's dramatic influence over the Indian anticolonial movement has long perplexed historians of colonial India. In an influential study, Judith Brown sought to demystify Gandhi's rise to power by focusing on his hold over various political networks and the capacity to leverage and unify otherwise disparate political groups.[143] From an opposite perspective, Shahid Amin has famously suggested that Indian peasants' perceptions of Gandhi were "at variance with those of local Congress and Khilafat leadership and clashed with the basic tenets of Gandhism itself."[144] The facts that Gandhi was adept at cutting through political division and that his popular appeal surpassed his words capture important aspects of his complex historical persona. But the intellectual source of his liberating impact on the anticolonial movement lay in his reworking of the ground of anticolonial action. His ethical turn to the self-authorizing actor in the context of the colonial paradox of people-hood freed anticolonial politics, if momentarily, from the constraints of developmental deferral of action. This is what imbued Gandhi's refusal to speak for, or in the name of, the people, with its democratic affect. In light of the formative debate over the meaning of swaraj, in this chapter I have thus also sought to offer an intellectual-historical account of Gandhi's paradoxical democratization of Indian anticolonial politics.

Earlier in the interwar era, as Gandhi took over the Indian political scene, the political future of the colonies suddenly appeared to be separable from the burden of a globe-spanning developmental journey. With the aim to overcome the telos of representative government, there emerged a new, federalist turn in Indian anticolonial political thought. The federalists broadly shared Gandhi's critique of developmentalism, even as they were driven by a set of commitments quite distinct from the Mahatma's. Gandhi sought to stand outside of developmentalism and popular sovereignty; the federalists aimed to reframe and reimagine these problems. Together, in the first quarter of the twentieth century, Gandhi and the federalists put up a formidable challenge to the political inheritance of the nineteenth century. Chapter 4 delves deep into the federalist search for another time for democracy in the colonial world.

BETWEEN THE MANY
AND THE ONE

The Anticolonial Federalist Challenge

UNTIL THE EARLY twentieth century, the institutional framework of parliamentary representation, grounded in the principle of popular sovereignty, stood as a relatively stable set of ideals for the majority of Indian anticolonial thinkers otherwise discontent with their imperial present. This vision of India's political future faced an ambitious challenge from a group of federalist political thinkers in the first quarter of the twentieth century. Writing in 1923, Radhakamal Mukerjee (1889–1968), a leading figure in the turn to pluralist federalism, anticipated an imminent demise of "the nineteenth-century . . . dogma of political sovereignty."[1] The inheritance from the nineteenth century lay, above all, in the framework of centralized sovereignty and the representative-represented hierarchy it instituted. Mukerjee felt that it was time for anticolonial politics to acknowledge and abandon the ruins of nineteenth-century political thought once and for all. Echoing his European pluralist contemporaries,[2] Mukerjee characterized this centralized form of sovereignty as monist.[3] Yet, with an emphasis distinct from his European counterparts, Mukerjee also located the source of

the expansionist drive of modern European empires in the logic of monist sovereignty.[4] Specifically, he suggested that the projection of representative government and centralized statehood as the ultimate goal
of all non-European political developments had been crucial to the
nineteenth-century legitimation of imperial rule. This constituted the
broader anticolonial stake of the critique of monist sovereignty.

Mukerjee and his colleagues advocated for a simultaneous turn to a
"multilinear" theory of historical development and to a many-willed conception of popular sovereignty. They found the germs of a pluralist theory
of popular sovereignty in the history of village republics in Asia. Only a
federal arrangement, they argued, could accommodate a democracy of
many peoples. Their vision was radically different from the modern centralized federalism associated with the American founding.[5] Nor did they
merely aspire to institute a decentralized form of federation among self-
governing states. These Indian federalists instead sought to ground sovereignty on the small scale of village republics, which would then be brought
together in a loose federal association. As a marker of multilinear developmental trajectories, the federation of village republics, they hoped,
would be a testament to the possibility that the historical trajectory of
Europe need not be repeated in the anticolonial pursuit of popular sovereignty.[6] Their wager sought to place popular sovereignty on a new footing
by way of splitting the figure of the people into a many-willed entity.
Though this federalist experiment enabled a new appreciation of direct
democracy in the form of village republics, it also struggled with the fact
that the meaning of modern popular sovereignty far surpassed the dichotomy of representative versus direct democracy.

Though Indian pluralist thought developed in critical dialogue with
European, especially British, pluralism, its origin lay in an arresting
late nineteenth-century critique of Hegel by Mukerjee's mentor, B. N.
Seal. Critiquing "unilinear" approaches to the development of non-
European political life, Seal's account of federalism—first broached at the
Universal Races Congress of 1911—transformed the question of pluralist
sovereignty into a debate over the trajectory of historical development
on a global scale. Seal observed that the positing of the centralized state
as the telos of political development across the globe underwrote the
normative incontestability of representative democracy. Insofar as village republics instantiate another way of exercising popular sovereignty,

the unilinear theory of development, Seal suggested, should give way to a multilinear approach. Seal's federalist invitation would be taken up by a host of anticolonial thinkers and actors, including Bipin Chandra Pal, Radhakamal Mukerjee, and C. R. Das. Although this anticolonial episode of pluralist federalism remains largely marginal in the global history of pluralist thought, its theoretical wager sharply revealed the constitutive tensions of pluralist political thought in the process of seeking to reconfigure the ideal of democracy for the colonial world.

The anticolonial career of the federalist project—brief, scattered, and historically unrealized—has lately generated substantial historiographical and theoretical interest.[7] The victory of anticolonial nationalism by the second half of the twentieth century was emphatic and overwhelming. The postcolonial revisiting of anticolonial political thought was thus motivated by a desire to trace the formation of the centralized nation-state. Unsurprisingly, then, the archives of federalist thought in Asia and Africa were left in the margins of historiography. Against this backdrop, the renewed appreciation of the federalist project has helped raise new questions regarding the political ideals of anticolonial movements. For Frederick Cooper, the federalist project, enabled by a divided conception of sovereignty, sought to democratize empire without traveling through the telos of the nation.[8] Gary Wilder argues that African anticolonial thinkers blended "pragmatic" and "utopian" approaches to theorize federalism as the best means available for reconciling self-government with socioeconomic equality.[9] Others, however, are less sanguine. While acknowledging the historical failures of the anticolonial nationalist project, Partha Chatterjee characterizes the interest in (post-)imperial federations as no more than an attempt to glorify "the possibility of a more benign empire where liberal colonized elites might share power with an enlightened imperial authority."[10] Although appreciative of the global reach of federalism in the era of decolonization, Samuel Moyn finds no historical evidence for the claim that federalism could have displaced anticolonial nationalism; he rightly observes that the recent revival of interest in federalism stems, in part, from the disappointments with the postcolonial nation-state.[11]

For both the champions and the critics of anticolonial federalism, its counterfactual archive has become a proxy to question the historical inevitability of the nation-state. My primary aim in this chapter is different. I revisit Indian federalist thought to explore how a far-reaching critique of unilinear developmentalism occasioned a rethinking of the modern ideal of popular sovereignty. The Indian federalists maintained that the question of popular sovereignty marks the fraught space between empire and post-imperial federations. Inspired by Seal's critique of the unilinear theory of development, they argued that the promise of future self-government in the manner of the British parliamentary system enabled evaluations of the "fitness" of the Indian people with reference to the ideals of nineteenth-century British democracy. What followed was a bold attempt to pluralize the concept of the people against the backdrop of an overarching imperial denial of Indian peoplehood. In particular, Mukerjee and Das argued that if one conceptualizes the people as many-willed and as the bearer of multilinear development, the two conditions that denied peoplehood to Indians—historical backwardness and national disunity—could be overcome. In this way, they hoped, the very premise of hierarchical peoplehood underlying the British Empire would be discredited in a federation of many peoples.

Yet the federalist ideal was also steeped in imperial narratives. As James Tully pointed out, the juridical theories of federalism coexisted with a developmental approach to non-European peoples in European imaginations of global federations since the eighteenth century.[12] In the American context, federalism helped facilitate the expansion of the settler-colonial state.[13] Closer to India, nineteenth-century British ideas of imperial federation generally excluded nonwhite colonies on developmental grounds.[14] This particular Indian tradition of federalism was born out of a philosophical refusal to tether the question of federalism to a unilinear theory of development. The pluralist theory of the village republic came to be central to this effort. The history of local self-rule in Asia—which had long fed into the discourse of oriental despotism— emerged as the marker of a misunderstood past and an alternative future. As the primary constituent unit of an expansive network of federated polities, the village republic appeared as living evidence of the claim that democracy requires neither a centralized state nor a homogeneous people. Such a reworking of the pluralist theory of sovereignty meant that the theoretical emphasis of the Indian federalists took a different form than that of the British pluralists. Whereas the defense of the real personality of groups over statist sovereignty preoccupied the British pluralists, the Indian federalists wedded pluralist sovereignty to a critique of the imperial narrative of democratization. Instead of being a relic of the past, the village republic, these federalists claimed, signified another trajectory of political development: to embrace pluralist sovereignty was to abandon the association of democracy with the developmental discourse of political fitness. Insofar as the village could be the foundation for democratic self-rule, the plurality and the apparent developmental backwardness of the Indian people need not be out of joint with the time of democracy.

Even though the Indian federalists departed from the institutional ideal of nineteenth-century democracy (namely, representative government), they shared its normative commitment to the principle of popular sovereignty. This attempt to reconcile pluralist federalism with the principle of popular sovereignty generated a powerful perspective on a constitutive dilemma of pluralist political theory: Could the people mean anything more than a collection of plural groups? The British pluralist grappling with the question remained indecisive. While acknowledging the revolutionary career of popular sovereignty, Harold Laski suggested that a workable theory of popular sovereignty should be centered on a plurality of wills. Laski was skeptical of the "prophetic announcements" attributed to one political will; he found it to be entangled in political metaphysics.[15] G. D. H. Cole recognized the necessity of a broader collective will beyond group wills,[16] but he rather unsatisfyingly defined it as the individual's loyalty to the wider community.[17] The pluralist hesitation regarding the question of collective will received sharp criticism from their contemporary critics across the political spectrum, from Carl Schmitt to Mary Parker Follett.[18]

From their colonial vantage point, the Indian federalists directly confronted the challenge of reconciling the ideal of popular sovereignty with a many-willed concept of the people. Mukerjee attempted to translate the group theory of sovereignty in terms of popular sovereignty, seeking to establish that the majoritarian and territorial dangers of monist popular sovereignty are best overcome in the federated structure of village republics. But the project of forging a dynamic conception of popular sovereignty—which would simultaneously signify a multilinear scheme of development and politically contest imperial sovereignty—was undercut by Mukerjee's organicist entanglements. The limits of the organicist approach were persuasively articulated by C. R. Das, who sought to foreground a transformative conception of peoplehood in the anticolonial federalist framework. In this project, Das found common ground with the American progressive thinker Mary Parker Follett, who held that the "one" and the "many" wills of the people could be reconciled through a process of gradual integration. Herself a friendly critic of British pluralism, Follett argued that a pluralist concept of the people is not necessarily opposed to collective will. If understood in a more dynamic sense, the effect of performing pluralist sovereignty would be a shared peoplehood with an integrated collective will. Building on Follett's account, Das argued that the enactment of democratic self-rule by many peoples would ultimately generate a collective will without undermining the premise of pluralist sovereignty. In other words, the federalist account of popular sovereignty could be more than a marker of an alternative developmental trajectory toward democracy; it would also tap into the possibilities of popular authorization for a new founding. The urgency of anticolonial resistance, however, would lead Das to politically reverse the temporal order he once proposed between the many and the one.

Das's turn to the "one people" as a provisional authorizer of a future of many peoples demonstrated the difficulty of invoking the name of the people without asserting its monist quality. As I argue, Das's grappling with the problem of collective will reveals, at once, the distinctive potential of anticolonial federalism and the theoretical challenges that beleaguered it in the age of national self-determination. The pluralist-federalist diagnosis of the limits of representative democracy perspicaciously captured its potential democratic deficit as well as its embroilment in the democratic legitimation of empire. It also showed remarkable theoretical acuity in its contention that the ideal of popular sovereignty could not be borrowed from the nineteenth century but must be transformed on the basis of a many-willed people. In marked contrast to contemporary appreciations of anticolonial federalism, these thinkers did not hold that a diffused and plural polity could be made plausible without fundamentally transforming the modern ground of democracy: popular sovereignty. The resultant dilemmas of anticolonial federalism, as I will argue below, are as instructive as its highly generative critique of representative democracy.

PATHWAYS OF PEOPLEHOOD: CRITIQUE OF "UNILINEAR" DEVELOPMENT AND THE TURN TO FEDERALISM

Brajendranath Seal was invited to the Universal Races Congress of 1911 in London as an Indian representative. The Races Congress was a watershed moment in the international history of anticolonial politics. One of the first international forums of its kind, the Congress brought together delegates from across the world. B. N. Seal delivered the first address of the Congress, following W. E. B. Du Bois's recitation of "Hymn to the Peoples." Seal's paper—"Meaning of Race, Tribe, Nation"—began with the bold claim that the evolving problems of empire and nationhood could no longer be understood in terms of either the "analytical methods of Aristotelian or Machiavellian politics" or the "so-called Historical Schools of Montesquieu and Vico."[19] Instead, he suggested, the study of the origins and developments of nations and empires should adopt a fluid approach to questions of racial and civilizational difference.[20] Seal proposed a plastic concept of "national personality," through which he sought to conceptually integrate a people's evolutionary, social, and cultural histories. His larger aim was to show that the historical trajectory of each people is singular and unamenable to easy comparison. According to Seal, the pursuit of "ideal ends" drives the development of the national personality, and the process is shaped by creative interaction with external environments, natural as well as social.[21] The centralized state is only a moment in the development process. As each people seeks to realize itself more fully, the state ceases to operate as a centralizing entity and gives in to the higher ideal of "universal humanity." If all nations were to realize their ends, the result would not be an exclusivist polity; instead it would lay the groundwork for global cooperation. Seal termed this union between different peoples "federationism."[22]

The dense arguments that Seal presented at the Races Congress were a culmination of two-decade-long reflections on the comparative study of historical development on a global scale. Seal was a professor of philosophy at the University of Calcutta, and the breadth of his polymathic expertise was legendary. Though he published only sporadically, the range of his work spans from political philosophy to art history. Seal had been deeply intrigued by the standards and methods of civilizational comparison. Is the pathway of Europe the only road to progress? This question preoccupied him since the 1890s. He soon grew critical of the assumption that development takes place in a linear series where each civilization could be compared and organized in an ascending series. Seal characterized this approach as the "unilinear" theory of development.[23]

The approach to civilizational difference through the development framework—where non-European concepts and ideas are treated as "backward" in contrast to their "advanced" European counterparts— struck Seal as fundamentally misleading. The comparative study of the non-European world, Seal wrote in 1899, had been dominated by the assumption that "all other race and cultures have been a preparation for the Greco-Roman-Gothic type, which is now the epitome of Mankind."[24] Seal mounted a critique of both the evolutionism of Herbert Spencer and historicism of the Hegelian philosophy of history. Thoroughly unimpressed by Spencer, Seal found the historical scope of the Spencerian teleology of "the military-industrial regime" to be singularly devoid of nuance. The Hegelian school fared better in its grasp of the dynamic process of development, its chief defect being the desire to derive an "abstract and arbitrary standard . . . from the history of European civilization."[25] In contrast, he argued that the main challenge of a historically capacious comparative method lay in overcoming the discourse of unilinear development.[26] Taking a cue from Darwin's contribution to the evolutionary sciences, Seal proposed that the comparative method should start from a multilinear and plural vision of development. The project of rescuing the world from its reduction into "mere European side-views of humanity" hinged on this renewed conceptualization of the developmental process.[27]

According to Seal, to render the world classifiable in a unilinear order, Hegel extracted certain representative ideals from various geographical-racial sites of the world and placed them in a successive order. This Hegelian translation of the universal in terms of world history was ultimately reliant on a presumed proximity between the Absolute Idea and the so-called highest stage of development—that is, Europe.[28] Insofar as comparative philosophy subscribes to a unilinear view of development, the complex network of global history transforms into a straight line. In contrast, a non-unilinear approach shows that historical development takes places along many lines and resembles a decentered network more than a linear trajectory of progress.[29] Contra Hegel, Seal went on to conclude that the universal is not to be "figured as the crest of an advancing wave, occupying but one place at any moment, and leaving all behind a dead level."[30]

What Seal suggested was not so much a qualification as a fundamental pluralization of the Hegelian universal. If different civilizations are to be compared, comparative philosophy must approach each civilization as a whole and in terms of its own immanent history. The access to the universal, Seal claimed, is not determined by the historical stage inhabited by a particular people. If each developmental schema is understood on its own intrinsic terms, the plural conceptions of development would make it possible to see the capacity of any people to participate in the universal. However, no particular people can ever fully embody the universal; only the respective self-realization of all peoples could ultimately enact universal humanity. This replacement of the Hegelian state with universal humanity was central to Seal's repurposing of the developmental logic of Hegel's philosophy of history. For the universal to arrive, each people must be allowed to realize itself in a creative exchange with others but not at the expense of any people losing its specificity. This also meant that no external ideal borrowed from a supposedly higher stage of development should be imposed on a people. The particular trajectory of a people's development thus posed no barrier to its capacity to enact self-rule.

World War I further deepened Seal's federalist commitments. Writing to William Rothenstein in 1916, he noted that the war had been the "supreme solvent, a merciless test, of all the values, social, political, spiritual, which you [Europeans] have standardized and made current in the West."[31] Connecting the Great War to the nation-state-based organization of the European political order, Seal hoped that the "still small voice" of India and China would finally receive the attention it deserved.[32] As he elaborated elsewhere, the histories of India and China show the centrality of group associations in political life beyond the duality of the state and the individual.[33] It is worth noting here that the counterexamples of India and China did not figure as compact, territorially organized polities. Seal accepted that the shared history of a given people could generate a distinct trajectory, but such developmental inheritances could not be territorially demarcated. In fact, the point that Seal tried to derive from the histories of India and China specifically concerned the limits of equating political sovereignty with territorial boundaries. The institution of the League of Nations only sharpened Seal's critique of territorial sovereignty. He argued in 1921 that the territorial notion of sovereignty was in profound tension with local practices of self-rule. Taking World War I as the natural conclusion of the territorial and monist conception of sovereignty, he noted that the key to a global federation dwelled in an "extraterritorial" account of political sovereignty.[34] In concrete terms, this would mean international recognition of political groups regardless of the status of their territorial sovereignty. He proposed that there should be an international conference of peoples unaffiliated with their respective central governments to discuss the terms of postwar international peace. Ultimately, he reminded his audience, the initiatives for international peace would be futile if the very ideal of centralized statehood was not reconsidered.[35]

As a philosopher, Seal's reflections on federalism were mostly speculative and appeared in the context of his larger preoccupation with the critique of the unilinear theory of development. The nearest institutional articulation of his pluralist federalism was the draft constitution he helped prepare for the princely state of Mysore in 1923 (when he was serving as vice chancellor of the University of Mysore). While the committee was tasked with formulating the institutional framework for integrating popular participation in an otherwise unitary state (a hereditary monarchy under British paramountcy), Seal took the opportunity to limn an extraterritorial account of group representation. The parliamentary representation of popular will in centralized states, the Seal Committee observed, straitjackets the plurality of popular groups into overarching categories of majority and minority. To remedy this problem, the Seal Committee advocated for the inclusion of functional and occupational groups (such as labor and industrial groups, traders, landholders, universities) in the representative and legislative assemblies.[36] The committee further argued that the tradition of extraterritorial representation could already be found in the history of ancient Indian political institutions, especially in the crucial role played by intermediary village communities and functional groups. The objective of drawing inspiration from those precolonial institutions, however, was not "a mediaeval State, nor even one of the nineteenth-century pattern."[37] Instead of framing the problem as one of the medieval tradition of pluralism versus modern centralization, the point of a twentieth-century constitution would be to synthesize lessons from the past with the demands of modern democratic norms.

Still, what Seal partially articulated in the report was an extraterritorial theory of representation and not a fully fleshed-out theory of pluralist federalism. It would be up to the next generation of Indian pluralists to elaborate on the project for the anticolonial context. Seal rarely engaged with his contemporary European pluralists, but the affinity between them did not go unnoticed. Benoy Kumar Sarkar—one of Seal's students, who himself explored a few federalist themes—observed that Seal "drank from the same [pluralist] cup as the German Gierke, French Duguit, and English Figgis."[38] Indeed, Seal's federalist lead was soon taken up by a number of his students and political associates. The legacy of Seal's conceptualization of federalism—as we shall see in the next two sections—would lie in the foregrounding of the critique of unilinear developmentalism.

RADHAKAMAL MUKERJEE AND THE COMPARATIVE HISTORY OF PLURALISM

Seal's critique of unilinear developmentalism paved the way for reconsidering the historical course of non-European political development. The uptake of his work, however, varied. The first Seal-inspired studies of federalism came from none other than Bipin Chandra Pal. Disavowing his earlier inclinations for monist sovereignty, Pal now characterized the swaraj episode as a necessary step toward "[awakening] a new self-consciousness in the people."[39] In an unmistakable rejoinder to John Stuart Mill's statement that representative government was only a possibility in advanced Europe and not in "Syria or Timbuctoo" (which I discussed in Chapter 1), Pal argued that "the masses in England no more govern themselves to-day than the masses in Russia or Tibet or Timbuktu."[40] In his revised argument, the rise of representative government had to do with a clash of power between the middle classes and the landed aristocracy; the name of the people was a mere instrument for the middle classes eager to seize power. With the aim to look beyond the ideal of representative government, Pal cautiously explored the possibility of transforming empires into global federations. Though he found the prospect of a pluralist global federation normatively preferable, Pal had his doubts concerning the possibility of democratically transforming the racial foundation of the British Empire.[41]

Pal's Swadeshi colleague Aurobindo Ghose also undertook a remarkably ambitious reconsideration of the federal idea amid the turbulence of the Great War. Much like Pal, Aurobindo now characterized the "nationalist" enthusiasm of the Swadeshi era as only a stage toward a more expansive horizon.[42] In *The Human Cycle* and *The Ideal of Human Unity*, Aurobindo mounted a critique of the merely "objective" view of development, while locating the distinctive contributions of India in the "spiritual" components of historical development. For Aurobindo, the "transition from the rationalistic and utilitarian period of human development" to a "greater subjective stage of society" signaled the emergence of a developmental imagination truer to the human condition.[43] Working independently of Seal's framings, Aurobindo's project raised questions about the prioritization of the objective over the subjective in theories of development.[44] Seal was not opposed to the critique of the primacy of the material, but his signature contribution consisted in a more fundamental problematization of the unilinear narratives of development.

The most important intellectual voice in the crowded pluralist wave was Radhakamal Mukerjee, whose interventions were preceded by his elder brother, Radhakumud Mookerji, who was also one of Seal's protégés. Radhakumud found evidence of the political and geographical unity of "Hindu civilization" in the history of local self-government in ancient India.[45] The younger Mukerjee largely avoided his brother's Hindu essentialist gloss on the history of ancient Indian local self-government and sought to bring together China, Japan, and the Middle East under a shared framework of what he called Eastern democracies. In parallel with the Indian fascination with a pluralist theory of development, the influential rise of British pluralism would also soon begin to travel back to India, as the Indian students of Laski published a number of pluralism-inflected histories of Indian politics.[46] Drawing primarily from Seal's approach to comparative philosophy and reckoning with the European critique of monist sovereignty, Mukerjee aimed to write what might be called a comparative history of pluralism.[47] He began to explore these issues in his mammoth *Foundations of Indian*

Economics (1916), followed by his two-volume *Principles of Comparative Economics* (1921–1922). The pinnacle of Mukerjee's study of comparative pluralism, however, was his 1923 volume *Democracies of the East: A Study in Comparative Politics.*

In the footsteps of Seal, Mukerjee singled out Hegel as the greatest theorist of unilinear developmentalism.[48] In Mukerjee's distinctive language, the Hegelian projection of the state as the embodiment of reason ultimately reflected the inherent tendency of a particular tradition, the "Romano-Gothic" civilization. Mukerjee not only questioned the philosophical ground of Hegel's historicism, but also aspired to particularize the universality of its norms. The latter move was crucial to the project of pluralizing the developmental trajectories of the world—in what Mukerjee termed a "multilinear" theory of development.[49] This also constituted his break with the comparative approach developed by nineteenth-century imperial historians and jurists, most notably Henry Maine. Unlike the Mills and other imperial liberals, Maine was critical of a direct transposition of the norms of supposedly advanced European societies on India.[50] But despite his sensitivity to the treatment of native societies, Maine did not question the unilinear theory of development: "The one path of human evolution which Maine chalked out ran from status to contract. The process to contract, which was readily assumed as universal, was superimposed upon a communal organization of life by an individualistic law, and disruptive tendencies . . . were hailed as the travails of progress."[51] Nevertheless, as Karuna Mantena has pointed out, Mukerjee shared Maine's centering of the village community in the Indian past.[52] While indebted to this aspect of Maine's work, Mukerjee was opposed to both the developmental framework and the normative orientation of Maine's account of the village community. Against Maine, Mukerjee argued that the critical salience of village communities did not so much lie in the observation that the premodern forms of status still dominated Indian political life; instead, the village republic was an embodiment of an altogether distinct developmental process whose normative possibility transcended Maine's narrative of status to contract.[53] Mukerjee's recalibration of pluralist sovereignty would be central to this project of extricating the village republic from the charges of backwardness.

For Mukerjee, the primacy of groups shaped the constitutively decentralized form of "Eastern" democracy. He maintained that the communal practices of group life in the East cannot be captured solely through the framework of territorial representation.[54] These groups—functional (guilds, occupational alliances, and such) as well as neighborhood-based— were overlapping and autonomous. Historically they had exerted a range of political power, from settling disputes to administering public services.[55] Crucially, for Mukerjee, economic interests were not the sole marker of group identity in India, Japan, and China; interest groups were one of many forms of groups and enjoyed no special privilege over other forms of associations. Mukerjee's attribution of interest-based group association to Europe dovetailed with a rather strong organicist reading of the history of group associations in the East. He claimed that Eastern groups grew independently of any centralized authority and required no bestowal of legal personhood from a higher sovereign entity.[56] As we shall see later, this organicist interpretation of village republics would eventually pose difficult questions for his political theory as a whole.

The turn to the federalist model emerged directly out of this picture of the village community. While self-sufficient in their formation, village communities were not self-enclosed; it was federalism that allowed for this union of autonomous political groups. Historically, village republics in the East formed a union of villages where the "principles of functional and territorial representation were fused."[57] The basis of such federation concerned matters that only affected several groups collectively, such as protection from invasion, founding new towns, and levying import duties. The primary function of the federal body was to coordinate cooperation between groups and to facilitate joint deliberation over issues that affected the groups as a whole. Even then, Mukerjee proposed that referendum should be preferred to decide issues of special importance in a future federation.[58] The federation, as it were, would presuppose the equality and prior sovereign rights of groups. The principle of representation would be fundamentally dispensed with, save the central body where proportional representation could be allowed. Mukerjee projected that the intermingling of diverse elements and groups would result in intersecting circles of authority.[59]

Mukerjee found the germs of the federalist polity in the Indian past as well as in extant political practices throughout Asia. The village and guild councils of India—and the cooperative associations of Chinese villages—carried the federalist spirit of Asia.[60] Mukerjee further claimed that the practices of communal democracy continue to survive among migrants from villages in the urban centers of colonial India.[61] In a sweeping survey, he also enlisted federalist evidence from the Islamic *majlis* and nomadic tribes in the Middle East.[62] Mukerjee contended that theorists of village communities such as Maine and Baden Powell had emphasized the isolated nature of village communities, thus erasing their federal history.[63] In other words, no utopian imagination was necessary to envisage the democratic future that had long eluded the so-called backward peoples. However, his point was not simply a return to a federalist past buried underneath the edifice of European empires. The polity of the future was yet to arrive, but it did not need to come from without. Far from disqualifying the claim to democracy, the Indian past could be in step with a federalist future. Mukerjee thus understood the proposed turn to pluralist federalism to be a rejection of both colonialism and the narrative of development that helped sustain it.

The question of caste particularly troubled this otherwise neat pluralist resignification of Indian village communities. Critical of the orientalist literature on the static and rigid nature of the Indian caste system, Mukerjee emphasized the changeable nature of caste groups. "There is," Mukerjee argued, "no truth in the ill-informed but common criticism that caste from its very nature is opposed to self-government."[64] He instead tried to show that most caste groups are autonomous and integrated into the democratic arrangements of village federalism. He acknowledged that the lower castes were oppressed by "specious doctrines," but whether federalism provided a sufficient answer to the problem of caste domination remained unexamined.[65] Mukerjee later developed a plastic theory of caste, arguing that economic and other forms of social transformations continually remake the order of caste groups.[66] Nevertheless, his account fell short of addressing the relationship of domination that would exist among otherwise autonomous caste groups in a federalist polity.

The imprint of British pluralism on Mukerjee's work is apparent; he self-consciously organized his arguments under the conceptual rubrics of monist and pluralist theories of sovereignty. For all the proximity to British pluralism, Mukerjee was anxious to demarcate his project from that of his European counterparts, especially Laski and Cole. He identified two major faults in British pluralism: a re-entrenched individualism and a mechanical conception of group association. Mukerjee notes, without citing any particular pluralist author, that there had been an individualist turn in British pluralism, centering an abstract individual at the heart of group associations.[67] He most likely had in mind Laski's affirmation of the impenetrable individual.[68] As Marc Stears shows, Laski (and Cole) began to reassert a version of individualism in the early 1920s following their dispute with the older pluralists, especially J. N. Figgis.[69] On the other hand, the premise of sectionalism—especially Cole's guild socialism—failed, in Mukerjee's reading, to account for the vital values that constitute the life of the community.[70] In contrast, Mukerjee portrayed Eastern groups as undergirded by a rooted solidarity that transcended the bonds of interest. The historically instilled value of group coordination, he further argued, would prevent competition among groups.[71]

In its organicist signification of pluralism, Mukerjee's argument, one might reasonably conclude, was closer to that of the German jurist Otto von Gierke. This, however, poses an interpretative conundrum. British pluralism famously began its intellectual project with the partial English translation of Gierke's *Das deutsche Genossenschaftsrecht* by the legal historian F. W. Maitland.[72] Maitland's interpretation of Gierke underplayed the organicist basis of his theory of *Genossenschaft* (fellowship), prioritizing instead the critical implication of Gierke's theory of group personality for the state-centric concept of sovereignty.[73] In fact, the British pluralists had been suspicious of organicist thought from the beginning, not least because of their identification of the monist theory of sovereignty with the British idealists' Hegel-inspired organicist statism. The British Idealist account of Hegel—culminating with the publication of Bernard Bosanquet's *The Philosophical Theory of the State* (1899)—centralized the organicist dimension of his political philosophy. While Bosanquet was open to acknowledging the importance of groups and associations, the state—he contended in a Hegelian vein—is a unified higher entity that subsumes "all the elements of a people's life . . . in it as an indivisible unity."[74] The organicism of the British Idealists was initially tethered to the Hegelian concept of ethical life, or *Sittlichkeit;* though, as Jeanne Morefield argues, their eventual turn to biological accounts of organicism would destabilize the Hegelian commitment.[75] Given this status of Hegelianism in England, the pluralists considered the organicist approach to associations to be embroiled in the problem of statism, and generally preferred a voluntarist notion of group formation.

From the textual evidence of *Democracies of the East*, it appears that Mukerjee was familiar with Gierke only through the Maitland translation.[76] Yet, much in the vein of Gierke, Mukerjee considered his Eastern groups to be rooted in a vital tradition of "plurality-in-unity" (as opposed to "unity-in-plurality"), where the whole precedes the parts.[77] His claim that local self-rule taps into the vital and communal elements organic to the East, and realizes its inherent possibilities, also had a Gierkean dimension. Gierke's theory of groups was steeped in Hegelian language, and he shared the philosopher's world-historical characterization of Germanic peoples.[78] J. N. Figgis—the most organicist of the British pluralists—also made a case for prioritizing the "life" of groups over "law."[79] But Figgis's organicism lacked the historicist dimension of Gierke's.[80] While Mukerjee did not share Gierke's celebration of the Germanic tradition, his organicist and historicist gloss on the developmental trajectory of Eastern groups was closer to Gierke than to the British pluralists or their Idealist rivals. However, given his inadequate knowledge of Gierke, it seems quite plausible that Mukerjee independently worked out similar arguments with the help of a different Hegelian influence—namely, Seal's pluralist reinvention of the discourse of development. Gierke's organicism was primarily concerned with the holistic nature of Germanic societies, whereas Mukerjee was more invested in the "multilinear" schemes of development suggested by post-Darwinian evolutionary organicism.[81] This is not all. Unlike Gierke, and echoing Seal, Mukerjee posited universal humanity, not the Gierkean-Hegelian *Rechtsstaat*, as the ultimate realization of the multilinear lines of development.

Given his Seal-inspired conception of pluralism, the monist theory of sovereignty posed a twofold problem for Mukerjee: the misrecognition of the nature of sovereignty and the universalization of European history as the norm. As we have seen above, Mukerjee was in broad agreement with the British pluralists with regard to the problem of monist sovereignty, even as he departed from what he considered their individualist and sectionalist tendencies. More fundamentally, Mukerjee found the British pluralists to be relatively unaware of the imperial drive enabled by a unitarian and territorial conception of sovereignty. The recognition of the imperial nature of monist sovereignty was indispensable if Europe hoped to overcome its statism. The force of this point would be acknowledged by Harold Laski in his later works.[82] To this extent, Mukerjee's multilinear theory of development also aspired to reverse the hierarchy that was once assumed between Western statehood and Eastern localism.

Mukerjee's project, notwithstanding its polemical attempt to reverse the civilizational scheme of nineteenth-century European political thought, was ultimately an attempt to articulate another developmental trajectory for democracy in the colonial world. This other time of peoplehood was a temporal scheme where Asian and global federations were the ultimate end. For Mukerjee, the ideals of popular sovereignty—a single, united, and "fit" peoplehood—were all imbricated in the unilinear theory of development. Once separated from this paradigm, the people could be diverse, scattered, and localized, yet sovereign in their exercise of political power as small groups. In particular, Mukerjee's account of communal-federal democracy had a direct implication for the majority-minority question. The tendency of modern popular sovereignty to devolve into majoritarianism was a well-recognized problem by the mid-nineteenth century. There was, however, another dimension to this problem in the colonial world. One of the justifications of colonial rule was predicated on the claim that India was not fit to rule over itself in part because of its national disunity, especially its division of India across regions and religions.

The immediate upshot of abandoning the ideal of unified peoplehood consisted in removing the lack of unity as a substantive impediment toward the institution of anticolonial democracy. In the small scale of self-rule, the burden of unity would dissolve in the autonomy bestowed upon each political group, rendering the nationally conceived notions of majority and minority groups superfluous. In practical terms, the adoption of pluralist federalism would mean a larger federation of India that would emerge from the coordination between small village communities. Mukerjee believed that the organic and communal grounding of eastern groups would resolve the difficulty of coordinating among many peoples, though he also suggested that certain techniques of modern European constitutionalism, such as referendum and delegation, could be borrowed to institute a federation on an all-Indian level.[83] Given that sovereignty would reside in groups rather than in a centralized state, the future federation of India would not rely on a territorial demarcation of its boundary for its political unity. Likewise, the regional federation—Indian, Chinese, or European—would build toward a federation of republics on a global scale without compromising the distinct traditions of a given people.[84]

Mukerjee's reclaiming of popular sovereignty—or what he called the "real will" of the people—thus critically hinged on the dissolution of the monist figure of the people into many peoples.[85] Although he sought to work out a pluralist conception of popular sovereignty more explicitly than his contemporary European pluralists did, the question of collective peoplehood ultimately dissolved into an organicist assumption. If India were left to its own devices, Mukerjee concluded, the "natural development" would be toward "a people's state, communal in its lower stratifications, and democratic and federal in its organization."[86] Colonialism, in political terms, amounted to an external invasion simply to be removed. Mukerjee eschewed the question of whether the pluralist theory of popular sovereignty could facilitate the anticolonial aspiration to displace imperial sovereignty: if the people in reality were composed of a plurality of wills, what form might an anticolonial movement of "many peoples" take? Mukerjee's critique of the unilinear developmentalism underlying modern imperialism was profound, but his organicist faith in the pluralist scheme of development in the East downplayed the challenge of making a federated people out of many peoples. As in the question of caste, his organicist approach to groups remained in tension with a dynamic and transformative conception of popular sovereignty.

COLLECTIVE WILL AND THE DILEMMA OF ANTICOLONIAL FEDERALISM

Mukerjee's distant companion in the federalist project, Chittaranjan Das—a major figure of the anticolonial movement in the 1910s and 1920s—confronted the problem of pluralist popular sovereignty directly amid the urgency of anticolonial resistance. C. R. Das, as he was commonly known, was a lawyer-turned-politician who rose to political fame in the late 1910s and earned the honorific *deshabandhu* (friend of the nation). As a Congress politician, the deshabandhu's influence was perhaps second only to Gandhi's in the early 1920s.[87] Das's turn to federalism took place independently and in parallel with Mukerjee's; he knew Bipin Chandra Pal's work well and was personally acquainted with B. N. Seal. Like Seal and Mukerjee, Das maintained that the ideal of representative democracy had colonized the future of the non-European world because of its conceptual complicity with the discourse of unilinear development. He eloquently observed that the very word "politics" had become inseparable from the former, as it "conjures up before our eyes the vision of English political institutions; and we feel tempted to fall down before and worship the precise form which Politics has assumed under the peculiar conditions of English history."[88]

Das, too, found new political possibilities in the critique of unilinear development. Federalism appeared to him to be more than a system of government; its meaning was equally determined by the counternarrative it offered to the imperial teleology of representative government. The reclaiming of the developmental narrative was so significant that Das preferred to theorize swaraj or self-rule as a people's claim to self-development: "Swaraj . . . is not to be confused with any particular system of government. . . . Swaraj begins when the true development of a nation begins."[89] Whether the system of government was representative or federal, the definition of self-rule could not simply be deduced from it. On the contrary, the unfolding of self-development, specific to each people, would determine the corresponding system of government. Self-rule was thus claimed to be a "relative notion."[90] This stress on historically singular trajectories of political development emerged from Das's abiding sensitivity to the antidemocratic implications of a unilinear discourse of development.

In spite of his regular protestations against the reduction of the question of democracy to a mere form of government, Das went on to offer a concrete institutional structure for the future government. In particular, his 1923 text *Outline Scheme of Swaraj* stands as a milestone in the Indian federalist tradition. In line with his predecessors, Das put the village at the center of this institutional arrangement.[91] Even while Das took the prevalent historiography of the village republic for granted, the institutional forms given— and the roles assigned— to the village republic avoided the temptation of organicism. As the primary unit of the government, the village center would have the power to make and execute laws, whereas the federated state's power would be exceptional and advisory. Within the village centers, the judiciary, legislative, and the executive must be strictly separated. The membership to the village republic should have no religious or gender barriers.[92] The relationship between these and the more central units would be nonhierarchical insofar as the latter would only seek to ensure coordination and mutual support among the primary units. Das specified two separate functions reserved for the government: protective and promotive. The first conception of government—negative in its essence—is merely concerned with the prevention of crimes and adjustment of wrongs. Most of the protective powers would be exercised by the village government; the arbitration court, which would be elected by members of the local center, would process both civil and criminal cases.[93] The promotive part of the government—positive and socialistic—would be concerned with developing social, economic, and cultural aspects of collective life.[94] Crucially, the standard of development would not be borrowed from the supposedly advanced stages of European life; the village republic would instead cultivate the drives of development already present in the people. The all-Indian federation, emerging out of the integration of village republics and provincial governments, would prioritize the task of coordinating among autonomous local centers. Crucially, the federal body would be a result of the unification of autonomous village centers and would not exist prior to the exercise of democracy by many peoples.

Das's scheme of democratic self-rule—self-developing in its political ontology and federalist in its constitutional projection—stood at odds with the idea of popular sovereignty as the one and undivided collective will of the people. Yet as a political actor, Das was faced with the limits of a strictly pluralist notion of popular sovereignty. Mere recourse to the plural and dispersed account of peoplehood—many peoples—left the popular authorization of the anticolonial demand scattered. If the people are dispersed into many wills, how could their diffused collective sovereignty be politically articulated and invoked for the sake of de-authorizing empire? Das was keenly aware of this problem. Unlike Mukerjee, he thus emphasized that the aim of pluralist federalism is dynamic: it seeks to generate a new collective will out of a myriad of local republics.[95]

In this project of reconciling the many (peoples) with the one (people), Das was greatly aided by the work of the contemporary American thinker Mary Parker Follett. Follett's The New State (1918) exerted significant influence in the American progressive era. Having studied with the British pluralists, Follett wrote her text partly as a critical advancement of the project in America. Follett shared the pluralist critique of centralized sovereignty, but she was critical of the discrete notion of groups proffered by Laski and his colleagues. Harold Laski adopted the term "pluralism" following William James's account of ontological pluralism (which he encountered during his time in the United States).[96] But the British pluralists, Follett observed, had fundamentally misunderstood the concept. Their appropriation of American pragmatism was one-sided insofar as they failed to understand how groups interact and create something new in the process: "[The pluralists] talk of the Many and the One without analyzing the process by which the Many and the One are creating each other."[97]

Follett argued that the practices of democracy within the bounds of neighborhoods do not stultify into self-enclosed provinces but instead open themselves up to the larger political community. Just as a given group is dynamically constituted by multiple perspectives, a new people could also emerge out of many groups. She reminded the pluralists on the other side of the Atlantic that the lesson of James is precisely that the distribution of sovereignty does not occlude the formation of collective sovereignty.[98] She agreed that there was no given popular will that we could simply summon. The concept of the people does not mean either a mere majority or the addition of all individual wills. It is instead "the integration of every development, of every genius, with everything else that our complex and interacting life brings about."[99] Insofar as the life of a group is not contained within a neighborhood, it is necessary that local groups deliberate and work at gradually ascending collective associations. The resulting collective will would emerge gradually, through concrete practices of democracy: "The reason we want neighborhood organization is not to keep people within their neighborhoods but to get them out."[100]

The arguments of Follett's *The New State* had far-reaching consequences for Das's own conceptualization of pluralist federalism. Presenting a lengthy summary of *The New State* in his presidential address at the eventful Gaya Congress Session of 1922, Das underscored the similarity between their visions of politics.[101] Drawing from Follett's arguments, he contended that the central problem of traditional theories of sovereignty had been their reliance on the idea of the collective will as a process of addition as opposed to a process of integration. He observed that a monist conception of collective will inevitably devolves into a war of particular wills. The process of integration, in contrast, emphasizes the dynamic interaction among neighborhood groups that ultimately forge a community beyond their small scale: "New democracy discountenances this process of addition, and insists on the discovery of detailed means and methods by which the different wills of a neighbourhood entity may grow into *one common collective will*."[102] Such an assimilation of Follett's argument helped Das to reconcile, however tentatively, the many and the one: the many peoples of village republics and the one people of the larger federation. Collective will could only emerge after the gradual integration of many wills into one will; the one people, to this extent, was an *effect* of the democratic practices of the many.

The precondition of the one was the many, yet the urgency of the anticolonial claim to sovereignty meant that the order could not be maintained. Frustrated with imperial repression of the anticolonial movement, Das resorted to the immediate sovereign authority of the collective people in a speech delivered the year before his death. Self-rule, he repeated, was not "any particular system of government." But instead of merely characterizing it as the spirit of the trajectory of India's self-development, Das declared: "What I want today is a clear declaration *by* the people of this country that we have got the right to establish our own system of government according to the temper and genius of our own people."[103] The reference to the genius of the people reiterated his faith in the federalist arrangement, which he considered suitable for India. What he now primarily invoked, though, was the constituent power of a collective will, which is not equivalent to the direct democracy of local self-rule but instead prior to it.[104] This call for a declaration of sovereignty by the people registered Das's hope for a collective authorization from the people prior to the institution of pluralist federalism.

This is a dilemma that Das encountered most profoundly in the aftermath of the Bengal Pact, a landmark event in the history of Indian anticolonial politics. Prior to the Pact, Bengal politics had grown increasingly acrimonious, destabilized by the conflict between socially dominant Hindus and Bengali Muslims emboldened by their numerical majority in the province. The group conflict also paved the way for the institution of separate electorates within the bounds of limited franchise. Das's response to this crisis, and the broader political stalemate it entailed, was the Bengal Pact between Hindus and Muslims, an arrangement that promised proportional distribution of legislative representation and administrative jobs and sought to bind the two communities through a shared commitment to respect each other's religious sentiments. The Pact was a remarkable experiment in addressing the rift between the Hindu and Muslim communities, and cemented Das's status as the leader of both communities.[105] Das also hoped to introduce the Pact at an all-Indian level, though it failed to receive much support from the Congress leadership.[106] Insofar as the Pact targeted asymmetries in the central legislative body and throughout provincial administrative appointments, Das hoped that it would reform rather than displace the central institutions. Still, the fundamental impulse of the Pact emerged precisely out of his federalist inclinations: instead of affirming the given (or pursuing the future) real unity of the people, Das considered group autonomy no hindrance to democratic self-rule.

Thus, when he was accused of pandering to the majority Muslims for political gains, Das responded in unequivocal terms: "For the last five years I have been thinking of this great idea [of federalism] . . . and I have been pointing out that the only foundation for self-government is the federation of Hindus and Muhammadans." The Bengal Pact, Das maintained, was a "suggestion" made to the people, who would, upon the institution of self-rule, accept the federal arrangement as a constitutional principle. Prior to the end of colonial rule, no such arrangement could be especially meaningful, given the reigning presence of imperial sovereignty. Setting "the constitutional charter of the federation between the Hindus and the Muhammadans" as the goal, Indians should first "shoulder to shoulder" and bring colonial rule to an end.[107] To institute dispersed federalist self-rule, then, Indians needed to act together for once: the one people collectively instituting a polity of many peoples. In other words, the reconciliation between the many and the one that Das conceptualized through Follett encountered a theoretical dilemma. If collective will could only emerge through the exercise of local self-rule, the appeal to, and prioritization of, the one people undermined the conceptual and temporal order underlying the theory of gradual integration. In embracing the dilemma, Das, however, opened up the possibility for pluralist federalism to politically incorporate the power of authorization associated with the voice of the people. Das seemed to have held that this theoretical dilemma, if deftly maneuvered, would have made it politically possible for pluralist federalism to facilitate a collective authorization for a postcolonial founding while setting sight on a democracy of many peoples. However, in the midst of these debates, C. R. Das passed away suddenly. With him, the popular career of pluralist federalism also came to an abrupt end.

Called upon to offer a popular life to anticolonial federalism, Das had to veer between the time of the one-and-undivided people and that of many peoples. After all, the claim of popular sovereignty, however incomplete and partial, derives its authorization in the name of *the* people. That the will of the people could be invoked to authorize and de-authorize constituted political bodies follows from the picture of the people as a sovereign agent speaking in one voice. Yet the same picture of the people has also proved to be an impediment to the project of instituting self-rule. As Hannah Arendt memorably argued, the construction of the people as a collective will renders it in the mold of an individual: united, indivisible, and willful.[108] Cannibalizing itself from within, the framework of collective will elevates politics to a space beyond political disputes, a self-evident body of truth that suppresses the worldly dimension of politics.[109] The Indian federalists reached this conclusion through a critique of nineteenth-century imperial thought, where the collective capacity to will was historicized and deployed in support of colonial rule. They argued that the monist view of sovereignty, whether it be statist or popular, institutes an insurmountable gap between the sovereign and the citizen, stifling the quotidian practices of democratic self-rule. Sidestepping the necessity to wait for the emergence of a "developed" and undivided people, these federalist thinkers attempted to reconceptualize the people as a plural entity.

The critique of the framework of collective will was shared by Euro-American as well as Indian pluralists, though their intellectual trajectories were not identical. The anticolonial federalists agreed with the pluralist argument that sovereignty should be dispersed rather than concentrated in a unitary state. But the distinct challenge of anticolonial founding led Das to realize that the question of collective will could not simply be bracketed as a metaphysical problem of "prophetic announcement" (as Laski would have it). On the one hand, Das argued that collective peoplehood is not given but must be brought into being; only the robust practice of democracy on a local scale could integrate discrete groups into a shared collective will. On the other hand, he responded to the urgency of anticolonial resistance by stretching and expanding the pluralist theory of sovereignty so as to be able to tap into the power of popular authorization associated with collective will. What is more, his political negotiation of the problem of the many and the one also showed that theoretical dilemmas need not block the work of politics. As we have seen, he was willing to hold on to the horns of the dilemma to carve out a political path for the anticolonial federalist project.

The emergence of the demand for an independent nation-state—centered on the promise of a planned development in order to "catch up" with the advanced nations[110]—would soon put an end to this tradition of federalist thought in colonial India in the mid-1920s. The politics of collective will would be seized by nonfederalist anticolonial thinkers such as Jawaharlal Nehru, who had no interest in the problem of many peoples.[111] The transformation of the nineteenth-century "imperial conception of empire" into that of a "national conception of empire" in the interwar era further weakened the speculative power of non-national visions.[112] Still, the question of federalism would haunt colonial India again in the 1940s, especially with the rise of the demands for Muslim autonomy. Muslim minority concerns about an assertive Hindu dominance both within the Indian National Congress and at the central legislative level were matched by the Congress leadership's dogged unwillingness to weaken its aspiration for a centralized planning state. The failure to find common grounds between these seemingly incommensurable demands paved the way to colonial India's partition, and the birth of two separate states (India and Pakistan)—and later a third (Bangladesh)—where the numerical superiority of each community assumed the form of what Bipin Chandra Pal once called an "isolated independent sovereignty."[113] These disputes, however, were far removed from the earlier innovative visions of local self-rule and many peoples. A centralized sovereign state was assumed to be inevitable, and the dispute as a whole consequentially concerned its share. Other projects of anticolonial federalism, unfolding in Africa and the Caribbean in the postwar era, were in fact closer to the Indian precedent, for they interrogated the limits of the nation-state itself (though their preoccupation with economic development was more contemporaneous to the Indian concerns of the 1940s).[114] Seen in light of this body of Indian federalist thought, the place of the nation-state in the history of anticolonial thought loses the aura of incontestability. But it also shows how the federalist wavering between the many and the one paved the way for its political eclipse by the project of unitary peoplehood and centralized statehood.

CONCLUSION

Federalism went through a conceptual expansion in the twentieth century. The American revolutionary history of federalism—central to the modern history of the concept—was marked by a commitment to the sovereignty of one national people, albeit within the limits of settler sovereignty.[115] The anticolonial agenda of overcoming globe-spanning empires with territorially expansive democratic federations destabilized scalar assumptions of modern federalism. As importantly, anticolonial thinkers found the possibility of transcending the developmental narrative of modern representative government in the federalist project. The Indian pluralist-federalist thinkers had further contended that the journey from representative democracy to a federation of many peoples required a reconfiguration of the ideal of popular sovereignty. Amid these debates, in the interwar period, federalism emerged, on a global scale, as a powerful avenue to reconsider sovereignty beyond the limits of the centralized nation-state. Reflecting on the political plight of European Jews, Hannah Arendt wrote in 1940 that "the only chance of all small peoples . . . lies in a new European federal system." The "territorial" conception of the nation, she added, was undergoing a much-needed revision.[116] Arendt also observed that the British Empire reveals the "rudiments of a new arrangement" in a "distorted form"—for different peoples had been coexisting under the shared commonwealth without losing their nationality.[117]

Arendt's prescient observation regarding the future of "small peoples" was shared by many anticolonial thinkers across Asia and Africa. However, while a rethinking of territorial nationhood was the catalyst for this global federal moment, the project stumbled on the difficult question of peoplehood. Against the grain of the observation that

European empires contained political possibilities beyond the bounded scale of the nation-state, the group of Indian anticolonial federalist thinkers I have studied in this chapter showed how the fundamental reliance of the British Empire on the discourse of unilinear development normatively troubled any hope of reinventing it. Modern empires were not antithetical but depended on the normative power of the principle of popular sovereignty: the coexistence of plural national groups in the empire was predicated on a simultaneous denial, and promise, of peoplehood to the colonies. That this group of anticolonial federalists could problematize not only the denial of peoplehood but also the promise itself owes to their profound critique of unilinear developmentalism. What was at stake was not the political expediency of transforming the British Empire into a democratic federal order, even as the Indian federalists were not fundamentally opposed to global federations. Their deeper aim was to ground federalism on a non-unilinear theory of development, thus directly positing federalism against the developmental justification of colonial rule.

This contention, then, paved the way for the original contribution that the Indian federalists made to pluralist political theory. The remarkable appeal of the nation-state in the twentieth century, after all, pertained to its absorption of the figure of the people in a territorially bounded and unified image. Pluralist federalism, therefore, could not simply ignore the monist history of modern popular sovereignty. Accepting the difficult challenge of reconciling pluralist federalism with the principle of popular sovereignty, the Indian federalists undertook the project of formulating an extraterritorial and many-willed concept of the people befitting a pluralist polity. From the thick of the anticolonial movement, C. R. Das in particular helped reveal the tension between the idealized account of many peoples and the alluring image of the one people sitting at the heart of modern political authorization, As we saw, Das hoped to politically navigate the fraught space between the many and the one by simultaneously upholding the ideals of a federal polity of many peoples and a collective will speaking in one voice. Das's dilemma remains instructive not only for understanding the internal tension that entangled the federalist pursuit of popular authorization for a postcolonial founding but also for the challenges involved in pluralizing or splicing the figure of the people.

The growth of pluralist federalism in early twentieth-century India took place in parallel with the rise of Gandhi on the broader political scene. Gandhi's arguably more influential critique of parliamentary democracy, coupled with the pluralist turn, burst open the political consensus that defined the age of Naoroji and Banerjea. The dream of a "Federation of India" acquired a wider life amid the unfolding of the Great War. As Sarojini Naidu argued at the Bombay Congress of 1915: "If the communities may keep their individual entities, it is only for the enrichment of the federated national life . . . subordinating all merely sectarian and racial interests to the larger hope and the higher vision of United India."[118] In any case, although the federalist and Gandhian moments were of a piece in their critique of monist sovereignty, these two contemporary attempts at renovating the anticolonial democratic project differed in their alternative political visions. Gandhi's break from the terms of collective peoplehood was decisive, and he had no inclination to reconstitute the figure of the people through the pluralist route. For all his occasional paeans to Indian civilization, Gandhi was neither an organicist nor a proponent of the multilinear theory of development. And the federalists had their reservations about the emerging Mahatma in the post–World War I era. Mukerjee would later note his disapproval of the moral overtones of Gandhi.[119] C. R. Das, of course, worked closely with Gandhi and often found common ground with his philosophy of nonviolence. Das's vision of anticolonial resistance, though, did not converge with Gandhi's, which led to the formation of Das-led Swaraj Party in the early 1920s. The political fracture between the Gandhian and federalist partisans of the anticolonial movement, however, would ultimately be remembered as a mere footnote in the historiography of Indian anticolonial politics. The questions posed by the federalists were not quite replaced with a more convincing ones, but there emerged a new answer to the problem of peoplehood: the case for accelerated development put forward by Jawaharlal Nehru. In Chapter 5 we turn to this most transformative moment of the anticolonial democratic project.

CHAPTER 5

TO "CARRY" THE PEOPLE THROUGH HISTORY

Postcolonial Founding and the Idea of Independence

WRITING FROM PRISON in the 1940s, Jawaharlal Nehru recounted a curious story from the days of his anticolonial mobilization in the Indian villages. Presented more in the form of a fable than as a specific event, the story exemplifies the narrativization of postcolonial founding as a sublime—almost descended-from-above—experience, especially for the masses in question. When Nehru reached political gatherings in remote villages, the crowd—mostly composed of peasants—would usually greet him with the chant "Bharat Mata ki jai" (Victory to Mother India). Nehru, in turn, would return their greeting with this question: What exactly is this *Bharat Mata,* or Mother India? Bemused and perplexed, the peasants would turn to one another for an answer. After a rather lengthy pause, someone would offer that the nation was *dharti,* or the earth. Nehru would follow up with more questions: "What earth? [Your] particular village patch, or all the patches in the district or province, or in the whole of India?" Others would join in and speculate further, but to no avail. Nehru invariably had to introduce *Bharat Mata* to "herself": "*Bharat Mata,* Mother India, was essentially these millions of

159

people, and victory to her meant victory to these people. You are parts of this *Bharat Mata*, I told them, you are in a manner yourselves *Bharat Mata*, and as this idea slowly soaked into their brains, their eyes would light up as if they had made a great discovery."[1]

The story synecdochally captures an account of postcolonial founding that had long been taken for granted, even though Nehru's account of founding itself does not entirely fit the gist of the story. The convergence between nationalist and democratic aspirations, as Rupert Emerson put it in an early articulation of the narrative in the 1960s, had resulted in the conferring of sovereignty on largely "illiterate" peoples. First worked out in Europe, the democratic ideal was, slowly and incompletely, disseminated in the rest of the world through colonial rule.[2] Writing at the height of decolonization, Isaiah Berlin could dismiss the question of anticolonial "liberty" with an inimitable self-confidence: "What they seek is . . . akin to what Mill called 'pagan self-assertion,' but in a collective, socialized form."[3] Following the lead of "Germans . . . Poles and Russians," postcolonial founders appeared to have sought mere glory in national independence.[4] Global historians of the idea of self-determination often unwittingly repeat a different version of the narrative. In an influential account of the rise of anticolonial self-determination, Erez Manela centers Woodrow Wilson's affirmation of the national right to self-determination as the critical event that facilitated the anticolonial claim for independent statehood. The right to self-determination—the argument goes—found its anticolonial claimants after Wilson's international authorization.[5] Even scholars critical of the derivative approach to anticolonial thought agree that the "gradual lifting of the constraints of class, rank, gender, race, caste etc." from "the idea of popular sovereignty" made it available to non-Europeans and led to the rise of "the general right of self-determination of nations."[6]

By all accounts, the era of decolonization had been one of the most important episodes of the twentieth century. The world map acquired entirely new boundaries, and international order and norms also changed—at least juridically. More importantly, the formation of the new states fundamentally transformed the experience of politics for most of the world. There is no need to belabor the singular historical importance of postcolonial independence. But the event itself—while overwhelming for those who experienced it—did not seem to have posed much of an interpretative conundrum. To sympathetic and critical observers alike, it was the extension of something already known or long in the process of becoming. It might have changed the course of history and altered the map of the world, but its theoretical significance was already familiar— a founding foretold.

The commonplace assumption that postcolonial founding emerged from a belated, naturalized identification of the people with the nation obscures more than it reveals. It is certainly true that juridical disqualifications of non-European claims to peoplehood were no longer a straightforward matter from the mid-twentieth century on. But rights-expansionist narratives, such as that of self-determination, do not quite get to the heart of postcolonial founding. In this chapter I argue that a new answer to the old problem of peoplehood was key to the Indian turn to independence. The key protagonist in this episode of Indian anticolonial thought was Jawaharlal Nehru. One of the first Congress politicians to take political independence as an immediate goal, Nehru ascribed his unflinching commitment to "complete independence" to the encounter with the *kisans* (peasants) in the early 1920s. Having been inspired by Gandhi to "go to the villages,"[7] Nehru's encounter with the Indian masses produced a distinctly non-Gandhian outlook. As he put it: "I had not fully realized what [the Indian villages] were and what they meant to India. . . . Ever since [these visits], my mental picture of India always contained this naked, and hungry mass."[8] From the "picture" of the "naked and hungry" masses, he derived authorization for an independent state that would act as the mediator between the backward masses and the sovereign people. What was new about Nehru's project, as we shall see, was the ambition to turn the time of development into an object of political sovereignty. In a crucial sense, Nehru's sovereign state—as opposed to simply a government of Indians—aspired to dictate the course of development so as to rapidly fulfill the preconditions of democracy proper.

The Gandhian and federalist moments significantly diminished the role of developmentalism in political mobilization, but the older terms of the problem of peoplehood remained in many ways the mainstream position. Interestingly, Nehru rediscovered the philosophical force of the social question from within the Gandhian political universe and in a new global context where the time of development seemed ready to be compressed. As the importance of the moral and educational components of development declined, the economy-centric conception of development began to enjoy a new vindication. But more than the return of the economy question, it was the revaluation of the role of the state in directing development that captivated Nehru and led to the formation of his agenda for postcolonial founding. Already in the nineteenth century, as we saw in Chapters 1 and 2, democratic theory found itself preoccupied with the time of representative democracy. One necessary consequence of centering the time of democracy was the evaluation of political institutions vis-à-vis the pace of social progress. "The territorial, representative, and mass democracies of modernity," argues Hartmut Rosa in his study of accelerationism and modernity, "developed against the background of a dynamic understanding of history according to which legislation in parliament was not an act to be completed once and for all . . . but rather a continuous task of progressively steering the path of societal development in the historical process."[9] Well before Nehru, Indian political actors were seriously engaged in critiquing the empire for failing to direct the course of India's development. Nehru, however, wanted to do more than steer the course of development: his vision of postcolonial founding involved nothing short of a mastery over the developmental trajectory so that the pace of progress itself could be accelerated. His rejection of empire was also a rejection of working within the existing pace of development.

Though very few in interwar India were readily persuaded to wait for the people to develop, the mere affirmation of independence for an underdeveloped people remained an answer too vague to generate immediate enthusiasm for a new founding. "Impatience" had been a well-understood vice of anticolonial radicals, and the record of the swaraj era stood as evidence of the difficulty involved in reconciling immediate self-government with the sovereignty of the "starving and ignorant" masses. Nehru's case for founding rendered the contrast between "patience" and "impatience" largely irrelevant. As opposed to the slow temporality of ordinary development, he posited the prospect of a fast-tracked development and connected it with the sovereign authority of the postcolonial state. Drawing on the Soviet example of planning, as well as contemporary futurological literature, Nehru fashioned postcolonial founding as a constitutional republic that would be simultaneously committed to parliamentary democracy and to an active planning organ run by the executive and experts. The political legitimation of the planning state lay in the promise to rapidly transport the masses from the age of deprivation to a developed future. As Nehru declared on the eve of Indian independence: "We must cover in five or ten years what other countries took generations to do and at the same time *carry* millions with us, not by compulsion or in any authoritarian way but with their consent."[10]

If Nehru had stopped there, his vision of founding would, at best, have been a creative reenactment of the commonplace twentieth-century tradition of prioritizing historical necessity over the autonomy of the political. Fully cognizant of the non-identity between "political democracy" and "economic democracy," his planning state did not seek to entirely instrumentalize the institution of constitutional democracy. Ephemeral and yet transformative, the planning state was to be authorized by the people and work with the government, without being identical to either. In a way, it was evocative of Rousseau's proverbial Lawgiver. In the eighteenth century, before popular sovereignty became entangled in developmentalism, Jean-Jacques Rousseau ran into a difficult problem that has vexed political theorists ever since. As is well known, Rousseau's will-centric idea of popular sovereignty took fundamental legislation as the medium through which the sovereignty of the people is enacted. But the people, he acknowledged, do not make good laws just by virtue of being sovereign: "For a nascent people to be capable of appreciating sound maxims of politics . . . the effect would have to become the cause, the social spirit which is to be the work of the institution would have to preside over the institution itself, and men would have to be prior to laws what they ought to become by means of them."[11] This dilemma led Rousseau to return to the enigmatic figure of the Lawgiver.[12] Perforce an extraordinary figure and unattached to power, the Lawgiver had to disappear after the initiation of the people into the art of legislation. Neither a sovereign nor a magistrate, the Lawgiver's power eluded positive descriptions and inspired some of Rousseau's most alluring contentions.[13]

Much like the Lawgiver, the planning state was meant to be a vanishing master, one that would shape the future of the republic without being codified into the constitution or being dragged into "squabbles and conflicts of politics."[14] It had to mediate between the before (the underdeveloped past) and the after (the developed future): its ultimate responsibility was to fashion the people without being one with them. In contrast to Rousseau and the eighteenth-century tradition of popular sovereignty, though, Nehru's theory of founding was relatively unconcerned with fundamental legislation. In fact, Nehru embraced the growing marginalization of the legislature in the mid-twentieth century. The engine of postcolonial state-form was located not in the legislative body but in a foresighted executive that would work in conjunction with the experts. In contrast, the role of universal suffrage and legislative representatives was to keep the planners in touch with the people and allow the latter to have some control over the process, albeit via the means of elections. The result was a form of democratic project that sought to carry the people and yet be authorized by them. What specifically propelled the project of postcolonial founding, then, was less a new picture of the people than the accelerationist project for bridging the two bodies of the colonial people: the one "naked and hungry," and the other free and developed.

To recover the novelty of this project of postcolonial founding, it is important first to situate the question of popular sovereignty in the broader discursive field of midcentury decolonization. Neither the juridical idea of independence nor the Wilsonian view of self-determination accounts for the intrinsic logic of founding as an act of asserting sovereignty over the time of development. The international background played an important role in the formation of the project of postcolonial founding, but it did not resolve the problem of peoplehood that had long clouded the aspiration for popular sovereignty. In the following section, I closely examine this problem. I then recover the way in which Nehru connected the figure of the starving masses with the idea of independence. Next, I trace the formation of Nehru's project of postcolonial founding as an accelerated resolution of the problem of peoplehood. In the final section, I take up the question of universal suffrage and the complex negotiations between the two meanings of democracy: political and economic. The chapter concludes with reflections on the intellectual challenges involved in retrieving the meaning of postcolonial founding.

SELF-DETERMINATION AND THE INTERNATIONAL ORIGIN NARRATIVE OF POSTCOLONIAL FOUNDING

Jawaharlal Nehru had earned some notoriety among his colleagues for his "obsession" with the international context of Indian politics. This fixation with international issues, charged Muhammad Ali Jinnah in 1938, led Nehru to "[think] in terms entirely divorced from realities which face . . . India."[15] Nehru was not apologetic about his preoccupation with international matters; the political future of India, he was convinced, was bound up with the rest of the world. He took pride in helping fashion the Congress's foreign policy and put great emphasis in tracing the emerging connections between developments in India and those in other colonial countries. This did not necessarily mean a subordination of the priorities of India's anticolonial movement to larger concerns. He, for instance, had no hesitation in joining resistance against the British during World War II—an event that he otherwise understood as a "war for democracy," albeit a democracy limited to Europe.[16] Though more internationally oriented than most of his peers, Nehru's approach to postcolonial founding is ultimately illustrative of the limits of the international origin narrative of postcolonial founding.

Central to the international origin narrative has been the idea of self-determination. The agenda of self-determination, which was forged in the chaotic context of World War I, is credited with transforming the overarching international consensus on the non-sovereignty of colonial peoples in the immediate aftermath of that conflict. The "expansionist" approach associated with the idea of self-determination, as I noted earlier, often contributes to the interpretation of postcolonial founding as a theoretical nonevent.[17] As we shall see, what the Wilsonian moment of self-determination facilitated was not so much a right to sovereignty as a right to self-government for those who were not yet fit to be sovereign. Nor could the international discourse of self-determination address the main form in which colonial rule legitimated itself: the disqualification of the popular *capacity* for sovereignty in the colonies. The crisis of anticolonial sovereignty required a more fundamental resolution than a mere extension of the idea that all nations have a right to self-determination.

To rehearse the familiar history, the principle of self-determination emerged as one of the centerpieces of the Paris Peace Conference of 1919 under the auspices of Woodrow Wilson. The concept of self-determination is of Enlightenment origin, but its early twentieth-century political meaning was initially shaped by the Marxist debates on the national question.[18] The "political" definition of self-determination—as V. I. Lenin argued in a series of articles written on the eve of the Great War (in part as a polemic against Rosa Luxemburg)—amounts to independent "national states."[19] He formulated this account of self-determination against the claim that the economic dependence of small nations would render the ideal of self-determination a meaningless proposition. On the contrary, Lenin claimed, the "national state" is "best" suited for the development of capitalism in backward nations. Though Lenin used the language of rights to describe self-determination, his affirmation of the ideal was undergirded by its simultaneous disavowal. The "norm" of self-determination—which ultimately meant a legitimation of intranational class exploitation—had to be kept in check so as not to undermine the international solidarity of the global proletariat.[20] Because the national state was a stage of capitalist development, the normative dimension of the right to self-determination was ultimately transient: "It is their [the proletariat's] task, in the interests of a successful struggle against all and every kind of nationalism among all nations, to preserve the unity of the proletarian struggle and the proletarian organizations . . . despite bourgeois strivings for national exclusiveness."[21] The ideal of self-determination, therefore, was a normatively provisional and even strategic goal. This is not to say that Lenin's argument failed to speak to anticolonial actors. Its purchase instead pertained to justifying the strategic necessity of self-determination rather than as a universally valid discourse of rights.[22]

Woodrow Wilson's appropriation of the Bolshevik concept of self-determination following World War I had helped quickly disseminate the term throughout the globe. While he used the language of rights less than Lenin, it was, ironically, Wilson who facilitated the rise of self-determination as a universal regulative ideal of international relations. At home with the British imperial language of political "fitness," Wilson had earlier disqualified the Philippines' demand for self-rule on the ground of its backwardness.[23] In his invocation of self-determination,

Wilson was primarily interested in addressing the imperial subjection of Eastern European peoples. The Fourteen Points mentioned the colonial question only once, suggesting that the "interests of the [colonial] population must have equal weight with the equitable government whose title is to be determined."[24] This resolution giving "equal weight" to imperial and colonial interests fell well short of the criterion of national self-determination, however restrictively defined. Take, for example, a definition of self-determination offered by the editor of a contemporary American collection of Wilson's war addresses: "Meaning the right of *any* people to determine for themselves under what rule they shall live—a new phrase for the 'consent of the governed.'"[25] Even as the scope of the concept was less than sovereignty and merely affirmed the power of a subject people to determine under whose and what rule they would live, there was no substantive safeguard against its global appropriation.[26]

The Indian reception of the idea of self-determination against this backdrop revealed the claimable nature as well as the restricted scope of the Wilsonian ideal. The annual session of the Indian National Congress in December 1918 was dominated by Wilson's Fourteen Points and their political possibilities for the anticolonial cause. The president of the session was the moderate congressman and Hindu Mahasabha leader Madan Mohan Malaviya. In his address, Malaviya produced a lengthy summary of Wilson's speeches to substantiate the argument that the "principle of self-determination" should be "extended to India."[27] The meaning of the term itself, however, proved to be open to interpretation:

> Let us make it clear what we mean when we talk of self-determination. There are two aspects of self-determination, and it has been spoken of in the Peace proposals. One is that the people of certain colonies and other colonies should have the right to say whether they will live under the suzerainty of one power or of another. So far as we Indians are concerned we have no need to say that we do not desire to exercise that election. Since India passed directly under the British Crown, we have owned [*sic*] allegiance to the Sovereign of England. . . . There is, however, the second and no less important aspect of self-determination, namely, that being under the British Crown, we should be allowed complete responsible government on the lines of the Dominions, in the administration of all our domestic affairs.[28]

As Malaviya helpfully elucidated, Wilson's defense of self-determination opened up two different possibilities. One possibility—the right of a people to choose who they would be ruled by—was markedly less than the proposition that any people should have the right to form their *own* government. The other possibility—self-government without sovereignty—was the avowed ideal of the Congress at least since Naoroji's swaraj speech in 1906. Malaviya avoided the language of "self-government" and pinned his hope on the more ambiguous term "responsible government." The Congress's resolution regarding self-determination also accepted the developmental criteria of the Wilsonian principle, and only affirmed India's place among the "progressive nations": "This Congress claims the recognition of India *by* the British Parliament and by the Peace Conference as one of the *Progressive Nations* to whom the Principle of Self-Determination should be applied."[29]

While Malaviya stopped short of calling for full self-government within empire, the more radical section of the Congress pushed the demand further. But they, too, invoked self-determination to embolden a preexisting demand rather than to forge a new one. Motilal Nehru—the moderate leader who was slowly disavowing his earlier faith in the policy of gradual reformism—offered another reading of self-determination: "Every nation in the world has a right to choose how they will be governed and by whom.—'Self-determination' is the new word that has been coined to give expression to this idea which itself is certainly not new at least to this country. . . . The fact is that it took hold of our imaginations no less than 33 years ago when the Indian National Congress was started."[30] The elder Nehru's speech was printed in the very first issue of the *Independent*—a short-lived Allahabad-based newspaper whose establishment was spurred by the enthusiasm around self-determination. In his own message for the *Independent*, C. R. Das echoed Motilal Nehru's point: "Self-Government has been the cry of the Indian National Congress for the last thirty-three years. Today Europe and America give it another name and call it 'Self-Determination' but we are old in history and the principle of Self-Determination is the one essential principle in our culture."[31]

Das and the elder Nehru's stress on the equivalence of "self-determination" and "self-government" registered a resistance to the idea that the norm of self-determination came to India from without. The semantic dispute was also prompted by the fear that a merely Wilsonian understanding of self-determination would pave the way for its assimilation into the moderate agenda of "responsible government." Lala Lajpat Rai—based in the United States at the time—voiced a similar opinion in an important pamphlet called *Self-Determination for India* (1919). Rai fiercely questioned the discourse of political fitness. England, he argued, may have taken six hundred years to be fit for self-rule, but it took only a generation for Athenians to institute democracy. He also rejected the assumption that India was an "infant nation," suggesting instead that the idea of the nation connotes a "moral and political being." Rai, nevertheless, did not call for severing the British connection. Granting India full self-government, he argued, would make it a "source of strength to the British commonwealth."[32]

It was not an anomaly that the enthusiasm for self-determination had practically disappeared by the next session of the Congress in December 1919. Having noted that Wilson's Fourteen Points had remained mere words, Jawaharlal Nehru, writing in mid-1919, found it fitting to reproduce Bertrand Russell's pessimistic note: "The Millennium is not for our time. The great moment has passed and for ourselves it is again the distant hope that must inspire us, not the immediate breathless looking for deliverance."[33] Gandhi, for his part, had no sympathy whatsoever for the Wilsonian program. He characterized the Paris Peace Conference as an exercise in armed peace. For the Mahatma, the primacy of imperial will in deciding the terms of self-determination was all too apparent.[34] The deployment of the ideal of self-determination for imperial ends, Gandhi noted in early 1920, had already corrupted its very meaning: "Is it the principle of self-determination that has caused cessation of Adrianople and Thrace to Greece? By what principle of self-determination has Smyrna been handed to Greece? . . . By the time the whole thing is finished, the very name self-determination will stink in one's nostrils."[35] As a result, by the end of 1920 the ideal of self-determination seemed to have retreated to its imperial origin. The term could barely be found in Gandhi or Jawaharlal Nehru's voluminous writings in the following decade. The discourse of self-determination became obsolescent as swiftly as it had emerged. The debate on the question of sovereignty instead came to be organized around the ideals of independence and dominion status.

Erez Manela's rich global history of the Wilsonian self-determination has renewed the academic appreciation of the moment, but his conclusion that the Wilsonian principle of the right of self-determination was "appropriated . . . by colonial nationalists" so as to posit "the self-determining nation-state as the sole legitimate entity in international relations" stems from a conflation of self-government with sovereign statehood.[36] As shown by the Indian history of self-determination (which constitutes one major site of Manela's narrative), the problem of anticolonial sovereignty was not especially clarified, let alone resolved, by the Wilsonian moment. The range of demands it enabled was tethered to the developmental gradation of sovereignty—from "responsible government" to "self-government within empire." From another perspective, Timothy Mitchell observed that the Wilsonian vision of self-determination, as an ideal, was "thin" and "lightweight."[37] Regardless of whether the "device" of self-determination was devised to reconsolidate imperial control (as Mitchell would have it), its portable nature helped embolden, however momentarily, the Indian pursuit of the preexisting demand for *self-government*. Importantly, however, the assimilation of self-determination into prior demands, such as for "responsible government" and "self-government," meant that the question of sovereignty remained unanswered. Postcolonial founding was still a distant horizon.

The Wilsonian moment of self-determination pales in comparison with its second arrival after World War II, when the discourse of self-determination began to be emphatically dissociated from its earlier absorption in the discourse of self-government. Between these two moments, however, the more consequential reconfiguration of the Indian approach to the international took place. Important to this transformation was the formation of the League Against Imperialism (LAI),[38] which emerged out of frustrations with the imperial hegemony over the League of Nations. At the opening conference in Brussels in 1927, a global cast of actors debated the principles and strategies of anti-imperial movements.[39] One of the key actors in the LAI was Jawaharlal Nehru. It was at this conference that Nehru first encountered anticolonial leaders from across Asia, Africa, and the Americas.

While the LAI's reach was far less than the Wilsonian international, its influence in India—via Nehru—was arguably more consequential. The LAI facilitated Nehru's reconsideration of the structure of international claim-making. He concluded that membership in the empire, in the form of "dominion status," no matter how equal, would mean complicity in the exploitation of other imperial subjects. A suggestive dispute between Nehru and his moderate colleagues at the Indian National Congress captured the critical salience of the LAI-inflected international. When Nehru singlehandedly pushed for a resolution about independence at the Congress's annual meeting in 1927, the rest of the party strongly criticized it. Two prominent Congress politicians—C. Vijayaraghavachariar and Rajendra Prasad—opposed the resolution on the ground that its passing would make the Congress the "laughing stock of the world."[40] For the critics of the resolution, India was not ready for sovereignty and such a premature declaration would only compromise its international standing. The power of the developmental discourse of political fitness, in other words, still lingered. What was new was the specific mode of Nehru's contestation of the deferral of Indian sovereignty. Nehru suggested that the opponents of the independence resolution should move away from judging Indian fitness for self-rule in light of the prehistory of European democracy ("17th and 18th centuries"). He reminded his colleagues that "countries such as Morocco, Turkey, Syria and Palestine were claiming independence." If they were not considered a "laughing stock" of the world, Nehru continued, neither should India be. Furthermore, if India were to stay within the British Empire, it would indirectly participate in "exploiting Egypt and Africa."[41] The demand for independence was no longer "silly" in the new world.[42]

This reframing of the question of the international facilitated a move away from the developmental prerequisites for belonging to the community of nations. This, however, was only a supplement, albeit an important one, to the turn toward independence in anticolonial political thought. Reflecting on the international origins of twentieth-century anticolonialism, Samuel Moyn observed that the hope of "postcolonial, collective liberation from empire," rather than "international rights," drove the anticolonial project.[43] Though the aspiration to transform the imperial international into an anticolonial one was an important concern, Moyn is right to prioritize the pursuit of collective sovereignty in anticolonial thought. The problem of collective sovereignty, however, takes us back to the problem of peoplehood. After all, what had long discursively prevented Indians from proclaiming hasty independence was

the doubt about its people's democratic capacity, rather than a rosy identification with the British. It is this problem that internally suspended
the project of postcolonial founding. The coming of postcolonial
founding was not the result of a sudden realization that developmental
description of the world is invalid. As it transpired, Indian anticolonial
thinkers—especially Jawaharlal Nehru—found a new avenue for democratic founding, by way of connecting postcolonial founding with the
possibility of asserting sovereignty over the time of development itself.
In this way, the ideal of independence and democratic founding ultimately came together for the colonial world. The figure of the people, as
we shall see, was crucial once again to this transformative episode of anticolonial political thought.

THE "STARVING MASSES" AND THE TURN TO INDEPENDENCE

"Independence," Jawaharlal Nehru wrote in January 1928 after moving
the independence resolution at the Madras Congress a month before, "is
certainly not a happy word." It was not a happy word because "isolation"
by itself was no longer a virtue in an increasingly international world.[44]
Yet it was necessary. The moral case for cutting off the British connection rested on the "reactionary" past and present of the British Empire.[45]
Independence was an inevitable step toward opening up to another
realm—the anticolonial world. This was a powerful argument in the interwar context when the lineaments of a global resistance against empire were becoming increasingly visible. But, as Nehru knew, the international examples would only remain an example without a pointed
answer to the problem of peoplehood.

The conventional definition of independence, notes David Armitage,
connotes "political separation of the kind that the representatives of the
United States asserted against King George III in 1776."[46] The juridical
notion of independence—influentially framed by Emer de Vattel in his
mid-eighteenth-century text *The Law of Nations*—essentially means "free"
and "sovereign" statehood. The "contagious consequences" of the American Declaration of Independence, Armitage rightly observes, acquired a
"near-universal significance" in the twentieth century. The generic and
juridical similarity between American and anticolonial declarations of
independence at a formal level constitutes an important thread in the

global history of independence.[47] But the temporal distance between the American and twentieth-century anticolonial visions of independence—separated by a century and a half—is no less striking. The model of independence instituted by the American Revolution was by no means unknown in nineteenth-century India. If it failed to generate urgency in the nineteenth century, it was not because of a lack of intellectual exposure to the ideal. Rather, the equation of independence with sovereignty itself came to be questioned in the twentieth century, transforming in the process the very meaning of independence.

The ideas of independence and postcolonial democratic founding were overlapping yet distinct. The keen recognition of the non-identity between independence and democracy already marked nineteenth-century Indian reflections on the problem. In fact, the vernacular public sphere from the mid-nineteenth century onward was saturated with reflections on the meanings of liberty and independence. Bankimchandra Chatterjee—a major nineteenth-century Indian thinker—could complain in 1873 that the Bengali encounter with European politics had resulted in endless ruminations on two words in particular: "liberty" and "independence."[48] A few years later, the poet Rabindranath Tagore—still a precocious teenager—commented similarly on the contemporary obsession over the word "swadhinata" (which translates as both "independence" and "liberty" in Bengali): "It is not that there was a preexisting idea of independence in our mind, which we later named accordingly; it is rather that we have picked up the word and have been worshipping it as though it is a thing."[49] Bankim, in particular, emphatically distinguished the idea of independence from that of liberty. If independence refers to territorial sovereignty, liberty concerns the equality of all, especially equality between the ruling and the ruled races. Under the British, Bankim concludes, India was both subjected and unfree. In the ancient era India was independent, but it was unfree thanks to its caste system. The ideal, therefore, had to be independence with equality and liberty. This conclusion was one reason certain nineteenth-century thinkers, such as Bankim, suspended the question of independence until the conditions for equality and liberty had been generated.[50] In any case, what these observations of Bankim and Tagore go on to show is that the idea of independence was simultaneously familiar (intellectually) and distant (politically) in nineteenth-century Indian political thought.

By the 1920s, Indian thinkers were too steeped in complex discourses of independence and liberty to be suddenly persuaded by a simply moral case for sovereignty. A new configuration of the relationship between independence and democracy was needed, and this was precisely what Nehru brought to the Indian political scene. Unsurprisingly, it was Nehru's renewed encounter with the masses—not as the self-determining people but instead as the repository of misery and poverty—that transformed the calculus of independence and democracy. As I have already underscored, Nehru essentially rediscovered the Indian people as a body of "starving" masses. Though Nehru shared this conception of the people with his predecessors, what he demanded from the people was different: the people did not have to prove their capacity for sovereignty but only had to express their readiness to authorize the acceleration of their own development. The desire for independence became one and inseparable from the popular authorization for accelerated development.

In the early 1920s, when the Gandhi-led Noncooperation and Khilafat movements took India by storm, Nehru found himself drawn to the distinctly modern pull of mass movements. Gandhi's masses, however, were no cipher for independence or sovereignty. Though Gandhi helped transform the anticolonial movement into a mass movement, his distinctive vision of individual self-rule steadfastly avoided the question of political sovereignty. Gandhi's call for boycotting British goods and institutions was directly related to his vision of making Indian villages self-sufficient. He also encouraged Congress workers to spend time in the Indian villages. One of Gandhi's recruits—his "first devotee" in North India[51]—was Jawaharlal Nehru. Having spent most of his youth in British boarding schools and universities, the younger Nehru's connection with the villages was more superficial than usual.

Nehru's encounter with the *kisans* (peasants) was to be the beginning of his departure from Gandhi. Prior to being swept away by Gandhi, Nehru's most notable political experience was acting as a secretary for Annie Besant's Home Rule League. Besant's League helped politically revive the Congress's demand for swaraj, albeit with a more emphatic defense of self-government within empire.[52] Nehru's intellectual world was also not immune to the critique of representative democracy flourishing in the wake of the Great War. In the aforementioned 1919 review of Bertrand Russell's *Road to Freedom,* he expressed his sympathy for Russell's diagnosis of the inadequacy of representative government. Still, he believed in developmental reasoning enough to conclude, "We in India have yet to travel over the long road of representative government before we can proceed on different lines."[53] The experience of the Noncooperation movement would embolden Nehru's republican investments. The true meaning of self-government, he declared in 1921, lies in the idea that "every Indian, every Hindu, Mussalman, Sikh or Christian, who lives in India and who is proud of calling it his motherland should be free and should have the right to take part in the government of the country."[54] This argument was enabled by Nehru's brief flirtation with the federalist critique of representative democracy: the rule of panchayat raj, or village republics.[55] This episode was short-lived partly because of Nehru's abiding skepticism regarding the relevance—real or metaphorical—of precolonial political forms. In any case, notwithstanding his conclusion that there could be no "real understanding" between India and Britain, Nehru could still observe in the same speech that the "last stage" of swaraj is "very far away."[56] This, of course, was an old script of Indian politics, where the rejection of the empire and the assertion of sovereignty were no logical corollaries.

Saying that his own outlook at that point had been "bourgeois," Nehru later recounted that the encounter with peasants was the beginning of his realization that Congress had been "cut off . . . from [the] people."[57] The Congress's account of "political freedom" was detached from "the peasantry," who were "a blind, poverty-stricken, suffering mass, resigned to their miserable fate and sat upon and exploited by all who came in contact with them—the Government, landlords, moneylenders, petty officials, police, lawyers, priests."[58] Nehru did perceptively underscore the great "sense of power" that the assembled masses generated.[59] He also celebrated the tenacious resistance showed by the peasants despite their misery. Nevertheless, in his judgment the weight of deprivation and destitution rendered the masses sociologically as well as politically incapable. The overarching lack of social freedom compromised the capacity to enact political freedom: "The Indian *kisans* have little staying power, little energy to resist for long."[60] For Nehru, the anticolonial project should neither ignore nor glorify the peasants. This realization would constitute one of his long-standing disagreements with the Mahatma. While poverty only accentuated the urgency of moral self-rule for Gandhi, Nehru was deeply irked by his elusive mentor's "glorification of poverty." (One of the expressions that Gandhi would often use when referring to the Indian poor was *daridranarayan*—"God that resides in the poor"). Nehru instead saw the burden of poverty as a "hateful thing, to be fought and rooted out and not to be encouraged in any way."[61]

Destitute and weak as the Indian masses were, the anticolonial project had no foundation except their future: "India is in the main the peasant and the worker, not beautiful to look at, for poverty is not beautiful."[62] The destitution of the masses was the responsibility of the empire, and the masses knew it: "the masses can never compromise with imperialism because their only hope lies in the freedom from its shackles."[63] He reminded his more reform-minded colleagues that "the day for palace intrigues and parlour politics and pacts and compromises passes when the masses enter politics."[64] In the years following the Noncooperation movement, the Indian masses had shown their transformation from a "subservient and demoralised people" into an agent with the "capacity [to] challenge the might of a great and entrenched empire."[65] Nehru's confidence followed from the newfound faith that the masses favored independence. The "mass will" in question concerned only independence and not necessarily a positive program of founding. It is for this reason that this new voicing of "mass will" could bypass the questions raised about the fitness of that will. Of course, Nehru was not the only actor invoking the interests of the masses in 1930s India. Increasingly his main political opponent, the Muslim League, also invoked an irresolvable difference written into the wills of the Indian majority and minority masses, including the maturity of (Hindu) majoritarian collective will. In response to the problems of mass incapacity and division, Nehru relied on the future claims latent in the will of the present masses. The more the "social and economic forces" developed in India, Nehru claimed, the more the masses would realize the nonsectarian basis of their unity.[66]

What we have in Nehru, then, are two different—if occasionally mutually competing—pictures of the people. On the one hand, he returned to the figure of the starving masses where suffering and deprivation are the key markers of their underdeveloped peoplehood. That this view of the masses—where "famines and epidemics come and slay them in their millions"[67]—led to a deflationary view of the popular capacity to act is hard to deny. On the other hand, Nehru's future-oriented reasoning convinced him that the masses were foreordained to realize their necessary contradiction with empire. The two poles of his figuration of the people were not quite a contradiction, for the dual argument allowed Nehru to posit his own founding agenda as precisely a mediator between the present destitute masses and the capable future people.

Having located the demand for independence in the masses, Nehru, suggestively, went on to specify the limits of independence. This shift to the demand for independence was directly sparked by the realization of its limit: "political independence meant, of course, political freedom only, and did not include any social change or economic freedom for the masses."[68] Independence was necessary but not sufficient. The vision of independence to which Nehru arrived afterward sought to move beyond the mere incidental benefit of severing the British connection—or even the assumption that "the removal of the financial and economic chains which bind us to the City of London, and this would have made it easier for us to change the social structure." This is because "real political freedom" was unlikely to result from mere independence.[69] Nehru also formulated a critique of the drain theory popularized by Dadabhai Naoroji. The source of the drain, he argued, is not just the British but the entire "economic structure" itself.[70] Owing to a superficial understanding of Indian backwardness, his predecessors at the Congress, especially the liberals, understood independence to be a mere change of political power. Returning to the recurrent "house" metaphor,[71] Nehru reflected on different visions of postcolonial founding:

> The British treated India as a kind of enormous country house (after the Old English fashion) that they owned. They were the gentry owning the house, while the Indians were consigned to the servants' hall, the pantry, and the kitchen. . . . [The Liberals] accept the country house in its entirety, admire its architecture and the whole edifice, but look forward to replacing the owners, one by one, by themselves. They call this Indianization. . . . They never think in terms of a new State.[72]

It was time for thinking about postcolonial founding in terms of a new sovereignty, as opposed to the framework of self-government that reduced the problem of founding to the Indian control of the administration.

Elsewhere, Nehru characterized the latter as "governmentarians."[73] The outstanding question, then, was this: What exactly is the new sovereignty that could be instituted in the name of the people and yet be an answer to the backwardness of the Indian masses?

SOVEREIGNTY OVER THE TIME OF DEVELOPMENT

It is perhaps telling that Nehru moved on to indicting his colleagues' understanding of the future right after renouncing the older program of self-government. Gandhi's political program, for instance, was based in "terms of scarcity" with no vision of a future political life where the people would be "abundantly supplied with the necessaries of life."[74] Yet, as Nehru knew, Gandhi's appeal owed to the exit he offered from the bondage of development, especially its blackmail of the future. The developmental process, subjected as it is to its own laws and requirements, had long been taken to be a slow process. How exactly would political sovereignty overcome the slow time of development? Nehru's answer to this conundrum was bold: the new state, once founded, would not so much work to correct the wrong policies of the British as strive to exert sovereignty over the time of development itself. This reframing of the founding project sought to revolutionize both the imagination of the developmental future and the state-form that would mediate the journey from "the present scarcity to future abundance."[75]

Nehru's encounter with Marxism and the Soviet Union was important to the formation of this agenda of founding. The cornerstone of Nehru's political thought—the world-historical power ascribed to "planned economy"—took shape in the period of his "fascination" with Soviet Russia.[76] Following his brief trip to the Soviet Union in November 1927, Nehru immersed himself in contemporary literature on the October Revolution and the Soviet Union. Between April and August of 1928, he wrote over a dozen articles on various aspects of the Russian experiment. Optimism generated by the Russian experiment led Nehru to declare in the mid-1930s: "I believe in the rapid industrialization of the country; and only thus, I think, will the standards of the people rise substantially and poverty be combated."[77] The question of planned economy in this era, as Quinn Slobodian has recently shown, was fiercely contested by early neoliberals, who quickly identified the importance of planning in decolonization projects and had their own alternative agenda for "de-planning" world economy.[78] Nehru was not unconcerned with the raging economic debates on planning, but its promise overwhelmingly out-weighed the risks involved:

> Are we going to solve this by petty tinkering and patchwork with all manner of vested interests obstructing us and preventing advance? Only a great planned system for the whole land and dealing with all these various national activities, coordinating them, making each serve the larger whole and the interests of the mass of our people—only such a planned system, with vision and courage to back it, can find a solution.[79]

For all its antipolitical elements, the Soviet model had shown that the developmental process, at least insofar as the economy was concerned, could be accelerated. In contrast, parliamentary democracy—Nehru wrote echoing the skepticism of the interwar critics of the Westminster model—was in "disrepute" and increasingly unable to speak to the greater "spirit of democracy."[80] His most substantive critique of parliamentary democracy, unsurprisingly, was temporal in character: "its methods were slow and cumbrous and unsuited to a period of rapid change."[81]

The uncertainty of planning was mitigated by Nehru's faith in the coming future of abundance, a projection that emerged out of his in-terest in interwar futurological literature. During his time in prison in the early 1930s and early 1940s, Nehru read a copious amount of work on the promise of scientific and technological revolution by Aldous Huxley, J. B. S. Haldane, H. G. Wells, and James Jeans, among others. As recent scholars of interwar futurology have pointed out, this was an era when utopian as well as dystopian projections into the future flourished simultaneously.[82] It is a commonplace that Nehru had a somewhat naive confidence in scientific rationalism—what Chatterjee described as his faith in "post-Enlightenment rationalism."[83] It is true that scientific reason underpinned Nehru's confidence in planning, notwithstanding the fact that he also was wary of the destructive potential of science, in-cluding the possibility that it could be appropriated by elites. The crux of the matter, however, lay elsewhere, beyond the predictable vacillation between the promise and the perils of science. From the aforementioned futurologists, Nehru imbibed the view that the ongoing progress of science would revolutionize technological capacity and lead to a dramatic expansion of power at the disposal of the state: "The technical achievements of science are obvious enough: its capacity to transform an economy of scarcity into one of abundance is evident."[84] This new future had no inherent drive to democratization for Nehru (he reminded his audience more than once that machines cause unemployment and also aid authoritarianism), but it opened up a new way of traveling to the long-awaited future. The importance of this vision for Nehru is perhaps best understood if we return to the nineteenth-century image of the future. That future of India, as Bernard Cohn felicitously put it, resembled the present of Europe and generated the expectation that India's journey must be as slow as the European precedent.[85] Nehru's vision of the future, in contrast, had promised to fold several centuries of industrial revolution into a brief period of postcolonial development. If Soviet Russia exemplified the possibility of planning and accelerating productive forces, the futuristic scientific literature signaled to him the onset of a new way of harnessing scientific power for a political end.

Armed with this vision of the future, Nehru posited the planning state as the guide to a postcolonial future of abundance. Though the example of Soviet Russia was the reason "the future was full of hope,"[86] there was no compelling reason for political democracy to be compromised for the sake of development. The phase of industrialization, by itself, was a process strewn with the "major evil" of exploitation. It could not be trusted to guide the political path, nor could it be fully decoupled from authoritarianism. Nehru concluded that a democratic form of planning—led by a republican state at the helm of economic production and distribution—would best facilitate the "onward march" to the future.[87] The mixed economy of Nehru's planning regime was far from a simple reproduction of the Soviet model. The Nehru-led National Planning Committee invoked this definition of planning: "Planning under democracy may be defined as the technical coordination by disinterested experts of consumption, production, investment, trade, and income distribution in accordance with social objectives set by bodies representative of the nation."[88] Nehru envisioned the planning organ as guided by experts and shielded from the burden of ordinary politics. The molding of the economy according to egalitarian ideals and rule of experts, Nehru hoped, would generate a faster process of economic and social development.

Importantly, the planning state was not simply a choice that Nehru made after deciding on the necessity of independence; it enabled the articulation of the idea of independence itself. This new vision of independence charged the successful campaign for *purna swaraj* (complete independence) at the 1929 Lahore Congress, rapidly accelerating the confrontation between the British Empire and its Indian adversaries.[89]

As a republican, Nehru had a commitment to the principle of popular sovereignty that was not simply instrumental. Its most immediate purchase, however, resided in ushering in the sovereignty of the planning state: the "large-scale state planning was impossible so long as the central government was not under popular control."[90] Political sovereignty would allow the new state to assert full control over the pace at which the masses were to be developed, even if the masses were unlikely to understand beforehand the logic and processes of the planning state. The simultaneous enlisting and subordination of the Russian peasants to the developmental project already made the problem clear to Nehru in the 1920s. The practice of collective farming, Nehru observed, was generating a new ethos of progress in Russia: "The tractor is almost a god in Russia today and it is the tractor that has led to large-scale cooperation on the land."[91] The Russian peasants prior to the revolution practiced no freedom and were "lazy and ignorant, demoralized and incapable of any great effort." It was the genius of the Russian leadership that "converted this poor human material into a strong, organized nation, full of faith in its mission and confidence in itself."[92] The point of Nehru's revolutionary zeal was not to keep the masses out of politics entirely; it was instead a hope that the people could be infused from above with the almost spiritual drive of development. "Democratic planning was meant to be different from communist planning," as Nikhil Menon observes in his history of Indian planning, in part because "persuasion and informed consents were its mantras."[93] The redistribution of lands and resources to the peasants itself, Nehru assumed, would not be enough to overcome their resistance to the rapid march of history. What was needed was a cultivation of the ethos of accelerated development. As Dipesh Chakrabarty put it while discussing the Nehruvian planning regime: "What Nehru's vision called for was faith in both the people of the country and in the project of modernization in the interest of unleashing popular energies in creating a nation."[94]

In Chapter 3, I explored how developmentalism rendered the Indian people unclaimable, complicating the rhetorical performance of sovereign peoplehood. The performative force of peoplehood relates essentially to its claimability—to be able to invoke and enact the people.[95] Although Nehru returned to the developmental premise, he also broke free of the impasse of an unclaimable people. He merely claimed authorization for independence from the people, rather than a fully formed program of democratic self-rule. The authorization for independence, in turn, was collapsed into that of the planning state. The destitute masses served both as the cause and the telos of the sovereign postcolonial state: the authorization for the developmental state was derived precisely from the gap between the immiserated and unfree people of the present and the developed and free people of the future. The otherwise scientific and progressive project of postcolonial founding acquired its political meaning by exploiting the gap between the two. While the principle of popular sovereignty would be constitutionally enshrined in the wake of postcolonial founding, it was hardly a reinstantiation of the classic eighteenth-century notion of popular sovereignty. Not primarily the lawmakers or the agents of rule, the people was instead that which licensed its own transformation.

It is a minor irony in Indian political thought that Nehru—for all his zealous assertion of the need to turn to the masses—would ultimately be seen as the standard bearer of what has come to be known as "elite nationalism." This conclusion by itself is not surprising. Nehru's idea of mass politics was not centered on delegating concrete political authority to the masses; they were instead an alibi for refashioning sovereignty as a vehicle of development. In his political theory there was no identity between a politics focused on the masses and a direct empowerment of them as decision makers. His later critics would locate many of the fault lines of the postcolonial age in this very non-identity. The only note worth adding here is that Nehru broadly shared the same paradigm of social analysis with many of his anti-elitist critics, even as he considered the question of political agency subservient to the structural priority of social transformation. In the era of Indian founding, those who refused the modern framing of the social question—in terms of the primacy of the economic and other objective positional indexes—also had plenty of discontent with Nehru's project. Imprisoned in their own dilemma of authorization, the offshoots of the pluralist-federalist moment continued to articulate critiques of representative democracy that lacked its erstwhile intellectual creativity and political appeal. Such charges against representative democracy fell flat in Nehru's Congress in part because his project of founding attenuated and disenthralled the role of representative institutions. Other proposals for directly turning to the masses struggled to translate their thick metaphysics of democracy and development into political life.[96] If Nehru's project of founding politically outmaneuvered these contesting accounts, it did so by reconfiguring older paradigms all while tethering an otherwise utopian dream of accelerated transformation to the concrete political future of India—namely, independence.

RECONSTITUTING THE IDEA OF DEMOCRACY: UNIVERSAL SUFFRAGE AND POPULAR SOVEREIGNTY

This particular vision of postcolonial sovereignty threw the very idea of democracy into sharp relief, as the distinction between sovereignty and government found a new shape in the gap between universal suffrage (one expression of popular sovereignty) and the planning state (whose authority transcended the will of the people). As India acquired independence with Nehru at the helm, "the central problem of Indian politics was the construction not of nationalism but of democracy."[97] The republic was to be a parliamentary democracy with universal suffrage and powerful planning organs. Yet, as we saw, Indian founding was born out of a reckoning with the limits of parliamentary democracy and under the shadow of the problem of peoplehood. True to his pre-independence diagnosis, in the years after independence Nehru continued to point out that the Indian people were still far from meeting the demand of democracy proper. A few years into the postcolonial era, when he was asked, "What is your principal problem?," Nehru replied: "We have got 360 million problems in India."[98] The number, 360 million, was a reference to the then-estimated population of the newly independent state.

What Nehru already realized in the 1940s—and what postcolonial democracies across the globe would all variously struggle with—was the difficult challenge of performing the formal norms of constitutional

democracy while directing substantive political power and imagination to developing the masses. To put it another way, postcolonial states
in India and elsewhere simultaneously enthroned the people as a norm
and sought to transform them as a fact. For all his prioritization of the
economic over the political, Nehru was not oblivious to the fact that
constitutional democracy—or what he called "political democracy"—
stood in the name of the people and enabled them to act in certain
ways.[99] He wanted the people to participate in and embody the spirit of
development, but the planned nature of accelerated progress also required a state guided by a sovereign "projection into the future."[100]
Nehru called the latter "economic democracy": economic development
was essentially a democratic problem because it concerned the development of the people. The people, then, turned out to be both the master
and the object of the postcolonial republic. Much like his generation of
postcolonial founders across Asia and Africa, Nehru took this dual pull
of democracy to be an unavoidable dilemma in an era of postcolonial
transition. But this larger postcolonial dilemma did not leave the idea
of democracy untouched.

The persistence of the grammar of the problem of peoplehood in the
postcolonial era need not be seen as antithetical to the institution of universal suffrage. For most of the nineteenth century, the demands for Indian political inclusion rarely involved the agenda of widespread popular
suffrage. In Britain itself, the anxiety over the progressive state of the metropolitan people boiled down to the question concerning the fitness of the
working-class masses for suffrage. In such a world, universal suffrage for
colonies such as India appeared to be impracticable—a question consigned
to the remote future. Amid the growing confrontation with the empire,
that distant future arrived in India without much birth pain. By the second
quarter of the twentieth century, the program of universal suffrage had
acquired wide acceptance among Indian political thinkers. From a moot
question in the nineteenth century, the rise of universal suffrage in India
ended up being almost simultaneous with its institutionalization in the
European world.[101] This achievement of postcolonial democracy has rightly
been understood as a special instance that defied the "imaginary waiting
room . . . of European historicist thought."[102]

The effect of universal suffrage proved to be far-reaching. As Pratap
Bhanu Mehta noted in reference to the institution of universal suffrage

in India: "The very mundane process of seeking majorities within a representative system, of building new coalitions, leads to the mobilization of new groups, unsettles existing power equations and produces new openings."[103] Elsewhere in the colonial world, especially in French Africa, the promise of universal suffrage embodied the hope for shifting the power of imperial centers; it was, Kevin Duong argues, a "dream" that promised to be a key part of the answer to metropolitan domination.[104] In newly founded postcolonial states, universal suffrage also marked an end to the racialization instituted by European empires.[105] In a way, the egalitarian promise of postcolonial founding, set against the backdrop of the imperial hierarchy of peoples, found its most pointed expression in the affirmation of universal suffrage for those who had long been deemed unfit for the sacred mantle of self-rule.

But as we just saw above, the problem of peoplehood only accentuated in the face of postcolonial founding. What, then, explains the decoupling of universal suffrage from developmentalist grounds? Responding to the charge that his simultaneous commitments to economic development and to formal democracy were in contradiction, Nehru observed in 1936, "I lay stress on adult franchise so that the mass elements in India may make their weight felt and thus divert attention to mass problems—poverty, unemployment, the land question, industry etc.—from the present upper middle class problems that largely fill our minds."[106] Universal suffrage was the means through which "mass problems" could occupy the center stage of electoral politics. On the one hand, the "idea" of democracy animating the anticolonial movement demanded that the "suffrage of [the] people" should be claimed unconditionally.[107] Any discrimination regarding suffrage would undermine the very principle that the anticolonial movement strove for. On the other hand, as Nehru would note a couple of years after Indian independence, "it has no meaning to give a vote to a starving man."[108] This is the split premise on which universal suffrage would be born in India.

No less salient to the rather uncontroversial rise of universal suffrage in India was the attendant problem of group representation. The direct implication of the boundary problem for legislative representation from the late nineteenth century meant that the question of suffrage was not far removed from the disputes concerning group representation. The Muslim League as well as lower-caste groups sought legislative representation on the basis of separate electorates as a safeguard against majoritarianism. The Congress's opposition to separate electorates gave way to the argument that universal suffrage offered better protection against majoritarianism than an unequal weightage of franchise. This argument partly substantiated the endorsement of universal suffrage in the Nehru Report of 1928—a draft constitution prepared by a committee led by Motilal Nehru. The report observed that any restricted suffrage based on property or literacy would especially affect the Muslim-majority provinces (given the advantage enjoyed by Hindus on these fronts). "Different electoral qualifications for different groups and communities," the report argued, would generate "grievance" in some communities.[109] Given such complexities of unequal suffrage in a splintered polity, the Nehru Report decided that universal suffrage was the most feasible means of counteracting majoritarianism.

But the (Motilal) Nehru Report neither proposed independence nor had any specific plans for accelerated development. Its reflections on the question of suffrage were almost entirely shaped by the disputes around group representation. Arguably the more decisive resignification of the universal suffrage question happened after the turn to independence crystallized. As the executive-led planning regime emerged as the foremost objective of the postcolonial state, the legislative was consigned to a less exalted position. Nehru, like other postcolonial founders, was attentive to the significance of this shift. He acknowledged that the struggle for democracy in nineteenth-century Europe was centered on the question of suffrage. It was only in the recent past that England itself began to experience a form of democracy beyond the "strict confines of certain classes."[110] Yet as this form of "political democracy" became consolidated, the problems facing political life radically expanded: "The problems of government have grown so enormously that sometimes one begins to wonder whether the normal parliamentary procedures are adequate to deal with them."[111]

The inherited conception of the legislative power pertained to the "police State," whereas in the twentieth century, especially for the postcolonial world, the function of government had now been redefined by the urgent tasks of "economic democracy." The foundation of a new society and a new economic order required a strong executive and an active people, leaving the legislature, as Udit Bhatia argues, with only the sec-

ondary responsibilities of cultivating the right political ethos and deliberative culture. For Nehru as for a great many of his contemporaries, the
role of the legislative body now mostly involved "political education"
rather than social transformation per se.[112] To be clear, beyond the pedagogic hierarchy of the representative-educator and the representative-
pupil, the Indian founders also underscored the participatory value of
universal suffrage.[113] The pedagogical resignification of the legislative
nevertheless signaled the coming of an era of universal suffrage that was
less defined by its command over lawmaking. What is more, Nehru also
read a Gandhi-inflected ethos of peaceful "self-discipline" into representative democracy. In empowering the individual, universal suffrage, Nehru
argued, encourages citizens to assume responsibility for themselves.[114]

At the moment of its triumph in India, then, universal suffrage was
understood in a way distinct from the transformative power once associated with it. Beyond the abstract affirmation of popular sovereignty
as a juridical principle, the value of universal suffrage now resided in its
facilitation of a "gradually increasing measure of economic democracy."[115] The issue at stake was not whether universal suffrage enforced
a certain form of popular control over the parliamentary wing of the government (which it did), but instead the role of the parliament itself.
Given the projection that popular sovereignty proper would arrive only
in a developed society of the future, universal suffrage assumed the role
of a moral compass for the developmental journey. Prior to the full development of now formal citizens into (a socially free) people, universal
suffrage was to be as much a vindication of "political democracy" as a
clarion call for attending to the still more urgent project of "economic
democracy."[116]

Throughout his post-independence writings and speeches, Nehru
would repeatedly return to the main challenge facing the postcolonial
state: the problem of the underdeveloped people. While he was seeking
to fashion the future in terms inherited from the colonial age, the masses
learned to exercise and channel new forms of power thanks to the institution of universal suffrage and electoral democracy.[117] The order that
Nehru wanted to maintain until the arrival of the age of abundance
would be disrupted by the postcolonial present. The apparent slow pace
of development—and the rapid dissolution of the promise of social
freedom into mundane governmentality—would radically problematize

the Nehruvian developmental regime. I will have more to say about this in the Conclusion of this book. Meanwhile, the postwar ideal of self-determination—influenced, in part, by the redefinition of independence by globally connected anticolonial thinkers such as Nehru—had brought the problem of economic development within its conceptual scope.[118]

CONCLUSION

In his coauthored book *India and Democracy* (1941), the British historian Guy Wint—not unsympathetic to the Indian cause—concocted an argument for independence through the voice of an imaginary Indian political thinker of the nineteenth-century mold. Ventriloquizing the Indian thinker, Wint wrote that "progress and parliamentary government are one and the same." The British and their Indian adversaries agreed on this point. The only difference was with regard to "the pace of advance."[119] In Wint's telling, the anticolonial pursuit of political freedom was not a dispute over the ideal; it only concerned the time of progress to that ideal. In fact, as Stuart Ward has argued, the advent of the discourse of "decolonization" in Europe pertained to the "rationalization" of the loss of empire.[120] By rendering postcolonial foundings as an expansion of European ideals, the political loss of colonies came to be synonymous with the intellectual conquest of European empires. The basic premise of Wint's argument continues to inform the dominant understanding of postcolonial independence and the attendant democratic founding. As we have seen in the section on self-determination, the international origin narrative of anticolonial sovereignty assumed that universalization of the right to self-determination resolved—or could resolve—the democratic legitimation of imperial subjection. The explanation of postcolonial founding as a gradual expansion of the universal ideal of free and sovereign statehood elides how the ideal itself had become contaminated by developmentalism in the wake of modern colonialism. The mere negation of colonial rule appeared to anticolonial thinkers themselves as normatively inadequate (even if indispensable) and not equivalent to democratic founding.

Instead, the question of democratic founding came to be inseparable from the problem of peoplehood, as developmentalism drove a wedge between the norm and the fact of democracy in the colonial world. The question inherited from the nineteenth century continued to resonate in late colonial India: Can India be democratic if the vast majority of its people are socially deprived, splintered, illiterate, and even unaware of the fact that they are the source of sovereignty? Through a new reading of Jawaharlal Nehru's political thought, I have in this chapter contended that the demand for independence acquired urgency only when anticolonial sovereignty could be reimagined as an accelerated path to a democracy yet to fully arrive. Postcolonial founding, therefore, was not merely an extension or belated realization of the universal ideal of independence. It is instead better understood as an inauguration of a new chapter in the history of modern democracy.

The messy—or even mundane—proliferation of democratic institutions and practices in the early postcolonial world were never quite removed from the philosophical weight of the grounding principle, popular sovereignty. If the concomitant aspiration to exercise sovereign will over the time of development was utopian, it "lived off," to quote Reinhart Koselleck, "points of connection not only in the realm of the fictive but in the empirically redeemable present."[121] As my reading of Nehru has suggested, the utopia of "real political freedom"—freed of social unfreedom—was squarely grounded on the figure of the destitute masses. In the founding narrative, the people thus appeared as the source of sovereignty who authorized the pursuit of "rapid progress" by the planning state. The source of authorization for this founding—the deprived masses—granted sovereignty to a developmental state that would not merely translate or represent its will; it would also work as an agent for the transformation of the people. In an apt summary of Nehruvian democracy, Sudipta Kaviraj noted that the postcolonial rulers operated with "a strong distinction between the state and the society it governed precisely to view the state as an instrumentality, rather than as an organic growth that should reflect society's cultural habits."[122] What this reading of Nehru shows is that the extraordinary power ascribed to the state stemmed not from any particular normative theory of statism but from the way in which it was positioned vis-à-vis the problem of peoplehood. This was further enabled by Nehru's break from the nineteenth-century view that the government should reflect the "advanced" section (who Naoroji and Banerjea characterized as "natural leaders" of the people) of the society—a natural mediator between the state and the society. Instead, Nehru sought the postcolonial state—its reliance on the rule of experts notwithstanding—to develop an "organic link" with the future lying outside of the existing social. The still-unfolding history of postcolonial democracy bears witness to the dilemma of turning democracy into a vehicle to an abundant future. The postcolonial wager for democracy was, and still is, a great experiment—a fraught bargain with the future.

My discussion so far has bracketed the most immediate consequence of Nehru's case for founding: the contentious struggle over the boundary of Indian peoplehood. I noted earlier in the chapter that Nehru's planning state—thanks to its self-understood objective to mediate between the eras of underdeveloped and developed peoplehood—generated its own constraints. The planning state's eagle-eyed focus on temporality rendered it particularly unsuited to reckon with the increasingly autonomous boundary problem of Indian peoplehood. Just when sovereignty over the time of development acquired urgency, it also subsumed the question of popular unity. Nehru's case for popular unity was no longer premised on the mere expectation that a developed people must be united. It had instead turned into a prior condition for instituting a centralized planning state. The narrative of accelerated transition to popular sovereignty was countered by Ambedkar's cautionary account of a people destined to dissolve into a splintered social. And M. A. Jinnah would go so far as to turn the premise of majoritarianism against the project of postcolonial founding itself. In Chapter 6 we will delve deep into the questions of the boundary problem and popular unity in the age of postcolonial founding.

THE TWO TIMES OF THE PEOPLE

The Boundary Problem, or the Burden of Unity

AS THE PROJECT of postcolonial founding took concrete shape, Indian political life turned decisively inward. At the very moment the ideal of independence emerged from the slumber that was its long-deferred future, the central preoccupations of Indian political life shifted away from intermittent confrontations with the British Empire to what appeared to be an increasingly irresolvable conflict between its two main religious communities. In the final decade of the Raj, India's British rulers, too, began to transition into the role of impatient mediators-in-chief between different Indian groups. This metamorphosis, on the British side, was as much triggered by the mounting pressure of anticolonial movements as it was forced by the intellectual exhaustion of the nineteenth-century democratic legitimation of empire. Yet, with the looming exit of the imperial sovereign, the long-groomed popular sovereign found itself not so much deferred as split from within.

It would not be an overstatement to say that the problem of popular unity was bursting at its seams in the years preceding India's independence. The long history of reckoning with the other problem of peoplehood—that is, the question of underdevelopment and the related doubt concerning democratic fitness—ceded center stage to the boundary problem at India's founding. By "boundary problem" I mean not simply the problem of drawing an external border of the political community, but, more generally, as Frederick Whelan specified, the problem of defining the "membership of the democratic body, or citizenry."[1] India's struggle with this eminently democratic problem intellectually manifested in the extraordinary purchase of the category of "nation" in those years. The challenge of developing the masses into a people capable of living up to the demands of democracy (including the condition of popular unity) had long guided Indian anticolonial politics. In contrast, the problem of adjudicating antagonistic claims of nationhood, inseparable as it was from the boundary problem, had seemingly begun to resist the developmental logic of growth and decay in the decades preceding India's Partition. The nation, at last, appeared to have subsumed the people. The shift of emphasis notwithstanding, the Indian Partition was not an exit from the problem of peoplehood; it was instead defined by a confrontation between competing conceptions of democratic peoplehood. In what follows, I trace how a dynamic tension between what one might call the two times of the people shaped the pursuit of unity and division in colonial India.

The dissolutions and schisms that consumed Indian political life had many actors and subplots, but the most significant one emerged by way of the face-off between the Indian National Congress (which adamantly claimed to speak for all Indians) and its long-dormant and only recently resurgent rival, the All-India Muslim League (which claimed to represent Indian Muslims and refused to accept the Congress's nonsectarian credentials). Their intractable political dispute came to stumble upon the boundary of the Indian nation. Take, for instance, this exchange between M. K. Gandhi, who was still the undisputed leader of the Congress, and Muhammad Ali Jinnah, the Bombay lawyer who had resurrected the League. In early 1940, Gandhi—philosophically distant from the new project of postcolonial founding but invested as ever in the question of Hindu-Muslim unity—wrote to congratulate Jinnah on the League's entry into a political alliance with a host of other political organizations, including the Hindu Mahasabha, in a variety of provincial governments. Gandhi's phrasings blurred the distinction between sincerity and irony—a mode of expression he was exceptionally adept at. In forming a coalition with non-Muslim groups, Gandhi wrote, Jinnah was "lifting the Muslim League out of the communal rut and giving it a national character."[2] The League's decision to share a platform with other groups opposed to the Congress implied that they had prioritized the political terms of alliance over sectarian differences. Such a political minority, Gandhi added, could one day become the political majority— a logic that amounted to an emphatic assertion of the "living unity of India."[3]

Jinnah, as usual, was not impressed by the subtle twists and turns of the Mahatma's arguments. He replied: "Your premises are wrong as you start with the theory of an Indian Nation that does not exist, and naturally, therefore, your conclusions are wrong."[4] The League might have accepted "strange bedfellows," but the fact remained that "India is not a nation, nor a country."[5] Elsewhere Jinnah claimed: "India is divided and partitioned by Nature. . . . Where is the nation which is denationalised? India is composed of nationalities, to say nothing about castes and subcastes."[6] For almost a century, Indians had struggled to answer questions concerning their fitness for self-rule as a people, including their standing as a unified people or a nation. The two times of the people—the one pertaining to their political fitness for self-rule, the other concerning the prior unity supposedly required for representative government in the face of a sneering colonial officialdom ever ready to underscore differences of language, religion, and caste—had raised different questions that Indians nevertheless sought to meld into the broader developmental project. As the Gandhi-Jinnah exchange shows, this was no longer the case in 1940s India. Now the two times of the people pulled in opposite directions. In fact, the premises of historical development and popular unity had come to a head and forced a choice for those who had embraced the tension as much as those who had denied its validity.

In the nineteenth century, when the developmental turn was at its peak, the tangible qualities of peoplehood—citizenship, political will, and institutional capacities—were more easily given a historical character. But the seemingly intangible fact of common bond defied the easy gloss of historical development and already raised intractable questions about the role of history in forging political belonging. The boundary of peoplehood involves a host of issues that are neither merely pre-political nor easily amenable to the willful work of politics: language, territoriality, religion, and, above all, the undefinable sentiment of common belonging. Considering the varying significance of these elements, John Stuart Mill concluded in the mid-nineteenth century that "none of these circumstances [race, religion, common history of political rule, etc.] however are either indispensable, or necessarily sufficient by themselves."[7] For every example of a nation springing out of ethnic, religious, or territorial homogeneity, there were always counterexamples. For instance, democratic Switzerland had been cobbled together from linguistically and ethnically different peoples, and nineteenth-century Italy found itself united despite the widely different historical experiences of its disparate lands.

If anything, Ernest Renan's oft-repeated 1882 observation that nations are defined more by forgetfulness than by memory was an apt recapitulation of the intellectual deadlock the question of nationality produced in the era. This difficulty of pinpointing the source of nationality was known to European and Indian thinkers alike.[8] Perhaps even more than their European counterparts, nineteenth-century Indian thinkers approached the question of nationality in close reference to the boundary of peoplehood. After all, one central feature of the modern self-discovery of India was its dizzying diversity. Not the pride of unity but the embarrassment of deep plurality mediated India's entrance into the democratic age. How to forge a bounded people out of heterogeneous communities was a founding question for modern Indian political thought. Though the progress of history was no sure guide to political unity, many nineteenth-century thinkers—Indian and British—hoped that the crucible of imperial subjection would eventually mold Indians into a united people. As Surendranath Banerjea put it: The mission of British rule was to "save, regenerate, emancipate from the chains of ignorance, error, and superstition ... 150 millions [sic] of human beings ... to reconcile the jarring conflicts of diverse Indian nationalities, to bring them together ... into a compact and homogeneous mass."[9]

The ambiguities of the boundary problem have not become any clearer following the manifold democratic experiences of the twentieth century, nor has the reliance on history disappeared. As Sofia Näsström notes, "who gets to be included in the people is not a democratic but a historical question" for most democratic theorists.[10] The point of this is not a surrender to the historically inherited boundary of the people (most contemporary theorists seek to bring it into the fold of legitimation, whether retroactively or not), but the apparent fact that the starting point for approaching the question of who the people are—as opposed to what the people is—is usually a product of contingent history. Habermas's observation is very much on point here: "Who gains the power to define the boundaries of a political community is settled by historical chance and the actual course of events—normally, by the arbitrary outcomes of wars and civil wars."[11] Addressing this problem of inherited political belongings in modern political life, Bernard Yack thus proposed that the conceptual labor of the nation is oriented to offering a temporal answer to who the people are—a question that the atemporal and "spatial" definition of the people cannot quite account for.[12] As I noted earlier contra Yack, the question of peoplehood in the global nineteenth and twentieth centuries was mired in temporal reasoning and expectations. The problem of the nation (and its constitutive boundary problem), too, was entangled in the developmental paradigm. The key difference concerned the extent to which nationalities could be willfully developed, in contrast to more historically pliant problems such as the social and moral condition of the masses. Less a dispute between the space and time of political community, the boundary problem, as we shall see, staged a confrontation between the two times of the people in the age of democracy's global expansion.

What rendered the Hindu-Muslim conflict a uniquely democratic problem in decades preceding Partition was the question of majoritarianism, a question that took shape under the developmental weight of the social question. To be sure, the rise of popular sovereignty in the early modern era had self-consciously accompanied a normative defense of the majority principle. As Richard Tuck puts it in reference to early modern theories of popular sovereignty: "the formation of a people immediately and necessarily implied a commitment to majoritarianism."[13] The germane philosophical claim of the majority principle was never quite sufficient to assuage the fear of majoritarianism. The eighteenth-century concern with the domination of the majority—as exemplified by James Madison, among others—centered on mitigating the risk of the factional capture of political institutions. Nineteenth-century preoccupations with majoritarianism had a different emphasis, at least if we consider two of the century's most influential democratic thinkers, Alexis de Tocqueville and John Stuart Mill. In reframing majoritarian domination in terms of the social question, they expanded its scope beyond the register of the separation of powers. Insofar as majoritarianism is a "problem of society, not of government," it required—Tocqueville argued—more than an institutional resolution.[14] This was also the reason Mill put so much weight on the advanced social conditions required for democratic rule. Mill did seriously explore institutional avenues for regulating majoritarianism, but what he was aiming at was restraining the political effect of the social rise of the masses (while also seeking to regulate their social progress through political institutions). Though familiar with the raging Euro-American concern with majoritarianism, nineteenth-century Indian thinkers had a completely different priority: to develop a majority commensurate with the time of democracy, rather than restrain majoritarian power. They certainly aspired to a future unity of the people, and they also hoped to reform the sectarian practices of the social majority. But priorities such as economic development and education also figured as preconditions of forging unity among Indians.

It was the founding of the Muslim League in 1906—and the institution of the separate electorate in 1909, which allowed Muslims to vote as a religious community—that turned the question of majoritarian domination into a permanent fixture of Indian political life. Nevertheless, as long as the monist people remained a distant horizon, the politics of the majority and the minority could compete in the relatively pluralistic space of empire without giving up on the hope of a future unity. It was only when a meaningful program for democratic founding emerged with Nehru that the question of majoritarianism moved swiftly to the center of Indian political life. At the same time, the global discovery in the interwar era of the reality that the progressive ethos of citizenship was no guard against the essentialism of race and religion— from Nazi Germany to India itself—gave credence to political agendas centered on resisting the upper-caste basis of Indian politics, from the Self-Respect Movement in the south to Ambedkar's Scheduled Castes Federation. In this new global context where the question of the minority was becoming the burning question of the era, Nehru's call for immediate independence—what he called the "here and now" necessity to sever the imperial bond[15]—had the paradoxical effect of accentuating the fault lines of the anticolonial movement. As we saw in Chapter 5, the postcolonial founding could not wait because the resolution of the problem of peoplehood required an acceleration of the development process. The urgency generated by this proposal affected not just the anticolonial cause but also the long-brewing problem of majoritarianism.

The most vocal critic of majoritarianism was Jinnah, once a reliably moderate member of the Congress and now the towering leader of the League.[16] The meaning of democratic founding in a backward nation was clear to Jinnah: the majority Hindu masses, he believed, would prioritize their communal interests and instrumentalize the postcolonial state for their own benefit. The "ignorant" and "untutored" majority of the Indian masses—he was convinced—would translate their "communal majority" into a "political majority."[17] Nehru's unduly optimistic, competing account of majoritarianism, in contrast, spoke past this developmentally deterministic account. Nehru was confident that the masses, precisely because of their underdevelopment, would ultimately align themselves along economic lines rather than religious ones.[18] Both of these contending arguments, in other words, were built on developmental assumptions. As independence became a palpable possibility, the choice in front of the leaders of the Indian independence movement collapsed into two extremes: the distribution of governmental power across strong provincial centers (which would have counteracted majoritarianism but weakened the guiding hand of the planning state) or a partition of the people so that the two different communities of India could be fully sovereign in their own realms. Before founding proper, popular unity had turned into a burden, forcing a choice between a divided people and weak sovereignty of the central state.

Although the Muslim League politically led the charge on the basis of the centralization of the boundary problem, the most profound intellectual work on the question came from the Dalit thinker Bhimrao Ramji Ambedkar, who was then the convener of India's premier Dalit association, the Scheduled Castes Federation. Through the lens of the boundary problem, the chapter also analyzes the implications of Ambedkar's critique of caste for the broader problem of Indian peoplehood. Standing politically distant from the Congress and the League, his investigation of the boundary problem—querying whether Indians shared enough in common to be considered a united people—remains the most powerful perspective on the bloody confrontation between the two times of the people in 1940s India. As the author of *Pakistan or the Partition of India*,

Ambedkar explored the problem in terms of the Hindu-Muslim question in an age when claims staked in one time of the people demanded a sacrifice from the other. His life's work, however, was focused on the caste question and its role in shaping the Indian social. This split character of the caste-centric social, Ambedkar argued, undermined the capacity of the Indian people to act as a cohesive political entity. Thanks to his keen awareness of the limits of the "economic interpretation of history," Ambedkar, as we shall see, went further than most in decoupling developmental progress from popular unity. The hierarchies intrinsic to the social, he prophesized, would reproduce themselves politically in the new state. For Ambedkar, the interdependence between the two times of the people necessitated a more robust vision of founding than what Nehru and the Congress had offered. With regard to the Muslim question, however, Ambedkar made a case for conceding the boundary problem and even the schemes of population transfer. At the same time, his recognition of the irreducibility of the two times of the people—especially when articulated vis-à-vis the caste question—led to the perspicacious conclusion that the boundary of peoplehood must be brought from its pre-political antechamber to an open stage of political life.

UNITY THROUGH DIVISION: MAJORITARIANISM IN THE ANTICOLONIAL AGE

There was a certain dilemma built into the British promise to prepare India for future self-government. As shown in Chapters 1 and 2, British rule came to ascribe its own validity to the eventual creation of a democratic people in India. Yet any declaration of the fulfillment of the developmental project undermined the very premise that legitimated foreign rule. Empire was supposed to be time-bound, but time itself moved rather slowly in the imperial imagination. The dutiful reports of the colonial administration on the "moral and material progress" of the Indian people operated under the assumption that the attributes of popular unfitness (illiteracy, poverty, sectarian ethos, and so on) would be overcome in a distant future. Where the British let their imagination range more freely was on the question of Indian nationality. That British rule was generating nationality in India was a claim that administrators and philosophers alike could indulge in without endangering the present. After all, if situated against the backdrop of the European democratic experience, the diversity of the Indian masses, from regions and religions to languages and castes, appeared to be astoundingly fissiparous. Reflections on the plurality of India, then, also doubled as a charge—that India was too heterogeneous to lay claim to modern nationhood. A text no less influential than J. R. Seeley's *Expansion of England* based its entire study of the "Indian Empire" on the question of absent Indian nationhood. Though Seeley's text was the most influential statement on the topic, diagnoses of India's absent sense of nationality abounded by the mid-nineteenth century.

"It is a mere European prejudice," Seely wrote in an arresting passage, "that since we do not rule *by* the will of the people of India, we must needs rule *against* their will."[19] The presence of certain "special" unity among the people of European nations such as England and France had generated the expectation that it was a universal feature of all peoples. Yet when applied to India, it amounted to nothing short of a "vulgar error."[20] Seeley's observation that the sociological features of India befitted more a continent than a nation was not exceptional, nor was his diagnosis that the absence of popular unity was related to the lack of democratic virtue: "Of liberty, of popular institutions, there exists scarcely a trace in the whole extent of Indian history or tradition."[21] He was also not breaking any new ground in approaching India as a nation-in-waiting. Rather, Seeley's most crucial departure from the older benchmark established by Macaulay and Mill concerned the standard of nationality. Whereas Macaulay or Mill would posit the fitness for self-government to be the criterion for Indian independence, Seeley's post-liberal-imperialist account posited a less morally burdened test. If India ever showed the signs of being the nation that many Europeans imagined it to be, Seeley famously observed, "we should recognise perforce the impossibility of retaining her."[22]

Even as India was still far from the horizon of nationalism, some germs of a future nationality could already be observed. If anything was bringing India together and transforming it into a "single national whole," Seeley argued, it was British rule itself.[23] This contribution of the British was also something that nineteenth-century Indian thinkers found easier to acknowledge. Surendranath Banerjea's observation on the

British-mediated formation of Indian nationhood, which I noted earlier, was fairly commonplace. A thinker no less than (post-Swadeshi) Bipin Chandra Pal—after having lost all faith in the colonial administration—could still observe as late as 1910 that "the greatest work that England had done in India, namely, the quickening of national self-consciousness in the people . . . English education, British laws and methods of administration, increased facilities of intercommunication,—had created [nationalism] in the country."[24]

So even as a people fit for democracy still seemed wanting, the nation was already declaring its arrival. However, as we saw in Chapter 3, the Swadeshi era, for all its so-called cultural nationalism, did not find the criterion of nationality to be a sufficient answer to the problem of peoplehood. What it had laid the foundation for was a way of thinking about nationality that did not need to be governed by the developmental logic of the social. From this period onward the two times of the people assumed different trajectories. One relevant example here is C. F. Andrews's 1920 pamphlet *Indian Independence: The Immediate Need,* which Nehru credited as an inspiration in his own journey toward independence. Andrews's text, Nehru noted, had none of the economic critique of empire that appealed to his own interests—it was "nationalism pure and simple." And yet Nehru found it to reflect "the inmost recesses of our hearts," giving an expression to the "half-formed desires" for independence.[25] Andrews's version of (Indian) "nationalism pure and simple," it turned out, was conceived on exactly the terms set by Seeley. He singled out select elements of Seeley's account—such as "[With] the expression of a universal feeling of nationality, at that moment all hope is at an end, as all desire ought to be at an end, of preserving our Empire"—to argue that such a desire could now be found in India, thanks to the dynamic influence of Gandhi.[26]

Andrews's gloss on Seeley was a creative, but not an exceptional, case for Indian independence on the premise of its nationhood. The discovery of the affective—and cultural—dimension of the political community, related to and yet independent of the demands of "larger and heavier responsibilities of free citizenship,"[27] had been flourishing since the Swadeshi movement. The resignification of the (Hindu) "old symbolism and ritualism of the people" as a well-spring of civil spirit had allowed for the possibility of affirming political unity.[28] It would not take long for leaders such as Pal to find out that the turn to the "old symbolism" of the masses divided the people as much as it united.[29] As the search for an affective basis of national unity—wittingly or unwittingly—stumbled on India's religious difference, the Muslim past of India figured as the source of its cultural as well as historical problems. When late nineteenth-century Hindu thinkers tried to make sense of what had made India stagnant in an era of European progressive dynamism, they often ended up holding the long history of Muslim rule responsible for the stagnation.[30] More than any mere disagreement with the ruling philosophy of the Muslim era, it was the purported stagnation of India under Muslim rule that turned the Muslim community itself into an embodiment of the medieval.

All this was taking place as political demands and aspirations were being articulated within the institutional order of the empire. Though the long-term vision was already set on a developmental commingling of the people into one cohesive entity, the diffused and overlapping jurisdiction of the empire facilitated forms of politics that otherwise would not have seamlessly fit with the ideals of modern peoplehood. The much-debated institution of the separate electorate in the post-Swadeshi era, for instance, operated in an imperial order of representation where communities, rather than the people, had juridical existence. Of course, the electoral reforms of 1909 and their undermining of the principle of numerical majority alarmed many Congress leaders. Still, as the veteran Congress leader Gopal Krishna Gokhale, despite sharing the objections to the separate electorate, reminded his colleagues: given the mere advisory role of the Legislative Council, "how many members were returned by any particular community was not of much consequence."[31] What really mattered was that those members had the "capacity" and "spirit" to serve as the "trustees" of the people.[32] This was also the era when the critique of representative democracy influenced many in the anticolonial movement. As we saw in Chapter 4, the framework of pluralist federalism offered a glimpse of an alternative to the already tiresome dialectic of (popular) unity and division in the post–World War I era. Gandhi's embracing of the Khilafat cause in the 1920s introduced a powerful ethical orientation to the Hindu-Muslim question. Before his new project of founding crystallized, even Nehru was open to the possibility that a form of self-rule that respected the demands of different communities would be preferable to "majority rule."[33] These floating alternatives to a strict requirement for national unity notwithstanding, the search for unity in the "old symbolism and ritualism of the people" developed in a steady stream throughout the interwar era. It did not require much ingenuity for organizations such as the Hindu Mahasabha to eventually reduce the very question of bounded peoplehood to an ahistorical narrative of a perennial fissure between Hindus and Muslims.

The collapse of the nationalism question into political majoritarianism quickly took place after Nehru's new synthesis of the two times of the people set the political agenda. Nehru's Marxisant faith in the primacy of the economic made him somewhat inattentive to the growing autonomy acquired by the culturalist imagination of the nation during this time. The affective register may not have offered an adequate answer to the problem of peoplehood, but it did allow for ways of conceiving Indian nationhood without the gradualist banister of developmentalism. In fact, the imagination of national oneness now meant a story of Indian division as much as anti-imperial unity: Hindu majoritarian organizations had, by then, transformed the question of unity into one of addressing the problem of internal others—above all, Indian Muslims. This also made it easy for minority groups like the League to conclude that independence would mean the consolidation of the power of the Hindu majority. The reframing of the question of national unity amid the anticolonial urgency of the interwar era in effect drove a wedge between the two times of the people. To be anti-British was no longer an answer to the internal fissures of Indians themselves. To be anti-majoritarian, on the other hand, cut against the pursuit of immediate independence. The traditional response to majoritarianism—the so-called constitutional safeguards—posed a uniquely political problem in 1940s India: it brought the British into play and rendered independence conditional on agreements between different communities. Nehru was quick to underscore this dynamic of anti-majoritarian politics, never failing to point out that the primacy given to the demand for various constitutional safeguards was delaying India's sovereign new beginning.

Nehru's answer was more than a call for national unity: he wanted to subsume the problem of popular unity into the broader agenda of economic development. He seemed to have genuinely believed that the importance of religion as a source of political identity would "soon disappear, or at any rate cease to have any political significance."[34] He was confident that if "the Muslim masses are consulted, they will lay far more stress on economic demands."[35] He asserted that the substantive basis of political unity—which could only emerge after a renewed "ideological fusion of Hindu, Muslim, Sikh and other groups in India"—would eventually develop "from below." It was for this reason, in Nehru's view, that the political agendas that solely focused on instituting safeguards for the religious minority missed the properly modern notion of the majority and the minority: the one based on the economic problem. Channeling his accelerationist vision, Nehru prognosticated that a dynamic interaction of "social and economic forces . . . will inevitably bring other problems to the front. They will create cleavages along different lines, but communal cleavage will go."[36]

Nehru tried to supplement this accelerationist vision with a competing account of the fundamental "cultural" unity across India's historical and geographical differences.[37] The plural and "tolerant" culture of India—he argued in a language evocative of Bergson[38]—assimilated many groups and religions, laying the foundation for its political unity. The long-winded, restless narrative of *Discovery of India* bears witness to how consumed he was by this question. Like many of his contemporaries in the decade prior to independence, Nehru ransacked the archives of the Indian past to find sources of Indian unity, even as he simultaneously denied the salience of cultural unity when isolated from the social question. If the Bergsonian language of creative assimilation helped Nehru to articulate the cultural oneness of India, it could also be conscripted easily to defend—as Muhmmad Iqbal did—an ontologically pluralist vision.[39] Indeed, insofar as political contestation over the cultural unity of the nation was concerned, the case for Indian unity could be forged as persuasively as the case for its disunity. Nehru's story of Indian unity, though by no means devoid of imagination, was neither new nor particularly effective in 1940s India.

Ultimately, however, the importance of political unity for Nehru resided in his understanding that it could not be practically separated from a true project of postcolonial development. For Nehru, the division of sovereignty between Hindus and Muslims would result in a weak centralized state with little power for organizing large-scale developmental projects. If sovereignty was divided, there would not only be "perpetual conflict but all planned economic and cultural progress would become impossible."[40] Nehru liked to remind his readers that the two ideals guiding the movement for Indian independence were democracy and unity.[41] Representing the two times of the people, unity and democracy came to be entangled in a difficult knot. The price of unity was a decentralized weak state, whereas the fulfillment of a developmentalist state potentially demanded the splitting of the Indian people.

For those opposed to Nehru and the Congress, the idea of national unity, at that time, was becoming increasingly indistinguishable from majoritarianism. Although Jinnah would later become emphatic in his affirmation of a natural fact of "two nations" in India,[42] his turn to the Pakistan project was propelled in no small part by a reckoning with the problem of (majoritarian) democracy *for* a backward people. Jinnah made no secret of the point that the core of the political antagonism between the Muslim League and the Congress concerned the question of "democracy in its strict application."[43] For representative democracy to work for everyone, Jinnah observed, the majority and the minority should be "alterable." In Jinnah's view, Indians—long beholden to the framework of British parliamentarism—had not realized the inapplicability of the social conditions of British democracy in their own backward country.[44] Because the nature of the majority was not plastic in India, "democracy" (i.e., majoritarian rule) was a "dead" system for India's Muslim minorities.[45]

Jinnah concluded that democracy was an unviable model for India, but not primarily because of any inherent limits of the model of representative government. It could be suitable for a "single nation" that was "harmonious and homogeneous."[46] The question of the people, once again, was the ground on which the argument turned. The source of the problem lay with the state of the Hindu masses—the "brute majority"[47]—themselves: "Having regard to the 35 millions of voters, the bulk of whom are totally ignorant, illiterate and untutored, living in centuries-old superstitions of the worst type, thoroughly antagonistic to each other, culturally and socially, the working of this constitution has clearly brought out that it is impossible to work a democratic parliamentary government in India."[48] In a republic predominantly composed of the underdeveloped masses, the elasticity and open-endedness presupposed by parliamentary democracy would be absent, and thus the only majority existing there would be a "permanent communal majority."[49] He had no qualms about chiding the British for forgetting the history of their own religious wars, a history that remained applicable to backward India.[50] When religion is reduced to a matter of private practice (as was the British inclination), it may seem superficial to the germane questions of peoplehood. But, Jinnah continued, the stake of the religion question in India consisted in the fact that "Hinduism and Islam . . . are definite social codes which govern not so much man's relation with his God as man's relation with his neighbour."[51] The religious difference, then, was inseparable from the social question. They were not simply inseparable because of their function as "social codes." The underdeveloped state of the masses directly reinforced the power of these codes. Jinnah was thus convinced that the line of division in India was going to be "horizontal" rather than "vertical."[52] As Faisal Devji has argued in his study of Pakistan, the Muslim League's argument for a separate state was partly based on the "problem of numbers," not least the assumption that "largely illiterate and superstitious" people of India would be unable to rise beyond their particularity and would ultimately reinforce a communal majoritarianism.[53]

This fundamental doubt about the plausibility of representative democracy in India underpinned Jinnah's rejection of Indian unity and his turn to the two-nation theory. Though Indian Muslims were scattered all over the subcontinent and differentiated by all sorts of ethnic and linguistic markers, for Jinnah they were "not a minority but a nation."[54] Jinnah was perfectly capable of characterizing the difference between Hindus and Muslims in essentialist terms. For instance, in response to the London Times's observation that "Indians will [eventually] be moulded into a single nation," he argued that if a thousand years' close contact had not unified them, a future independent republic would also certainly fail to do so.[55] Between Nehru's passionate narrative of Indian unity and Jinnah's plain rejection of its past (and future) existence, perhaps no arbitration was rationally possible. But it would be a mistake to locate Jinnah's case for Pakistan in the facticity of the Indian past. His arguments for a separate nationhood of Indian Muslims often invoked a claim regarding their "future destiny."[56] What united the past and future of the Muslim minority, however, was the old problem of developmentalism. Jinnah presented Indian Muslims as a numerical minority who were "educationally backward, and economically nowhere," and squarely connected the prospect of the development of the Muslim masses to the demand of Pakistan.[57] Interestingly, one of the common elements of the Congress's charge against Jinnah was that he was standing in the way of the "progress" of the Indian people by delaying the negotiations over independence. Jinnah, on his part, emphatically returned the change: the Congress's refusal to concede Muslim autonomy made them "wholly responsible for blocking the progress of India."[58] The debate over majoritarianism thus found itself mired in the problem concerning the "speed of the progress."[59] For Jinnah, to separate from the Hindu masses was also to develop the social and political conditions of the Muslim masses. By the same token, it meant a liberation from the burden of India's divided past. The Pakistan movement's claim of sovereignty over the Muslim minorities was, then, also inflected by a desire to assert sovereignty over the time of their development.

The relative autonomy once acquired by the nation question crumbled under the normative weight of majoritarianism: If Nehru posited the unity of the people as a whole to be the prior condition of postcolonial sovereignty, Jinnah found it to be the usurper of the political sovereignty of the minority in an all-Indian context. These different approaches to the question of majoritarianism came to a head in the 1940s especially because the political orientations Nehru and Jinnah represented both had a shared faith in centralized sovereignty. The irony of this fateful dissensus between Nehru and Jinnah lay in the fact that neither disagreed with the developmental essence of postcolonial sovereignty. Nor did Jinnah have any essential objection to the majoritarian principle as long as both Hindus and Muslims could form the majority in their respective domains. It is owing to this reason that the boundary of the people turned into a problem requiring resolution prior to postcolonial founding so as to offer a free passage to postcolonial development. By separating the time of the bounded people from that of economic and social development, the collision between the two times of the people had to be forestalled. Precisely for this reason, what Partition involved was not primarily a territorial division. It required a still more foundational partition of the people.

Unable to reconcile, the Muslim League and the Congress confronted each other throughout the 1940s over a variety of byzantine schemes of power sharing, poorly umpired by the jaded British. The resultant haggling and bartering of politicians in drawing rooms over all

manner of schemes was perhaps an odd finale to an anticolonial movement that had been forged in the fire of mass mobilization. This episode
of Indian anticolonial history, centered on the mad rush of negotiations
between the Congress and the League, has since enveloped narratives of
India's Partition in an aura of counterfactual possibilities. To an extent,
the territorial and institutional outline of independent South Asia could
easily have taken a different shape. That the prior boundary problem of
peoplehood had presented too foundational a deadlock for mere diplo-
matic negotiations to resolve remains inadequately appreciated. As it
turned out, the project of accelerating mass development and the efforts
to forestall the dangers of majoritarianism pulled in opposite directions.
Ultimately, Jinnah and his League were not the only ones arguing for
a necessary relationship between division and unity. The triumph of
the boundary problem would also manifest in the recalibration of the
political rhetoric of the Indian National Congress, especially by figures
such as Sardar Patel. As Shruti Kapila argues in reference to Patel, the
act of fratricidal confrontation became one with the institution of a
"unitary" vision of popular sovereignty.[60] What necessitated unity also
forced division.

Historians of modern India have written a great deal on the colonial origins of Hindu-Muslim conflict. Studies of the role of the epistemic hierarchy of sentiments and reasons in constructing communal
identities, as well as the transformation of "fuzzy boundaries" into a
hardened boundary through techniques of modern governmentality,
have moved the understanding of India's communal conflict beyond the
tenacious hold of the "divide-and-rule" framework.[61] The making of the
territorial imagination of India has also received substantive treatment.[62]
From within the world of political thought, what particularly stands
out is that the confrontation between the Congress and the League, and
the growing rift between Hindus and Muslims, sharply exemplified
a problem that was constitutive of majoritarianism in the age of democracy's global expansion. The numerical majoritarianism of modern
politics could inspire unity as much as disunity: narratives of India's
popular unity were no less incoherent than those of its essential disunity.
As we have seen, the political difficulty of the problem of majoritarianism
at India's founding could not be separated from the parallel problem of
developing the people. The established measures generally understood

to constitute a restraining check on the majority will, such as the separation of powers, were rejected as inadequate not simply because of their own normative limits. Rather, the developmental knot between the social question and political majoritarianism spliced the figure of the people into two irreparable fragments. Popular unity, even at the cost of dividing the people, appeared to be so essential because of its purported role in facilitating sovereignty over the time of development. For this reason, the ideal of popular unity weighed heavier in colonial India, compounding as it did the inescapable problem of majoritarianism in modern democracies.

The Hindu–Muslim conflict, however, was not the only site of the boundary problem. The question of caste was another fault line, one that caused an even greater dismay about the future of popular unity. In the following section, I turn to the political thought of B. R. Ambedkar. Ambedkar was not entirely distant from the range of arguments I have considered above; in fact, he helped popularize some of them. What makes his reflections on the topic particularly powerful—beyond his analysis of the caste question—is the keen attention he paid to the difficult problem of rendering the boundary problem into a politically contestable problem.

AMBEDKAR, THE SOCIAL QUESTION, AND THE BOUNDARY PROBLEM

"Indians are not a nation," noted Ambedkar in his classic book *Annihilation of Caste,* "they are only an amorphous mass of people."[63] The Congress's relentless affirmation of Indian nationhood was rooted in the assumption that "nationality had a most intimate connection with the claim for self-government." In the modern era, a people without a claim to nationhood—Ambedkar noted, invoking H. G. Wells—was akin to a "man . . . without his clothes in a crowded assembly."[64] For all the doubt concerning Indian peoplehood, the affirmation of the Indian nation, as we saw, had become quite commonplace by the time Ambedkar came of age. He was critical of this conviction. Indians, he observed, never took a moment to ask if "nationality was merely a question of *calling* a people a nation or was a question of the people *being* a nation."[65] Ambedkar had no faith in essentialist conceptions of the nation. He noted elsewhere that words such as "nation" are necessarily "amorphous," and it was futile to look for an overarching sociological unity to define the category.[66] Instead, "nationality is a social feeling . . . it is a feeling of corporate sentiment of oneness."[67] In an unmistakably Deweyian vein,[68] Ambedkar suggested that what was at stake was not whether Indians had similar inheritances, but instead whether they "[possess] things in common, . . . and the only way by which men can come to possess things in common with one another is by being in communication."[69]

As the demand for independence intensified, Ambedkar launched a searching critique of the demos underlying the project of postcolonial founding. His renewed critique of Indian peoplehood followed the trail of the colonial history of the social, which he sought to both redefine and re-center. The normative touchstone of Ambedkar's reconsideration of the social question was the ideal of popular unity. He connected the disunity of India to the internal order of Hindu society, pushing back against the prevalent wisdom on Indian peoplehood—be it the Nehruvian anticipation of a national unity guaranteed by economic development or that of Nehru's Mahasabha critics, who argued India's nationhood was warranted by its hoary cultural inheritance. For Ambedkar, at the core of Hindu society—and in fact, Indian society at large—lay the caste system. As a fundamentally "antisocial" institution, it foreclosed the possibility of India "becoming a society with unified life and a consciousness of its own being."[70] The caste system formed a gradation of sovereignty and divided the social into fragments that resisted polarization. In such a society, the "parts" never become "one whole."[71] It is almost as though each caste is a "nation" itself.[72] Ambedkar suggested that the figure of the Brahmin was evocative of the Nietzschean superman, as members of the Brahmin caste enjoyed the superior right to live, rule, and fashion norms for the rest.[73] In the image of Nietzsche's proverbial superman, the Brahmin was incompatible with the modern ideals of "liberty, equality and fraternity." This is precisely why the institution of political sovereignty would only result in Hindu majoritarianism in free India. In concurring with Jinnah's conclusion, Ambedkar also implied that the prioritization of the time of development over that of the fragmented social was a self-defeating choice for the minorities.

Ambedkar moored his analysis of the caste system to the argument that political revolution without social revolution was meaningless, even dangerous. Presenting evidence from ancient Rome and ancient India, he contended that a political revolution would only accentuate the social discord. Given the fracture within, a nation made of castes could neither defend itself against aggressors nor lay the groundwork for unity. The social, as it were, was destined to determine the political. Ambedkar further contended that what the "politicals" did not realize was that "democracy [is] not a form of Government: it [is] essentially a form of society."[74] If a similar realization led the Jacobins to attempt to politically regenerate the torn social fabric,[75] Ambedkar was occasionally tempted to come to the opposite conclusion: to redeem the social before instituting political sovereignty. Unless "Hindu society becomes a casteless society," he concluded, political freedom would only be a "step towards slavery."[76]

Ambedkar was well familiar with contemporary scholarship on nationality, ranging from Ernest Renan to Arnold Toynbee. He agreed with Renan that nationality is more often a product of historical "forgetfulness" than of natal bonds.[77] Distinguishing "nationality" from "nationalism," Ambedkar also underscored that the presence of national "consciousness" does not always result in a demand for political sovereignty.[78] Regardless of the source of nationality, the "will to live as a nation," he concluded, was an essential requirement.[79] In his sympathetic study of the demand for Pakistan, Ambedkar emphasized the voluntary dimension of the nation more than the role of inherited conditions such as language and territory.[80] There was, however, a certain tension to this will-centric view of the nation. Whereas he found the will to live together to be sufficient for the legitimacy of the Pakistan demand, this condition turned out to be inadequate for the caste society. Absent a remaking of the Hindu social, no voluntary expression of unity would be sufficient. Indian Muslims could withdraw from the Hindu social, but Dalits had to work to transform and tame it from within.

In his voluminous writings from the 1930s and 1940s, Ambedkar would challenge again and again the identity assumed between the people and the nation, posing a new set of questions for the project of postcolonial founding. The theoretical handle for his intervention was the social question, whose contours had changed quite a bit between the age of Naoroji and that of Nehru. In nineteenth-century India, the social meant "social reform," the project of abrogating some of India's more iniquitous practices current in upper-caste households—child marriage, polygamy, the enforced celibacy of widows, and widespread prohibition on women's education all being common targets—in the name of a new, fairer society. The concern of "social reformers" with the treatment of women occasioned a great deal of debates and reflections in their own era: in fact, in the wake of the Ilbert Bill controversy in 1883, the arguments supporting the political unfitness of Indians, as Mrinalini Sinha has shown, took an increasingly gendered form.[81] The formation of the early Congress was very much against the backdrop of what Prathama Banerjee has aptly characterized as "the unhappy question of the social" in India, where "social reform" tended to take precedence over self-government.[82] As the Congress-led movement began to make claims for political participation, starting in the late nineteenth century, this order between the social and the political—we saw in Chapter 2—faced resistance. In the interwar era, as we saw in Chapter 5, the social question came more and more to refer to the economic condition of the masses. The older, nineteenth-century Indian meaning of the social, in contrast, would be consigned to the margins.

Revisiting the crucial decade of the 1890s, Ambedkar engaged in a revealing posthumous debate with W. C. Bonnerjee, the first president of the Congress. Speaking at the annual session of the Congress in 1892, Bonnerjee had questioned the disqualification of Indians from political office on the ground of their civilizational backwardness: "I for one have no patience with those who say we shall not be fit for political reform until we reform our social system. . . . Are we not fit because our widows remain unmarried, . . . because we do not send our daughters to Oxford and Cambridge?"[83] Some half a century later, Ambedkar returned the question to Bonnerjee: "Are we fit for political power even though you do not allow a large class of your own countrymen like the Untouchables to use public schools? . . . Are you fit for political power even though you do not allow them the use of public streets?"[84] The separation of the political from "the social" had ensured that the Congress did not have to confront the problem of caste.

For Ambedkar, the twentieth-century incarnation of Bonnerjee's argument was the economic interpretation of history. Although not unsympathetic to socialism, Ambedkar found the positing of property as the "source" of all power thoroughly unconvincing.[85] Forms of power exercised by religion and culture could not quite be captured by turning to the economic. Nor could such an approach meaningfully encapsulate the challenge facing the politics of resistance. Insofar as the socialist ideal of revolution presupposed the possibility of unity among the proletariat, it ignored how the graded hierarchy of the Indian caste system would make such a development impossible. India never had a "social revolution" because the caste system had rendered the "lower classes of India . . . disabled for direct action." "Social war," Ambedkar concedes, is universal, but the distinctive inheritance of India is that the weak were deprived of all three "weapons" of change: physical, political, and moral.[86]

Unlike Nehru, Ambedkar registered a profound distrust in the onward march of history. Mere progress would exacerbate rather than mend the social fracture, as the very essence of the Hindu social was anti-collectivist. The problem with mainstream anticolonial politics' restless desire to claim sovereignty was its growing inability to grapple with "the untaught multitude."[87] For Ambedkar, anticolonial leaders either glorified the ways of the backward multitude or sought to take advantage of their ignorance. In Gandhi he saw nothing but veiled attempts to vindicate inherited Indian ways.[88] Turning to Burke, Ambedkar reminded his contemporaries absorbed in the anticolonial project that "there is no method found for punishing the multitude."[89] Once again, then, the limit of the anticolonial democratic project boiled down to the state of the Indian (non-)people.

The history of the American Revolution—and the experience of American democracy—was crucial to Ambedkar's reflections on the relationship between the social and the political. A "frugal" government of the Jeffersonian variety, the function of which was to police and to maintain the rights of the people, would be an "absurdity" in India because preexisting rights in the Indian social were split between those who had an excess of rights (i.e., Brahmins) and those who had none (i.e., Untouchables). The more meaningful option was to found a new polity and distribute new rights to the people. This "idea of fundamental rights" conferred by a new constitution, however, carried its own problems in India. Insofar as rights are safeguarded by the "moral and social conscience of the society" and not just by laws, the introduction of new rights, however egalitarian, would be undone by the deeper hierarchies of the social. Just as African Americans had no use for their newfound rights, a similar fate would await the Indian Untouchables. The experience of the American Civil War further illustrated this point. The United States owed the preservation of its union to African Americans who constituted a large chunk of the military. While the Thirteenth, Fourteenth, and Fifteenth Amendments legally abolished slavery and conferred citizenship, the continued social exclusion of African Americans from civic life withheld those rights in practice. In fact, the American Republicans ultimately formed a "compact" with the Southern Democrats at the expense of Black Americans—betraying the substantive military and civic contribution of African Americans to the very preservation of the same Union during the Civil War. "The Untouchables," concludes Ambedkar, "cannot forget the fate of the Negroes."[90]

Ambedkar's diagnosis of the fractured social generated two, often mutually uneasy, political possibilities: the politics of waiting for the social to mend or of disrupting the neat order of postcolonial founding by inserting the figure of the Dalit into the quest for future. Ambedkar's adoption of the program of the separate electorate was designed to resist the (majoritarian) oneness of the people. When Gandhi moved to oppose this institutional resolution of what he took to be the moral problem of untouchability at the Poona Pact of 1932, Ambedkar was faced with the perennial plight of the minority in the age of representative democracy. If the numerical majority is destined to devolve into a "communal majority," the principle of popular sovereignty is a dangerous foray into the future for the minority. Yet the temporal resolution of the problem—to wait for the reconstitution of the social—was mired in the imperial premise.[91] As proposals for separate electorates came to naught, the alternative Ambedkar found himself considering—that is, to delay Indian independence in order to reform the social—was a path all too often frequented by the partisans of empire.[92]

Though Ambedkar wrote that Indians' desire to cut off the British connection was understandable, the celebration of the ideal of independence merely for the sake of it still befuddled him.[93] Echoing Pal's early warning about the "disastrous consequences" of the French Revolution, he argued, on one occasion, that the lesson of the "premature" Chinese Revolution of 1911 should serve as a lesson to Indians vying for independence.[94] Indeed, Ambedkar corresponded with Winston

Churchill and W. E. B. Du Bois at the same time to recruit imperial as well as left-international support for the Dalit cause.[95] But he had no anachronistic faith in imperial sovereignty, nor did he find the ideal of independence normatively undesirable.[96] Rather, his skepticism toward the Congress program was a response to the ways in which the urgency attributed to independence subordinated the caste question and Dalit demands. Beyond the temporal calculus of the social and the political, Ambedkar's argument for an immanent political quality of the caste question directly pertained to the boundary problem:

> It is wrong to say that the problem of the Untouchables is a social problem . . . it is a problem of securing to a minority liberty and equality of opportunity at the hands of a hostile majority, which believes in the denial of liberal and equal opportunity to the minority and conspires to enforce its policy on the minority . . . the problem of the Untouchables is *fundamentally* a political problem.[97]

At their critical edge, Ambedkar's proposals for representation and constitutional safeguards for Dalits were designed to *politically* resist the power of the (communal) majority. Given the absence of a substantive basis of common peoplehood, the coexistence of the majority and the minority as representatives of a splintered people struck him as a preferable alternative.[98] That said, Ambedkar did not turn to agonism for its own sake. Acutely attentive to the fissures internal to India, he did not believe that social disunity would magically dissolve in the unity of the state. Precisely because of his diagnosis that the fault lines of the social would be manifested in the state, Ambedkar considered the active presence of Dalit representatives in the legislature and the executive necessary for the political project of remaking of the social.[99]

To be sure, as his qualified support for the Pakistan demand illustrated, he was willing to concede the partition of a people if a part of them had a strong desire to live together as a distinct nation and if their continued coexistence "[retarded the growth of their] moral and material resources."[100] The main current of his writings on the caste problem, however, advocated for the difficult, if desirable, project of bringing the boundary problem into the realm of political action, in part because the caste minority had no viable option for exit from the bounds of Indian peoplehood. The other important point to underscore here is that the scope of the caste problem for Ambedkar was not reducible to the remit of political institutions. As Anupama Rao has argued, "Dalits' status as a territorially dispersed, suffering minority rendered them incommensurable. As a figure of singularity, Ambedkar's Dalit was both a subject constituted by a hurtful history and a portent of the future, a constant reminder of the inadequacy of a merely political response to the violence of caste."[101] Insofar as the source of the problem lay deep within the society, political inclusion or empowerment could not be a panacea. More attentive to the two-way traffic between the social and the political than his contemporaries, Ambedkar's own analysis of caste established that it is constitutive of the very (Hindu) social. But in bringing the boundary problem from the recesses of the social into the public light of politics, he radically questioned the aspiration to externally guide, rather than immanently struggle with, the social.

Ambedkar may not have fully overcome the profound tension between the two times of the people, but he certainly went further than any of his contemporaries in stressing the irreducibility of the boundary problem to the project of postcolonial development. As is well known, Ambedkar ultimately not only participated in the founding of postcolonial India but was one of its central figures—he would, in fact, become the chairman of the Constitution Drafting Committee. Although his proposal for separate electorates was not taken up, the Indian constitution legally abolished untouchability. Like Nehru, Ambedkar bolstered the sovereignty of the central state within the federal structure of postcolonial India.[102] Whereas Nehru wanted to institute centralized sovereignty to shepherd the process of planning, Ambedkar's immediate concern was to institute centralized safeguards for minorities against the dangers of localized majoritarianism. The possibility of a loose federation appeared to be synonymous with both the slow pace of development and the caste oppression in scattered provinces.

Upon the completion of the draft of the Indian constitution, Ambedkar declared that India was still not a nation: "I remember the days when politically-minded Indians resented the expression 'the people of India.' They preferred the expression 'the Indian nation.' I am of the opinion that in believing that we are a nation, we are cherishing a great delusion. How can [a] people divided into several hundreds of castes be a nation?"[103] The incomplete people—or rather what he earlier called an "amorphous mass"—was the inheritance of the new state. True to his pre-independence convictions, Ambedkar's political agenda in post-independence India critically hinged on organizing India's Dalits so they would be serious contenders for "political power."[104] In fact, insofar as the arrival of independence ruptured the connection between backwardness and the deferral of sovereignty, the social question acquired immediate and inescapable political salience. Ambedkar's own prioritization of the social—now understood as parallel with, and dependent on, the Dalit pursuit of political power—did not disappear but acquired new urgency and import. Before his death, Ambedkar converted to Buddhism and declared that the philosophy of "liberty, equality, and fraternity" Indians ought to seek was not to be borrowed from the French Revolution but to be "root[ed] in religion," and found in the egalitarianism of Buddhism, a faith he hoped would free Indians from the caste order.[105] This was to be the last *political* act of Ambedkar's career.

CONCLUSION

At India's founding, the two times of the people were evidently disjointed. Not the suspense of wresting sovereignty from the British, but open confrontations between Hindus and Muslims and the negotiations between the Congress and the League gripped the country's imagination in the final years of the Raj. The anxious wait for the fate of "the nation" overshadowed the long-awaited enthronement of the people. Whether explicitly focused on the Pakistan moment or not, the historiography of colonial India has never quite escaped the obfuscating projections of this event—a formative moment when the language of nationhood eclipsed and assimilated the democratic dilemmas that had long haunted the Indian struggle for freedom. In a way, this was a reversal of the nineteenth-century framing of the problem of peoplehood, where the challenge of developing the people in time had subsumed the boundary problem in its fold. In both instances, of course, the two times of the people were in principle recognized, even as the emphasis varied. The significance of the variation of emphasis (on fitness and unity), though, has often eluded the scholarly gaze, leading to a conflation of peoplehood and nationhood. It is no accident that the term "anticolonial nationalism" has stood—perhaps more confounding than revealing—as a portmanteau for the entire history of the anticolonial movement in India, from Rammohun Roy to Jawaharlal Nehru.

As we have seen, it was not so much the perceived identity but the difference of the two times of the people that brought the boundary problem to the forefront of pre-Partition India. Precisely because of the wide acceptance of the agenda set up by Nehru—namely, the understanding that the postcolonial state would prioritize the development of the people in social and economic terms—the other concern relating to the boundary of peoplehood became critically salient. No less instrumental to this story had been the colonial career of the distinction between sovereignty and government, which I discussed earlier in the book. The conception of government as that which would develop the people meant that the so-called constitutional safeguards appeared to be a wholly inadequate answer to the minority problem. What Jinnah and even Ambedkar sought was the certainty that the minority would have as much control over the time of development as the majority did. That demand inevitably came to loggerheads with the majority principle of representative democracy. What troubled Indian minorities was not so much the majority principle itself, but the premonition that a backward majority would not be capable of rising beyond its group identity. In dividing the people along their religious boundary, the minority critics of the project of postcolonial founding hoped to escape the fate of languishing in the darkness of majoritarian progress. Far too often reduced to a uniquely South Asian tragedy, the event of Partition was ultimately a spectacular exhibition of the limits of modern popular sovereignty in defining its own remit.

In this shadow war, Indian political actors across the spectrum struggled to render the boundary problem into the broad view of political contestation. Their difficulty, at one level, was not exceptional. Democratic theorists have also long been stuck with the same difficulty. In different ways, Nehru, Jinnah, and Ambedkar all struggled to subject the boundary problem to the agential labor of politics. That struggle was not primarily over the shadowy presence of the past or the ephemeral vista of the future. In order for the boundary problem to be an independent site of politics, it had to be extricated, however tentatively, from the project of developing the people in social and economic terms. Ambedkar's keen dissection of the problem offered one generative experiment in turning the boundaries of the fissiparous masses into an open-ended field of political action. There is also the example of Ambedkar's adversary, Gandhi.[106] More fundamentally skeptical of the claims of history and thoroughly uninterested in foreknowing the future, Gandhi, too, refused to treat the one time of the people as a means of another (even as his simultaneous reluctance to speak in terms of the social question obscured the power of his approach for a great many of his contemporaries).

The two times of the people—much like the two faces of the proverbial Janus—had resisted, and continue to resist, a single answer. Nehru's progressivist hope that the boundary problem would retract into a shared social question meant little during or after the age of founding. In fact, the great sacrifice made for the boundary of the people to coincide with sovereign states meant that postcolonial polities in South Asia inherited scant resources from the founding era that could politically enliven the space between the majority and the demos. One lesson of Indian founding was that, as political unity is made into a prior condition of popular sovereignty, it could only generate political meaning by splitting itself. Contrary to the prediction of Seeley and his Indian interlocutors, the "nation" announced its arrival by crushing and splitting not so much the British as Indians themselves. To not evaluate one time of the people by another was—and remains—a distinctive challenge of postcolonial democracy.

CONCLUSION

The Futures of Anticolonial Political Thought

WHEN THE FIRST waves of decolonization hit British India and fatefully splintered it into two new states in 1947, India's founders were already aware that their "star of freedom" was shared with the rest of "the east."[1] Postcolonial foundings were scattered across continents, and yet their abiding preoccupations had plenty in common. Much like other modern foundings, these postcolonial republics in their early days maneuvered through political avenues still besieged by competing claims of sovereign authorization. Though rapidly retracting, the specter of empire, too, found new expressions. Some of the new polities were born with uncertain borders; colonial rule had remade and left behind often intractable group conflicts.[2] The challenge of development, however, rose above all other dramas of postcolonial founding and cast its shadow over every other concern, from building new states to writing new constitutions. From New Delhi to Accra, new postcolonial regimes understood development to be their monumental responsibility. The five-year-plan project dominated the early years of the Republic of India. In Ghana, Kwame Nkrumah launched an ambitious seven-year plan, while Julius Nyerere of Tanzania declared that "freedom and development are as completely linked together as are chickens and eggs!"[3] Invariably uttered in the same breath, democracy and development together led the entrance of Asian and African peoples into the postcolonial age. The global conquest of democracy happened neither in the name of general will nor in the name of equality strictly construed but in the name of the development of the people. And it is a name that traveled remarkably well from the epic age of anticolonialism to the prosaic era of the postcolonial.

This was an entirely new chapter in the modern history of democracy. In the European world, the obsolescence of the older notion of democracy—a people directly ruling over itself—had much to do with the emergence of the people as a representational figure. The modern diagnosis that the scattered and numerous people could not be assembled in one place led to a distinction between sovereignty and government, paving the way for the rise of representative democracy.[4] Postcolonial democracy inherited the representational ambiguity of modern peoplehood, but it also encountered a challenge of its own: the people appeared to be not just spatially unassembled but also temporally short of the demands of popular sovereignty. Postcolonial founders were well aware of the historical significance of overthrowing imperial sovereignty and vindicating the anticolonial norm of the equality of peoples. Yet they also maintained, as we saw in Chapter 5, that the end of colonial rule did not readily amount to democracy. The developmental state was thus tasked with the goal of making the people one with itself. To quote Nyerere again: "For the truth is that development means the development of *people*. Roads, buildings, the increases of crop output, and other things of this nature are not development: they are only tools of development."[5] The outstanding question, once again, was this: How could postcolonial democracy simultaneously be the form of rule that was to transform a people and yet be authorized and performed by the very people it was to transform? The simultaneous centralization of mass underdevelopment and affirmation of the juridical principle of popular sovereignty constituted the two pulls of the postcolonial state-form.

The postcolonial revolution did not require the rejection of the diagnosis of mass underdevelopment; on the contrary, this diagnosis helped make sense of the challenge ahead. But it unhesitatingly repudiated the long-held consensus that underdevelopment necessitated external tutelage. Though severed from the legitimation of empires, the idea of development did not cease to be any less of a global category; after all, underdevelopment is philosophically a meaningful framing only in light of a developed future present elsewhere. At the same time, the meaning of development also changed in significant and decisive ways in the wake of postcolonial founding. When the developmental legitimation of empire was disavowed, it spelled an end to the idea that the moral and intellectual qualities of a people have a bearing on their claim to sovereignty. One palpable expression of this shift was the institution of universal suffrage in India and across the postcolonial world. It was partly because of the rejection of the moral implication of backwardness that the economic (or the broader "material") indexing of development could be decoupled from its imperial history. As we saw, since the formative early decades of the nineteenth century, Indian and British political thinkers alike had understood the developmental process to be composed of both moral and material elements. The contrasting fortunes of the two registers of developmentalism could already be seen by the end of the nineteenth century. As I noted in Chapter 6, the status of the moral question declined in proportion with the recognition that the affective elements of the political community could transcend the labor of historical development. Arguments underscoring the role of a morally transformative education for the cultivation of peoplehood lost further plausibility in India after the rise of Gandhi and his insistence on the immediacy of moral self-rule. But concerns with economic development withstood Gandhi's criticism and in fact emerged as a commonplace with Nehru (hardly alone in scoffing at the idealism of Gandhian economics) before being fluidly assimilated into the language of the new postcolonial state. These transformations were key to the reinvention of developmentalism amid its exhaustion as a justificatory device for imperial rule.

Nor did the collapse of European empires mean the evanescence of the orientation to the future that developmentalism had generated. On the contrary, as argued in Chapters 5 and 6, postcolonial founding tied future sovereignty to a newer possibility of mastering the time of development. At times the developmental orientation to the future would require sacrificing the present for the future. More often this orientation helped make sense of the unsettled and messy present of postcolonial democracy, inasmuch as it signified the shortcomings of the present as an unavoidable part of the journey to the future. Above all, it was an orientation that helped sustain the idea in the postcolonial age that economic development is inseparable from the development of the people. That the relationship between the people and their government in the postcolonial world continues to be conceived in terms of development has to do more with the persistence of this orientation to the future than with the success of concrete developmental agendas. By the persistence of the developmental orientation to the future, I do not mean the continuation of the accelerationist utopia that marked the age of postcolonial founding. Fully absorbed in the quotidian practices of postcolonial democracy, developmentalism had shed much of its accelerationist and utopian visions in the decades after independence.[6] If seen from the perspective of the promises made in the heydays of anticolonialism, the postcolonial present may resemble a graveyard of utopias—or, at the very least, "a superseded future, one of our futures past."[7] The pessimistic note on which the anticolonial era is usually revisited has to do with the disappearance of the enchanted future that Nehru's generation once found conquerable. Though the anticolonial dream of rapid progress has faded away in the postcolonial age, what remains is the expectation that democratic politics must simultaneously be a vehicle for development (of the people). It is an expectation that has survived the collapse of the febrile developmental imagination of the early postcolonial age.

Soon after the postcolonial foundings, new democracies across Asia and Africa witnessed the reversal of the order of progression idealized by Nehru and his contemporaries: instead of shaping the people from above, developmental projects themselves began to be shaped by popular politics.[8] The balance between "political" and "economic" democracy (to invoke Nehru's framing) was fragile, as the unraveling of the hope for an accelerated journey through the treacherous road of historical development demonstrated. In postcolonial India, the developmental project simultaneously empowered the technocratic planners and unleashed a great wave of popular participation, while, in many other postcolonial states, economic development became a pretext to suspend or curtail "political" democracy. Notably, the dispute regarding who was to be included in the people—and who was not—kindled a more effervescent, and often violent, democratic energy compared to the sacrificial project of developing the people in time. "The deepening of democracy in India," Thomas Blom Hansen argues, "has produced ever-stronger assertion of the legitimate power of majorities . . . without any concomitant percolation of liberal-democratic values."[9] Postcolonial founders' utopia of condensing the time of peoplehood through an accelerated development free of the constraints of ordinary politics seems to have given way to a perverse tradition of violently reenacting the boundary of the people so as to affirm its sovereign core. From intermittently interrupting the developmental narratives of new postcolonial states, majoritarian violence has now become another means of condensing history into the immediacy of transgressive self-assertion. The two times of the people—much in the tradition that I reconstructed in Chapter 6—continue to vie for the future of postcolonial democracy, all while feeding off each other.

When independence and popular sovereignty were juridically enshrined and the masses entered into electoral politics, the loud question of the colonial era—"Are we developed enough to rule ourselves?"—gradually ceded the center stage to a set of more prosaic questions concerning poverty eradication and measurable indices of human development. Both a problem and a solution, developmentalism left no corner of imperial or anticolonial thought untouched, even while the political import of developmental reasoning was fiercely debated. In the postcolonial era, the developmentalist paradigm continues to constitute, albeit in new ways, the very horizon of democratic expectation for the colonial world. The critical core of Indian anticolonial political thought, as we saw in the foregoing chapters, was defined by its spirited exploration of the idea that democratic self-rule in the colonial world should mean the development of the people. It is thus fitting to conclude this book by way of reflecting on the postcolonial career of democracy and the legacies that anticolonial thinkers left behind for global political thought.

DEMOCRACY AND DEVELOPMENT IN THE POSTCOLONIAL AGE

Just as new postcolonial states were seeking to accelerate the time of development through rapid industrialization and institution-building, development acquired a new life in the international domain. The postcolonial history of developmentalism has been the result of the confluence of two separate, often politically antagonistic, projects: the ambitious "catching-up" projects of the newly independent states—always and invariably framed as projects of development—and the comprehensive reimagining, under the sign of "development," of the international role of new global hegemons and erstwhile imperial powers in political and economic governance. The roots of the ambitious developmental projects undertaken by the newly independent states lay, unsurprisingly, in the anticolonial aspiration to overcome the developmental unevenness of the modern world. The first generation of postcolonial statesmen also paid keen attention to the interdependence of their national aspirations and the international order. The international experiments of the 1950s and 1960s—from the Bandung Conference to the New International Economic Order—had generated much hope for democratizing the international order. But the promises of the 1950s and 1960s remained unfulfilled: throughout the postcolonial world, domestic political crises were matched by the undoing of the hope to remake the international. Sovereignty over the time of development also turned out to be much harder to accomplish than once anticipated. Authoritarianism abounded, and an avalanche of famines, coups, and civil wars seemed to have transformed the postcolonial utopia into a nightmare.

In a new world dotted with postcolonial states, the international order itself went through a developmental remaking. With the rise of the "Truman doctrine" in the postwar era, the role of the Western nations in a quickly decolonizing world took a new form. The stated goal was no longer the denial of sovereignty but the promise of peaceful and sustained development of backward nations. New international organizations such as the World Bank and the International Monetary Fund adopted the ideal of developmentalism as the political bedrock of their economic policies, while international law and diplomacy became saturated with developmental reasoning.[10] As the state-led developmental projects foundered by the final quarter of the last century, the Bretton Woods institutions began to dictate the terms of postcolonial developmental policies. These endeavors, too, have mostly ended in failures, often resulting in further impoverishment and even in the subversion of postcolonial democracies. The flourishing of developmental economics in the postwar era, as Albert Hirschman once observed, presumed an account of economic growth divorced from the work of politics: "The Western economists who looked at them [underdeveloped countries] at the end of World War II were convinced that these countries were not all that complicated. . . . With the new doctrine of economic growth, contempt took a more sophisticated form: suddenly it was taken for granted that progress of these countries would be smoothly linear if only they adopted the right kind of integrated development program! In sum, like the 'innocent' and *doux* trader of the eighteenth century, these countries were perceived to have only interests and no passions."[11] James Ferguson memorably characterized this developmental regime as an "anti-politics machine." The global developmental apparatus, Ferguson argued, expands and entrenches "bureaucratic state power" while pushing the problem of development outside of the political domain.[12] In contrast to the early postcolonial states that hoped to straddle the domains of "political" and "economic" democracy, the global developmental apparatus found it far easier to reduce politics into technocracy. By the end of the twentieth century, its dominance was such that the idea of the "Third World" itself appeared to be inseparable from developmentalism.[13]

These two different springs of developmentalism together gave a profound depth to its popular life. The popular uptake of developmental motifs in the postcolonial world—a history that is as rich as it is paradoxical—has defied almost all expectations of postcolonial founders. In the postcolonial era, the "rational" planning of the postcolonial state and "irrational" mass politics both relied on developmental claims for democratic legitimation.[14] Underdevelopment was no longer simply a marker of the location of the postcolonial people in a global order; it had also become "a form of identity," informing the normative aspirations of popular politics.[15] The suspension of popular will for the sake of future development has met with mass resistance in postcolonial South Asia and elsewhere.[16] The immediacy of popular action finds itself invariably in tension with the drawn-out time of development, even when what the popular actors demand is development itself.[17] The institution of popular sovereignty as a juridical principle was not inconsequential either. As Rohit De shows, it enabled popular claim-making in the legal domain, facilitating a form of popular constitutionalism that bypassed the developmental governmentality of the postcolonial state.[18] Eventually, developmentalism would also bolster a distinct proliferation of judicial authority in postcolonial India. The developmental urgency has facilitated new ways for the court to speak for the people and even led to the emergence of "mass destitution" as a foundational source of judicial authorization.[19]

The entwined philosophical careers of development and democracy outlasted the raging skepticism that enveloped academic study of developmentalism in the late twentieth century. While not uncritical of the global developmental apparatus, Amartya Sen has offered perhaps the strongest normative case for wedding democracy to the developmental framework. For Sen, the problem of poverty should be framed as the deprivation of "basic capabilities" rather than merely as low income.[20] His broader argument is directed against the view that development stands in contradiction with freedom—and that the authoritarian regimes are best suited for economic development (what is known as the "Lee thesis," after the former Singaporean prime minister Lee Kuan Yew). The Lee thesis, of course, is the postcolonial reincarnation of an older argument that goes back to nineteenth-century liberal imperialism. Sen finds no justification for making a choice between economic development and political democracy, because it is only in a democracy that the right kind of development flourishes.[21] Sen's case for development makes or requires no explicit commitment to a strong theory of historical development. Instead, he argues that the dual exercise of development and democracy expands the scope of "freedom"—social, political, and economic. The resignification of poverty as the developmental lack of capability cannot, however, fully escape a gradational comparison between different capabilities. What requires particular underscoring here is the dependence of the normative case for democracy on the developmental touchstone of "capabilities." Indeed, the discussion of democracy in the postcolonial world, normative or otherwise, remains inextricably tied to the parallel problem of development.

The foundational role of the idea of historical development in making the globe thinkable for a great deal of modern social and political theories has not ceased to inspire reflections either. Thomas McCarthy's measured arguments for continuing with the framework of development are a case in point. McCarthy is aware of the violent history of developmentalism and its deep entanglement with imperialism. Still, it is no less true, McCarthy argues, that "the idea of human development is not exhausted by the misuse to which it has been put; that there is much more than a kernel of truth in the view that human history evinces considerable advances in learning, problem solving, practical reasoning, functional differentiation, economic production, the rule of law, political organization, and other respects."[22] In other words, "developmental thinking is irrepressible" and constitutes an "inescapable" fact of the modern world.[23] The question is no longer whether societies should choose to modernize or not, for modernization is already a fait accompli. The question instead is "which forms of modernity to develop, in light of structural constraints and pressures emanating from the global system."[24] The normative hope invested in the idea of development is often, as in McCarthy's account, directly related to its status as a "fact" of the world.[25] In the nineteenth century, as we saw in Chapter 1, the developmental justification of colonial rule was predicated on the theoretical move that rendered norms (self-government) dependent on the fact of development. Unlike Mill, McCarthy, of course, is critical of the imperial uses of development; the fact of development is instead meant to support the norm of global democracy. That said, McCarthy's commitment to a progressive philosophy of history is not entirely based on descriptive reasons. The achievement of "multicultural universalism" requires "multiple forms of sociocultural modernity united by an overlapping consensus."[26] The possibility of a globally valid democracy is thus claimed to be ultimately dependent on a thin but normatively valuable framework of development.

Inescapable though the developmental order might be, the recognition of its ubiquity does not make the challenges posed by it to democratic politics any easier. Although no longer tethered to the deferral of sovereignty, the conception of postcolonial democracy as a vehicle of development continues to split the people into its deficient present and its developed future. Much like the "democratic consummation of the fantasy of recognition," the aspiration for a consummated development has historically looked forward to "a dream of the moment at which ruler and ruled, seer and seen, become identical."[27] This conflation of democracy with (temporal) mastery, much more than the failings of weak postcolonial institutions, has rendered postcolonial democracy vulnerable to a distinct form of authoritarianism—an authoritarianism that promises to usher in the future precisely because of its independence from the institutional and normative constraints of the present. Beyond the danger of authoritarianism, the developmental figuration of the people has led to a conception of democratic government where the rule of the people and the responsibility to carry the people into a fuller future tend to become indistinguishable. Democracy in its postcolonial iteration may have succeeded in articulating claims and concerns in the language of development, but the difficult problem of establishing a democratic reciprocity between (popular) sovereignty and (self-)government has proven to be a stubborn challenge.

Though the crisis in the developmental mediation between sovereignty and government now appears to be far removed from the political agendas of the anticolonial age, the theoretical preoccupations of anticolonial democratic thought, as we saw in foregoing chapters, were not far from this question. The Indian entry into the debate on the historicity of democracy in the nineteenth century was part of a broader global moment: the establishment of a correspondence—not just formal but also temporal—between the social condition of the people and their political institutions had gripped democratic thought since the nineteenth century. Tocqueville's travel through America convinced him (and a great many other observers of democracy ever since) that the irresistible progress of the social—the gradual rise of the equality of conditions—underlies the democratic revolution of the age. This broader framing not only helped generate a historical self-understanding for modern democracy but also captured one of its constitutive anxieties: the temporal discord between democracy as a form of rule and as a form of society. It is arguable, however, that it was in the colonial world that democracy had the most extraordinary reckoning with its own time, not least because of the (colonial) people's resignification as a marker of temporal backwardness. Democracy arrived in India as an idea and an aspiration, and anticolonial attempts to make a home for it there generated a profound anxiety about enthroning a set of norms without supplying its concomitant historical entailments.

Out of this anxious struggle, Indian anticolonial political thinkers crafted a set of answers that remain instructive as ever to think through the global career of democracy. An animating concern with a democracy not blackmailed by the future was the defining wager of the development-critical tradition of Indian anticolonial political thought. They warned that the approach to democracy as a means to the end of a sovereign future burdens it with encumbrances that undermine the very ideal of self-rule. Gandhi's turn to the universally available possibility of self-rule—in place of an authorization from the higher realm of progress—was the most arresting formulation of this argument. Temporal imagination, of course, is an unavoidable foundation of politics; there is no escape from the need to bridge possible futures with the narratives of the past. This consideration underpinned B. N. Seal's proposal to approach development as a dynamic immanent in the people. What the critical tradition within Indian political thought teaches us is that the developmental description of the world is a source of heteronomy precisely because of its tendency to summon political authorization from an idealized future inaccessible to democratic politics. The political languages of Gandhi, Seal, or Das are not necessarily redeemable from the dead, and it is not of much value to lament over paths not taken. But their critical diagnosis of the temporal logic underlying the (colonial) split between sovereignty and government remains a generative point of departure.

Others like Naoroji, Nehru, and Ambedkar bear testament to the appeal of developmentalism—that its role in rendering legible the discontent with the present in the pursuit of a democratic vision is too entrenched (and important) to simply abandon. It would be unjustifiably idealistic to deny that developmentalism offered a powerful perspective into the diagnosis of India's political predicament, whether it be caste inequality or poverty. As Ambedkar exemplified, the act of learning from developmental perspectives need not result in a surrender to the sovereign claims of the future. For better or worse, developmentalism has now become more a language of politics than a problem with determinable normative content. While one may still take a stance for or against developmental reasoning, it is unlikely to settle anything important about the layered and perplexing history of its uses. Where the work of political theory proves indispensable is in disclosing the ways in which developmentalism has shaped the imagination of peoplehood and continues to define the orientation to democracy for most of the world. To be more precise, narratives of development morph into a political problem when the people are taken to be the historical marker of (under)development. To disentangle the two, of course, is not an easy challenge, nor is it always simple to isolate this from other pressing concerns of postcolonial democracies. But, as a problem of foundational nature, the entwined story of peoplehood and developmentalism is unlikely to disappear any time soon. The history of Indian anticolonial political thought has left behind many lessons, but one remains particularly relevant for postcolonial democracy: the pursuit of a people whose time is not a source of its subjection, imperial or otherwise.

THE GLOBAL CLAIMS OF ANTICOLONIAL POLITICAL THOUGHT

The global reach of the concepts and categories of modern political thought has been all-encompassing. Democracy, popular sovereignty, constitutionalism, and their cognate concepts have been governing political institutions and reasoning all over the world at least since the imperial unification of the globe in the nineteenth century. And yet political theory has been one of the last disciplines to reckon with the political thought from the colonial and postcolonial world. The disciplinary marginality of the history of modern non-European political thought has more than representational consequences. It obscures the global life of political thought from its disciplinary scope, which in turn impoverishes our appreciation of the vast landscape on which modern political ideas transformed, deepened, expanded, and contracted. As I argued in Chapter 5, one important methodological basis for the marginalization of anticolonial thought has been the assumption that the theoretical goals of the anticolonial democratic project were already normatively validated ideals elsewhere. The undermining of the theoretical scope of anticolonial political thought has equally been characteristic of historical studies of anticolonialism. The predominance of the framework of nationalism meant that the archive of anticolonial thought has mostly been read in light of the seemingly inexorable rise of the nation-state.[28] As a master category, nationalism subsumed the questions of sovereignty, government, and peoplehood. The success of this approach has been so great that "anticolonial nationalism" came to be a shorthand for anticolonial thought in general.

Close readings of the history of anticolonial political thought amply demonstrate that it was neither a delayed restaging of universal questions nor simply a straightforward reflection of the internal contradictions of modern empires. As we saw in Chapters 1 and 2, when the

European and non-European worlds came together through a global ordering of peoplehood, it led Indian political thinkers to the realization that the universal claim of modern political ideals could not be extricated from the developmentalist paradigm. This did not mean that the origin of political ideas was the problem, or that they should be identical across colonial and metropolitan space. Rather, the key problem that Indian anticolonial thinkers had directly or indirectly wrestled with was the hierarchical, developmental assumptions encoded in the globalization of political ideas. Though we are now acutely aware of the moral problems of denying self-government to a people because of their putative backwardness, this formative entanglement between modern political ideas and the developmental vision of the global remains little appreciated, in part because the stake of the question is usually framed in terms of political support or opposition to empire.

It is in this theoretical context that the global claims of Indian anticolonial political thought should be situated. The reconstitution of political thought for an imperial-global world, these political thinkers understood, requires being attentive simultaneously to the global condition and to the conceptual content of modern political thought. Being situated in an all-pervasive imperial hierarchy, Indian political thinkers were drawn to the questions of global difference from the early decades of the nineteenth century. The reason-centric navigation of global difference that Rammohun Roy and Dakshinaranjan Mukherjee exemplified unraveled as the century reached its developmentalist heights. A developmentally integrated picture of the globe had overshadowed the horizon for the likes of Naoroji and Banerjea as they sought to reconfigure the terms of (anti-)imperial politics. For those who appeared in Naoroji and Banerjea's wake, the trials and tribulations of Indian liberalism would generate a profound realization: that the act of turning developmentalism against the empire was a Faustian bargain. As most powerfully illustrated by Gandhi, the anticolonial project could not simply claim universal rights but must first question the principles and terms through which the time and place of the colonies were determined. This insight propelled the powerful interventions of Seal and his fellow pluralists, and even tempered the renewed developmentalism of Nehru. One clear thread of argument emerges from this history: a democratic theory that is not alert to the global background of modern peoplehood reproduces developmental hierarchy and fails to appreciate the challenges involved in placing the people in historical time.

Through their struggle with the problem of peoplehood, Indian anticolonial political thinkers recognized that that modern colonialism derived its legitimacy from a picture of the globe that itself needed to be challenged and recast. The ultimate source of imperial legitimation lay in—to use B. N. Seal's felicitous phrase—the "unilinear" conception of global development. The unilinear assumptions of modern political thought amounted to, at once, a politically dubious and theoretically impoverished view of the historical requirement for the realization of democratic self-rule. To this end, Naoroji, Dutt, and Nehru theorized how the global claims of development paradoxically sprang from the exploitation of the colonies. Seal and Mukerjee demonstrated how the logic of development superimposes external standards to render global differences chronological. Gandhi endeavored to theorize political action in opposition to the demand of historical progress. These otherwise different thinkers shared the overarching goal of rendering colonial "backwardness" commensurate with the time of democracy. But they also invited us to reflect on the global assumptions of modern democratic thought—assumptions that are often unarticulated and buried in the interstices of the positive theoretical content of democratic theory. The salience of this contribution for the political thought of our own era—striving as it is to come to terms with its own global condition—requires no belaboring.

Though a diverse intellectual tradition, anticolonial political thought is broadly united by its pursuit of democratic self-rule. What is more, this pursuit yielded a singular set of perspectives into the ways in which historical assumptions and normative ideals of modern democratic thought have co-constituted each other. Far too often reduced to a mere critique of foreign domination, anticolonial political thought was arguably just as invested in addressing the problems of modern democratic theory from its own context.[29] Instead of taking questions of democracy or the nation-state for granted, the anticolonial political thinkers I have discussed in this book vigorously deconstructed those questions and dissected their normative and historical presuppositions. Because they so dramatically experienced the temporal lag between (popular) sovereignty and (democratic) government, these thinkers were naturally attuned to the struggle of modern democracy to unite its norms with divergent histories of peoplehood. Bipin Chandra Pal's turn to self-reliance, Gandhi's self-authorizing action, and C. R. Das's diffused self-rule were various attempts at accounting for the rupture between democratic self-rule and the ground of popular sovereignty. Closer to the moment of postcolonial founding, B. R. Ambedkar's proposal to foreground the boundary of peoplehood as a site of continuous struggle has proved to be prescient, thanks to his keen awareness of the fissiparous social body of the people and the tendency of modern peoplehood to divide itself from within. These reflections on peoplehood, for all their internal tensions and dilemmas, offer valuable resources for grappling with one of the foundational challenges of modern democratic theory: the necessity to creatively bridge the fraught space between practices of self-rule and the abstract ideal of popular sovereignty. Neither a mere juridical premise of democratic government nor a historical fact deducible from social and cultural contexts, the problem of peoplehood is what decided the fortunes of the anticolonial democratic project and may very well critically shape the future of democracy in a global age when the norm of democracy is increasingly out of joint with its plural and conflicting histories.

Waiting for the People has eschewed the familiar trope of taking anticolonial political thought merely as providing answers to the moral deficit of empire. What the rich history of anticolonial political thought demands—and what I have let myself be guided by in this book—is an appreciation of its theoretical problems and dilemmas on their own terms. In the process of rendering most of the world subject, modern colonialism dislocated the cherished ideals of democracy and popular sovereignty from their prior histories. In reckoning with this inheritance, Indian anticolonial thinkers arrived at the conclusion that the enactment of democracy in the colonial world required an answer to the developmental narrative of these political ideals as much as the liberation from foreign rule. This dual endeavor of anticolonial political thought constituted its distinctive character, while also enabling it, one may add, to carry the burden of the globe on its shoulder. For postcolonial democracies, the history of anticolonial political thought remains an indispensable resource to make sense of their present and of possible futures. For the history of modern political thought, it remains an archive to mine for understanding how modern democracy came to be as it is, and a constant reminder to not take the globe for granted.

NOTES

INTRODUCTION

1. Bipin Chandra Pal, *Indian National Congress* (Lahore: Anarkali, 1887), 7 (emphasis in original). On Pal's status as a "prophet of nationalism," see Sri Aurobindo, *Bande Mataram* (Pondicherry: Sri Aurobindo Ashram Publication Department, 2002), 911–914.

2. Edwin Arnold, *Marquis of Dalhousie's Administration of British India,* vol. 2 (London: Saunders, Otley and Co., 1865), 388.

3. B. R. Ambedkar, *Three Historical Addresses of Dr. Babasaheb Ambedkar* (New Delhi: Dr. Ambedkar Foundation Research Cell, 1999), 54–55.

4. Pierre Rosanvallon, *Counter-Democracy: Politics in an Age of Distrust* (Cambridge: Cambridge University Press, 2012), 83.

5. Hannah Arendt, *On Revolution* (London: Penguin Books, 1990), 94.

6. See also Hannah Arendt, "The Freedom to Be Free," *New England Review* 38, no. 2 (2017): 56–69. To be clear, my aim is not to criticize Arendt's salutary insight that "the conquest of poverty is a prerequisite for the foundation of freedom, but also . . . liberation from poverty cannot be dealt with in the same way as liberation from political oppression" (66). Instead, the point is to question the assumption that material deprivation of the masses acquired the same political signification in the colonial world as it did in eighteenth-century France.

7. John Dunn, *Democracy: A History* (New York: Atlantic Monthly Press, 2005), 15. On the wide reach of the "democratic idiom" beyond ostensibly

democratic political agendas, see Ian Shapiro, *Democracy's Place* (Ithaca, NY: Cornell University Press, 1996), 1–3.

8. For a history of how popular sovereignty co-opted and replaced the theory of divine kingship, see Edmund Morgan, *Inventing the People: The Rise of Popular Sovereignty in England and America* (New York: W. W. Norton, 1989).

9. Jürgen Habermas, *Between Facts and Norms: Contributions toward a Discourse Theory of Law and Democracy,* trans. William Rehg (Cambridge, MA: MIT Press, 1998), 136.

10. See Stephen Holmes, *Passions and Constraint: On the Theory of Liberal Democracy* (Chicago: University of Chicago Press, 1995); David Held, *Models of Democracy* (Stanford, CA: Stanford University Press, 2006).

11. For representative accounts, see Sheldon Wolin, "Norm and Form: The Constitutionalizing of Democracy," in *Athenian Political Thought and the Reconstruction of American Democracy,* ed. Peter Euben and John Wallach (Ithaca, NY: Cornell University Press, 1994), 29–58; Jacques Rancière, "Ten Theses on Politics," in *Dissensus: On Politics and Aesthetics,* ed. and trans. Steve Corcoran (New York: Continuum, 2010), 35–52.

12. Habermas, *Between Facts and Norms,* 136, 486–487. See also Seyla Benhabib, *Dignity in Adversity: Human Rights in Troubled Times* (Cambridge: Polity Press, 2011), 77–93, 117–137.

13. For a mapping of the debate, see Bonnie Honig, "Between Decision and Deliberation: Political Paradox in Democratic Theory," *American Political Science Review* 101, no. 1 (2007): 1–17.

14. Richard Tuck, *The Sleeping Sovereign: The Invention of Modern Democracy* (Cambridge: Cambridge University Press, 2015), x (emphasis in original).

15. Daniel Lee, *Popular Sovereignty in Early Modern Constitutional Thought* (Oxford: Oxford University Press, 2016), 1–23.

16. Jason Frank, *Constituent Moments: Enacting the People in Post-Revolutionary America* (Durham, NC: Duke University Press, 2010).

17. Bryan Garsten, "Representative Government and Popular Sovereignty," in *Political Representation,* ed. Ian Shapiro et al. (Cambridge: Cambridge University Press, 2009), 90–110.

18. Patchen Markell, "'The Caricature of the People': Arendt, the Mob, and Democracy" (unpublished manuscript).

19. On the "folk foundationalism" of popular sovereignty, see Kevin Olson, *Imagined Sovereignties: The Power of the People and Other Myths of the Modern Age* (Cambridge: Cambridge University Press, 2016).

20. See Ludwig Wittgenstein, *Philosophical Investigations,* trans. G. E. M. Anscombe, P. M. S. Hacker, and Joachim Schulte (West Sussex, UK: Wiley-Blackwell, 2009), §217; Ludwig Wittgenstein, *On Certainty,* ed. G. E. M. Anscombe and G. H. von Wright (London: Harper Torchbooks, 1969), §144.

21. See Nicholas Dirks, *The Scandal of Empire: India and the Creation of Imperial Britain* (Cambridge, MA: Harvard University Press, 2006).

22. See Robert Travers, *Ideology and Empire in Eighteenth-Century India: The British in Bengal* (Cambridge: Cambridge University Press, 2009).

23. Bernard Yack, "Popular Sovereignty and Nationalism," *Political Theory* 29, no. 4 (2001): 517–536.

24. For a classic statement, see Emmanuel-Joseph Sieyès, *What Is the Third Estate?*, in *Political Writings,* ed. Michael Sonenscher (Indianapolis: Hackett, 2003), 94–144; see also Arendt, *On Revolution,* 53–110.

25. On the modern tension between the people as a "political abstraction" and as a "sociological fact," see Pierre Rosanvallon, "Revolutionary Democracy," in *Democracy Past and Future* (New York: Columbia University Press, 2006), 79–97; see also Sheldon Wolin, "The People's Two Bodies," *Democracy* 1, no. 1 (1981): 9–24.

26. For a representative account, see Bipan Chandra, *Nationalism and Colonialism in Modern India* (New Delhi: Orient Longman, 1979).

27. Adam Smith, *An Inquiry into the Nature and Causes of the Wealth of Nations* (New York: Modern Library, 1937), 416.

28. See Anthony Pagden, *Lords of All the World: Ideologies of Empire in Spain, Britain, and France, 1500–1800* (New Haven, CT: Yale University Press, 1995); Sankar Muthu, ed., *Empire and Modern Political Thought* (Cambridge: Cambridge University Press, 2012).

29. Lea Ypi, "What's Wrong with Colonialism," *Philosophy and Public Affairs* 41, no. 2 (2013): 158–191. The point I am underscoring here concerns not so much the substance of Ypi's powerful moral arguments but the fact that modern colonialism's claim to rule was predicated on a set of questions directed at the very legitimacy of a straightforward moral critique.

30. John Stuart Mill, *The Collected Works of John Stuart Mill,* vol. 1, *Autobiography and Literary Essays,* ed. John M. Robson and Jack Stillinger (Toronto: University of Toronto Press, 1981), 169 (emphasis in original).

31. Of note here is the debate between postcolonial scholars and the "Cambridge school" of South Asian history in the final decade of the twentieth century. For an overview, see Gyan Prakash, "Subaltern Studies as Postcolonial Criticism," *American Historical Review* 99, no. 5 (1994): 1475–1490; Dipesh Chakrabarty, "A Small History of Subaltern Studies," in *A Companion to Postcolonial Studies*, ed. Henry Schwarz and Sangeeta Ray (Oxford: Basil Blackwell, 2005), 467–485; Nicholas Dirks, "The Burden of the Past: On Colonialism and the Writing of History," in *Castes of Mind: Colonialism and the Making of Modern India* (Princeton, NJ: Princeton University Press, 2001), 303–316; Rosalind O'Hanlon and David Washbrook, "After Orientalism: Culture, Criticism, and Politics in the Third World," *Comparative Studies in Society and History* 34, no. 1 (1992): 141–167.

32. See especially Karuna Mantena, *Alibis of Empire: Henry Maine and the Ends of Liberal Imperialism* (Princeton, NJ: Princeton University Press, 2010).

33. See, in particular, Uday Singh Mehta, *Liberalism and Empire: A Study in Nineteenth-Century British Liberal Thought* (Chicago: University of Chicago Press, 1999); Jennifer Pitts, *A Turn to Empire: The Rise of Imperial Liberalism in Britain and France* (Princeton, NJ: Princeton University Press, 2005); Matthew P. Fitzpatrick, ed., *Liberal Imperialism in Europe* (New York: Palgrave Macmillan, 2012); Duncan Bell, *Reordering the World: Essays on Liberalism and Empire* (Princeton, NJ: Princeton University Press, 2016); Thomas McCarthy, *Race, Empire, and the Idea of Human Development* (Cambridge: Cambridge University Press, 2009).

34. The relative absence of the question of democracy in this body of work has lately received scrutiny. Writing on popular sovereignty and the making of American settler-colonialism, Adam Dahl has contrasted the "antidemocratic imperialism" of British liberalism to the "democratic imperialism" of settler colonialism. While Dahl rightly emphasizes the mutual imbrication between native "dispossession" and popular sovereignty in the settler-colonial context, it is also arguable that "liberal imperialism" in the Asian and African contexts, too, relied fundamentally on a justification of empire on democratic terms. Adam Dahl, *Empire of the People: Settler Colonialism and the Foundations of Modern Democracy* (Lawrence: University Press of Kansas, 2018), 8. See also Inés Valdez, "Empire, Popular Sovereignty, and the Problem of Self-and-Other-Determination," *Perspectives on Politics* 21, no. 1 (2023): 109–125.

35. John Stuart Mill, *Considerations on Representative Government,* in *The Collected Works of John Stuart Mill,* vol. 19, *Essays on Politics and Society,* pt. 2, ed. John M. Robson and Jack Stillinger (Toronto: University of Toronto Press, 1981), 413.

36. J. B. Bury, *The Idea of Progress* (London: Macmillan, 1920), 324–325.

37. H. W. Arndt, "Economic Development: A Semantic History," *Economic Development and Cultural Change* 29, no. 3 (1981): 457–466.

38. See Ranajit Guha, *Dominance without Hegemony: History and Power in Colonial India* (Cambridge, MA: Harvard University Press, 1997), 30–39; Partha Chatterjee, *The Nation and Its Fragments* (Princeton, NJ: Princeton University Press, 1993), 95–115; Brian Hatcher, *Idioms of Improvement: Vidyāsāgar and Cultural Encounter in Bengal* (Oxford: Oxford University Press, 1996).

39. Jugannath Sunkersett, quoted in Bimanbehari Majumdar, *History of Indian Social and Political Ideas* (1934; Calcutta: Bookland, 1967), 195.

40. See Ranajit Guha, *Elementary Aspects of Peasant Insurgency in Colonial India* (Durham, NC: Duke University Press, 1999).

41. Dipesh Chakrabarty, *Provincializing Europe: Postcolonial Thought and Historical Difference* (Princeton, NJ: Princeton University Press, 2000), 3–23.

42. On this point, see Duncan Kelly, "Popular Sovereignty as State Theory in the Nineteenth Century," in *Popular Sovereignty in Historical Perspective,* ed. Richard Bourke and Quentin Skinner (Cambridge: Cambridge University Press, 2016), 270–296.

43. See Gregory Conti, *Parliament the Mirror of the Nation: Representation, Deliberation, and Democracy in Victorian Britain* (Cambridge: Cambridge University Press, 2019).

44. Surendranath Banerjea, *A Nation in Making: Being the Reminiscences of Fifty Years of Public Life* (London: Oxford University Press, 1925), 67.

45. See Christopher A. Bayly, *Recovering Liberties: Indian Thought in the Age of Liberalism and Empire* (Cambridge: Cambridge University Press, 2012), 1–25.

46. Dadabhai Naoroji, *Essays, Speeches, Addresses, Writings* (Bombay: Caxton Printing Works, 1887), 295, 361, 112.

47. See especially Claude Lefort, "The Question of Democracy," in *Democracy and Political Theory* (London: Polity Press, 1988), 9–21.

48. For an interest-based interpretation, see Judith M. Brown, *Gandhi's Rise to Power: Indian Politics, 1915–1922* (Cambridge: Cambridge University Press, 1972); for a history of Gandhi's free-floating reception among the peasants, see Shahid Amin, "Gandhi as Mahatma," in *Selected Subaltern Studies,* ed. Ranajit Guha and Gayatri Chakravorty Spivak (New York: Oxford University Press, 1988), 288–348; for an account of his "spiritualization" of politics, see Raghavan N. Iyer, *The Moral and Political Thought of Mahatma Gandhi* (New York: Oxford University Press, 1973).

49. M. K. Gandhi, *"Hind Swaraj" and Other Writings,* ed. Anthony J. Parel (Cambridge: Cambridge University Press, 1997), 117 (emphasis added).

50. Gandhi, *"Hind Swaraj,"* 17.

51. On the formation of popular sovereignty as a discourse of resistance, see Edmund Morgan, *Inventing the People: The Rise of Popular Sovereignty in England and America* (New York: W. W. Norton, 1989); Michel Foucault, *Society Must Be Defended* (New York: Picador, 2003), 43–140; Margaret Canovan, *The People* (Cambridge: Polity Press, 2005), 10–39.

52. W. E. B. Du Bois, "To the World: Manifesto of the Second Pan-African Congress," in *W. E. B. Du Bois: International Thought,* ed. Adom Getachew and Jennifer Pitts (Cambridge: Cambridge University Press, 2022), 57. Such a practice-centric account of democratic self-government was not in fundamental contradiction with developmentalism. In the same work, Du Bois, for instance, made a case for empowering the "natural leaders" of colonial peoples for the sake of their development: "For the purpose of raising such peoples to intelligence, self-knowledge and self-control, their intelligentsia of right ought to be recognized as the natural leaders of their groups" (56).

53. V. I. Lenin, *Selected Works in Three Volumes,* vol. 2 (Moscow: Progress Publishers, 1970), 372.

54. Chittaranjan Das, *India for Indians* (Madras: Ganesh and Co., 1918), 99.

55. Arturo Escobar, *Encountering Development: The Making and Unmaking of the Third World* (Princeton, NJ: Princeton University Press, 1995), 5.

56. See, in particular, Sudipta Kaviraj, "Democracy and Development in India," in *Democracy and Development,* ed. Amiya Kumar Bagchi (New York: St. Martin's Press, 1995), 92–130; Pranab K. Bardhan, *The Political Economy of Development in India* (Oxford: Basil Blackwell, 1984); Amartya Sen, *Development as Freedom* (New York: Oxford University Press, 1999); Sundhya Pahuja, "From Decolonization to Developmental Nation State," in *Decolonizing International Law* (Cambridge: Cambridge University Press, 2011), 44–94; Nils Gilman, *Mandarins of the Future: Modernization Theory in Cold War America* (Baltimore: Johns Hopkins University Press, 2003); Begüm Adalet, *Hotels and Highways: The Construction of Modernization Theory in Cold War Turkey* (Stanford, CA: Stanford University Press, 2018).

57. Jawaharlal Nehru, "Bullock Cart, Motor Lorry, Jet Plane," in *Jawaharlal Nehru's Speeches,* vol. 3, *March 1953–August 1957* (Delhi: Ministry of Information and Broadcasting, Government of India, 1958), 60.

58. Nehru, "Government and the People," in *Speeches,* 3:138–139.

59. See Sudipta Kaviraj, "A State of Contradictions: The Post-Colonial State in India," in *The Imaginary Institution of India: Politics and Ideas* (New York: Columbia University Press, 2010), 210–233; Chatterjee, *The Nation and Its Fragments,* 210–219.

60. That "colonialism" came to be the descriptive term in the twentieth century for this critical period of global history was a result of rapid semantic shifts, connections, and theoretical expediencies. As Barbara Arneil argues, theorists must be attentive to the ways in which the term can conflate different forms of colonialism, lumping together the connected yet separate histories of territorial occupations, population transfers, and domestic segregation. See Barbara Arneil, *Domestic Colonies: The Turn Inward to Colony* (Oxford: Oxford University Press, 2017).

61. Adom Getachew, *Worldmaking after Empire: The Rise and Fall of Self-Determination* (Princeton, NJ: Princeton University Press, 2019).

62. Benedict Anderson, *Imagined Communities: Reflections on the Origin and Spread of Nationalism* (London: Verso, 2006), 5.

63. Partha Chatterjee, *Nationalist Thought and the Colonial World: A Derivative Discourse?* (London: Zed Books, 1986), 11.

64. Chatterjee, *Nationalist Thought,* 30.

65. Chatterjee, *Nationalist Thought,* 38.

66. Majumdar, *History, of Indian Social and Political Ideas,* v.

67. Majumdar, *History of Indian Social and Political Ideas,* iii.

68. Majumdar, *History of Indian Social and Political Ideas,* v.

69. This issue was not unique to India. For an account of nineteenth-century Chinese grappling with the problem, see Leigh Jenco, "Histories of Thought and Comparative Political Theory: The Curious Case of 'Chinese Origins of Western Knowledge,' 1860–1895," *Political Theory* 42, no. 6 (2014): 658–681.

70. On the comparative dimension of works that are not usually categorized as "comparative political theory," see Andrew March, "What Is Comparative Political Theory?," *Review of Politics* 71, no. 4 (2009): 531–565; on the disciplinary specificity of comparative political theory in the broader context of comparative studies, see Joshua Simon, "Institutions, Ideologies, and Comparative Political Theory," *Perspectives on Politics* 18, no. 2 (2020): 423–438; on the idea of "tradition" in comparative political thought, see Humeira Iqtidar, "Redefining 'Tradition' in Political Thought," *European Journal of Political Theory* 15, no. 4 (2016): 424–444.

71. Leigh Jenco, "Introduction: On the Possibility of Chinese Thought as Global Theory," in *Chinese Thought as Global Theory: Diversifying Knowledge Production in the Social Sciences and Humanities,* ed. Leigh Jenco (Albany: State University of New York Press, 2017), 11.

72. David Scott, *Conscripts of Modernity: The Tragedy of Colonial Enlightenment* (Durham, NC: Duke University Press, 2004).

73. Scott, *Conscripts of Modernity,* 6.

74. Scott, *Conscripts of Modernity,* 6.

1. A GLOBAL HIERARCHY OF PEOPLES

1. Abul Fazl, *The History of Akbar,* trans. Wheeler M. Thackston, vol. 5, *1590–1602* (Cambridge, MA: Harvard University Press, 2019), 81. A few years later Akbar would officially invite the Jesuits to the Mughal court to discuss Christian theology. The story of his first encounter thus should not be taken to imply a dogmatic Mughal sense of superiority. On the Mughal-Jesuits exchange, see Muzaffar Alam and Sanjay Subrahmanyam, "Mediterranean Exemplars: Jesuit Political Lessons for a Mughal Emperor," in *Machiavelli, Islam, and the East: Reorienting the Foundations of Modern Political Thought,* ed. Lucio Biasori and Giuseppe Marcocci (London: Palgrave Macmillan, 2018), 105–130.

2. Even as the Mughal imagination of politics had no space for the juridically sovereign category of the people, the rise of the urban masses in eighteenth-century India—as Abhishek Kaicker shows—put a novel emphasis on popular politics and exerted significant pressure on the Mughal framework of imperial sovereignty. See Abhishek Kaicker, *The King and the People: Sovereignty and Popular Politics in Mughal Delhi* (Oxford: Oxford University Press, 2020); on the precolonial imaginations of the "peopling" of Hindustan, see Manan Ahmed Asif, *The Loss of Hindustan: The*

Invention of India (Cambridge, MA: Harvard University Press, 2020), 143–180.

3. P. J. Marshall, "The Seventeenth and Eighteenth Centuries," in *The Raj: India and the British, 1600–1947,* ed. C. A. Bayly (London: National Portrait Gallery Publications, 1990), 19.

4. See Sanjay Subrahmanyam, *Europe's India: Words, People, Empires, 1500–1800* (Cambridge, MA: Harvard University Press, 2017), 286–325.

5. On the minor beginning of British rule and its eventual signification as historical inevitability, see Ranajit Guha, "A Conquest Foretold," in *The Small Voice of History: Collected Essays* (Ranikhet: Permanent Black Press, 2009), 373–390.

6. See Robert Travers, *Ideology and Empire in Eighteenth-Century India: The British in Bengal* (Cambridge: Cambridge University Press, 2007), 207–249.

7. On the emergence of a significant economic gap between Europe and Asia in the nineteenth century, see Kenneth Pomeranz, *The Great Divergence: China, Europe, and the Making of the Modern World Economy* (Princeton, NJ: Princeton University Press, 2000).

8. Anthony Pagden, *European Encounters with the New World: From Renaissance to Romanticism* (New Haven, CT: Yale University Press, 1993), 17–49; see also Pagden, *Lords of All the World: Ideologies of Empire in Spain, Britain, and France, c. 1500–c. 1800* (New Haven, CT: Yale University Press, 1995); Richard Tuck, *The Rights of War and Peace: Political Thought and International Order from Grotius to Kant* (Oxford: Oxford University Press, 1999).

9. See Francisco de Vitoria, "On the American Indians," in *Political Writings,* ed. Anthony Pagden and Jeremy Lawrance (Cambridge: Cambridge University Press, 1991), 233–292. See also Antony Anghie, *Imperialism, Sovereignty and the Making of International Law* (Cambridge: Cambridge University Press, 2004), 13–31.

10. See Ronald Meek, *Social Science and the Ignoble Savage* (Cambridge: Cambridge University Press, 1976), 1–4, 68–176; for an account of the limits of approaching non-Europeans as "natural humanity," see Sankar Muthu, *Enlightenment against Empire* (Princeton, NJ: Princeton University Press, 2003), 11–71.

11. Muthu, *Enlightenment against Empire,* 1–71, 259–283.

12. See C. A. Bayly, *Imperial Meridian: The British Empire and the World, 1780–1930* (London: Longman, 1989).

13. For studies on the rise of development and progress from the perspective of the history of political thought, see Uday S. Mehta, *Liberalism and Empire: A Study in Nineteenth-Century British Liberal Thought* (Chicago: University of Chicago Press, 1999); Jennifer Pitts, *A Turn to Empire: The Rise of Imperial Liberalism in Britain and France* (Princeton, NJ: Princeton University Press, 2005); for an examination of the problem around the questions of modernity and colo-

nialism, see Dipesh Chakrabarty, *Provincializing Europe: Postcolonial Thought and Historical Difference* (Princeton, NJ: Princeton University Press, 2000); Priya Satia, *Time's Monster: How History Makes History* (Cambridge, MA: Harvard University Press, 2020); on the role of imperial episteme in the making of modern Indian historiography, see Asif, *The Loss of Hindustan*.

14. Jürgen Osterhammel, *The Transformation of the World: A Global History of the Nineteenth Century* (Princeton, NJ: Princeton University Press, 2014), 45–113.

15. Rammohun Roy, "Letter to Mr. Buckingham," in *The English Works of Rammohun Roy,* vol. 1, ed. Jogendra Chunder Ghose (Calcutta: S. K. Lahiri and Co., 1906), 352.

16. See Lynn Zastoupil, *Rammohun Roy and the Making of Victorian Britain* (New York: Palgrave Macmillan, 2010), 1–8.

17. Rammohun Roy, "Additional Questions respecting the Condition of India," in Ghose, *The English Works of Rammohun Roy,* 1:295–296.

18. Rammohun, "Additional Questions," 1:295–296.

19. Rammohun, "Additional Questions," 1:299.

20. Andrew Sartori, *Bengal in Global Concept History: Culturalism in the Age of Capital* (Chicago: University of Chicago Press, 2008), 68–108.

21. Zastoupil, *Rammohun Roy,* 1. A pamphlet submitted to the US Congress by the abolitionists in the early 1830s was signed as "Rammohun Roy." The author of the pamphlet added: "In closing this address, allow me to assume the name of one of the most enlightened and benevolent of the human race now living, though not a white man, Rammohun Roy." See Adrienne Moore, *Rammohun Roy and America* (Calcutta: Sadharan Brahmo Samaj, 1942), 52.

22. For an account of Rammohun's early intellectual formation, see Sophia Dobson Collet, *The Life and Letters of Raja Rammohun Roy,* 2nd ed. (Calcutta: A. C. Sarkar, 1913), 5–9.

23. On this debate, see Dilipkumar Biswas, *Rammohan Samiksha* [Surveying Rammohan] (Kolkata: Saraswata Library, 1983), 48–63 (in Bengali).

24. Rammohun Roy, *Tuhfat-ul-Muwahhidin* [A gift to monotheists] (Calcutta: S. K. Lahiri and Co., n.d.), iii.

25. Rammohun, *Tuhfat-ul-Muwahhidin,* 20.

26. Rammohun, *Tuhfat-ul-Muwahhidin,* 24. This account of prophetic revelation—and especially the centrality of "deception" to the origin of prophethood—is quite unmistakably Voltairean. Voltaire was widely available in English translation in the period. It is worth noting, however, that according to the testimony of one of his acquaintances, John Digby, Rammohun had an imperfect command of English at the time of the conventional dating of the Tuhfat (c. 1803–1804; this dating is contested). It is not clear if he entirely lacked reading knowledge of English in that period (as Digby also notes, Rammohun started learning English in the mid-

1790s). On Digby's testimony, see Collet, *The Life and Letters of Raja Rammohun Roy*, 15. For a broad survey of Voltaire on priestcraft, see John Marshall, "Voltaire, Priestcraft and Imposture: Christianity, Judaism, and Islam," *Intellectual History Review* 28, no. 1 (2018): 167–184.

27. Rammohun, *Tuhfat-ul-Muwahhidin*, 10.

28. The distinction of the *Tuhfat*'s "psychological and sociological" rationalism from the prevalent "speculative" rationalism of eighteenth-century Indian thought has been perceptively underscored by the unnamed author of "Date of the *Tuhfat*," which accompanied the D. N. Pal edition of the text. See "Date of the Tuhfat," in Rammohun, *Tuhfat-ul-Muwahhidin*, xxxiii.

29. Rammohun Roy, introduction to "Translation of the Cena Upanishad," in Ghose, *The English Works of Rammohun Roy*, 1:4, 41.

30. Rammohun Roy, "Precepts of Jesus," in Rammohun Roy, "Extracts from a Letter on Grant's Jury Bill," in *The English Works of Raja Rammohun Roy*, ed. Kalidas Nag and Debajyoti Burman, pt. 5 (Calcutta: Sadharan Brahmo Samaj, 1948), 1–54.

31. Rammohun, introduction to "Translation of the Cena Upanishad," 41.

32. Brajendranath Seal, "Hints on the Study of Raja Rammohun Roy," in *Raja Rammohun Roy* (1896; reprint, Kolkata: Banglar Mukh, 2018), 17.

33. Rammohun Roy, "Sahamaran Bishaye Prabartak o Nibartaker Dwityiya Sambad" [A second conference between an advocate for, and an opponent of, the practice of burning widows alive]," in Rammohun Roy, *Rammohan Rachanabali* (Kolkata: Rammohan Mission, 2008), 231 (in Bengali).

34. Rammohun Roy, "Abstract of the Arguments regarding the Burning of Widows," in Ghose, *The English Works of Rammohun Roy*, 1:355–366.

35. Rammohun Roy, "Brief Remarks regarding Modern Encroachments on the Ancient Right of Females," in Ghose, *The English Works of Rammohun Roy*, 1:359–370.

36. Rammohun Roy, "The Brahmunical Magazine," in Ghose, *The English Works of Rammohun Roy*, 1:170.

37. Biswas, *Rammohan Samiksha*, 343–345.

38. Rammohun, "Brief Remarks," 1:368.

39. Rammohun Roy, introduction to "Translation of Ishopanishad," in Ghose, *The English Works of Rammohun Roy*, 1:85.

40. Sartori, *Bengal in Global Concept History*, 79.

41. Sartori, *Bengal in Global Concept History*, 87; see also C. A. Bayly, *Recovering Liberties: Indian Thought in the Age of Liberalism and Empire* (Cambridge: Cambridge University Press, 2012), 53.

42. James Mill, *The History of British India*, vol. 1 (London: Baldwin, Cradock, and Joy, 1826), 159.

43. Rammohun Roy, "Ram Doss's Reply to the Christian," in Ghose, *The English Works of Rammohun Roy*, 1:285.

44. See "Appendix 7," in Biswas, *Rammohan Samiksha,* 621. The Rammohun scholar Dilipkumar Biswas recovered this little-known exchange between Rammohun and Owen from the archives of New York Public Library. These letters appeared in the appendix to his Bengali monograph on Rammohun.

45. Biswas, *Rammohan Samiksha,* 622–623.

46. See Alan D. Hodder, "Emerson, Rammohan Roy, and the Unitarians," in *Studies in the American Renaissance,* ed. Joel Myerson (Charlottesville: University of Virginia Press, 1988), 133–148.

47. For a particularly suggestive example of Rammohun's critique of the missionaries, see his "A Dialogue between a Missionary and Three Chinese Converts," in Ghose, *The English Works of Rammohun Roy,* 1:291–294.

48. Rammohun Roy, "Extracts from a Letter on Grant's Jury Bill," in *The English Works of Raja Rammohun Roy,* ed. Kalidas Nag and Debajyoti Burman, pt. 4 (Calcutta: Sadharan Brahmo Samaj, 1947), 40. To my knowledge, this is Rammohun's only documented reference to James Mill. This indirect encounter between Rammohun and James Mill seems to have been entirely missed by scholars so far.

49. This argument directly paralleled James Mill's censure of the legal system instituted by the Company in India, especially its reliance on native agents: the codification of law and its application is "one of the most difficult tasks to which the human mind can be applied, a work to which the highest measure of European intelligence is not more than equal, could be expected to be tolerably performed by the unenlightened and perverted intellects of a few Indian pundits." See James Mill, *The History of British India,* vol. 5 (London: Baldwin, Cradock, and Joy, 1826), 513.

50. Untitled editorial, *Morning Chronicle,* July 24, 1832, 2.

51. Grant's reproduction of Rammohun has also been underscored by Lynn Zastoupil. See Zastoupil, *Rammohun Roy,* 118.

52. Charles Grant, "Letter from the Right Hon. Charles Grant, MP to the Chairman and Vice-Chairman of the East India Company," in *Raja Rammohun Roy and Progressive Movements in India: A Selection from Records, 1775–1845,* ed. Jatindra Kumar Majumdar (Calcutta: Art Press, 1941), 381–385.

53. Rammohun Roy, "Questions and Answers on the Judicial System of India," in *The English Works of Rammohun Roy,* vol. 2, ed. Jogesh Chunder Ghose (Calcutta: Aruna Press, 1887), 534–537.

54. Bimanbehari Majumdar, I think, was correct in his assessment that "the western political philosophers who seem to have influenced the mind of the Raja were not Rousseau and Thomas Paine but Montesquieu, Blackstone and Bentham." See Bimanbehari Majumdar, *History of Indian Social and Political Ideas* (1934; reprint, Calcutta: Bookland, 1967), 26–28.

55. Rammohun Roy, "Appeal to the King in Council," in Ghose, *The English Works of Rammohun Roy*, 1:451. For a similarly phrased argument in Montesquieu, see *The Spirit of the Laws* (Cambridge: Cambridge University Press, 1989), 157.

56. Rammohun, "Appeal to the King in Council," 1:451.

57. Rammohun, "Appeal to the King in Council," 1:458. For a detailed discussion of this issue, see Majumdar, *History of Indian Social and Political Ideas*, 32–36.

58. Rammohun Roy, "Brief Remarks regarding Modern Encroachments on the Ancient Rights of Females," in Ghose, *The English Works of Rammohun Roy*, 1: 359–360.

59. See, in particular, V. C. Joshi, ed., *Rammohun Roy and the Process of Modernization in India* (New Delhi: Vikas Publishing House, 1975).

60. Rosinka Chaudhuri, "'On the Colonization of India' (1829): Public Meetings, Debates and Later Disputes," *Indian Economic and Social History Review* 55, no. 4 (2018): 463–489.

61. Rammohun Roy, "Remarks on Settlement in India by Europeans," in Ghose, *The English Works of Rammohun Roy*, 2:116.

62. Rammohun, "Remarks on Settlement," 2:114.

63. Rammohun, "Remarks on Settlement," 2:115.

64. Rammohun, "Remarks on Settlement," 2:117.

65. In a brief piece on the forms of government, Rammohun critiqued both absolute monarchy and (direct) democracy, arguing that instead an aristocracy with a publicly responsive executive body is the ideal political arrangement. Excerpt from *Mirat ul-Akhbar, Calcutta Journal*, May 2, 1822.

66. On Montesquieu's nondistinction between sovereignty and government, see Richard Tuck, *The Sleeping Sovereign: The Invention of Modern Democracy* (Cambridge: Cambridge University Press 2015), 123–124.

67. Rammohun Roy, "Anti-Suttee Petition," in Ghose, *The English Works of Rammohun Roy*, 1:48.

68. Rammohun Roy, "Letter to William Rathbone, Esq," in Ghose, *The English Works of Rammohun Roy*, 2:355.

69. Rammohun, "Extracts from a Letter," in Nag and Burman, *The English Works of Raja Rammohun Roy*, pt. 4, 39.

70. Rammohun, "Extracts from a Letter," pt. 4, 41.

71. Bipin Chandra Pal attributed the origin of the idea of swaraj to Roy. See Bipin Chandra Pal, *The Brahmo Samaj and the Battle for Swaraj in India* (Kolkata: Sadharan Brahmo Samaj, 1945).

72. Partha Chatterjee, *The Black Hole of Empire: History of a Global Practice of Power* (Princeton, NJ: Princeton University Press, 2012), 158.

73. Rammohun Roy, "A Letter on English Education," in Ghose, *The English Works of Rammohun Roy*, 1:473.

74. For an early history of the idea of improvement, see Paul Warde, "The Idea of Improvement, c. 1520–1700," in *Custom, Improvement, and the Landscape in Early Modern Britain,* ed. Richard Hoyle (Farnham, UK: Ashgate, 2011), 127–148.

75. Jogendra Chunder Ghose, "Introduction," in Ghose, *The English Works of Rammohun Roy,* 1:xxvi.

76. Majumdar, *History of Indian Social and Political Ideas,* 32.

77. Travers, *Ideology and Empire,* 50.

78. Travers, *Ideology and Empire,* 16–20; see also Ranajit Guha, *A Rule of Property for Bengal: An Essay on the Idea of Permanent Settlement* (Ranikhet: Permanent Black Press, 2016), 21–22.

79. While Burke and Hastings differed with regard to how India was to be politically treated, both worked within the pluralist framework of ancient constitutionalism and shared a certain respect for "Indian tradition." On Burke and Hastings's different notions of pluralism, see Jennifer Pitts, *Boundaries of the International: Law and Empire* (Cambridge, MA: Harvard University Press, 2018), 92–117.

80. Eric Stokes, *English Utilitarians and India* (Oxford: Oxford University Press, 1959). 8. As Stokes further argues, the Permanent Settlement Act institutionalized by Cornwallis and administrative reform along the British tradition suggested by his successor, Richard Wellesley, faced resistance from a group of British administrators (Munro, Malcolm, Metcalfe, et al.) who preferred to view India through the Burkean lens of "human society as a continuous community of the past, present, and future" (15).

81. Thomas Metcalf, *Ideologies of the Raj,* vol. 3, pt. 4 of *The New Cambridge History of India* (Cambridge: Cambridge University Press, 1995), 25.

82. Burton Stein, *Thomas Munro: The Origins of the Colonial State and His Vision of Empire* (Delhi: Oxford University Press, 1989), 358.

83. Pitts, *A Turn to Empire,* 123–133.

84. James Mill, *The History of British India,* vol. 2 (London: Baldwin, Cradock, and Joy, 1826), 190.

85. On this point, see Jurgen Osterhammel, "'Peoples without History' in British and German Historical Thought," in *British and German Historiography, 1750–1950: Traditions, Perceptions, and Transfers,* ed. Benedikt Stuchtey and Peter Wende (Oxford: Oxford University Press, 2000), 265–287. For a discussion of the plural intellectual sources of Victorian historicism, see Mark Bevir, "Historicism and the Human Sciences in Victorian Britain," in *Historicism and the Human Sciences in Victorian Britain,* ed. Mark Bevir (Cambridge: Cambridge University Press, 2017), 1–20.

86. See, for instance, G. W. F Hegel, *Lectures on the Philosophy of World History,* vol. 1, ed. Robert F. Brown and Peter C. Hodgson (Oxford: Clarendon Press, 2011), 277–286.

87. See Metcalf, *Ideologies of the Raj;* Jon Wilson, *The Domination of Strangers: Modern Governance in Eastern India, 1780–1835* (London: Palgrave Macmillan, 2008), 133–160.

88. Mill, *The History of British India,* 5:538.

89. The classic critique of James Mill is Macaulay's "Mill on Government," in *Miscellaneous Writings of Lord Macaulay,* vol. 1 (London: Longman, Green, Longman, and Roberts, 1860), 282–322. James Mill did consider representative institutions to be the best means for the end of individual happiness. But for backward peoples, Mill argued, good government should instead be prioritized. It is worth noting that in a letter to David Ricardo, Mill speculated if the societies in a "low state of civilization" were left to their own devices, their own representative government might have been more beneficial than "any other government that would *emanate from themselves.*" Having noted this point, Mill concluded that rule by an advanced civilization, despite all its evils, is preferable to native rule—representative or not. In any case, James Mill's preference for representative government was primarily on utilitarian grounds—he did not value it for its intrinsic worth in the way Macaulay and the younger Mill would. See "Mill to Ricardo (14 August 1819)," in *The Work and Correspondence of David Ricardo,* vol. 8 (Indianapolis: Liberty Fund, 2005), 52–53 (emphasis added). On James Mill's view of representation, see Richard Krouse, "Two Concepts of Democratic Representation: James and John Stuart Mill," *Journal of Politics* 44, no. 2 (1982): 509–537.

90. For an account of the convergence between the elder Mill and Macaulay's progressivist views of Indian history against the backdrop of their general philosophical divergence, see Stefan Collini, Donald Winch, and John Burrow, "The Cause of Good Government: Philosophic Whigs versus Philosophic Radicals," in *That Noble Science of Politics: A Study in Nineteenth-Century Intellectual History* (Cambridge: Cambridge University Press, 1983), 91–126.

91. Macaulay, *Miscellaneous Writings of Lord Macaulay,* 162.

92. Macaulay, *Miscellaneous Writings of Lord Macaulay,* 142.

93. Macaulay, *Miscellaneous Writings of Lord Macaulay,* 160.

94. Macaulay, *Miscellaneous Writings of Lord Macaulay,* 163 (emphasis added).

95. John Stuart Mill, *The Collected Works of John Stuart Mill,* 33 vols. (hereafter cited as *CWJSM*), vol. 1, *Autobiography and Literary Essays,* ed. John M. Robson and Jack Stillinger (Toronto: University of Toronto Press, 1981), 177 (emphasis added).

96. Lynn Zastoupil, "Intellectual Flows and Counterflows: The Strange Case of J. S. Mill," in *Colonial Exchanges: Political Theory and the Agency of the Colonized,* ed. Burke A. Hendrix and Deborah Baumgold (Manchester: Manchester University Press, 2017). A decade later, Mill would forward a sig-

nature of Rammohun Roy to Thomas Carlyle (which was sought by someone Carlyle knew). As Zastoupil notes, this is the only evidence we have of the younger Mill's knowledge of Rammohun.

97. *CWJSM,* 18:119. In *A System of Logic,* Mill also suggestively distinguished "progress" from "improvement." The former connotes the historical movement of society, the point that "in each successive age the principal phenomena of society are different from what they were in the age preceding, and still more different from any previous age." Improvement, on the other hand, has a moral dimension, as it connotes a "better and happier state" for humans. Despite the analytical distinction (and he was not always precise in his deployments of these terms), Mill believed that improvement and progress generally were not in tension. See *CWJSM,* 8:913–914.

98. *CWJSM,* 18:121.

99. *CWJSM,* 18:123.

100. *CWJSM,* 18:123.

101. *CWJSM,* 18:127–128.

102. *CWJSM,* 18:128.

103. Syria and Timbuktu, of course, shared certain commonalities as Muslim communities and as centers of Sunni learning. But their shared Islamic traditions do not seem to be what Mill had in mind here. In fact, the coupling of vastly different non-European places was not unique to this instance (he would also lump together "Malays and Bedouins" to make the point regarding the improbability of democracy among backward peoples in *Considerations on Representative Government;* see *CWJSM,* 19:394). On this point, see also Pitts, *A Turn to Empire,* 252–253.

104. *CWJSM,* 19:380.

105. *CWJSM,* 19:413.

106. *CWJSM,* 19:416.

107. *CWJSM,* 19:414.

108. *CWJSM,* 19:415.

109. *CWJSM,* 19:377.

110. For a subtle appreciation of Mill on nationality, see Pratap B. Mehta, "Liberalism, Nation, and Empire: The Case of J. S. Mill," in *Empire and Modern Political Thought,* ed. Sankar Muthu (Cambridge: Cambridge University Press, 2012), 232–260.

111. *CWJSM,* 19:418.

112. Although Mill confessed that he had not read Kant and Hegel directly, he also noted that the works by their "English and French interpreters" had been "extremely useful" to him. John Stuart Mill, "Letter to Auguste Comte" (March 13, 1843), in *The Correspondence of John Stuart Mill and Auguste Comte,* trans. Oscar A. Haac (New Brunswick, NJ: Transaction Publishers, 1995), 140.

113. *CWJSM*, 10:318.

114. *CWJSM*, 19:399.

115. For alternative readings, see Inder Marwah "Two Concepts of Liberal De-velopmentalism," *European Journal of Political Theory* 15, no. 1 (2016): 97–123. See also Margaret Kohn and Daniel I. O'Neill, "A Tale of Two Indias: Burke and Mill on Empire and Slavery in the West Indies and America," *Political Theory* 34, no. 2 (2006): 192–228.

116. John Stuart Mill, "First Draft of a Court of Directors' Public Department Dispatch to India," in *The Great Indian Education Debate: Documents Relating to the Orientalist-Anglicist Controversy, 1781–1843,* ed. Lynn Zastoupil and Martin Moir (Surrey, UK: Curzon Press, 1999), 232.

117. On Mill and nationality, see Georgios Varouxakis, *Mill on Nationality* (London: Routledge, 2002).

118. *CWJSM*, 19:408–410.

119. See *CWJSM*, 21:87–95.

120. *CWJSM*, 19:413.

121. *CWJSM*, 19:418. Mill is not always precise in his uses of terms such as "stage of civilization," "state of society," "national character," and so on. While he generally employed "stage/state of civilization" and "state of society" interchangeably and distinguished this from the question of "character," there are occasional instances when he also folded the question of "na-tional character" into the "state of society." Mill was a friendly critic of Comte's account of the three stages of progress, on the ground of its inad-equate scientific substantiation, but his own attempt to articulate a more empirically minded approach to the interaction between "history" (that is, changes in the "state of society") and "human nature" in the developmental process was left unresolved in the *Logic* (and he never revisited the problem with systematic intent).

122. *CWJSM*, 19:295.

123. *CWJSM*, 19:419.

124. *CWJSM*, 19:396–398.

125. *CWJSM*, 19:550.

126. *CWJSM*, 19:564; see also Duncan Bell, "John Stuart Mill on Colonies," *Political Theory* 38, no. 1 (2011): 34–64.

127. See Nadia Urbinati, "The Many Heads of the Hydra: J. S. Mill on Despo-tism," in *J. S. Mill's Political Thought: A Bicentennial Reassessment,* ed. Nadia Urbi-nati and Alex Zakaras (Cambridge: Cambridge University Press, 2007), 78.

128. For a rich study of the "language of capacity" in nineteenth-century lib-eral thought, see Alan S. Kahan, *Liberalism in Nineteenth-Century Europe: The Political Culture of Limited Suffrage* (New York: Palgrave Macmillan, 2003).

129. On the crucial place of the stationary state in Mill's democratic thought, see Georgios Varouxakis, "Mill on Democracy Revisited," in *A Companion to*

Mill, ed. Christopher Macleod and Dale E. Miller (Oxford: Wiley-Blackwell, 2016), 454–471. Mill's more robust defense of gender equality, as Linda Zerilli argues, was related to his developmental approach to the English working class: "On closer examination ... [Mill's] argument for [female] suffrage turns out to be justification for increased intervention into the social. Women would be the executors of reform, the volunteers who would reduce the crushing expense of reform, and the superintendents of Poor Law reform." Linda M. G. Zerilli, *Signifying Woman: Culture and Chaos in Rousseau, Burke, and Mill* (Ithaca, NY: Cornell University Press, 1994), 124.

130. See, for instance, *CWJSM* 19: 323.

131. Hannah Arendt, *The Human Condition* (Chicago: University of Chicago Press, 1958), 250.

132. See Jimmy Casas Klausen, "Violence and Epistemology: JS Mill's Indians after the 'Mutiny,'" *Political Research Quarterly* 69, no. 1 (2016): 96–107.

133. "The English in India," *The Westminster Review* 68–69 (1857–1858): 110–111.

134. Grish Chunder Ghose, "Who Are the People of India?," in *Selections from the Writings of Grish Chunder Ghose*, ed. Manmathanath Ghosh (Calcutta: Indian Daily News Press, 1912), 283.

135. Ghose, "Who Are the People of India?," 284.

2. THE BIRTH OF THE PEOPLE

Epigraph: Rabindranath Tagore, "Ebar Firao More" [Turn me back now], in *Chitra* (Kolkata: Kalidas Chakrabarty, 1896), 18–19. All translations from Bengali, unless otherwise stated, are my own.

1. On the rise of "economic nationalism" in India in the second half of the nineteenth century, see also Bipan Chandra, *The Rise and Growth of Economic Nationalism in India: Economic Policies of Indian National Leadership, 1880–1905* (1966; reprint, New Delhi: Har-Anand, 2010); and Manu Goswami, *Producing India: From Colonial Economy to National Space* (Chicago: University of Chicago Press, 2004), 209–241.

2. Pierre Rosanvallon, *Democracy Past and Future,* ed. Samuel Moyn (New York: Columbia University Press, 2006), 82.

3. For a reading of Indian liberalism as a "caricature" of European "bourgeois" liberalism, see Ranajit Guha, *Dominance without Hegemony: History and Power in Colonial India* (Cambridge, MA: Harvard University Press, 1997), 4–5; for an account that portrays late nineteenth-century Indian political effort as self-interested collaboration, see Anil Seal, *The Emergence of Indian Nationalism: Competition and Collaboration in the Later Nineteenth Century* (Cambridge: Cambridge University Press, 1971).

4. C. A. Bayly, *Recovering Liberties: Indian Thought in the Age of Liberalism and Empire* (Cambridge: Cambridge University Press, 2012), 4; see also Ro-

chana Bajpai, "Liberalism in India: A Sketch," in *Liberalism as Ideology: Essays in Honour of Michael Freeden,* ed. Ben Jackson and Marc Stears (Oxford: Oxford University Press, 2012), 53–76.

5. Andrew Sartori, *Bengal in Global Concept History: Culturalism in the Age of Capital* (Chicago: University of Chicago Press, 2008), 73.

6. On the central place of representative government in nineteenth-century European liberal thought, see William Selinger and Gregory Conti, "The Lost History of *Political* Liberalism," *History of European Ideas* 46, no. 3 (2020): 341–354.

7. To give one example, in 1874 the Bengali essayist and novelist Bankim-chandra Chatterjee published a satirical dialogue between an English-educated *babu* (gentleman) who was excited by the prospect of self-government, and a monkey (who featured, at once, as a wild animal and a devotee of the Hindu god Rama) that also claimed to perform "self-government" as a free animal. Consider, for instance, this exchange: "Babu: '... The point is, you're the slave of Rama, and I am of the English. Is your Rama greater or my English? My English kingdom is bringing a new entity into being—local self-government. Did your *Ramarajya* [Kingdom of Rama] have it?' Monkey: 'What is this thing called self-government? Is it like a [delicious] banana?' Babu: 'No, not that. It means ruling over oneself.'" In what followed, the cunning monkey demonstrated the folly of the babu's definition of self-government, on the ground that the babu sought self-government without having any share in sovereignty. See Bankimchandra Chattopadhyay, *Lokarahasya* [Essays on society], in *Bankimrachanabali,* vol. 2 (Kolkata: Sahitya Akademi, 1954), 39–40.

8. Dadabhai Naoroji, *Dadabhai, Essays, Speeches, and Writings on Indian Politics* (Bombay: Caxton Printing Works, 1887), 26.

9. Surendranath Banerjea, *A Nation in Making: Being the Reminiscences of Fifty Years of Public Life* (London: Oxford University Press, 1925), 67.

10. Duncan Bell, "What Is Liberalism?," *Political Theory* 42, no. 6 (2014): 682–715.

11. Rammohun Roy, "Judicial and Revenue Systems of India," in *The English Works of Rammohun Roy,* vol. 2, ed. Jogesh Chunder Ghose (Calcutta: Aruna Press, 1887), 515.

12. For a cultural history of Young Bengal, see Rosinka Chaudhuri, *Freedom and Beef Steaks: Colonial Calcutta Culture* (Hyderabad: Orient Blackswan, 2012).

13. See "Government of the Company," in *Selections from Jnanannesan,* ed. Suresh Chandra Moitra (Calcutta: Prajna, 1979), 61–64.

14. "Employment of the Natives in the Public Service," in Moitra, *Selections from Jnanannesan,* 60.

15. James Mill quoted in Moitra, *Selections from Jnanannesan,* 59.

16. For a rich intellectual history of the reinvention of the very idea of morality in nineteenth-century Bengal, see Thomas Newbold, "The Critical Age: Modern Periodization and Moral Revaluation in Colonial Bengal" (PhD diss., University of Chicago, 2022).

17. Dakshinaranjan Mukherjee's name was spelled in a variety of ways ("Dukhina Ranjan" "Duckinarungun," "Dukinarungun," etc.) in his own lifetime. Given the lack of consistency of the old spellings of his name, I will stick to its modernized English rendition (namely, Dakshinaranjan Mukherjee).

18. *Bengal Hurkaru,* March 2, 1843.

19. *Bengal Hurkaru,* March 2, 1843.

20. *Bengal Hurkaru,* March 2, 1843.

21. *Bengal Hurkaru,* March 2, 1843.

22. *Bengal Hurkaru,* March 3, 1843.

23. *Bengal Hurkaru,* March 3, 1843.

24. *Bengal Hurkaru,* February 13, 1843.

25. *Bengal Hurkaru,* February 13, 1843.

26. *Bengal Hurkaru,* February 13, 1843.

27. *Bengal Hurkaru,* February 13, 1843.

28. "Review of Eastern News," *Asiatic Journal and Monthly Register for British and Foreign India, China, and Australasia* 40 (January–April 1843): 190.

29. *Friend of India,* February 16, 1843.

30. *Bengal Hurkaru,* February 9, 1843.

31. Quoted in "Hindoo Opinions on the Revolt," *The Aberdeen Journal,* October 21, 1857.

32. Quoted in "Hindoo Opinions on the Revolt."

33. Editorial, "What Is the Government of India?," *Mahratta* 1, no. 18 (1881): 1–2. (Accessed at the Nehru Memorial Museum and Library, New Delhi.)

34. Editorial, "Are We Represented in the British Parliament?," *Mahratta* 1, no. 20 (1881): 1.

35. Bankimchandra Chatterjee, *Anandamath* (Kolkata: Ananda Publishers, 1983), 189 (in Bengali).

36. For instance, see Bankimchandra Chatterjee, "Bangla Shasaner Kal" [The machinery for ruling over Bengal], in *Bankimrachanabli,* vol. 2 (Kolkata: Sahitya Samsad, 1954), 327–330 (in Bengali). On the "illiberal" underpinnings of British rule in India, see Jon Wilson, *The Domination of Strangers: Modern Governance in Eastern India, 1780–1835* (London: Palgrave Macmillan, 2008).

37. John Crawfurd, "On the Physical and Mental Characteristics of the European and Asiatic Races of Man," in *Transactions of the Ethnological Society of London,* vol. 5 (London: John Murray, 1867), 81; on Crawfurd and India, see Onur Ulas Ince, "Deprovincializing Racial Capitalism: John

Crawfurd and Settler Colonialism in India," *American Political Science Review* 116, no. 1 (2022): 144–160.

38. Dadabhai Naoroji, "Observations on Mr. Crawfurd's Paper on the European and Asiatic Races, Read before the Ethnological Society on February 13th, 1886," in *Transactions of the Ethnological Society of London,* 5:146. For an insightful reconstruction of the debate, see Dinyar Patel, *Naoroji: Pioneer of Indian Nationalism* (Cambridge, MA: Harvard University Press, 2020), 131–135.

39. Naoroji, "Observations on Mr. Crawfurd's Paper," 5:146–149.

40. Dadabhai Naoroji, *Poverty and Un-British Rule in India* (London: Swan Sonnenschein and Co., 1901), 583.

41. For a rich study of Naoroji's drain theory in the context of broader nineteenth-century political-economic thought, see Vikram Visana, *Uncivil Liberalism: Labour, Capital and Commercial Society in Dadabhai Naoroji's Political Thought* (Cambridge: Cambridge University Press, 2022), esp. 97–122. On the Maharashtran predecessors of Naoroji's drain theory, see J. V. Naik, "Forerunners of Dadabhai Naoroji's Drain Theory," *Economic and Political Weekly* 36, no. 46–47 (2001): 4428–4432. Naoroji's drain theory, in a way, prefigured twentieth-century accounts of European underdevelopment of Asia and Africa, including dependency theory. The challenge to insert the colonial people into this story, too, persisted and inspired different answers. For a recent exploration of these questions through Walter Rodney, see David Myer Temin, "Development in Decolonization: Walter Rodney, Third World Developmentalism, and 'Decolonizing Political Theory,'" *American Political Science Review* 117, no. 1 (2023): 235–248.

42. See B. N. Ganguli, *Dadabhai Naoroji and the Drain Theory* (Bombay: Asia Publishing House, 1965), 136.

43. Naoroji, *Dadabhai, Essays, Speeches,* 212.

44. Naoroji, *Poverty and Un-British Rule,* 185.

45. Naoroji, *Poverty and Un-British Rule,* 62.

46. Naoroji, *Poverty and Un-British Rule,* 247.

47. Naoroji, *Poverty and Un-British Rule,* 203.

48. Naoroji, *Dadabhai, Essays, Speeches,* 37.

49. Naoroji, *Poverty and Un-British Rule,* 217.

50. For other contemporaneous reflections on the relationship between the moral and the intellectual, see Kissory Chand Mittra, "Rammohun Roy," *Calcutta Review* 4 (December 1845): 355–393; Bankimchandra Chatterjee, "Samya [Equality]," in *Bankimrachanabali,* vol. 2 (Kolkata: Sahitya Akademi, 1954), 381–406.

51. Surendranath Banerjea, *Speeches of Surendranath Banerjea,* vol. 6 (Calcutta: S. K. Laihir and Co., 1908), 121.

52. Banerjea, *Speeches of Surendranath Banerjea,* 237.

53. Surendranath Banerjea, *Speeches and Writings of Hon. Surendranath Banerjea* (Madras: G. A. Natesen and Co., 1917), 216.

54. Banerjea, *Speeches and Writings,* 216.

55. Banerjea, *Speeches and Writings,* 214–215.

56. Banerjea, *Speeches and Writings,* 227–228.

57. Banerjea, *Speeches and Writings,* 398.

58. Banerjea, *Speeches and Writings,* 24.

59. Naoroji, *Dadabhai, Essays, Speeches,* 295.

60. Alexis de Tocqueville, *The Ancien Régime and the French Revolution,* trans. Arthur Goldhammer (Cambridge: Cambridge University Press, 2011), 160.

61. Tocqueville, *The Ancien Régime,* 160.

62. Rosanvallon, *Democracy Past and Future,* 93.

63. Bipin Chandra Pal, *Writings and Speeches of Bipin Chandra Pal,* vol. 1, pt. 1 (1889; reprint, Calcutta: Yugayatri Prakashak Limited, 1954), 14, 19. Appreciations of the French Revolution for its "impatience" were rare, but not entirely absent. Pal's future colleague Aurobindo Ghose was unique in defending the French revolutionary lessons against the British story of democratization as early as 1893: "Rather we know that the first step of that fortunate country towards progress was not through any decent and orderly expansion, but through a purification by blood and fire. It was not a convocation of respectable citizens, but the vast and ignorant proletariate, that emerged from a prolonged and almost coeval apathy and blotted out in five terrible years the accumulated oppression of thirteen centuries." Sri Aurobindo, "New Lamps for the Old—IV," in *Bande Mataram* (Pondicherry: Sri Aurobindo Ashram Publication Department, 2002), 29.

64. Arendt, *On Revolution* (London: Penguin Books, 1990), 59–114.

65. For a representative and influential version of this argument, see T. B. Macaulay, *Speeches of Lord Macaulay: Corrected by Himself* (London, 1860), 76.

66. Surendranath Banerjea, *Speeches and Writings of Hon. Surendranath Banerjea* (Madras: G. A. Natesen and Co., 1917), 12–13; see also M. G. Ranade, *Miscellaneous Writings of the Late Honourable Justice M. G. Ranade* (New Delhi: Sahitya Akademi, 1992), 114–121.

67. Dadabhai Naoroji, *Selected Speeches and Writings of Dadabhai Naoroji* (Madras: G. A. Natesan and Co., 1917), 3–4.

68. On the decline of liberal imperialism as an imperial ideology in Britain, see Karuna Mantena, *Alibis of Empire: Henry Maine and the Ends of Liberal Imperialism* (Princeton, NJ: Princeton University Press, 2010).

69. See Theodore Koditschek, *Liberalism, Imperialism, and the Historical Imagination: Nineteenth-Century Visions of a Greater Britain* (Cambridge: Cambridge University Press, 2011), 263–313.

70. Rabindranath Tagore, "Chhoto o Baro" [The little and the great], in *Kalantar* (Kolkata: Visvabharati, 1355), 83–112.

71. The most comprehensive study of Mill's reception in nineteenth-century India is S. Ambirajan, "John Stuart Mill and India," in *J. S. Mill's Encounter with India,* ed. Martin I. Moir, Douglas M. Peers, and Lynn Zastoupil (Toronto: University of Toronto Press, 1999), 221-264.

72. Naoroji, *Dadabhai, Essays, Speeches,* 37.

73. Naoroji, *Dadabhai, Essays, Speeches,* 37.

74. On Indians and imperial citizenship, see Sukanya Banerjee, *Becoming Imperial Citizens: Indians in the Late-Victorian Empire* (Durham, NC: Duke University Press, 2010); for an insightful reading of Naoroji and his colleagues regarding their investment in imperial sovereignty, see Mithi Mukherjee, *India in the Shadow of Empire: A Legal and Political History* (Delhi: Oxford University Press, 2010).

75. On the exclusion of nonwhite colonies from the projects of Greater Britain, see Duncan Bell, *The Idea of Greater Britain: Empire and the Future of World Order, 1860–1900* (Princeton, NJ: Princeton University Press, 2007).

76. R. C. Dutt, *England and India: A Record of Progress during a Hundred Years, 1785–1885* (London: Chatto and Windus, 1897), x.

77. Dutt, *England and India,* x.

78. Naoroji, *Poverty and Un-British Rule,* 206 (emphasis in original).

79. Naoroji, *Dadabhai, Essays, Speeches,* 251-252.

80. Naoroji, *Dadabhai, Essays, Speeches,* 251-252.

81. Though it is not clear if Naoroji was aware of Mill's argument against involving the English people in the administration of India (especially in the final chapter of *Considerations on Representative Government*).

82. See Naoroji, *Dadabhai, Essays, Speeches,* 83-96.

83. Surendranath Banerjea, "The Vernacular Press Act," in *Speeches and Writings of Babu Surendranath Banerjea, 1876–1880* (Calcutta: Bose Press, 1880), 108.

84. Banerjea, "The Vernacular Press Act," 109.

85. Banerjea, "The Vernacular Press Act—Second Meeting," in *Speeches and Writings of Babu Surendranath Banerjea,* 114. Naoroji also argued similarly for the political priority of campaigning in Britain. See Patel, *Naoroji,* 108-119.

86. Koditschek, *Liberalism, Imperialism,* 291.

87. Bimanbehari Majumdar, *History of Indian Social and Political Ideas* (1934; reprint, Calcutta: Bookland, 1967), 98.

88. Tagore, "Chhoto o Baro," 83-112 (emphasis added).

89. Aurobindo, "The Effect of Petitionary Politics," in *Bande Mataram,* 459.

90. Jawaharlal Nehru, *Toward Freedom: The Autobiography of Jawaharlal Nehru* (New York: John Day, 1941), 51.

91. Nehru, *Toward Freedom,* 261.

92. *Report of the Proceedings of the Second Session of the All India Conference of the Moderate Party Held at the Town Hall, Calcutta on the 30th and 31st December, 1919 and 1st January, 1920* (Calcutta, 1920), 22.

93. Consider, for example, this passage from Buch's *Liberalism:* "The essential mission of the Indian Liberal Party was to translate the great social and political ideas for which the Western Government in its highest conception stood into the lives and thoughts, first, of the educated people of India and, through them, of the masses. These ideals they saw in the march of, first, English and, then, European and American history." Maganlal Buch, *The Rise and Growth of Indian Liberalism* (Baroda: Atmaram Press, 1938), 313.

94. Buch, *The Rise and Growth of Indian Liberalism,* 174.

95. V. N. Naik, *Indian Liberalism: A Study, 1918–1943* (Bombay: Padma Publications, 1945), 1.

96. K. M. Panikkar, *In Defence of Liberalism* (Bombay: Asia Publishing House, 1962), 2.

97. James Fitzjames Stephen, "Liberalism," *Cornhill Magazine,* January 1862, 70–83.

98. See Jörn Leonhard, "From European Liberalism to the Languages of Liberalisms: The Semantics of Liberalism in European Comparison," in *Redescriptions: Yearbook of Political Thought and Conceptual History* 8 (2004): 17–51.

99. K. T. Telang, "The Ilbert Bill Question," in *Selected Writings and Speeches* (Bombay: K. R. Mitra, 1916), 194.

100. Bal Gangadhar Tilak, "Tenets of the New Party," in *Speeches and Writings of Bal Gangadhar Tilak* (Madras: Ganesh and Co., 1919), 57–58.

101. Ranajit Guha, "Neel-Darpan: The Image of a Peasant Revolt in a Liberal Mirror," *Journal of Peasant Studies* 2, no.1 (1974): 43.

102. See Sumit Sarkar, "Rammohun Roy and the Break with the Past," in *Rammohun Roy and the Process of Modernization in India,* ed. V. C. Joshi (New Delhi: Vikas, 1975), 46–68.

103. See, in particular, Uday Singh Mehta, *Liberalism and Empire: A Study in Nineteenth-Century British Liberal Thought* (Chicago: University of Chicago Press, 1999); Jennifer Pitts, *A Turn to Empire: The Rise of Imperial Liberalism in Britain and France* (Princeton, NJ: Princeton University Press, 2005); Catherine Hall, *Civilising Subjects: Metropole and Colony in the English Imagination, 1830–1867* (Chicago: University of Chicago Press, 2002).

104. Bayly, *Recovering Liberties,* 1.

105. Banerjea, *Speeches of Surendranath Banerjea,* 33, 36.

106. Banerjea, *A Nation in Making,* 67.

107. Banerjea, *A Nation in Making,* 44.

3. THE COLONIAL PARADOX OF PEOPLEHOOD

1. Dadabhai Naoroji, *Speeches and Writings of Dadabhai Naoroji* (Madras: G. A. Nathesen and Co., 1917), 73.

2. Naoroji, *Speeches and Writings,* 79.

3. A. C. Mazumdar, *The Indian National Evolution: A Brief Survey of the Origin and Progress of the Indian National Congress and the Growth of Indian Nationalism* (Madras: G. A. Natesen & Co., 1917), 103.

4. Quoted in Shyamji Krishnavarma, "Home Rule Is 'SVARAJYA,'" *Indian Sociologist* 3, no. 3 (March 1907): 11.

5. Aurobindo, "The Results of the Congress" (December 31, 1906), in *Bande Mataram: Political Writings and Speeches* (Pondicherry: Sri Aurobindo Ashram, 2002), 208.

6. Krishnavarma, "Home Rule Is 'SVARAJYA,'" 11.

7. See Jason Frank, *Constituent Moments: Enacting the People in Post-Revolutionary America* (Durham, NC: Duke University Press, 2010); Angélica Bernal, *Beyond Origins: Rethinking Founding in a Time of Constitutional Democracy* (New York: Oxford University Press, 2017).

8. Frank, *Constituent Moments*, 3.

9. Fred Dallmayr, "What Is Swaraj? Lessons from Gandhi," in *Gandhi, Freedom, and Self-Rule*, ed. Anthony J. Parel (New York: Lexington Books, 2000), 105; Raghavan N. Iyer, *The Moral and Political Thought of Mahatma Gandhi* (New York: Oxford University Press, 1973), 347; Parel, "Editor's Introduction," in Gandhi, *"Hind Swaraj" and Other Writings* (Cambridge: Cambridge University Press, 1997), xxx.

10. Partha Chatterjee, *Nationalist Thought and the Colonial World: A Derivative Discourse* (London: Zed Books, 1986), 110; Uday Mehta, "Gandhi on Democracy, Politics and the Ethics of Everyday Life," *Modern Intellectual History* 7, no. 2 (2010): 371; Bhikhu Parekh, *Gandhi's Political Philosophy: A Critical Examination* (Notre Dame, IN: University of Notre Dame Press, 1989), 203–205.

11. See Sumit Sarkar, *Swadeshi Movement in Bengal, 1903–08* (Ranikhet: Permanent Black Press, 2010).

12. There were only a handful of open-air public meetings in Kolkata, the capital of British India, in the nineteenth century. This would dramatically proliferate with the rise of the mass anticolonial movement in the early twentieth century, beginning with the Swadeshi movement. See Sarkar, *Swadeshi Movement in Bengal*, 216.

13. Aurobindo, *Bande Mataram*, 173–175.

14. Aurobindo, *Bande Mataram*, 150.

15. Naoroji, *Speeches and Writings*, 93.

16. Naoroji, *Speeches and Writings*, 96.

17. Naoroji, *Speeches and Writings*, 79.

18. In addition to the Colonies, Naoroji—as Vikram Visana notes—also "compared Indian 'self-government' to the status that Indian native states like Baroda and Mysore enjoyed." See Vikram Visana, *Uncivil Liberalism: Labour,*

Capital and Commercial Society in Dadabhai Naoroji's Political Thought (Cambridge: Cambridge University Press, 2022), 148.

19. See Naoroji, *Speeches and Writings,* 201. Even though the discourse of Greater Britain never quite took off in colonial India (and it was also generally excluded from the British discussions on the topic), Naoroji's career as a member of the British Parliament likely inflected his argument with the aspects of the Greater Britain project. See Duncan Bell, *The Idea of Greater Britain: Empire and the Future of World Order, 1860–1900* (Princeton, NJ: Princeton University Press, 2007).

20. Naoroji, *Speeches and Writings,* 92.

21. Naoroji, *Speeches and Writings,* 78.

22. Mazumdar, *The Indian National Evolution,* 103–104.

23. Mazumdar, *The Indian National Evolution,* 103, liv.

24. Mazumdar, *The Indian National Evolution,* liv.

25. Bal Gangadhar Tilak, *Bal Gangadhar Tilak: His Writings and Speeches* (Madras: Ganesh and Co., 1922), 57.

26. Tilak, *Bal Gangadhar Tilak,* 61–63.

27. Aurobindo, "The *Times* on Congress Reforms," in *Bande Mataram,* 139.

28. Bipin Chandra Pal, *Speeches of Bipin Chandra Pal, Delivered at Madras* (Madras: Ganesh and Co., 1907), 31–32.

29. Pal, *Speeches of Bipin Chandra Pal,* 32.

30. Pal, *Speeches of Bipin Chandra Pal,* 36–37.

31. Pal, *Speeches of Bipin Chandra Pal,* 31.

32. Pal, *Speeches of Bipin Chandra Pal,* 63.

33. Pal, *Speeches of Bipin Chandra Pal,* 62–63.

34. Pal, *Speeches of Bipin Chandra Pal,* 64.

35. Pal, *Speeches of Bipin Chandra Pal,* 72.

36. Pal, *Speeches of Bipin Chandra Pal,* 73 (emphasis in original).

37. Bipin Chandra Pal, *Swadeshi and Swaraj* (Calcutta: Yugayatri Prakashak, 1954), 69–70.

38. Pal, *Speeches of Bipin Chandra Pal,* 109 (emphasis added).

39. Pal, *Speeches of Bipin Chandra Pal,* 27.

40. Pal, *Speeches of Bipin Chandra Pal,* 69.

41. Sarkar, *Swadeshi Movement in Bengal,* 39–53.

42. Pal, *Swadeshi and Swaraj,* 71–72, 217.

43. Pal, *Swadeshi and Swaraj,* 64.

44. Tilak, *Bal Gangadhar Tilak,* 61–65.

45. Tilak, *Bal Gangadhar Tilak,* 64.

46. Tilak, *Bal Gangadhar Tilak,* 82–83.

47. Tilak, *Bal Gangadhar Tilak,* 43.

48. Tilak, *Bal Gangadhar Tilak,* 43.

49. Bal Gangadhar Tilak, "The Real Meaning of the Bomb," in *Full and Authentic Report of the Tilak Trial: Being the Only Authorised Verbatim Account of the Whole Proceedings with Introduction and Character Sketch of Bal Gangadhar Tilak* (Bombay: N. C. Kelkar, 1908), 46.

50. Tilak, "The Real Meaning of the Bomb," 45.

51. Tilak, "The Real Meaning of the Bomb," 42.

52. On the sedition case and its crucial place in Indian political history, see Shruti Kapila, *Violent Fraternity: Indian Political Thought in the Global Age* (Princeton, NJ: Princeton University Press, 2021), 14–52.

53. See Shabnum Tejani, *Indian Secularism: A Social and Intellectual History, 1890–1950* (Ranikhet: Permanent Black Press, 2007), 53–110. As Shruti Kapila observes, Tilak did not so much "revive" religious motifs in Indian politics but represent "the initial, foundational, and open interplay between a religion and a politics that the imperial state not only sought to separate, but whose separation it zealously policed." Kapila, *Violent Fraternity,* 17.

54. Tilak, *Bal Gangadhar Tilak,* 56.

55. Tilak, *Bal Gangadhar Tilak,* 68 (emphasis added).

56. Bal Gangadhar Tilak, "The Secret Meaning of the Bomb," in *Full and Authentic Report of the Tilak Trial: Being the Only Authorised Verbatim Account of the Whole Proceedings with Introduction and Character Sketch of Bal Gangadhar Tilak* (Bombay: N. C. Kelkar, 1908), 55.

57. Tilak, *Bal Gangadhar Tilak,* 74–75.

58. Tilak, *Bal Gangadhar Tilak,* 108.

59. Tilak, *Bal Gangadhar Tilak,* 113–114 (emphasis in original).

60. Tilak, *Bal Gangadhar Tilak,* 185.

61. On the limits of universalizing the terms of founding inherited from European political thought, see Leigh Jenco, *Making the Political: Founding and Action in the Political Theory of Zhang Shizhao* (Cambridge: Cambridge University Press, 2010), 12–15, 45–71.

62. Jean-Jacques Rousseau, *The Social Contract and Other Later Political Writings* (Cambridge: Cambridge University Press, 1997), 71.

63. For a keen dissection of these paradoxes, see Bonnie Honig, "Between Decision and Deliberation: Political Paradox in Democratic Theory," *American Political Science Review* 101, no. 1 (2007): 1–17; see also William Connolly, *Political Theory and Modernity* (Oxford: Basil Blackwell, 1988), 53–57; Seyla Benhabib, "Deliberative Rationality and Models of Democratic Legitimacy," *Constellations* 1, no. 1 (1994): 26–52; Chantal Mouffe, *The Democratic Paradox* (London: Verso, 2000); Alan Keenan, *Democracy in Question: Democratic Openness in a Time of Political Closure* (Stanford, CA: Stanford University Press, 2003); Jason Frank, "'Unauthorized Propositions': 'The Federalist Papers' and Constituent Power," *Diacritics* 37, no. 2–3 (2007): 103–120; Kevin Olson, "Paradoxes of Constitutional Democracy," *American Journal of*

Politics Science 51, no. 2 (2007): 330–343; Paulina Ochoa Espejo, *The Time of Popular Sovereignty: Process and the Democratic State* (University Park, PA: Pennsylvania State University Press, 2011).

64. Emmanuel-Joseph Sieyès, *What Is the Third Estate?*, in *Political Writings*, ed. Michael Sonenscher (Indianapolis: Hackett, 2003), 94–144.

65. For a sensitive historical study of these dilemmas in the context of seventeenth- and eighteenth-century France, see David Bell, *The Cult of the Nation in France: Inventing Nationalism, 1680–1800* (Cambridge, MA: Harvard University Press, 2001), 5.

66. See, for example, Judith Brown, *Gandhi's Rise to Power: Indian Politics, 1915–1922* (Cambridge: Cambridge University Press, 1974).

67. M. K. Gandhi, *The Collected Works of Mahatma Gandhi* (electronic books), 98 vols. (New Delhi: Publications Division, Government of India, 1999), https://www.gandhiashramsevagram.org/gandhi-literature/collected -works-of-mahatma-gandhi-volume-1-to-98.php (hereafter cited as *CWMG*), 6:208 (emphasis in original).

68. *CWMG*, 8:457.

69. *CWMG*, 8:458.

70. *CWMG*, 8:458.

71. Parel, "Editor's Introduction," xxx.

72. Dallmayr, "What Is Swaraj?," 105. The notable exception is Dalton. Dalton acknowledges the influence of Pal, Aurobindo, et al. on Gandhi's theory of swaraj, although his focus is primarily on their efforts to reconcile "spiritual" (positive) and "political" (negative) meanings of swaraj. See Dennis Dalton, *Mahatma Gandhi: Non-Violent Power in Action* (New York: Columbia University Press, 2012), 2–7.

73. See Jonathan Hyslop, "An 'Eventful' History of *Hind Swaraj*: Gandhi between the Battle of Tsushima and the Union of South Africa," *Public Culture* 23, no. 2 (2011): 299–319.

74. "A Natal Journal's Attitude toward *The Indian Sociologist*," *The Indian Sociologist* 6, no. 12 (1910): 47–48.

75. "The Indians in the Transvaal Get Their Deserts," *The Indian Sociologist* 4, no. 1 (1908): 1.

76. See Inder Marwah, "Rethinking Resistance: Spencer, Krishnavarma, and *The Indian Sociologist*," in *Colonial Exchanges: Political Theory and the Agency of the Colonized*, ed. Burke Hendrix and Deborah Baumgold (Manchester: Manchester University Press, 2017), 43–72.

77. "India House," *The Indian Sociologist* 1, no. 10 (1905): 38.

78. "Education Not Necessary for Self-Government," *The Indian Sociologist* 2, no. 9 (1906): 34.

79. "English Tribute to Indian Martyrdom: Garibaldi's Advocacy of Wholesale Political Assassination," *The Indian Sociologist* 5, no. 9 (1909): 37.

80. Gandhi originally wrote *Hind Swaraj* in Gujarati in 1909. He published the English version in 1910 under the title of "Indian Home Rule."

81. Gandhi, *Hind Swaraj*, 28.

82. Gandhi, *Hind Swaraj*, 29.

83. See Stanley Wolpert, *Gandhi's Passion: The Life and Legacy of Mahatma Gandhi* (Oxford: Oxford University Press, 2001), 43.

84. Gandhi, *Hind Swaraj*, 35–38.

85. Gandhi, *Hind Swaraj*, 67. Gandhi's polemical defense of Indian "civilization" against Western "civilization" should be understood in this context. As he argues, India's "immovable" state—generally seen as the marker of "uncivilized" backwardness—is a manifestation of its rejection of the primacy of material progress. The rejection of the ideology of progress, for Gandhi, enables self-rule, leading him to the claim that Indian "civilization" is truer than its modern "progressive" European counterpart. See Gandhi, *Hind Swaraj*, 66–70.

86. Gandhi, *Hind Swaraj*, 48.

87. Gandhi, *Hind Swaraj*, 48.

88. Gandhi, *Hind Swaraj*, 95.

89. Gandhi, *Hind Swaraj*, 73.

90. Gandhi, *Hind Swaraj*, 73.

91. *CWMG*, 21:280.

92. Gandhi, *Hind Swaraj*, 73.

93. See Farah Godrej, "Gandhi, Foucault, and the Politics of Self-Care," *Theory and Event* 20, no. 4 (2017): 894–922.

94. Gandhi, *Hind Swaraj*, 118.

95. See Alex Livingston, "Fidelity to Truth: Gandhi and the Genealogy of Civil Disobedience," *Political Theory* 46, no. 4 (2018): 511–536; Uday Mehta, "Patience, Inwardness, and Self-Knowledge in Gandhi's *Hind Swaraj*," *Public Culture* 23, no. 2 (2011): 417–429.

96. On this history of Gandhi's idea of nonviolence, see Eijiro Hazama, "Unravelling the Myth of Gandhian Non-violence: Why Did Gandhi Connect His Principle of Satyāgraha with the "Hindu" Notion of Ahiṃsā?," *Modern Intellectual History* 20, no. 1 (2023): 116–140.

97. Gandhi, *Hind Swaraj*, 90.

98. Gandhi, *Hind Swaraj*, 92–93.

99. Gandhi, *Hind Swaraj*, 70.

100. Gandhi, *Hind Swaraj*, 92.

101. *CWMG*, 23:71–72.

102. Gandhi, *Hind Swaraj*, 82.

103. Complementary to this argument is Gandhi's claim that action must be indifferent to its "fruits." Taken together, they instantiate the extent to which

Gandhi was willing to go to liberate moral action from its reliance on external authority or incentive. See Gandhi, *The Gospel of Selfless Action, or the Gita according to Gandhi* (Ahmedabad: Navajivan Publishing House, 1946), 132.

104. *CWMG,* 21:101.
105. Gandhi, *Hind Swaraj,* 118.
106. Gandhi, *Hind Swaraj,* 73.
107. *CWMG,* 75:178–179.
108. See Anthony J. Parel, *Gandhi's Philosophy and the Quest for Harmony* (Cambridge: Cambridge University Press, 2006), 57; Parel, *Pax Gandhiana: The Political Philosophy of Mahatma Gandhi* (Oxford: Oxford University Press, 2016), 73–93; Dalton, *Mahatma Gandhi,* 21.
109. *CWMG,* 22:260. On this caveat, see also Dipesh Chakrabarty and Rochona Majumdar, "Gandhi's Gita and Politics as Such," *Modern Intellectual History* 7, no. 2 (2010): 345.
110. *CWMG,* 16:117.
111. See esp. *CWMG,* 81:355–357.
112. See Karuna Mantena, "Another Realism: The Politics of Gandhian Non-Violence," *American Political Science Review* 106, no. 2 (2012): 455–470.
113. See Faisal Devji, *The Impossible Indian* (Cambridge, MA: Harvard University Press, 2012); Shruti Kapila, "Self, Spencer and Swaraj: Nationalist Thought and Critiques of Liberalism, 1890–1920," *Modern Intellectual History* 7, no. 2 (2007): 109–127.
114. Bal Gangadhar Tilak, "L. Tilak's Letter," *Young India* 2, no. 1 (1920): 3.
115. *CWMG,* 19:331, 11:38–42.
116. Iyer, *The Moral and Political Thought of Mahatma Gandhi,* 48.
117. Chatterjee, *Nationalist Thought,* 92, 108.
118. Lloyd Rudolph and Susan Rudolph, *Postmodern Gandhi and Other Essays* (Chicago: University of Chicago Press, 2006), 152.
119. See Mehta, "Gandhi on Democracy."
120. Karuna Mantena, "Gandhi's Critique of the State: Sources, Contexts, Conjectures," *Modern Intellectual History* 9, no. 3 (2012): 559.
121. *CWMG,* 88:325.
122. Ajay Skaria, *Unconditional Equality: Gandhi's Religion of Resistance* (Minnesota: University of Minnesota Press, 2016), 91–93.
123. *CWMG,* 83:113.
124. *CWMG,* 91:326.
125. *CWMG,* 91:326.
126. Akeel Bilgrami. "Gandhi, the Philosopher," *Economic and Political Weekly* 38, no. 39 (2003): 4162.
127. Nehru, *Toward Freedom: The Autobiography of Jawaharlal Nehru* (New York: John Day, 1941), 74.

128. On Gandhi's intellectual struggle to reconcile nonviolence with the act of recruiting Indian soldiers for the imperial army, see Thomas Weber and Dennis Dalton, "Gandhi and the Pandemic," *Economic and Political Weekly* 55, no. 25 (2020).

129. *CWMG*, 17:10.

130. *CWMG*, 17:10. On Gandhi's argument concerning a simultaneous sacrifice for and "detachment" from empire, see Faisal Devji, "Gandhi's Great War," in *India and World War I: A Centennial Assessment*, ed. Roger D. Long and Ian Talbot (London: Routledge, 2018), 191–206.

131. Mahadev Desai, *Day-to-Day with Gandhi*, vol. 1 (Varanasi: Sarva Seva Sangh, 1968), 128.

132. The Khilafat movement was forged in the global tumults around self-determination, albeit in a rather unexpected form. Indian Muslims claimed that the undermining of the sovereignty of the Ottoman emperor by the victorious Allied forces would compromise their religious standing, since the Ottoman emperor stood as the religious figurehead of Sunni Muslims (who composed the majority of Indian Muslims).

133. See Nazmul S. Sultan, "Moral Empire and the Global Meaning of Gandhi's Anti-Imperialism," *Review of Politics* 84, no. 4 (2022): 545–569.

134. For an account of Gandhi's "failure" to influence the formation of the post-colonial project, see Sandipto Dasgupta, "Gandhi's Failure: Anticolonial Movements and Postcolonial Futures," *Perspectives on Politics* 15, no. 3 (2017): 647–662.

135. Jawaharlal Nehru, *A Bunch of Old Letters: Written Mostly to Jawaharlal Nehru and Some Written by Him* (Delhi: Oxford University Press, 1988), 509.

136. Nagendrakumar Guha Roy, ed., *Swaraj Sadhanay Bangali* [Bengalis in pursuit of swaraj] (Kolkata: Saraswati Library, 1922).

137. *CWMG*, 61:393.

138. Jawaharlal Nehru, "Swaraj and Socialism," in *Selected Works of Jawaharlal Nehru*, vol. 3 (Delhi: B. R. Publishing, 1972), 426.

139. Nehru, "Swaraj and Socialism," 371.

140. Reinhart Koselleck, "Introduction to Geschichtliche Grundbegriffe," *Contributions to the History of Concepts* 6, no. 1 (2011): 19 (emphasis added).

141. On this point, see Ernesto Laclau, *On Populist Reason* (London: Verso, 2005).

142. Enrique Dussel, *Twenty Theses on Politics* (Durham, NC: Duke University Press, 2008), 73.

143. Judith Brown, *Gandhi's Rise to Power: Indian Politics, 1915–1922* (Cambridge: Cambridge University Press, 1974).

144. Shahid Amin, "Gandhi as Mahatma," in *Selected Subaltern Studies*, ed. Ranajit Guha and Gayatri Chakravorty Spivak (New York: Oxford University Press, 1988), 342.

4. BETWEEN THE MANY AND THE ONE

1. Radhakamal Mukerjee, *Democracies of the East: A Study in Comparative Politics* (London: P. S. King and Son, 1923), v.
2. On the influential role of pluralist sovereignty in early twentieth-century European political thought, see Jeanne Morefield, "Urgent History: The Sovereignty Debates and Political Theory's Lost Voices," *Political Theory* 45, no. 2 (2017): 164–191.
3. Mukerjee, *Democracies of the East,* 11.
4. Mukerjee, *Democracies of the East,* 67. Mukerjee elaborated on this point further in one of his Bengali texts: "The Utilitarians—Bentham, Mill, et al.—thought that the world could be transformed into a heaven (of the European image) through the dissemination of the ideas of popular self-government and education under the leadership of the British." For Mukerjee, the idealistic aim of nineteenth-century European imperialism to uplift the "backward peoples" is central to understanding its historical specificity. With the erosion of this discourse, European imperialism had transformed into a blatant striving for territorial sovereignty. Mukerjee's hope about the imminent demise of territorial sovereignty partly emanated from this historical diagnosis. It might be worth noting that Mukerjee wrote this article a few months before the start of World War I for the Bengali periodical *Prabasi.* The editor of the journal added a note apologizing for the delayed publication of the article, as Mukerjee correctly predicted the beginning of the Great War! See Radhakamal Mukerjee, *Manomay Bharat* (1914; reprint, Kolkata: Indian Book Club, 1924), 1–5.
5. For an overview of centralized federalism and the importance of its American origins, see William H. Riker, *The Development of American Federalism* (Boston: Kluwer Academic Publishers, 1987).
6. Mukerjee, *Democracies of the East,* 116.
7. For a recent survey of federalist literature, see Merve Fejzula, "The Cosmopolitan Historiography of Twentieth-Century Federalism," *The Historical Journal* 64, no. 2 (2021): 477–500.
8. Frederick Cooper, *Citizenship between Empire and Nation: Remaking France and French Africa, 1945–1960* (Princeton, NJ: Princeton University Press, 2014), 10.
9. Gary Wilder, *Freedom Time: Negritude, Decolonization, and the Future of the World* (Durham, NC: Duke University Press, 2015), 1–16.
10. Partha Chatterjee, "Empires, Nations, Peoples: The Imperial Prerogative and Colonial Exceptions," *Thesis Eleven* 139, no. 1 (2017): 95.
11. Samuel Moyn, "Fantasies of Federalism," *Dissent* 62, no. 1 (2015): 145–151.
12. James Tully, *Public Philosophy in a New Key,* vol. 2, *Imperialism and Civic Freedom* (Cambridge: Cambridge University Press, 2009), 145.

13. See Adam Dahl, *Empire of the People: Settler Colonialism and the Foundations of Modern Democratic Thought* (Lawrence: University Press of Kansas, 2018), 23–46. On the racial foundations of federalist sovereignty in revolutionary and post-revolutionary America, see also Lawrie Balfour, "Reading Publius with Morrison and Melville," *Polity* 47, no. 4 (2015): 550–557.

14. Duncan Bell, *The Idea of Greater Britain: Empire and the Future of World Order, 1860–1900* (Princeton, NJ: Princeton University Press, 2007), 3–12.

15. Harold Laski, "The Theory of Popular Sovereignty," *Michigan Law Review* 17, no. 3 (1919): 201–215.

16. See, in particular, G. D. H. Cole, "Conflicting Social Obligations," *Proceedings of the Aristotelian Society* 15, no. 1 (1915): 140–159; see also Cole, *Social Theory* (London: Methuen, 1921), 133.

17. Cole, "Conflicting Social Obligations," 154; on Cole's career-long grappling with the problem of the general will, see Peter Lamb, "G. D. H. Cole on the General Will: A Socialist Reflects on Rousseau," *European Journal of Political Theory* 4, no. 3 (2005): 283–300. Cole was more sympathetic to Rousseau than Laski was, though they both agreed that Rousseau's concept of popular sovereignty was unworkable in practice. Laski, in particular, thought that it would inevitably result into a straightforward majoritarian rule.

18. Schmitt noted that the British pluralists were motivated by the desire to evade the "dilemma" of "popular sovereignty," but he found them at fault for reducing the problem of sovereignty to one of associations. See Carl Schmitt, *The Concept of the Political* (Chicago: University of Chicago Press, 2007), 43–44.

19. Brajendranath Seal, "Meaning of Race, Tribe, Nation," in *Papers on Inter-Racial Problems Communicated to the First Universal Races Congress*, ed. G. Spiller (London: P. S. King and Son, 1911), 1.

20. This aspect of Seal's argument strikingly paralleled Franz Boas's paper in the next session of the Congress. Boas also questioned the static notion of race and the assumption of "hereditary superiority" associated with it. See Franz Boas, "The Instability of Human Types," in Spiller, *Papers on Inter-Racial Problems*, 99–103.

21. Seal, "Meaning of Race, Tribe, Nation," 12–13.

22. Seal, "Meaning of Race, Tribe, Nation," 12.

23. Brajendranath Seal, *New Essays in Criticism* (Calcutta: Som Brothers, 1903), i.

24. See B. N. Seal, *Comparative Studies in Vaishnavism and Christianity and an Introduction on the Historico-Comparative Method* (Calcutta: Hare Press, 1899), i.

25. Seal, *Comparative Studies*, iii–iv.

26. Seal, *Comparative Studies*, iv.

27. Seal, *Comparative Studies*, 5.

28. Seal, *Comparative Studies*, 18–19.

29. Seal, *Comparative Studies*, i–ii.
30. Seal, *Comparative Studies*, v–vi.
31. B. N. Seal to W. Rothenstein, January 4, 1916, British Library, India Office Records and Private Papers, MSS EUR / B / 213 / 42. For a brief discussion of the Seal–Rothenstein exchanges, see Jennifer Pitts, *Boundaries of the International: Law and Empire* (Cambridge, MA: Harvard University Press, 2018), 186–187.
32. Seal to Rothenstein, January 4, 1916, British Library.
33. Brajendranath Seal, "Visvabharati Parishad-Sabhar Pratishtha–Utsabe Sabhapatir Abhibhasan" (presidential address at the celebration of the founding of the Council of Visvabharata University), in *Bangla Rachana* (Kolkata: Patralekha, 2013), 39.
34. Seal, "Visvabharati Parishad," 38–39.
35. Seal, "Visvabharati Parishad," 37–38.
36. *Constitutional Developments in Mysore: Report of the Committee Appointed to Work Out the Details of the Scheme* (Bangalore: Government Press, 1923), 41.
37. *Constitutional Developments in Mysore*, 2–3.
38. Benoy Kumar Sarkar, *Benoy Sarkarer Baithake* [In the salon of Benoy Sarkar], vol. 1 (Kolkata: Chakrabarty, Chatterjee and Co., 1944), 66.
39. Bipin Chandra Pal, *Nationality and Empire: A Running Study of Some Current Indian Problems* (Calcutta: Thacker Spink and Co., 1916, x.
40. Pal, *Nationality and Empire*, 197.
41. Pal, *Nationality and Empire*, xxxiii.
42. As Aurobindo puts it: "The nation or community is an aggregate life that expresses the Self according to the general law of human nature and aids and partially fulfils the development and the destiny of mankind by its own development and the pursuit of its own destiny according to the law of its being and the nature of its corporate individuality." Sri Aurobindo, *The Human Cycle*, in *The Complete Works of Sri Aurobindo*, vol. 25 (Pondicherry: Sri Aurobindo Ashram Trust, 1997), 70.
43. Aurobindo, *The Human Cycle*, 29.
44. Aurobindo seems to have believed that Seal tended to read "modern" ideas into the resources of India's past. See Sri Aurobindo, *Evening Talks with Sri Aurobindo* (Pondicherry: Sri Aurobindo Ashram Trust, 1982), 357–358.
45. See especially Radhakumud Mookerji, *Local Government in Ancient India*, 2nd ed. (Oxford: Clarendon Press, 1920). For a critical analysis of Mookerji's account of Indian unity in the broader context of the debates around national unity and kingship, see Milinda Banerjee, *The Mortal God: Imagining the Sovereign in Colonial India* (Cambridge: Cambridge University Press, 2018), 188–189. On Radhakumud's political invocations of Indian antiquity, see Tejas Parasher, "Federalism, Representation, and Direct Democracy

in 1920s India," *Modern Intellectual History* (First View), doi: 10.1017/ S1479244320000578.

46. See, for instance, Brij Mohan Sharma, *The Indian Federation* (Lucknow: Upper India Publishing House, 1932). Laski served as the examiner of Sharma's dissertation, on which the book was based.

47. See Radhakamal Mukerjee, *India, the Dawn of a New Era: An Autobiography* (New Delhi: Radha Publications, 1997), 88.

48. Radhakamal Mukerjee, *Principles of Comparative Economics,* vol. 2 (London: P. S. King and Son, 1922), 57.

49. Mukerjee, *Principles of Comparative Economics,* 32.

50. On Maine and the question of the native society see Karuna Mantena, *Alibis of Empire: Henry Maine and the Ends of Liberal Imperialism* (Princeton, NJ: Princeton University Press, 2010).

51. Mukerjee, *Democracies of the East,* 297.

52. See Karuna Mantena, "On Gandhi's Critique of the State: Sources, Contexts, Conjectures," *Modern Intellectual History* 9, no. 3 (2012): 535–563.

53. Mukerjee, *Democracies of the East,* 296–297.

54. Mukerjee, *Democracies of the East,* 15–16.

55. Mukerjee, *Democracies of the East,* xvi.

56. Mukerjee, *Democracies of the East,* 157.

57. Mukerjee, *Democracies of the East,* 211.

58. Mukerjee, *Democracies of the East,* 155.

59. Mukerjee, *Democracies of the East,* 10.

60. Mukerjee, *Democracies of the East,* 93, 211.

61. Mukerjee, *Democracies of the East,* 280.

62. Mukerjee, *Democracies of the East,* 174–179.

63. Mukerjee, *Democracies of the East,* 201–202.

64. Mukerjee, *Democracies of the East,* 274.

65. Mukerjee, *Democracies of the East,* 347.

66. See, in particular, Radhakamal Mukerjee, "Caste and Social Change in India," *American Journal of Sociology* 43, no. 3 (1937): 377–390.

67. Mukerjee, *Democracies of the East,* 344–345.

68. Harold Laski, *Authority in the Modern State* (New Haven, CT: Yale University Press, 1919), 65–66.

69. Marc Stears, *Progressives, Pluralists, and the Problem of the State* (Oxford: Oxford University Press, 2002), 100.

70. Mukerjee, *Democracies of the East,* 345.

71. Mukerjee, *Democracies of the East,* 350–351.

72. Otto von Gierke, *Political Theories of the Middle Age,* trans. F. W. Maitland (Cambridge: Cambridge University Press, 1900).

73. On the undermining of the organicist and Hegelian elements of Gierke's thought in England, see David Runciman, *Pluralism and the Personality of the State* (Cambridge: Cambridge University Press, 1997), 54–85;

Charles Turner, "Organicism, Pluralism and Civil Association: Some Neglected Political Thinkers," *History of the Human Sciences* 5, no. 3: 175–184.

74. Bernard Bosanquet, *The Philosophical Theory of the State* (London: Macmillan, 1965), 264. For Laski's critique, see Laski, "Theory of Popular Sovereignty," 207–208.

75. See Jeanne Morefield, "Hegelian Organicism, British New Liberalism and the Return of the Family State," *History of Political Thought* 33, no. 1 (2002): 141–170.

76. Mukerjee refers to Gierke only twice in the text (in the same paragraph). On both occasions, he groups Maitland and Gierke together as exponents of the "group theory of rights." In the next sentence he again implies that Maitland and Figgis in England and Gierke in Germany were advancing the same project. Mukerjee, *Democracies of the East,* 342.

77. For an elaborate discussion of Gierke's distinction between "unity-in-plurality" and "plurality-in unity," see Runciman, *Pluralism,* 37–43; see also Sobei Mogi, *Otto von Gierke: His Political Teaching and Jurisprudence* (London: P. S. King and Son, 1932), 191–193.

78. See Otto von Gierke, *Community in Historical Perspective,* ed. Antony Black (Cambridge: Cambridge University Press, 1990), 116–117.

79. On Figgis's model of "organic coordination (as opposed to later pluralists such as Cole and Laski's "contractual integration"), see Cécile Laborde, *Pluralist Thought and the State in Britain and France, 1900–1925* (London: Palgrave Macmillan, 2000), 45–68.

80. On Gierke's Hegel-inflected historicism, see Gierke, *Community in Historical Perspective,* 2–4.

81. On Gierke's "organism," see Gierke, *Political Theories of the Middle Age,* 22–30. For an account of the uses of Darwinian evolutionary organicism in early twentieth-century Indian thought, see Inder Marwah, "Provincializing Progress: Developmentalism and Anti-Imperialism in Colonial India," *Polity* 51, no. 3 (2019): 498–531.

82. Laski's sensitivity to this point developed after the publication of Mukerjee's work. On Laski's reflections on the association between the nation-state and imperialism, see Jeanne Morefield, "Harold Laski on the Habits of Imperialism," in *Lineages of Empire: The Historical Roots of British Imperial Thought,* ed. Duncan Kelly (Oxford: Oxford University Press, 2009), 213–237.

83. Mukerjee, *Democracies of the East,* 154–155.

84. Mukerjee, *Democracies of the East,* 362–363.

85. Mukerjee, *Democracies of the East,* xii.

86. Mukerjee, *Democracies of the East,* 154.

87. Benoy Kumar Sarkar—writing in 1928—noted that C. R. Das, Sun Yat-Sen of China, and Zaghlul Pasha of Egypt were the three most important voices

of "Young Asia." See Benoy Kumar Sarkar, "Chittaranjan Das and Young Asia," in *The Political Philosophies since 1905* (Madras: B. G. Paul and Co., 1928), 333–373.

88. C. R. Das, "Bengal and the Bengalees," in *Deshabandhu Chitta Ranjan: Brief Survey of Life and Work, Provincial Conference Speeches, Congress Speeches* (Calcutta: Rajen Sen, B. K. Sen, 1926), 8; see also C. R. Das, *India for Indians* (Madras: Ganesh and Co., 1917), 41.

89. Das, *Deshabandhu Chitta Ranjan*, 195.

90. Das, *Deshabandhu Chitta Ranjan*, 217.

91. C. R. Das, *Outline Scheme of Swaraj* (Kolkata: Department of Information and Public Relations, Government of West Bengal, 1973), 31.

92. Das, *Outline Scheme of Swaraj*, 45.

93. Das, *Outline Scheme of Swaraj*, 20.

94. Das, *Outline Scheme of Swaraj*, 35.

95. C. R. Das, *Freedom through Disobedience* (Madras: Arka, 1922), 41.

96. On William James's pluralism and the problem of empire, see Alexander Livingston, *Damn Great Empires! William James and the Politics of Pragmatism* (Oxford: Oxford University Press, 2016).

97. Mary Parker Follett, *The New State: Group Organization the Solution of Popular Government* (New York: Longmans, Green and Co., 1918), 271–272.

98. Das, *Outline Scheme of Swaraj*, 266.

99. Das, *Outline Scheme of Swaraj*, 220.

100. Das, *Outline Scheme of Swaraj*, 249.

101. Das, *Deshabandhu Chitta Ranjan*, 217–218. Das fell out with Gandhi's agenda at the Gaya Congress Session following a dispute over the form of noncooperation the organization should adopt. In 1923 he went on to found the Swaraj Party (within the Congress), which held significant sway over the anticolonial movement for the next couple of years.

102. C. R Das, *Freedom through Disobedience*, 41–43 (emphasis added).

103. Das, *Deshabandhu Chitta Ranjan*, 274 (emphasis in original).

104. On the distinction between constituent power and direct democracy, see Lucia Rubinelli, *Constituent Power: A History* (Cambridge: Cambridge University Press, 2020), 1–32.

105. See Leonard Gordon, *Bengal: The Nationalist Movement, 1876–1940* (New Delhi: Manohar, 1979), 194–201; Semanti Ghosh, *Different Nationalisms: Bengal, 1905–1947* (New Delhi: Oxford University Press, 2017), 138–145. For a contemporary account of the Muslim support for the Bengal Pact, see Maulavi Abdul Karim, *Letters on Hindu-Muslim Pact* (Calcutta: Oriental Printers and Publishers, 1924).

106. See Gordon, *Bengal*, 197–198.

107. Bengal Legislative Council, *Bengal Legislative Council Proceedings* 14, no. 4 (March 12–14, 1924): 85–87.

108. Hannah Arendt, *On Revolution* (London: Penguin Books, 1990), 94; on Arendt's view of constituent power, see Rubinelli, *Constituent Power,* 176–205.

109. For a critical survey of Arendt on the will, see Linda Zerilli, "From Willing to Judging: Arendt, Habermas, and the Question of '68," in *A Democratic Theory of Judgment* (Chicago: University of Chicago Press, 2016), 184–207.

110. On the reconsolidation of the ideal of "rapid progress" led by an independent planning state, see Jawaharlal Nehru, "The Peasantry," in *Selected Works of Jawaharlal Nehru,* vol. 3 (New Delhi: Orient Longman, 1972), 412–416; see also Partha Chatterjee, *Nationalist Thought and the Colonial World* (London: Zed Books, 1986), 131–166.

111. On Nehru's critique of federalism as a "feudal" reaction, see Rama Sundari Mantena, "Anticolonialism and Federation in Colonial India," *Ab Imperio* 3 (2018): 36–62.

112. On the rise of the "national conception of empire," see Mrinalini Sinha, "Whatever Happened to the Third British Empire? Empire, Nation Redux," in *Writing Imperial Histories,* ed. Andrew S. Thompson (Manchester: Manchester University Press, 2013), 168–187.

113. Pal, *Nationality and Empire,* xxxiii.

114. See Adom Getachew, *Worldmaking after Empire: The Rise and Fall of Self-Determination* (Princeton, NJ: Princeton University Press, 2019), 107–141.

115. See Jason Frank, *Publius and Political Imagination* (Lanham, MD: Rowman and Littlefield, 2014), 25–46; Joshua Miller, "The Ghostly Body Politic: *The Federalist Papers* and Popular Sovereignty," *Political Theory* 16, no. 1 (1988): 99–119.

116. Hannah Arendt, "The Minority Question," in *The Jewish Writings* (New York: Schocken Books, 2007), 129–130.

117. On Arendt's federalism, see Gil Rubin, "From Federalism to Binationalism: Arendt's Shifting Zionism," *Contemporary European History* 24, no. 3 (2015): 393–414; William Selinger, "The Politics of Arendtian Historiography: European Federation and *The Origins of Totalitarianism,*" *Modern Intellectual History* 13, no. 2 (2016): 417–446.

118. Sarojini Naidu, *Speeches and Writings of Sarojini Naidu* (Madras: G. A. Natesen and Co., 1918), 234.

119. Mukerjee, *India, the Dawn of a New Era,* 125–135.

5. TO "CARRY" THE PEOPLE THROUGH HISTORY

1. Jawaharlal Nehru, *The Discovery of India* (Delhi: Oxford University Press, 1985), 60–61.

2. Rupert Emerson, *From Empire to Nation: The Rise to Self-Assertion of Asian and African Peoples* (Cambridge, MA: Harvard University Press, 1962), 227.

3. Isaiah Berlin, *Liberty: Incorporating Four Essays on Liberty,* ed. Henry Hardy (Oxford: Oxford University Press, 2002), 205.

4. Isaiah Berlin, "The Bent Twig: A Note on Nationalism," *Foreign Affairs* 51, no. 1 (1972): 18. Elie Kedourie makes a similar argument in his introduction to the influential anthology *Nationalism in Asia and Africa,* ed. Elie Kedourie (New York: Meridian Books, 1970), 28–29.

5. Erez Manela, *The Wilsonian Moment: Self-Determination and the International Origins of Anticolonial Nationalism* (Oxford: Oxford University Press, 2007).

6. Partha Chatterjee, *Politics of the Governed: Reflections on Popular Politics in Most of the World* (New York: Columbia University Press, 2004), 27–29.

7. Jawaharlal Nehru, *Toward Freedom: The Autobiography of Jawaharlal Nehru* (New York: John Day, 1941), 75.

8. Nehru, *Toward Freedom,* 60.

9. Hartmut Rosa, *Social Acceleration: A New Theory of Modernity* (New York: Columbia University Press, 2015), 251.

10. Jawaharlal Nehru, *Selected Works,* 2nd ser. (New Delhi: Jawaharlal Nehru Memorial Fund, 1984–), 1:587 (emphasis added).

11. Jean-Jacques Rousseau, *The Social Contract and Other Later Political Writings,* ed. and trans. Victor Gourevitch (Cambridge: Cambridge University Press, 1997), 71.

12. On Rousseau's Lawgiver problem, see Jason Frank, *The Democratic Sublime: On Aesthetics and Popular Assembly* (New York: Oxford University Press, 2021).

13. Of the Lawgiver's office, Rousseau says: "This office which gives the republic its constitution has no place in its constitution" (*The Social Contract,* 69). Of his power: "Thus, since the Lawgiver can use neither force nor reasoning, he must of necessity have recourse to an authority of a different order, which might be able to rally without violence and to persuade without convincing" (71).

14. Nehru, *The Discovery of India,* 399.

15. Muhammad Ali Jinnah, "Jinnah to Nehru—12 April 1938," in *Nehru: The Debates That Defined India,* ed. Tripurdaman Singh and Adeel Hussain (London: William Collins, 2021), 121.

16. Nehru, *The Discovery of India,* 18–20.

17. To give one prominent late twentieth-century example, Hedley Bull characterized the anticolonial struggle as a "revolt against Western dominance" in the name of "ideas and values that are themselves Western." Hedley Bull, "The Revolt against the West," in *The Expansion of International Society,* ed. Hedley Bull and Adam Watson (Oxford: Clarendon Press, 1984), 222–223.

18. On the Enlightenment origin of the concept of self-determination and the concept's transformation from an individualist notion to a collective

one, see Eric Weitz, "Self-Determination: How a German Enlightenment Idea Became the Slogan of National Liberation and a Human Right," *American Historical Review* 120, no. 2 (2015): 462–496.

19. Vladimir Ilyich Lenin, *The Right of Nations to Self-Determination,* in *Collected Works of V. I. Lenin,* ed. J. Katzer (Moscow: Progress Publishers, 1964), 396.

20. Lenin, *The Right of Nations,* 400.

21. Lenin, *The Right of Nations,* 454.

22. The debate between Lenin and M. N. Roy—the Indian voice in the Third International—is suggestive here. Against the argument that the communist movements in colonial countries should strategically support "bourgeois-democratic liberation" projects, Roy proposed that Indian communists should immediately strive for the same communist end as their Western counterparts. See M. N. Roy, "The Situation in India: The Report of Comrade Roy," in *The 2nd Congress of the Communist International: As Reported and Interpreted by the Official Newspapers of Soviet Russia* (Washington, DC: Government Printing Office, 1920), 42–44.

23. See Woodrow Wilson, "The Ideals of America," *Atlantic Monthly,* December 1902, 721–734.

24. "President Woodrow Wilson's Fourteen Points," January 8, 1918, The Avalon Project: Documents in Law, History and Diplomacy, https://avalon.law.yale.edu/20th_century/wilson14.asp.

25. Woodrow Wilson, *War Addresses of Woodrow Wilson,* ed. Arthur R. Leonard (Boston: Ginn, 1918), 129 (emphasis added).

26. Wilson's apprehensive secretary of state Robert Lansing recognized that the term was "loaded with dynamite" and could be appropriated by unintended addressees. Norman Levin, *Woodrow Wilson and World Politics: America's Response to War and Revolution* (Oxford: Oxford University Press, 1964), 248.

27. Madan Mohan Malaviya, "Delhi Congress Presidential Address," in *Speeches and Writings of Pandit Madan Mohan Malaviya* (Madras: G. A. Natesen and Co., 1918), 524–525.

28. Malaviya, *Speeches and Writings,* 384–385.

29. "Resolutions Adopted by the Congress," in *The Encyclopaedia of the Indian National Congress,* vol. 7, *1916–1920,* ed. A. M. Zaidi (New Delhi: S. Chand and Co., 1960), 400 (emphasis added).

30. Motilal Nehru, "Let Your Indignation Flame," *The Independent,* February 5, 1919. The *Independent*'s mission statement cited Woodrow Wilson approvingly: "*The Independent* . . . joins President Wilson in saying: 'The select classes of mankind are no longer the governors of mankind. The fortunes of mankind are now in the hands of the plain people of the whole world'" (*The Independent,* February 5, 1919).

31. C. R. Das, "Welcome to *The Independent,*" *The Independent,* February 9, 1919.

32. Lala Lajpat Rai, *Self-Determination for India* (New York: India Home Rule League, 1919), 13.

33. Jawaharlal Nehru, "Roads to Freedom," in *Selected Works of Jawaharlal Nehru* (hereafter cited as *SWJN*), ed. S. Gopal et al. (Delhi: Orient Longman, 1970–), 1:143.

34. M. K. Gandhi, "Letter to C. F. Andrews," in *Collected Works of Mahatma Gandhi* (New Delhi: Publications Division, Ministry of Information and Broadcasting, Government of India, 1958–), 17:300–301.

35. M. K. Gandhi, "Criticism of Muslim Manifesto," in *Collected Works*, 21:17.

36. Manela, *The Wilsonian Moment*, 61–62.

37. Timothy Mitchell, *Carbon Democracy: Political Power in the Age of Oil* (London: Verso, 2011), 68, 85. For another account of Wilsonian self-determination as a "mask for the right of conquest," see Joseph Massad, "Against Self-Determination," *Humanity: An International Journal of Human Rights, Humanitarianism, and Development* 9, no. 2 (2018): 166–170.

38. For the post–World War II history of self-determination, see Adom Getachew, *Worldmaking after Empire: The Rise and Fall of Self-Determination* (Princeton, NJ: Princeton University Press, 2019).

39. See Michele L. Louro, *Comrades against Imperialism: Nehru, India, and Interwar Internationalism* (Cambridge: Cambridge University Press, 2018).

40. *SWJN,* 3:4.

41. *SWJN,* 3:4.

42. *SWJN,* 3:58.

43. Samuel Moyn, *The Last Utopia: Human Rights in History* (Cambridge, MA: Harvard University Press, 2010), 85.

44. *SWJN,* 3:21.

45. *SWJN,* 3:21.

46. David Armitage, *The Declaration of Independence: A Global History* (Cambridge, MA: Harvard University Press, 2007), 4.

47. However, as Emma Mackinnon has noted, the genres of twentieth-century rights declarations were not identical or in a "static" continuity with the earlier American and French Declarations. See Emma Mackinnon, "Declaration as Disavowal: The Politics of Race and Empire in the Universal Declaration of Human Rights," *Political Theory* 47, no. 1 (2019): 57–81.

48. Bankimchandra Chatterjee, "Bharatbarsher Swadhinata o Paradhanita" [Liberty and the subjection of India], in *Bankim Rachanabali,* vol. 2 (Kolkata: Sahitya Samsad, 1954), 211. For a brief study of nineteenth-century Bengali debates on the meaning of freedom and independence, see Nazmul S. Sultan, "Independence, Freedom, Liberation: The Promise of Bangladesh's Founding," *Economic and Political Weekly* 56, no. 44 (2021): 41–43.

49. Rabindranath Tagore, *Rabindra Rachanabali,* vol. 17 (Kolkata: Visvabharati Granthalay, 2001), 369.

50. Bankim was not alone in this regard. His more radical successors would continue to acknowledge the normative poverty of independence without democracy. Aurobindo Ghose, for instance, observed that the meaning of "swadhinata" concerns both external and internal freedom: "As long as there is foreign rule, a people is not free. At the same time, until a popular republic has been founded, the people of a given nation cannot be considered free either." Those who demanded immediate independence in the wake of the Swadeshi movement—such as Shyamji Krishnavarma's *Indian Sociologist*—found it necessary to explicitly disavow the equal importance of democratic founding. Sri Aurobindo "Swadhinatar Artha" [The meaning of liberty], in *Writings in Bengali and Sanskrit* (Pondicherry: Sri Aurobindo Ashram Publication Department, 2017), 116; "India House," *The Indian Sociologist* 1, no. 10 (1905): 38.

51. A. S. Iyengar, *Role of Press and Indian Freedom Struggle: All through the Gandhian Era* (New Delhi: A. P. H. Publishing, 2001), 23.

52. On Annie Besant and the Home Rule League, see Mark Bevir, "The Formation of the All-India Home Rule League," *Indian Journal of Political Science* 52, no. 3 (1991): 341–356.

53. *SWJN*, 1:144.

54. *SWJN*, 1:180.

55. Referring to this speech, Judith Brown argues that in the early 1920s Nehru conceptualized swaraj "partly in political terms and partly in cultural terms." I would suggest that Nehru's invocation of panchayat raj is less a culturalist reference and more an invocation of the federalist project. Nehru was reading federalist literature at this point and also registered a sympathy for a version of pluralism (guild socialism) in his 1919 review of Russell's *Road to Freedom*. See Judith Brown, *Nehru: A Political Life* (New Haven, CT: Yale University Press, 2003), 63.

56. *SWJN*, 1:182.

57. Nehru, *Toward Freedom*, 59. Nehru, for his part, did underscore the crucial role of this encounter: "I have sometimes wondered what would have happened if I had not [encountered the peasants]. Very probably I would have been drawn to the *kisans* anyhow, sooner or later, but the manner of my going to them would have been different, and the effect on me might also have been different." Nehru, *Toward Freedom*, 56.

58. Nehru, *Toward Freedom*, 54.

59. Nehru, *Toward Freedom*, 57.

60. Nehru, *Toward Freedom*, 64.

61. Nehru, *Toward Freedom*, 143.

62. Nehru, *Toward Freedom*, 274.

63. Jawaharlal Nehru, *Recent Essays and Writings on the Future of India Communalism and Other Subjects* (Allahabad: Kitabistan, 1934), 68.

64. Nehru, *Recent Essays,* 21.

65. Nehru, *Recent Essays,* 40.

66. Nehru, *Recent Essays,* 58. On mass will, see also 35, 42.

67. Nehru, *Toward Freedom,* 64.

68. Nehru, *Toward Freedom,* 115.

69. Nehru, *Toward Freedom,* 115.

70. *SWJN,* 2:350–351.

71. For a study of the homology between the household and the social in modern imperial thought, see Patricia Owens, *The Economy of Force: Counterinsurgency and the Historical Rise of the Social* (Cambridge: Cambridge University Press, 2015). For a qualification of the homology as a "creative transposition" of the techniques of household rule to the social (as opposed to the idea that the house is the "archetype" of the social), see Patchen Markell, "Domestic Homologies and Household Politics: A Comment on Patricia Owens's *Economy of Force,*" *Security Dialogue* 47, no. 3 (2016): 193–200.

72. Nehru, *Toward Freedom,* 264–265.

73. Nehru, *The Discovery of India,* 19.

74. Nehru, *Toward Freedom,* 143.

75. Nehru, *Toward Freedom,* 346–347.

76. *SWJN,* 2:381. As Nikhil Menon also argues, Roosevelt's New Deal policies, too, spurred the Indian faith in planning. Nikhil Menon, *Planning Democracy: Modern India's Quest for Development* (Cambridge: Cambridge University Press, 2022), 6.

77. Nehru, *Toward Freedom,* 399.

78. Quinn Slobodian, *Globalists: The End of Empire and the Birth of Neoliberalism* (Cambridge, MA: Harvard University Press, 2018).

79. Nehru, *Toward Freedom,* 427.

80. Nehru, *Toward Freedom,* 324.

81. Nehru, *Toward Freedom,* 324.

82. See Peter J. Bowler, *A History of the Future: Prophets of Progress from H. G. Wells to Isaac Asimov* (Cambridge: Cambridge University Press, 2017).

83. Partha Chatterjee, *Nationalist Thought and the Colonial World: A Derivative Discourse?* (London: Zed Books, 1986), 139; see also Ashis Nandy, "Science as Reason of State," *Science and Culture* 1, no. 7 (1989): 69–83. For a close historical study of the role of scientific and technological reasoning in Nehru's conception of development, see Benjamin Zachariah, *Developing India: An Intellectual and Social History, c. 1930–1950* (Oxford: Oxford University Press, 2005).

84. Nehru, *The Discovery of India,* 31.

85. Bernard Cohn, *Colonialism and Its Forms of Knowledge* (Princeton, NJ: Princeton University Press, 1996), 78.

86. Nehru, *Toward Freedom*, 398.

87. *SWJN*, 3:220.

88. *Report of the National Planning Committee* (New Delhi: Indian Institute of Applied Political Research, 1938), 16.

89. The rise of militant socialist politics in the period, as Kama Maclean shows, exerted pressure on the moderate as well as Gandhian wings of the Congress, and politically backed up Nehru's efforts to push the agenda of independence within the Congress. See Kama Maclean, *A Revolutionary History of Interwar India: Violence, Image, Voice and Text* (Cambridge: Cambridge University Press, 2015), 147–204.

90. Nehru, *The Discovery of India*, 375.

91. *SWJN*, 2:439.

92. Jawaharlal Nehru, *Glimpses of World History* (1934; reprint, London: Lindsay Drummond, 1939), 656.

93. Menon, *Planning Democracy*, 4.

94. Dipesh Chakrabarty, "Planetary Crisis and the Difficulty of Being Modern," *Millennium: Journal of International Studies* 46, no. 3 (2017): 277; see also Dipesh Chakrabarty, "Legacies of Bandung: Decolonization and the Politics of Culture," in *Making a World after Empire: The Bandung Moment and Its Afterlives,* ed. Christopher J. Lee (Athens, OH: Ohio University Press, 2010), 45–68.

95. See Jason Frank, *Constituent Moments: Enacting the People in Post-Revolutionary America* (Durham, NC: Duke University Press, 2010); Jacques Derrida, "Declarations of Independence," *New Political Science* 15 (1986): 7–15.

96. The notable thinker here is M. N. Roy, who disavowed his earlier Marxism in favor of what he called "radical humanism." A fringe figure at India's founding, Roy proposed delinking planning from the delegation of power to the national state, arguing instead for a form of democracy that distributed power among the people. Yet Roy's proposal, too, felt the need to put forward a mediating authority ("Council of State") that would guide the backward masses into the future. Roy's political theory relied on a philosophy of humanity according to which "the quest for freedom is the continuation, on a higher level—of intelligence and emotion—of the biological struggle for existence" (53). Apart from the metaphysical baggage of "radical humanism," Roy's proposal also failed to wed the new founding to the necessity of independence (in fact, he considered "national government" to be a "greater evil" than the continuation of British rule). Nehru's intellectual feat, on the contrary, was making the vision of democratic founding conditional on the achievement of independence; this explains a great deal of the purchase of Nehru's founding project. On the metaphysical assumptions underlying Roy's radical democracy, see M. N. Roy, *New Humanism: A Manifesto* (Delhi: S. Balwant, 1981), 53; on "national government"

versus "popular government," see Roy, *National Government or People's Government?* (Calcutta: Renaissance Publishers, 1944). For an insightful discussion of Roy's "Council of State" and its developmental assumptions, see Udit Bhatia, "The Pedagogical Account of Parliamentarism at India's Founding," *American Journal of Political Science*, February 3, 2023, https://doi.org/10.1111/ajps.12768.

97. Sudipta Kaviraj, *The Trajectories of the Indian State: Politics and Ideas* (Ranikhet: Permanent Black Press, 2010), 32.

98. Jawaharlal Nehru, *Jawaharlal Nehru's Speeches*, vol. 3, *March 1953–August 1957* (Delhi: Ministry of Information and Broadcasting, Government of India, 1958), 4.

99. On Nehru's emphasis on constitutional "elasticity," see Madhav Khosla, *India's Founding Moment: The Constitution of a Most Surprising Democracy* (Cambridge, MA: Harvard University Press, 2020), 40–41.

100. Uday S. Mehta, "The Social Question and the Absolutism of Politics," India Seminar, https://www.india-seminar.com/2010/615/615_uday_s_mehta.htm.

101. For a history of the institutionalization of universal suffrage in post-independence India, see Ornit Shani, *How India Became Democratic: Citizenship and the Making of the Universal Franchise* (Cambridge: Cambridge University Press, 2017).

102. Dipesh Chakrabarty, *Provincializing Europe: Postcolonial Thought and Historical Difference* (Princeton, NJ: Princeton University Press, 2000), 10.

103. Pratap Bhanu Mehta, *The Burden of Democracy* (Gurgaon: Penguin Books, 2003), 11.

104. Kevin Duong, "Universal Suffrage as Decolonization," *American Political Science Review* 115, no. 2 (2021): 412–428.

105. Adom Getachew, "Democracy in the Age of Decolonization," in *The Cambridge History of Democracy*, vol. 3, ed. Samuel Moon and Christopher Meckstroth (Cambridge: Cambridge University Press, forthcoming).

106. *SWJN*, 7:354.

107. *SWJN*, 8:2.

108. Nehru, *Selected Works*, 2nd ser., 13:336.

109. The Committee Appointed by the All Parties' Conference, *The Nehru Report: An Anti-Separatist Manifesto* (New Delhi: Michiko and Panjathan, 1975), 92–93.

110. Nehru, *Speeches*, 3:138.

111. Nehru, *Speeches*, 3:140.

112. Bhatia, "Parliamentarism at India's Founding."

113. On this point, see Khosla, *India's Founding Moment*, 10–15.

114. Nehru, *Speeches*, 3:139.

115. Nehru, *Speeches*, 3:138.

116. As Niraja Gopal Jayal has shown, backwardness itself would eventually be integrated into the very idea of citizenship (and broader "political democracy," to use Nehru's parlance) in postcolonial India. It would also allow for making demands on the state in ways unforeseen by founders such as Nehru. See Niraja Gopal Jayal, *Citizenship and Its Discontents: An Indian History* (Cambridge, MA: Harvard University Press, 2013), 229–253.

117. On this point, see Dipesh Chakrabarty, "'In the Name of Politics': Democracy and the Power of Multitude in India," *Public Culture* 19, no. 1 (2007): 35–57.

118. On the importance of the question of economic development in post–World War II accounts of self-determination, see Getachew, *Worldmaking after Empire*, 107–175.

119. George Schuster and Gary Wint, *India and Democracy* (London: Macmillan, 1941), 93.

120. Stuart Ward, "The European Provenance of Decolonization," *Past and Present* 230, no. 1 (2016): 227–260.

121. Reinhart Koselleck, "The Temporalization of Utopia," in *The Practice of Conceptual History: Timing History, Spacing Concepts* (Stanford, CA: Stanford University Press, 2002), 88.

122. Sudipta Kaviraj, "On the Enchantment of the State: Indian Thought on the Role of the State in the Narrative of Modernity," *European Journal of Sociology / Archives Européennes de Sociologie* 46, no. 2 (2005): 289.

6. THE TWO TIMES OF THE PEOPLE

1. Frederick G. Whelan, "Prologue: Democratic Theory and the Boundary Problem," *Nomos* 25 (1983): 13–47; see also Arash Abizadeh, "On the Demos and Its Kin: Nationalism, Democracy, and the Boundary Problem," *American Political Science Review* 106, no. 4 (2012): 867–882.

2. Gandhi, "A Welcome Move," in *Collected Works of Mahatma Gandhi* (New Delhi: Publications Division, Ministry of Information and Broadcasting, Government of India, 1958–), 77:222.

3. Gandhi, "A Welcome Move," 77:223.

4. Mohammad Ali Jinnah, *Some Recent Speeches and Writings of Mr. Jinnah* (Kashmiri Bazar, Lahore: Sh. Muhammad Ashraf, 1942), 120.

5. Jinnah, *Some Recent Speeches*, 120.

6. Jinnah, *Some Recent Speeches*, 163–164.

7. John Stuart Mill, *Considerations on Representative Government*, in *The Collected Works of John Stuart Mill*, vol. 19, *Essays on Politics and Society*, pt. 2, ed. John M. Robson and Jack Stillinger (Toronto: University of Toronto Press, 1981), 546.

8. For a perceptive, turn-of-the-century Indian reckoning with Renan and the obscure sources of nationhood, see Rabindranath Tagore, "Nation ki?" [What is the nation?], in *Atmashakti* [Self-empowerment] (Kolkata: Majumdar Press, 1905), 1–8.

9. Surendranath Banerjea, *Speeches of Surendranath Banerjea*, vol. 1 (Kolkata: Indian Association, 1970), 36–37.

10. Sofia Näsström, "The Legitimacy of the People," *Political Theory* 35, no. 5 (2007): 625.

11. Jürgen Habermas, *Inclusion of the Other: Studies in Political Theory*, ed. Ciaran Ciaron and Pablo de Greiff (Cambridge, MA: MIT Press, 1998), 116.

12. Bernard Yack, "Popular Sovereignty and Nationalism," *Political Theory* 29, no. 4 (2001): 517–536.

13. Richard Tuck, *The Sleeping Sovereign: The Invention of Modern Democracy* (Cambridge: Cambridge University Press, 2015), 97.

14. See Morton I. Horwitz, "Tocqueville and the Tyranny of the Majority," *Review of Politics* 28, no. 3 (1966): 293–307.

15. Jawaharlal Nehru, *Recent Essays and Writings on the Future of India Communalism and Other Subjects* (Allahabad: Kitabistan, 1934), 21.

16. On Jinnah's early career as a moderate congressman, see Ayesha Jalal, *The Sole Spokesman: Jinnah, the Muslim League, and the Demand for Pakistan* (Cambridge: Cambridge University Press, 1985), 7–34.

17. Jinnah, *Some Recent Speeches*, 86.

18. Nehru, *Recent Essays and Writings*, 21.

19. John Robert Seeley, *The Expansion of England* (Boston: Little, Brown and Co., 1905), 264 (emphasis in original).

20. Seeley, *The Expansion of England*, 254–255.

21. Seeley, *The Expansion of England*, 265.

22. Seeley, *The Expansion of England*, 264.

23. Seeley, *The Expansion of England*, 271.

24. Bipin Chandra Pal, *The Spirit of Indian Nationalism* (London: Hind Nationalist Agency, 1910), 10–11.

25. Jawaharlal Nehru, *Toward Freedom: The Autobiography of Jawaharlal Nehru* (New York: John Day, 1941), 67.

26. C. F. Andrews, *Indian Independence: The Immediate Need* (Madras: Ganesh and Co., 1920).

27. Pal, *The Spirit of Indian Nationalism*, 3.

28. Pal, *The Spirit of Indian Nationalism*, 35.

29. For Pal's retrospective consideration of how the turn to Hindu cultural resources affected communal relationship in Bengal, see Bipin Chandra Pal, *Nabajuger Bangla* [Renaissance Bengal] (Kolkata: Bipin Chandra Pal Institute, 1964), 212–233.

30. See, for instance, Tanika Sarkar, "Imagining a Hindu Nation: Hindu and Muslim in Bankimchandra's Later Writings," *Economic and Political Weekly* (1994): 2553–2561.

31. Gopal Krishna Gokhale, "The Hindu-Mahomedan Question," in *Speeches of Gopal Krishna Gokhale* (Madras: G. A. Natesen and Co., 1920), 1000.

32. Gokhale, *Speeches of Gopal Krishna Gokhale*, 1000–1001.

33. Jawaharlal Nehru, "Roads to Freedom," in *Selected Works of Jawaharlal Nehru*, ed. S. Gopal, vol. 1 (Delhi: Orient Longman, 1970), 144.

34. Nehru, *Recent Essays and Writings*, 62.

35. Nehru, *Recent Essays and Writings*, 67.

36. Nehru, *Recent Essays and Writings*, 58.

37. Jawaharlal Nehru, *The Unity of India: Collected Writings, 1937–40* (New York: John Day, 1941), 15.

38. Nehru read Bergson's *Creative Evolution* when he was imprisoned at Ahmadnagar Fort and made use of it in *Discovery of India* while discussing India's past. As Sunil Khilnani rightly notes, there is a certain similarity between Nehru's idea of Indian unity and Bergson's notion of *élan vital*. Sunil Khilnani, introduction to *Discovery of India* by Jawaharlal Nehru (Haryana: Penguin Random House, 2010), xxii.

39. On Iqbal and Bergson, see Soulemane Bachir Diagne, *Postcolonial Bergson* (New York: Fordham University Press, 2019).

40. Nehru, *Discovery of India*, 308. This argument became a commonplace among those opposed to the partition of India. Even Radhakamal Mukerjee, once a critic of centralized sovereignty (as we saw in Chapter 4), concluded in the 1940s that "without the unity of the whole country, economic planning will be difficult, and agricultural Hindus and Muslims will be in greater misery and . . . will fight more bitterly with one another." Radhakamal Mukerjee, *An Economist Looks at Pakistan* (Bombay: Hind Kitabs, 1944), 23.

41. Nehru, *Discovery of India*, 384.

42. Jinnah, *Some Recent Speeches*, 163.

43. Jinnah, *Some Recent Speeches*, 86.

44. Jinnah, *Some Recent Speeches*, 41.

45. Jinnah, *Some Recent Speeches*, 190.

46. Jinnah, *Some Recent Speeches*, 240.

47. Jinnah, *Some Recent Speeches*, 44.

48. Jinnah, *Some Recent Speeches*, 86.

49. Jinnah, *Some Recent Speeches*, 86.

50. Jinnah, *Some Recent Speeches*, 113.

51. Jinnah, *Some Recent Speeches*, 113.

52. Jinnah, *Some Recent Speeches*, 113.

53. Faisal Devji, *Muslim Zion: Pakistan as a Political Idea* (Cambridge, MA: Harvard University Press, 2013), 86.

54. Jinnah, *Some Recent Speeches,* 131.

55. Jinnah, *Some Recent Speeches,* 151–152.

56. Jinnah, *Some Recent Speeches,* 110, 125, 158.

57. Jinnah, *Some Recent Speeches,* 25.

58. Jinnah, *Some Recent Speeches,* 88.

59. Tej Bahadur Sapru, "Letter from Sir Tej Bahadur Sapru to Mr. Jinnah," in *Leaders' Correspondence with Jinnah,* ed. Syed Sharifuddin Peerzada (Bombay: Sh. Nazir Ahmad, 1944), 176.

60. Shruti Kapila, *Violent Fraternity: Indian Political Thought in the Global Age* (Princeton, NJ: Princeton University Press, 2021). 237.

61. See especially Gyanendra Pandey, *The Construction of Communalism in Colonial North India* (Oxford: Oxford University Press, 2006); Sudipta Kaviraj, *The Imaginary Institution of India: Politics and Ideas* (New York: Columbia University Press, 2010).

62. See Manu Goswami, *Producing India: From Colonial Economy to National Space* (Chicago: University of Chicago Press, 2004).

63. B. R. Ambedkar, *Annihilation of Caste,* in *Dr. Babasaheb Ambedkar: Writings and Speeches* (New Delhi: Dr. Ambedkar Foundation, 2014) (hereafter cited as *BAWS*), 1:50.

64. Ambedkar, *Pakistan or the Partition of India,* in *BAWS,* 8:29–30.

65. Ambedkar, *Pakistan or the Partition of India,* in *BAWS,* 8:30 (emphasis in original).

66. Ambedkar, *What Congress and Gandhi Have Done to the Untouchables,* in *BAWS,* 9:201–202.

67. Ambedkar, *Pakistan or the Partition of India,* in *BAWS,* 8:31.

68. Ambedkar studied with John Dewey at Columbia University and was deeply influenced by his approach to the question of political community. Ambedkar's uses of Dewey have been studied by a number of scholars. See, in particular, Arun P. Mukherjee, "B. R. Ambedkar, John Dewey, and the Meaning of Democracy," *New Literary History* 40, no. 2 (2009): 345–370; Scott R. Stroud, "What Did Ambedkar Learn from John Dewey's *Democracy and Education?,*" *The Pluralist* 12, no. 2 (2017): 78–103; Keya Maitra, "Ambedkar and the Constitution of India: A Deweyan Experiment," *Contemporary Pragmatism* 9, no. 2 (2012): 301–320.

69. Ambedkar, *Annihilation of Caste,* in *BAWS,* 1:51.

70. Ambedkar, *Annihilation of Caste,* in *BAWS,* 1:51.

71. Ambedkar, *Ranade, Gandhi and Jinnah,* in *BAWS,* 1:234.

72. Ambedkar, "Thoughts on Linguistic States," in *BAWS,* 1:169.

73. Ambedkar, *Philosophy of Hinduism,* in *BAWS,* 3:74–77. Ambedkar was aware that the philosophy of Hinduism differed from that of Nietzsche. In fact,

he considered Hinduism to be more "odious" than Nietzsche because of its reliance on birth as opposed to a will to power (77).

74. Ambedkar, *Ranade, Gandhi and Jinnah,* in *BAWS,* 1:222.
75. On this point, see Kevin Duong, "The People as a Natural Disaster: Redemptive Violence in Jacobin Political Thought," *American Political Science Review* 111, no. 4 (2017): 786–800.
76. Ambedkar, *Annihilation of Caste,* in *BAWS,* 1:80.
77. Ambedkar, *Pakistan or the Partition of India,* in *BAWS,* 8:34–37.
78. Ambedkar, *Pakistan or the Partition of India,* in *BAWS,* 8:38–39.
79. Ambedkar, *Pakistan or the Partition of India,* in *BAWS,* 8:39.
80. Ambedkar, *Pakistan or the Partition of India,* in *BAWS,* 8:39.
81. Mrinalini Sinha, *Colonial Masculinity: The "Manly Englishman" and the "Effeminate Bengali" in the Late Nineteenth Century* (Manchester: University of Manchester Press, 1995).
82. Prathama Banerjee, *Elementary Aspects of the Political: Histories from the Global South* (Durham, NC: Duke University Press, 2020), 30.
83. Quoted in Ambedkar, *Annihilation of Caste,* in *BAWS,* 1:39.
84. Ambedkar, *Annihilation of Caste,* in *BAWS,* 1:39.
85. Ambedkar, *Annihilation of Caste,* in *BAWS,* 1:44.
86. Ambedkar, *Annihilation of Caste,* in *BAWS,* 1:63.
87. Ambedkar, *Annihilation of Caste,* in *BAWS,* 1:94.
88. Ambedkar, *Annihilation of Caste,* in *BAWS,* 1:95.
89. Ambedkar, *Ranade, Gandhi, and Jinnah,* in *BAWS,* 1:222.
90. Ambedkar, *Ranade, Gandhi and Jinnah,* in *BAWS,* 1:173–177.
91. On the heightened imperial as well as Indian effort in the early twentieth century to domesticate the caste question to "the social," see Rupa Viswanath, *The Pariah Problem: Caste, Religion, and the Social in Modern India* (New York: Columbia University Press, 2014), 217–239.
92. On the imperial uses of the social, see Patricia Owens, "The Colonial Limits of Society," in *The Economy of Force: Counterinsurgency and the Historical Rise of the Social* (Cambridge: Cambridge University Press, 2015), 131–172.
93. Ambedkar, *Ranade, Gandhi and Jinnah,* in *BAWS,* 1:234.
94. Ambedkar, *Ranade, Gandhi and Jinnah,* in *BAWS,* 1:234–235.
95. On the Ambedkar–Churchill correspondence, see Jesús Francisco Cháirez-Garza, "'Bound by Hand and Foot and Handed Over to the Caste Hindus': Ambedkar, Untouchability, and the Politics of Partition," *Indian Economic and Social History Review* 55, no. 1 (2018): 1–28. For a comparative study of Ambedkar's and Du Bois's thought, see Anupama Rao, "Deprovincializing Anticaste Thought: A Genealogy of Ambedkar's Dalit," in *The Postcolonial Contemporary: Political Imaginaries for the Global Present,* ed. Jini Kim Watson and Gary Wilder (New York: Fordham University Press, 2018), 126–146.

96. See, for example, B. R. Ambedkar, "I Don't Want Just Freedom but a Complete Independence," in *Ambedkar Speaks,* vol. 3, ed. Narendra Jadhav (New Delhi: Konark Publishers, 2013), 331.

97. Ambedkar, *What Gandhi and Congress Have Done to the Untouchables,* in *BAWS,* 9:190 (emphasis added).

98. Ambedkar's strong commitment to popular unity thus paradoxically reinforced a turn to agonism. On Ambedkar's agonism, see Shruti Kapila, "Ambedkar's Agonism: Sovereign Violence and Pakistan as Peace," *Comparative Studies of South Asia, Africa, and the Middle East* 39, no. 1 (2019): 184–195.

99. On Ambedkar's approach to "state action," see Hari Ramesh, "B. R. Ambedkar on Caste, Democracy, and State Action," *Political Theory* 50, no. 5 (2022): 723–753; on his proposals for incorporating Dalits into the executive and the legislative bodies of the independent state, see *States and Minorities,* in *BAWS,* 1:412–426.

100. Ambedkar, *Pakistan or the Partition of India,* in *BAWS,* 8:340.

101. Rao, *The Caste Question,* 124–125.

102. For a detailed account of Ambedkar's reflections on federalism as a constitutional principle, see his "Federation versus Freedom," in *BAWS,* 1:279–354. On the vision of sovereignty underpinning Ambedkar and Nehru's conceptions of the unitary state, see Uday Mehta, "Indian Constitutionalism: Crisis, Unity, History," in *The Oxford Handbook of the Indian Constitution,* ed. Sujit Choudhry, Madhav Khosla, and Pratap Bhanu Mehta (New York: Oxford University Press, 2016), 38–54.

103. B. R. Ambedkar, *Three Historical Addresses of Dr. Babasaheb Ambedkar* (New Delhi: Dr. Ambedkar Foundation Research Cell, 1999), 54–55. The terms "people" and "nation" here should be understood in the context of a dispute over the cultural unity of Indians. The problem that "politically-minded Indians" had with the term "people" was that, purely descriptively, it connoted a collection of different groups devoid of any preexisting unity. Ambedkar's suggestion obviously did not entail the argument that Indians should aim toward a pre-political cultural unity; it instead concerned the necessity to develop a cohesive community—a people not socially divided across the lines of caste and religion.

104. Ambedkar, "Organise under One Leader, One Party, One Programme," in *BAWS,* vol. 17, pt. 3, 390.

105. Quoted in Christophe Jaffrelot, *Dr. Ambedkar and Untouchability: Analyzing and Fighting Caste* (London: Hurst, 2005), 133.

106. On Gandhi on the Hindu-Muslim conflict, see Faisal Devji, *The Impossible Indian: Gandhi and the Temptation of Violence* (Cambridge, MA: Harvard University Press, 2012).

1. Jawaharlal Nehru, "A Tryst with Destiny," in *Selected Works of Jawaharlal Nehru,* 2nd ser., vol. 3, ed. S. Gopal (New Delhi: Oxford University Press, 1987), 136.

2. See Mahmood Mamdani, *Citizen and Subject: Contemporary Africa and the Legacy of Late Colonialism* (Princeton, NJ: Princeton University Press, 2018).

3. Julius Nyerere, "Freedom and Development," in *Man and Development* (New York: Oxford University Press, 1974), 25. This was broadly true for the generation of postcolonial founders in Africa. As Frederick Cooper put it: "No word captures the hopes and ambitions of Africa's leaders, its educated populations, and many of its farmers and workers in the post-war decades better than 'development.'" See Frederick Cooper, *Africa since 1940: The Past of the Present* (Cambridge: Cambridge University Press, 2002), 91.

4. On the difference between "ancient" and "modern" notions of democracy and the transition to representative government, see Bernard Manin, *The Principles of Representative Government* (Cambridge: Cambridge University Press, 1997).

5. Nyerere, "Freedom and Development," 26 (emphasis in original).

6. See Aditya Nigam, *Desire Named Development* (New Delhi: Penguin, 2011).

7. David Scott, *Conscripts of Modernity: The Tragedy of Colonial Enlightenment* (Durham, NC: Duke University Press, 2004), 210.

8. See Partha Chatterjee, *Politics of the Governed: Reflections on Popular Politics in Most of the World* (New York: Columbia University Press, 2004).

9. Thomas Blom Hansen, "Democracy against Law: Reflections on India's Illiberal Democracy," in *Majoritarian State: How Hindu Nationalism is Changing India,* ed. Angana P. Chatterjee, Thomas Blom Hansen, and Christophe Jaffrelot (Oxford: Oxford University Press, 2019), 39; see also Thomas Blom Hansen, *Saffron Wave: Democracy and Hindu Nationalism in Modern India* (Princeton, NJ: Princeton University Press, 1999).

10. On the rise of developmentalism in international law, see Sundhya Pahuja, "From Decolonization to Developmental Nation State," in *Decolonizing International Law* (Cambridge: Cambridge University Press, 2011), 44-94; Antony Anghie, *Imperialism, Sovereignty, and the Making of International Law* (Cambridge: Cambridge University Press, 2004), 196-272. On the nineteenth-century origins of historicism in international law, see Jennifer Pitts, *Boundaries of the International: Law and Empire* (Cambridge, MA: Harvard University Press, 2018), 148-184.

11. Albert O. Hirschman, "The Rise and Decline of Development Economics," in *The Essential Hirschman,* ed. Jeremy Adelman (Princeton, NJ: Princeton University Press, 2013), 69-70.

12. James Ferguson, *The Anti-Politics Machine: Development, Depoliticization, and Bureaucratic Power in Lesotho* (Minneapolis: University of Minnesota Press, 1994), xiv.

13. Arturo Escobar, *Encountering Development: The Making and Unmaking of Theory of the Third World* (Princeton, NJ: Princeton University Press, 1995), 4.

14. Partha Chatterjee, *The Nation and Its Fragments* (Princeton, NJ: Princeton University Press, 1993), 219.

15. Akhil Gupta, *Postcolonial Developments: Agriculture in the Making of Modern India* (Durham, NC: Duke University Press, 1998).

16. On this point, see Nusrat Sabina Chowdhury, *Paradoxes of the Popular: Crowd Politics in Bangladesh* (Stanford, CA: Stanford University Press, 2019); for a reading of postcolonial democracy as a tension between conflicting aspirations of development and popular "empowerment," see Jeffrey Witsoe, *Democracy against Development: Lower-Caste Politics and Political Modernity in Postcolonial India* (Chicago: University of Chicago Press, 2013).

17. See Dipesh Chakrabarty, "Rajnitir Rasta: Path Abarodh o Ganatantra" [The road of politics: Road blockade and democracy], in *Itihasher Janajiban o Ananya Prabandha* [The public life of history and other essays] (Kolkata: Ananda, 2011), 79–91.

18. Rohit De, *A People's Constitution: The Everyday Life of Law in the Indian Republic* (Princeton, NJ: Princeton University Press, 2018).

19. See Anuj Bhuwania, *Courting the People: Public Interest Litigation in Post-Emergency India* (Cambridge: Cambridge University Press, 2017), 28–31; Sayantan Saha Roy, "Legal Lives in the Post-Colony: Sovereignty, Absolutism, and the Rule of Law in India" (PhD diss., University of Chicago, 2019).

20. Amartya Sen, *Development as Freedom* (New York: Alfred A. Knopf, 2000), 20.

21. Sen, *Development as Freedom,* 20.

22. Thomas McCarthy, *Race, Empire, and the Idea of Human Development* (Cambridge: Cambridge University Press, 2009), 241–242.

23. McCarthy, *Race, Empire,* 15, 221, 242.

24. McCarthy, *Race, Empire,* 233.

25. On this point, see Amy Allen, *The End of Progress: Decolonizing the Normative Foundations of Critical Theory* (New York: Columbia University Press, 2016).

26. McCarthy, *Race, Empire,* 18–19.

27. Patchen Markell, *Bound by Recognition* (Princeton, NJ: Princeton University Press, 2003), 188; on the relationship between sovereignty and mastery, see also Anna Jurkevics, "Contested Territory: A Political Theory of Land and Democracy beyond Sovereign Bounds" (unpublished manuscript).

28. Bipin Chandra Pal's brief appearance in Benedict Anderson's *Imagined Communities*—perhaps the most widely engaged-with text in scholarship on anticolonial nationalism—is exemplary of how the anticolonial archive be-

came grist to the mill of the cultural and social history of nationalism. Anderson turned to Pal—whose work I have discussed in Chapters 3 and 4—to illustrate the limits of anglicization in the British colonies. He focused on Pal's description of the estrangement of Indian civil service officials from their own society in order to drive home the point regarding the "inner incompatibility of empire and nation." Having situated the possibility of Pal's argument in the historical constitution of the British Empire, Anderson strangely—but suggestively—moved on to pluralizing Pal. The internal contradiction of the empire, he noted, "produced thousands of Pals all over the world." Anderson's main objective was to establish that "these Pals" could not be accounted for in terms of racism because they also existed in the white colonies. The immediate irony of such a claim lies in the fact that Pal, in one of the first book-length studies of federalism, argued against the ideal of the nation-state. My concern, however, is not to fault Anderson for his inadequate understanding of Pal or for the larger point that there was an internal contradiction between empire and nation. What is suggestive here is how a foundational anticolonial thinker like Bipin Chandra Pal was turned into a mere mirror for tracing the inevitable emergence of the nation-state form. In the wake of Anderson's agenda-setting work, even scholars critical of Anderson's account continued to circumscribe anticolonial thought in the world of nationalism and its dilemmas. Benedict Anderson, *Imagined Communities: Reflections on the Origin and Spread of Nationalism* (London: Verso, 2006), 93.

29. On this point, see Adom Getachew and Karuna Mantena, "Anticolonialism and the Decolonization of Political Theory," *Critical Times: Interventions in Global Critical Theory* 4, no. 3 (2021): 359–388.

ACKNOWLEDGMENTS

I have incurred many debts to many people and institutions in the course of writing this book. The initial research for this book was generously funded by the University of Chicago's Department of Political Science, Division of Social Sciences; the Committee on Southern Asian Studies; the Nicholson Center for British Studies; and the Mellon Foundation. Further support from Christ's College, University of Cambridge, and the University of British Columbia (UBC) was essential to the development of the book.

It has been a pleasure to complete the manuscript in the supportive and collegial environment of the Political Science Department at the University of British Columbia. My colleagues—Afsoun Afsahi, Bruce Baum, Arjun Chowdhury, Katia Coleman, Glen Coulthard, Antje Ellerman, Alan Jacobs, Anna Jurkevics, Yves Tiberghien, Mark Warren, and Mike Weaver, among others—have warmly welcomed me into the department and engaged enthusiastically with this project. Special thanks are owed to Barbara Arneil—who has been a pillar of support since I joined UBC—for her help with putting together a highly generative manuscript workshop. I am also fortunate to have been reunited with Hasan Siddiqui—who has been a wonderful interlocutor over the last few years—and Naveena Naqvi at UBC.

Much of the revision and refinement of the manuscript took place at the University of Cambridge, where I spent a couple of years as a Research Fellow at Christ's College. Cambridge proved to be an ideal place to think through this book, not least because of the support provided by colleagues and staff at Christ's. I am especially indebted to Duncan Bell, whose engagement with the project has enriched it in a number of ways. Conversations with John Dunn were always generative and instructive; I also wish to thank him for his helpful comments on parts of the manuscript. I am also grateful to Shruti Kapila for spirited conversations on and around the history of Indian political thought. Susan Bayly, Richard Bourke, Chris Brooke, Salmoli Choudhuri, Sean Fleming, Duncan Kelly, Adam Lebovitz, Emma Mackinnon, Giovanni Mantilla, David Reynolds, Lucia Rubinelli, Amar Sohal, Jane Stapleton, Benjamin Tan, and Sam Zeitlin have all been wonderful colleagues and have enabled my thinking on the book in different ways.

Above all, this book owes a great deal to the sharp engagement and abundant encouragement of Patchen Markell and Jennifer Pitts, who co-supervised the project when it began at the University of Chicago. Patchen's astute reading and sharp insights improved each of the chapters; the depth of his intellectual engagement with the project propelled much of the early research for this book. Jennifer shared her wealth of knowledge in empire and the history of political thought at every step of the way and enriched my research in more ways than I can count. Adom Getachew has been an exemplary mentor. Her keen insights into the history of anticolonial political thought, and generous attention to the project, were indispensable to its development into a book. Linda Zerilli helped me see the broader stakes of the project from early on. Finally, Dipesh Chakrabarty has been an indispensable and inspiring interlocutor. I am grateful to him for his friendship and for all the conversations we have had about the past and present of South Asia.

At Chicago, the project also benefited from the suggestions of and conversations with numerous colleagues and friends: Suchismita Das, Supurna Dasgupta, Alex Haskins, Mannat Johal, Emily Katzenstein, Steven Klein, Harini Kumar, Matt Landauer, Will Levine, Rochona Majumdar, William Mazzarella, John McCormick, Sankar Muthu, Tejas Parasher, Sarath Pillai, Steven Pincus, Lucas Pinheiro, Sanjukta Poddar, Sayantan Saha Roy, Madeline Smith, Lisa Wedeen, and Jim Wilson. A

special word of thanks to the librarians and staff of the Regenstein Library; this book would have been much harder to write without its extraordinary collection of South Asian resources. I must also thank the librarians at the Asiatic Society (Kolkata), the British Library, the National Library of India, the Nehru Memorial Museum and Library, and the National Archives of India.

A manuscript workshop at UBC yielded rich insights and suggestions, for which I thank the participants, including Barbara Arneil, Kevin Duong, Anna Jurkevics, Sudipta Kaviraj, Duncan Kelly, Karuna Mantena, and Pratap Bhanu Mehta. Karuna Mantena read different chapters of the manuscript over the years and unfailingly offered incisive comments and invaluable suggestions. Kevin Duong, who generously engaged with the project in its various stages, has been an essential interlocutor. Faisal Devji's suggestions were invariably illuminating, as were our conversations in London and Vancouver. In the broader world of political theory and intellectual history, the project stands enriched from the engagements and suggestions of numerous colleagues who have read parts of the project or engaged in important conversations on the project: Rochana Bajpai, Lawrie Balfour, Udit Bhatia, Dennis Dalton, Aniket De, Rohit De, Leonard Feldman, Jason Frank, Humeira Iqtidar, Leigh Jenco, Abhishek Kaicker, Alex Livingston, Rama Mantena, Robyn Marasco, Inder Marwah, Jeannie Morefield, Joshua Simon, Anurag Sinha, Mrinalini Sinha, and James Tully.

At Harvard University Press, I am profoundly indebted to Sharmila Sen for her unerring advice on all things related to the book, and for guiding the book through the publication process with utmost expertise and kindness. I am also grateful to Ian Malcolm, who embraced the project early on. I also wish to thank Samantha Mateo and Olivia Woods for their help with the publication process. Two anonymous readers for the Press offered rich, encouraging, and genuinely helpful comments on the manuscript; I am grateful to them both.

Parts of Chapter 3 were published as "Self-Rule and the Problem of Peoplehood in Colonial India," *American Political Science Review* 114, no. 1 (2020): 81–94. Most of Chapter 4 was first published as "Between the Many and the One: Anticolonial Federalism and Popular Sovereignty," *Political Theory* 50, no. 2 (2022): 247–274.

Three friends deserve special mention. Nusrat Chowdhury's friendship has enriched my life and work in profound ways. She championed the project from the beginning and patiently read countless drafts over the years. My debt to Shefali Jha is immeasurable. She read almost all of the book, and unfailingly posed sharp questions and offered keen insights. Many of the arguments that went into the book were first discussed with Thomas Newbold. His profound and always-generative engagement with the project was one reason the process of writing the book was often enjoyable.

The manuscript has traveled with me over the past few years as I moved between cities and continents. My friends scattered through New York, Chicago, and Dhaka have been the most critical source of support. Without Krithika Ashok and Sannoy Das's care and friendship, the quarantine months, when a large chunk of the book was written, would have been a far greater ordeal. The extraordinary friendships of Imtiaz Hossain and Ahmed Shamim have been a source of immense joy and meaning for almost a decade. My other friends in New York, including Tirtho Dutta, Humayun Kabir, and William Cheung, have also helped make the city a pleasant escape. I owe particular thanks to my Bangladesh friends—especially Arastu Lenin Khan and Priyam Paul—for their camaraderie from near and far.

My parents have lovingly endured my work on the book over the past few years and have eagerly looked forward to its publication. This book is dedicated to them. For their unquestioned support, I am grateful in equal measure to my siblings, Sharmin, Nasrin, and Anzim, and my brother-in-law, Suddha. Many thanks also to my parents-in-law, who have warmly welcomed me into their family and have never failed to inquire about the progress of the book. Potol and Casey provided me with necessary distractions but were also faithful writing companions when needed.

Finally, my debt to Muhsina is beyond measure. Her love has transformed my world and has made possible a great many things, including the writing of this book.

INDEX

action, 100, 121-122, 262n103
affect, 75, 129, 200, 202, 221
Africa, 185, 220, 285n3
African Americans, 213
agonism, 284n98
Akbar, 36, 241n1
Ambedkar, B. R., 2, 23, 197-198, 208-216, 233, 282n68
American Revolution, 172-173, 212
Amin, Shahid, 128
Anandamath (The Abbey of Bliss, novel), 79
ancient constitutionalism, 53. *See also* constitution
Anderson, Benedict, 29, 286n28
anticolonialism, 29; as diffusionist narrative, 30; Gandhi's importance for, 123; and nationalism, 29-30, 216-217, 230, 286n28; in political theory, 28-35; and self-rule, 123, 232; success of, 10
anticolonial thought: in Africa, 132; and democracy, 228-229; development-

affirming/developmental-critical, 19-20, 22-24; global claims, 230-233; historiography of, 33-34; margin-alization of, 230; postcolonial, 132; scholarship on, 69
Arendt, Hannah, 4, 64, 156, 235n6
Armitage, David, 172
Arneil, Barbara, 240n60
Arnold, Edwin, 1
Asiatic Journal (journal), 76
Aurobindo, Sri, 91, 98, 141, 255n63, 267n42, 275n50
authoritarianism, 180, 224, 227
authorization, 4-5, 27, 87, 99; collective to the self, 100-101; in Gandhi's thought, 20, 119; for independence, 182; popular, 104-112; and popular sovereignty, 154; and self-government, 102; sovereign, 109. *See also* swaraj

backwardness: and citizenship, 279n116; and civilization, 81, 262n85; colonial, 232; and cultural identity, 30; and

184; and developmentalism, 225–226; and empire, 39, 80; Follett on, 151; Gandhi on, 158; vs. government, 210; historicity, 228; ideal of, 160; in India, 204; vs. liberalism, 93; Mill on, 58; normative foundations of, 12–13; in political thought, 11; political vs. economic, 163–164; and postcolonialism, 223–230; temporal visions in, 32; theory, 217, 219–220, 238n34

derivativeness, 30

despotism, 11–12

developmentalism, 13; as abstraction, 33–34; appeal of, 229; vs. colonialism, 3; critiques of, 20–21, 80, 133, 141; and democracy, 225–226; and difference, 38; and empire's democratic legitimation, 9, 40; Gandhi on, 116–117, 129; history of, 26, 54–55; and imperialism, 65, 226–227; as language, 229; and liberality, 77; in nineteenth century, 36–66; and otherness, 38; and political thought, 38–39; postcolonial politics of, 26–28, 224–225; scholarship on, 226; and self-government, 90; unilinear, 142. *See also* underdevelopment

Devji, Faisal, 205

Dewey, John, 282n68

discrimination, 83

divide-and-rule framework, 207

division, unity through, 198–208

drain theory, 81–82, 177, 254n41

Du Bois, W. E. B., 24, 136, 214, 237n52

Duong, Kevin, 185

Dussel, Enrique, 128

Dutta, Akshaykumar, 31

Dutt, R. C., 15, 68, 80, 87–88

education, 83, 87, 221

Emerson, Ralph Waldo, 46

Emerson, Rupert, 160

empire: abstract ideologies, 55; ancient constitutionalism, 53; critiques of, 38, 162; and democracy, 39, 80; institu-tional aspects, 201; as irredeemable, 90–91; of Mughals, 36; and people-hood, 66, 71–72, 78–86; promise of, 80, 94; and representative government, 62

English language, 84

English literature, 86, 95

English people, 16, 62–64, 72, 76, 88–90

Enlightenment, Age of, 9–10, 38

essentialism, 80–81, 205

"ethics of everyday life," 122

Europe and Europeans, 9, 11, 36–37, 199

evolutionism, 137

expansionist approach, and self-determination, 165

Fanon, Frantz, 32

Fazl, Abul, 36

federalism, 21, 130–158; critique of collective sovereignty, 34; imperial narratives, 133; nation-state as ending, 155; vs. representative government, 149; Seal on, 139; as theory, 131–132, 156–157; and village republics, 143. *See also* pluralism

Ferguson, James, 225

Figgis, J. N., 145–146

Follett, Mary Parker, 134, 135, 150–151

France, 61

Frank, Jason, 6, 99

freedom, 175, 219, 226

freedom of speech, 49

French Revolution, 84, 111, 213, 216, 255n63

Friend of India (journal), 76

Gandhi, Mohandas Karamchand, 19–21, 34; action, theory of, 100, 121; on authority, 119; against colonial modernity, 117; and Das, 270n101; on democracy, 158; on English government, 116; Gandhian turn, 113–125; and Jinnah, 192–193; moral philosophy, 121; nationalism, 117; political life, 120–121, 124–125, 158, 174–176,

Kaicker, Abhishek, 241n2
Kapila, Shruti, 207
Kaviraj, Sudipta, 189
Kedourie, Elie, 29
Khilafat movement, 125, 174, 201, 264n132
Khilnani, Sunil, 281n38
Koditschek, Theodore, 89–90
Koselleck, Reinhart, 127, 189
Krishnavarma, Shyamji, 98, 114–115

land, redistribution of, 181
language: of capacity, 63; developmentalism as, 229
Lansing, Robert, 273n26
Laski, Harold, 134, 145, 147, 151, 266n17
Lawgiver, 163, 272n13
League Against Imperialism (LAI), 170–171
Lee thesis, 226
Lenin, V. I., 24–25, 166
liberal imperialism, 41, 52–64, 95
liberalism, 11; British, 71; and Cold War, 94; conceptual formation, 92–96; vs. democracy, 93; history of, 92–93; Indian, 69, 90–91; liberality before, 72–78; scholarship on, 95; twentieth-century (Bell), 70; universality of, 13
liberality, 72–78
liberty, 173

Macaulay, T. B., 2, 46, 55–56, 80, 86, 199
Mackinnon, Emma, 274n47
Mahratta (journal), 78
Maine, Henry, 142
Maitland, F. W., 145
majoritarianism, 147, 195–197, 202, 206, 215
Majumdar, Bimanbehari, 30–32, 52, 90, 245n54
Malaviya, Madan Mohan, 167
Manela, Erez, 160, 170
Mantena, Karuna, 122, 142

Marxism, 178, 202, 277n96
masses, 2, 14, 68, 84, 101, 176, 200–201
Mazumdar, A. C., 103
Mazzini, Giuseppe, 83
McCarthy, Thomas, 226–227
Mehta, Pratap Bhanu, 184–185
Mehta, Uday, 122
mendicant method of politics, 102–103
Menon, Nikhil, 181, 276n76
Mill, James, 46–48, 54–55, 245n48, 247n89
Mill, John Stuart, 1–2, 10–11, 39–40; democracy, rise of, 58; against essentialism, 80; in India, 86–91; liberal imperialism of, 41; and majoritarianism, 195–196; on a people's stage of civilization, 57, 60; on progress, 57, 60–61; reception of work, 63; on representative government, 56, 58–59; on self-government, 56–57, 199; on work of politics, 194; writings, 57–59, 61–62, 64
Mitra, Dinabandhu, 94
moderatism, 92, 94
modernization, 227
monarchy, 246n65
monism, 43, 130, 140, 146
Montesquieu, 37, 49, 136, 246n55
Morefield, Jeanne, 145
Mother India, 159–160
Moyn, Samuel, 132, 171
Mughals, 36, 241n1
Mukerjee, Radhakamal, 21–22, 130–131, 134, 141–148, 232.
Mukherjee, Dakshinaranjan, 71, 74–77, 231
Muslims, 264n132; communities, 249n103; conquest of India, 74–75, 77, 79; Hindu relations, 117, 152–153, 195, 198, 201–202, 205, 207–208; *majlis*, 144; Muslim League, 185–186, 192, 196, 205–207
Mysore, 139

Naidu, Sarojini, 158
Naik, V. N., 93
Naoroji, Dadabhai, 2; critiques of, 177; developmentalism, 80–81; on English rule, 86; on imperial sovereignty, 88; on the masses, 68, 70; Pal's response to, 105; political life, 99, 259n19; and self-government, 15–17, 87, 90, 96, 101–103; swaraj, call for, 103; use of "swaraj" term, 97–98, 127
Näsström, Sofia, 194
nationalism: anticolonial, 216–217, 230, 286n28; conceptual scope of, 29–30; Gandhi's, 117; and majoritarianism, 202; vs. nationality, 210; and Pal, 1, 109; and popular sovereignty, 8–9; scholarship on, 29
national personality, 136
National Planning Committee, 180
nationhood, 192; as body of people, 111; and imagination, 198; of Indians, 208; and memory, 194; Mill on, 61; theories on, 199–200; unity, 201, 204
nation-state, 155–156, 166
natural law, 37
Nehru, Jawaharlal, 2; and developmentalism, 24; and formation of liberalism, 92; and Gandhi, 124–125; on independence, 172; legacy of, 161, 165, 182; majoritarianism, 197, 202; and the people, 19; planning, 179–180; political life, 22–23, 161, 174, 181, 186–187, 190, 202–204; and popular sovereignty, 181; theory of founding, 164, 177; writings of, 159
Nehru, Motilal, 168
Nehru Report (1928), 186
neoliberalism, 178–179
New International Economic Order, 224
New Testament, 44
Nietzsche, Friedrich, 282n73
Nkrumah, Kwame, 219
Noncooperation Movement, 124, 174–176

nonviolence, 100, 119, 122, 126
Nyerere, Julius, 219–220

October Revolution, 178
organicism, 135, 148, 229
Orientalist discourse, 30
Osterhammel, Jürgen, 38
otherness, 30, 38, 53–54
Owen, Robert, 46–47

Pagden, Anthony, 37
Pakistan, 155, 204–206, 210, 214, 216
Pal, Bipin Chandra, 1, 17, 98–99, 104–107, 140–141, 155, 200, 233, 286n28
panchayat raj, 275n55
Panikkar, K. M., 93
Parel, Anthony, 114
Paris Peace Conference, 166
parliamentary representation, 130, 139
Partition of India, 155, 217, 219
passive resistance, 119
peasants, 181
people, the, 67–96; as absent, 2–3, 14, 17, 65, 99, 112; colonial world, emergence in, 7; contestability of, 99; descriptive vs. normative, 17; developmental conception of, 112; and government, 221–222; in Indian political thought, 68; as legitimizing, 6–7; masses, 2, 14, 68, 84, 176, 200–201; as norm and as fact, 184; as not-yet, 2, 18, 61, 68, 78, 99; oneness and unity of, 23; pluralist concept of, 151; political status of, 128; and popular sovereignty, 134; progress embodied in, 56, 58–59; social body of, 68, 78–86; spatiality of, 7–8; as speechless, 67–68; suffrage of, 185; temporality of, 8, 56, 218, 222–223; transformation of, 111
peoplehood, 2, 97–129; boundary problem, 190–218; collective, 123; colonial problem of, 13–18; colonial paradox of, 97–129; of the colonized,

98; critiques of, 209; democratic, 59; and empire, 66, 71–72; "fit" for, 8, 14, 23, 128, 147; hierarchy of, 39–40, 56, 58, 100; language of, 112; and liberal imperialism, 52–64; pathways of, 136–140; performativity of, 182; pluralist reconceptualization of, 21–22; postcolonial founding and, 184–185; as problem, 122; progress and, 60, 206; recognition of, 65; and representative government, 58–59, 61; subjection as result of, 86; tangible qualities, 193; unified, 147

Permanent Settlement Act, 247n80

pluralism, 131, 151; comparative history, 141–148; creative assimilation, 203; critiques of, 135, 144–145; growth of, 158; in Mukerjee's work, 144–145; ontological, 151; scholarship on, 145. *See also* federalism

political thought, 230; anticolonialism in, 28–35; democracy in, 11; and developmentalism, 38–39; global vs. European, 32, 34; improvement and betterment in, 52; liberal, 90; people in, 68; temporal visions in, 32

Poona Pact, 213

Pope, Alexander, 76

popular authorization, 4–6, 112, 157

popular sovereignty: as abstract norm, 112; anticolonial search for, 30; and authorization, 4–6, 154; danger of, 213; and decolonization, 164; globally, 3–9; the government vs. the people, 77; vs. imperial sovereignty, 128; legitimation of, 7; vs. majoritarianism, 147; Mukerjee on, 147–148; nationalist claim to, 8–9; and Nehru, 181; and people, 134; pluralist theory of, 131; public legitimacy of, 6; revolutionary origins, 4; scholarship on, 99; and self-government, 17–18; and self-rule, 233; suffrage and, 184–188; unitary vision, 207; and the will, 163

popular unity, 191, 208

postcolonial democracy, 26–28. *See also* democracy

postcolonial founding: cross-continental comparisons, 219; as republic, 162–163; and sovereignty, 221; theory of, 159–160, 177, 188–189

postcoloniality, 25, 159

poverty, 81–82, 176, 226

powers, separation of, 50, 208

priestcraft, 46, 56, 75

Proclamation of 1858, 87, 94

progress: distrust in, 212; end of under imperial rule, 62; as norm, 12–13; optimism about, 30; and people-hood, 56, 59–60, 206; as result of self-government, 25; and self-rule, 117; Mill on, 57, 60, 62

property, 212

public opinion, 47–48

Purna Swaraj, 127. *See also* swaraj

Rai, Lala Lajpat, 169, 216

Rammohun Roy, 31, 243n21; biographical details, 41–43; empire of liberty, 41–52; global difference, 231; good government, 40, 51, 57; liberalism in work, 72; political thought, 47–52; reception, 39–43, 45–46, 51–52, 93; theological writings, 43–45

Rao, Anupama, 215

rationalism, 188, 243n28

reason and tradition, 43

Rebellion of 1857, 14, 64–65, 77

Reform Acts, 93

Reform Bill of 1832, 42, 51, 57

reforms, 43, 51

religious conflict, 74–75, 77, 79, 191

Renan, Ernest, 194, 210

representation, 16, 130, 139, 214. *See also* group representation

representative democracy, 56, 205. *See also* representative government

swaraj, 97–98, 111, 116; as divine democracy, 106; Gandhi, association with, 100; Gandhian recasting, 100–101, 113–114, 116, 118–120, 122–126; institutional form, 124; meanings, 106, 126–127; Naoroji's call for, 103; parliamentary vs. individual, 120–121; popular authorization for, 112; vs. self-government, 119; use in print, 114; and visible government, 110; from word to event, 101–104. *See also* self-government
swaraj movement, 17, 23
Swaraj Party, 158
swaraj resolution, 103–104
Switzerland, 194
Syria, 58, 249n103

Tagore, Rabindranath, 67, 86, 91, 173
Tanzania, 219
Telang, K. T., 93–94
temporality: of anticolonialism, 32, 97, 122; of backwardness, 56, 63, 228; of democracy, 32, 227; of empire, 198; of the people, 8, 56, 218, 222–223; and political thought, 32; of reformism, 99
Tennyson, Alfred, 95
theology, 43–45
Tilak, Bal Gangadhar, 2, 17, 78, 94, 99, 107–111, 121, 260n53
Timbuktu, 58, 140, 249n103
Tocqueville, Alexis de, 84, 195–196, 228
Toynbee, Arnold, 210
Travers, Robert, 53
Truman doctrine, 224
Tuck, Richard, 5, 195
Tully, James, 133

underdevelopment, 220–221, 229. *See also* developmentalism
unity through division, 198–208
universalism, 46–47
Universal Races Congress, 131, 136–137
Untouchables, 212–213
Urbinati, Nadia, 62

Vattel, Emer de, 172
villages: councils, 143; and federalism, 143; Nehru's visits, 159; pluralist theory of, 133, 150; as political form, 122–123, 125, 131–132; theorists of, 144
Voltaire (François-Marie Arouet), 244n26

Ward, Stuart, 188
wars: civil, 213; social, 212. *See also* World War I; World War II
Wellesley, Richard, 247n80
Wells, H. G., 208
Whelan, Frederick, 192
widow-burning (*sati*), 45
Wilder, Gary, 132
Wilson, Woodrow, 160, 166–167, 273n30
Wint, Guy, 188
World Bank, 224
World War I, 25, 124, 138–139, 141, 158, 165–166, 174
World War II, 170, 225

Yack, Bernard, 7–8, 195
Young Bengal Group, 73
Ypi, Lea, 237n29

Zastoupil, Lynn, 57, 249n96
Zerilli, Linda, 251n129